TOMBS, TEMPLES, & ANCIENT ART

TOMBS

By Joseph Lindon Smith

TEMPLES

Edited by Corinna Lindon Smith

& ANCIENT

With paintings by the author

ART

University of Oklahoma Press: Norman

By Corinna Lindon Smith

Rising Above the Ruins in France (New York, G. P. Putnam's Sons, 1920)

Tombs, Temples, and Ancient Art, with Joseph Lindon Smith

(Norman, University of Oklahoma Press, 1956)

Library of Congress Catalog Card Number: 56-5999

Copyright 1956 by the University of Oklahoma Press,
Publishing Division of the University.
Composed and printed at Norman, Oklahoma, U.S.A.,
by the University of Oklahoma Press.
First edition, June, 1956.
Second printing, September, 1956.

To Rebecca, Frances, and Lois—

my companions in art and acting

since their childhood.

CONTENTS

CONTENTS

AT SAQQARAH AND ABYDOS, 1933–1938

THE EGYPTIANS TAKE OVER, 1946–1950

THE ANCIENT NEAR EAST

THE MAJESTY OF PERSIA

THE CLASSICAL WORLD

QUEST IN THE FAR EAST

ANCIENT MONUMENTS OF THE AMERICAS

ILLUSTRATIONS

PREFACE

I N MY HUSBAND's art student days, he kept a casual journal to send
to his mother. So ingrained became this habit formed in his youth
that it persisted throughout his painting career. He jotted down in
a loose-leaf notebook, which he always kept about him, events in which
the subject he was painting had figured, or interesting information he
had gathered about the period of a piece of sculpture or other art or
architecture which he was rendering. The information might be drawn
from conversations with archaeologists and other scholars at the moment
of a rediscovery—a procedure which, as George A. Reisner, the archaeologist, put it, made the recording of high factual significance.

These rough notes were invaluable to him as the source materials for
the innumerable lectures he gave on his art experiences in many lands.
Moreover, he always wrote, in preparation for a lecture, precisely what
he intended to say, even though he never looked at it again. "This way,"
he said, "the data are fixed in my mind." It is fortunate he worked in
this fashion, for from his informal notes and his formal presentation of
ideas and developments we have the essential fabric of the book that
follows. He had begun to give it shape as early as 1946, as the second
world war closed.

The end of archaeological concessions under the auspices of foreign
museums was one of the many changes in postwar Egypt. Reisner had
died in 1942, Harvard Camp, from which so much fruitful work had
come, was closed, and the expedition of the Metropolitan Museum was

in process of being dismantled. Even so, Joe decided he wanted to be a part of the "new" Egypt which the Egyptians were making for themselves.

When we sailed in December, 1946, Joe had celebrated his eighty-third birthday, and his doctor issued an ultimatum that he must restrict his daily painting regime to six hours, instead of his customary eight. Faced with the dilemma of how to occupy his time after emerging from a session of tomb painting until bedtime in desert surroundings, he accepted my suggestion of reliving his own past through the study and ordering of the files on his travels.

Our baggage contained a formidable array of carefully labeled large manila envelopes, classified by countries, and consisting of journals, lectures, letters, and newspaper articles about his career. He became interested, and on our return home in May, 1950, he had revised his material into a consecutive narrative sufficient to fill a number of volumes, which, however, he intended to condense into one. His customary active summer made it necessary for him to lay aside further work on the manuscript until our expected return to Egypt that fall.

But, as with so many human plans and aspirations, Joe's book was not to be finished, for he died on October 18, 1950. In the years since, I have simply condensed what he set down, checking always against the notebooks, letters, and other data, in order that the spirit of what he intended should be fulfilled and the utmost accuracy achieved. The task has been a rewarding one for me, inasmuch as it has permitted me to witness for a long second time the exciting and notable events that we shared together in ancient lands for half a century. I hope that the record will prove not only interesting for itself but, in some measure at least, significant for the details it provides in a history which is not as yet fully recorded.

A word about spellings, dates, and chronology in general may be in order here. Archaeology is constantly changing the facts and sequence of things in areas of prehistory and ancient history. Moreover, not all research institutions and scholars are in agreement at any given moment on either the data or the interpretations. But I have adopted, generally speaking, the spellings and chronology preferred by the Museum of Fine Arts, Boston, in its most recent publications. At many points, however, I have had before me, and have used, the great fund of technical information made available by the Metropolitan Museum of Art in New York City.

To these and many other museums, I wish to express my appreciation for help freely given me, and for supplying photographs of my husband's paintings required for illustrations in this book. I am particularly indebted to Dows Dunham, William Stevenson Smith, and Kojiro Tomita of the Museum of Fine Arts, Boston; to John A. Wilson of the Oriental Institute of the University of Chicago; to Richard A. Parker of Brown University; and to John D. Cooney of the Brooklyn Museum.

I owe special thanks also to the Carnegie Institution of Washington, the owner of a number of my husband's Maya paintings as large as billboards, whose staff ever so cheerfully took them down from over an enormous main stairway and from other inaccessible places to be photographed. I am also grateful to the staffs of the Peabody and Fogg museums of Harvard University; to Richard Tetlie, formerly of the State Department, for assistance in checking references; to Karl Kup of the New York Public Library and William C. Hayes of the Metropolitan Museum of Art for helpful suggestions in handling the difficult problems of chronology and bibliography; and to Gordon Ekholm of the Natural History Museum, New York, for bibliographical aid in the Maya field.

I am very appreciative of the encouragement and advice given me by Florence Waterbury and Rufus G. Poole, and I wish to thank Katherine E. Berry, Shirley Worth, Grace E. Miller, Ruth Wight, and Carol Davison for typing the manuscript.

But my deepest personal sense of gratitude is for the patience of the experienced staff of the University of Oklahoma Press in training me to become an editor.

CORINNA LINDON SMITH

New York City
January 15, 1956

TOMBS, TEMPLES, & ANCIENT ART

THE WAY TO EGYPT

1863-1898

1. *Decisive Influences*

FOR MORE than half a century, my life and career have been associated with the tombs and monuments of the classical past—in Egypt, Mesopotamia, Iran, Greece, Turkey, Italy, Japan, China, Indo-China, Siam, and Java—and of the Maya of Honduras, Guatemala, and Yucatán. As an artist with perhaps some small gifts for literal detail, my privilege was to be present when some of the great tombs of antiquity were reopened by modern archaeologists and to assist them in their work. What I saw I recorded with brushes and paint on canvases. Mine has been a happy life not only of opportunity in art, but of adventure, which can be understood more from the narrative that follows than from the paintings done by me, which, like myself, are often on the move, as a study series, on loan, from one museum to another.

It all began in the most unconventional of ways. Soon after landing in Egypt for the first time, in December, 1898, I was in Nubia on the Upper Nile, camping out at Abu Simbel. This marvel of temples, cut out of the living rock, with a façade of four seated colossal figures, was built by King Ramesses II, whose long active reign started in 1301 B.C.

I was far too absorbed in painting a profile view of the finest of these Ramesses heads to wonder who might be on board a private steamer being moored to the near-by sandbank. I was startled on seeing a rather elderly, intelligent-looking woman peering over my shoulder.

3

"What do you want for that picture?" she asked.

Her abruptness and business-like manner threw me off guard.

"I don't know," I stammered. Then, pulling myself together, added, "I have not yet thought of a price for something that is for me entirely new."

My explanation satisfied her, and she ended by buying the eight pictures I had already painted and she said she also wanted any others I did. I had no idea who she was until I read by the flickering light of a candle in my tent her signature on a check. She was Mrs. Phoebe A. Hearst, well known as a generous patron of the fine arts, who at the time was financing an important archaeological expedition at the Pyramids of Giza for the University of California.

The late Dr. George A. Reisner was in charge, and later, when he saw these paintings in Cairo, admitted with a blunt frankness which subsequently proved to be characteristic that he had not been particularly keen to see any artist's attempt to reproduce temple bas-reliefs, because he thought it could not be done. He greatly encouraged me by saying my work made him feel differently, and that he hoped I would specialize in interpreting ancient art to students who came to museums. "You've accomplished the impossible," he told me. "Each painting is an archaeological record correct in details, but beautiful as a picture." If a young man needed encouragement, I had had it.

I was born in Pawtucket, Rhode Island, October 11, 1863. My father was proprietor and manager of a lumber yard on the near-by Blackstone River, and mother was a cousin of the poet John Greenleaf Whittier, on her mother's side. This was a connection that was destined to have a continuing influence on my career.

To mother, "play acting," as it was then called, was a favorite pastime. She persuaded father to build a stage in one room of the large barn that was a part of the house on School Street where I grew up. She wrote and produced the comedies in which the performers were myself and classmates in Mr. Wheeler's private school. At the age of eight I was taking the lead because of an aptitude for pantomime and a quickness in improvisation that compensated for a lack of capacity in memorizing lines. I also had a vivid imagination and a power of mimicry that made me an apt pupil to my mother's versatility in creating characters. In addition to the drama, I was enthusiastic about my piano lessons. But, here again, I memorized the score by ear rather than learning to read at sight. Grandfather Gideon Smith, an elder in the Friends Meeting House in Providence, kept a collection of my pictures in which I had expressed my wants with a pencil when too little to make myself understood by the spoken word. All in all, my tendencies in my formative years were in the creative line rather than the intellectual.

Out of deference to my father's wishes, I managed to squeeze through the entrance examinations to Brown, but during the ensuing summer months became greatly depressed at the prospect of an academic routine, and I persuaded my mother to take me to Amesbury to appeal to Cousin John Whittier to intercede in my behalf against a college career. I stated to him with determination, "I want to be an artist, continue with the drama, but no book-learning, and the piano must go." Thanks to Cousin John's eloquence, father accepted a compromise to which I also agreed. Professor Ware, who taught architecture in the Massachusetts Institute of Technology, was a friend of Whittier's, and at the poet's instigation was willing to admit me into one of his classes as a "listener." Unfortunately, in class, instead of using my ears to pay attention to what the Professor was explaining, I used my eyes to look at the boys, and my hand to draw sketches of their faces. One day Professor Ware summoned me to his desk and said, "I notice you are always diligent; may I examine your notes?" He did so, smiling a little on recognizing a kindly pencil portrait of himself, then remarked, "The Boston Museum School of Fine Arts is where you belong; we'll have to see what your Cousin John can do about getting you admitted."

Whittier succeeded and broke the news to my father, who considered the prospects of an artist in the family as a tragedy. He was somewhat consoled when, after a few weeks, I won a scholarship and the reports from my art teachers, Frederick Crowninshield and Otto Grundmann, were consistently favorable. It was obvious I had found my *métier*. I also found a life-long friend in a fellow classmate, Frank W. Benson of Salem. He and I studied during the winters of 1883 and 1884, at the Académie Julien, on the Rive Gauche in Paris, under the French masters Lefebvre and Boulanger. Thus, in an atmosphere of the glamour of the present in Paris, I began the course of training from which I later deliberately departed to devote my art career to depicting the glories of the past.

By the fall of 1885 I was in Boston, where my parents had joined me from Pawtucket. I hired a studio and was ready to start painting portraits and landscapes for any clients who showed up. I had painted an oil sketch of my father seated in a wheelbarrow that was on exhibition in a Boston gallery. There was something in the way of my handling sunshine that attracted the attention of Denman Ross, then professor of fine arts at Harvard University. He told me he recognized a technique he had hitherto found lacking in modern art, and asked me to give him lessons in it. Later he summed up the situation by saying, "I am trying to teach a form of art expression that to you comes instinctively." He became interested in my future career and offered to take me abroad as his guest to see the great German, Dutch, Spanish, Flemish, and Italian masterpieces before I settled down to be a portrait painter and to do landscapes.

For three successive years, we traveled together seeing the great traditional art of the ancient world, and I taught Ross how to paint architectural and sculptural details in water colors by a technique that was impossible to distinguish from oils. In Spain and Italy our subjects, for the most part, were architecture in churches, while in Greece we painted sculptures. He learned my method of painting landscape as well, and became so skillful as the pupil-professor that, unless the pictures were signed, no one could tell which of us had done them.

In 1887 I had been appointed instructor in the decorative arts class of the Boston Museum School of Fine Arts as assistant to C. Howard Walker. This position I was to hold for four years, and it gave me sufficient leisure to execute private commissions at home and abroad. Later the same fortunate combination was repeated when I taught water-color painting in the architectural department at Harvard. Next year I was exhibiting my work in the galleries of the Museum and at the St. Botolph Club. Catalogs listed a versatility in my choice of subjects and medium. There were water-color details of churches and other buildings, landscape sketches and street scenes, copies of old masters, many pencil drawings, and, in oil, portraits from life and rather ambitious canvases of the scenery in Mexico.

A disagreeably phrased item about one of the exhibitions in a leading newspaper touched me to the quick. I rushed to Cousin John Whittier in his home at Amesbury for consolation. Without preamble I burst out indignantly that the newspaper stated, "Mr. Smith's work was without merit" and went on to say I, as an "aspiring young artist," was fortunate in "pleasing the fancy of Commonwealth Avenue," and that the purchasers of my carelessly executed sketches read like a "page in Boston's *Blue Book*." When I paused for breath, Cousin John laid an affectionate hand on my shoulder and said, "To have thy first exhibition completely ignored by the press and public would have given thee cause to worry, and remember, Joseph, poor folk can't buy pictures."

I was furious about having my commissions to paint portraits of Professor Shaler and Professor Joseph Lovering attributed to the fact that they were colleagues of Professor Denman Ross's at Harvard, who never missed an opportunity to "push his protégé from Rhode Island," and that I had got the order to do the portrait of the poet for the Whittier Club of Haverhill because of relationship, and not artistic qualifications.

This personal insinuation against Cousin John's motives he met by saying that the picture was to hang in the room of the old homestead where he had been born, and that was where family sentiment came in. Then, looking me straight in the eye, he told me solemnly that he had recommended me to the club because he felt confident my portrait would be a good likeness and have high artistic merit. He had been justified by the results, he assured me. I was never to forget, he said with great earnestness, that Denman Ross and others who were giving me their support in starting a career did so because they (like himself) believed I was a "born artist."

He commented that the critics as an unit had acclaimed my painting of the head of the famous bronze equestrian statue of Bartolommeo Colleoni, in the center of Venice, as "portraiture." He was greatly amused on hearing of the circumstances of my being the first artist to paint the heroic-sized, rugged face at close view. I had taken advantage of a ladder, placed against the statue and not yet removed after some repairs to the head. No one had protested as I had mounted it, and I returned to climb it again with a roll of canvas and paints. Three days later I had completed the picture without being ejected by officials. I was about to roll up my canvas when a cultivated woman's voice called up to me asking what I was doing.

"Painting the portrait of a great Venetian General," I answered.

"Come down and steady the ladder for me!" she said.

Her manner was that of a woman with the habit of command. I obeyed at once and stood beside her, impressed by the elegant simplicity of her gown and the magnificent ruby at her throat, and above all by the charm of her personality.

She went up the ladder without effort and perched in the uncomfortable seat I had vacated. It was almost half an hour before she rejoined me.

"You have caught the strength and courage Verrocchio got into the features and the delicious greenish patina of the bronze," she said, and ordered me to bring the picture and any other studies I had to the Palazzo Barberini. "I am Mrs. John L. Gardner," she turned to say, and was off.

This chance meeting was to mean much to me. I subsequently traveled with the Gardners abroad on many trips, assisted her in the creation of the Isabella Stuart Gardner Museum on the Fenway in Boston, and made numerous purchases for it. She always addressed me as "Colli" in her letters.

When I had finished telling him of these adventures, Cousin John's face began to look drawn and white, and I rose to say "good night."

"Not yet," he said with a detaining hand. "I wish to discuss a past age thy brush makes live again."

There was about him at that moment an irresistible persuasiveness that frequently had broken down my youthful defenses when he showed strong feeling. Such was now the case. He was obviously pleased at criticisms that referred, over-generously, to my "perfect understanding of the fifteenth-century Italian spirit," and in my painting of marble heads on tombs "conveying an almost miraculous feeling of eternal rest sought by the sculptor."

"But most of the critics will not accept thy gift as 'interpretive' and 'creative'!" he exclaimed. "I can't see what earthly difference it makes whether thy sitter is Gaston de Foix lying peacefully in marble on his tomb or Mrs. B. seated bolt upright, with an insipid smile on her face not worth perpetuating on canvas."

Under thirty my art interests were so varied that they led to indecisiveness as to my future. Both Sargent and Abbey encouraged me to devote myself exclusively to murals, based on traditional themes. This was after I had decorated a large alcove in the Boston Public Library (1894), and had been commissioned to do murals for the Horticultural Hall in Philadelphia. It was to be an outdoor frieze, at the time the longest mural to adorn the outside of a building ever awarded to an American painter. I was also continuing portraiture and landscape painting.

Primarily it was to be Cousin John's influence even more than Ross's that determined my selection of a highly specialized field of art in which I used what came to be termed a "new" technique in reproducing old wood and stone. This was reflected in a letter I wrote to my mother from Abu Simbel six years after Whittier's death. It read:

Cousin John was always patient and helped me with sound advice at various phases of my life. Therefore I wish he might have been the first one to know of a decision I have made that will greatly affect my future activities in art. He realized that I was not altogether happy in portraiture. My sitters were never on time, they invariably wriggled, and always had husbands or wives, mothers, and other relatives, each of whom had some criticism of the mouth, the nose, or the chin.

Now Ramesses the Great is posing for me, and he is the sort of a sitter I enjoy. He will always be on time, he won't wriggle, and his relatives, like himself, are in stone. Moreover, Dr. Reisner, the greatest of American

Egyptologists, has just seen my pictures painted in Egypt and advised me to continue this kind of work as a study series for museums. It looks very much as though thy son Joseph had found a "purpose in life."

2. *Lord Cromer's Cairo*

AT THE END of November, 1898, I was on a German steamer bound for the Mediterranean. I intended to disembark at Naples and remain in Italy until the following spring, to execute painting commissions of the art of the past. Instead of carrying out this program, I yielded to a sudden impulse to study the great temples and sculptured reliefs of the Nile Valley and, changing steamers, continued on to Alexandria.

This chance decision was destined to change my whole future career.

The first sight of the Orient stirred within me a thrill of eager expectancy unequaled in any of my previous travels. The sun was hot, the sky cloudless, and the sea streaked with many shades of brilliant blues, as beyond picturesque shipping of the port of Alexandria shone the white walls of houses, tall palms, and desert sands. Natives swarmed all over the ship as she approached the dock, vaulting aboard with extraordinary leaps, their movements apparently unhampered by long skirts. White teeth flashed in black faces as these odd-looking creatures struggled to possess themselves of the passengers' luggage laid out on the decks. The din was deafening, but the ship was a place of calm and order when compared to what happened as the passengers descended the gangplank to the dock.

One had to be agile to avoid buffaloes hitched to narrow carts, kneeling camels with wide loads adjusted to their backs, *galli galli* magicians calling attention to their exhibitions with shrill cries, and also not being caught unaware, in stooping to retrieve a valise, by a cobra with its head appearing out of a basket. I got to a cleared space and, seated on my modest luggage, looked about me until I was retrieved by a Cook's agent, who summoned a passing carriage, placed me and my belongings in it, and got us started for the railroad station.

When I reached Cairo, I settled myself in a modest room at Shepheard's Hotel and from the terrace watched the Orient drift by in the street below. Animals and humans mixed together in fascinating groups seen for a delightful moment, to be replaced by others equally memorable. Types that appealed to my paint brush appeared and went in bewildering confusion, and in an interesting variety of garments and headgear. A Persian miniature came to life for a second, an East Indian potentate passed, or a dramatic Arab posed instinctively. Nubians were in close proximity to some Scotch in kilts, English ladies and gentlemen, dressed for dinner, in open landaus were conspicuous from having all around them men in baggy trousers and long shirts and dignitaries in wide-sleeved, flowing robes and enormous turbans. These were indescribable scenes for color and, beyond all else, a mingling of indefinable cries and unfamiliar sounds.

There are not many foreigners left in Egypt who remember Cairo before it developed into a growing Levantine city with a number of features like those of other world capitals. There were no motors and but few European shops. In the heart of the city, in the vicinity of Opera Square, casual avenues were soft surfaced, which water carriers, sprinkling from pigskin sacks, turned into muddy pools difficult to cross. And along the edges, pedestrians had to avoid pitfalls in loosened earth around recently watered large trees. Near these thoroughfares there was a dignity in residential quarters, where old mansions and ornate palaces had high walls that gave rambling gardens an air of aloofness that was charming in itself. Cairo was an amusing sight at dusk, when from the spreading branches of banyan trees or sycamores, with a loud fluttering of wings, vulture-like birds swept down from a high perch to serve as town scavengers.

The able-bodied of all nationalities, male and female, rode through the streets on tall white donkeys from Assiut or imported from Syria. Smart, two-wheeled, high carts, with a spirited Arab pony between the shafts, were frequent sights among old-time landaus drawn by well-matched pairs. All equipages, with foreigners or important Turkish dignitaries in them, were preceded by outrunners richly garbed in wide, baggy trousers and short jackets of blue or red cloth heavily embroidered in gold, and very full, long white linen sleeves waving in the breeze.

11

These *sais,* as they were called, kept up steady shouts of "Clear the way," an order they were prepared to enforce with a heavy stick held high. Natives and livestock scattered promptly. Even more interesting were carriages with veiled ladies and, seated beside the drivers, eunuchs, who kept a watchful eye on any male who ventured to approach within speaking distance.

On certain days of the week, a four-in-hand coach, under English management, was driven between Shepheard's and Mena House, on which a place had to be reserved in advance. One sped along over a narrow dirt road, with its entire length from Giza to the Pyramids attractively shaded by a double row of sweet-scented acacia trees meeting overhead. Strings of well-groomed polo ponies frequently passed through the streets led proudly by native attendants on their way to the British Sports Club. Solid-looking Englishmen in smart riding attire and mounted on superb thoroughbreds volubly expressed their annoyance if held up even briefly by a surging crowd, in which the young town *effendi,* wearing a fez and European clothes, were not yet self-assertive with nationalistic ideas exciting them.

All in all, one got the feeling of being in a city, oriental in its char-acter and population, but dominated by the British way of life. There was much in the way of display and passing pageantry that simple Egyptians loved, especially on the wide parade grounds at the Kasr el-Nil barracks, where maneuvers took place with the traditional cere-mony of British troops throughout her Empire.

Lord Cromer was of an imposing stature, very dignified, stern-eyed, and with a haughty mien. His was a personality that did not court intimacy among his colleagues, and among Egyptians of all classes he inspired fear as a symbol of the British occupation of Egypt. He was an impressive sight in the streets, seated in an enormous open landau drawn by superb horses, and with an escort of Englishmen and many outrunners.

Several times I watched a moving crowd of natives stop in their tracks to stare in awe at the great Englishman, while none of them had seemed to notice their ruler's passage through the same streets. I could not but wonder whether His Highness the Khedive resented the contrast in the attitude of the populace or, with a Moslem's resignation, accepted the situation as the will of Allah.

Blinding sunlight, deep shadows, and a riot of color made me forget the filth and signs of poverty in the native quarter of the town. Most of all I lingered in the bazaars, where I was carried along in a surging crowd composed of many races, or stopped to admire some simple object of local manufacture I longed to own. The sense of rhythm in both the moving throngs and the pounding on metal, the clashing of cymbals, and the crashing of looms was exhilarating.

For some time I stood facing the Gami' el-Ghari Mosque. The doorway was very high and narrow and the ornamentation rich with Eastern intricacy, a splendid piece of lettering from the Koran topped the lintel, and above was the blue sky—and such a blue! It would have been a superb subject, but I was in no mood for painting with amusing scenes being enacted all about me to distract attention from the complete concentration such a study required.

I wandered from mosque to mosque and found much to admire as an artist but nothing that tempted my brush.

Then I drove to Giza, and no words could describe my thoughts when, on the edge of yellow desert, I saw my first pyramid. I went from it and sat in the hot sand and gazed into the battered and mutilated face of the Sphinx, as so many millions of other human beings had done before me. I tried to imagine the scene if all who had ever looked at the Sphinx were seated there together, forming an enormous living carpet covering the great desert stretch of sand.

I knew *I* would be back again and again.

3. *Destination—Upper Egypt*

I HAD TELEGRAPHED a distinguished American artist friend of Denman Ross's named Henry Newman, whose home was in Florence but who, with his wife, spent the winter months on the Nile living on a *dahabieh,* painting year after year in the Temple of Philae at Assuan. When he telegraphed back a cordial invitation to join them, I made my plans accordingly.

Within three days I was actually on my way to Upper Egypt on a small, inexpensive tourist steamer, the *Columbia,* which was attempting to compete with Cook's monopoly of travel for foreigners. It proved to be a memorable experience to see nearly a thousand miles of the Nile from the deck of a steamer.

I never tired of the native boats, built for trade on the same lines since ancient times, with a broad stern and a fine, curved upsweep to a high prow. When they moved along with a favoring northerly wind, their tall white sails were spread out like the wings of a huge bird in flight. And towards dusk, after the wind fell, was the enjoyable, though less dramatic, sight of river craft with furled sails drifting downstream, aided by a swift current and long sweeps or a pole. I liked to see the great black hulls, motionless against mud banks from sunset on, and also signs of activity among the crew and native passengers which began soon after dawn.

On both sides of the river high, distant cliffs frequently stretched the length of one's vision, pink or red where the sun's rays touched them, dark blue in the shadows. The variety of the skies was endless, at times like those Giovanni Bellini loved to paint, green and wonderfully translucent, or of an unbelievable blue. And delicate white cumulus clouds had edges aflame at sunrise and again at the last gasp of the dying day. I had never seen stars as brilliant except in Mexico, and even the moon failed to dim their radiance.

I saw, unchanged through the centuries, desert wastes, black earth, and the ever-moving river, and along the banks were fields of waving sugar cane or other growing crops that glistened in the warm light, golden green in color, and water from a lower level was being raised by man power or by creaking large wheels and trickled through narrow ditches among the crops in which men sang and laughed as they patiently toiled from daybreak till dark.

I found an instant charm that defied definition in low mud houses, stately palms and sunt trees, drab human beings, strange and familiar domestic animals, poverty, flies, and ageless dust, a combination that ever has been village life in Egypt—a charm that I knew could be recaptured by a reminiscent odor or sound as long as I lived.

Trips ashore, to this tomb and that temple, meant long donkey rides during the glare and heat in the company of a dozen fellow passengers, Baedeker in hand, who kept interrupting the droning voice of our energetic dragoman with eager questions. Wonderful monuments were scattered over the Theban Plain across the river, situated at great distances from one another. In the town of Luxor there was an important temple, and ruins in near-by Karnak.

Ahmose I, founder of the New Kingdom (1570–1085 B.C.) made Thebes the capital city of Egypt. He dedicated to an already existing god, Amon, the temple at Karnak, that was to be the greatest of all the New Kingdom monuments, with each ruler in turn recording his deeds in self-glorification in courts, colonnades, and lesser temples added to the main building.

I had listened to our dragoman telling which king had done what over a period of two thousand years, in temples covering an area sufficiently large to accommodate Notre Dame in Paris, and returned to the *Columbia* in a mood of rebellion. But it was a night of full moon, and without waiting for supper I slipped off to Karnak again by myself. There I sat alone in the great Hypostyle Hall. And as the moonlight picked out delightful details on the tall columns, I dreamed my dreams of Egypt's former splendor.

After two more days of river I reached my destination, Assuan, where the first cataract blocked passage into Nubia. There was only one hotel for tourists, large and very expensive, run by Cook. And I was greatly relieved when the steamer manager got me into a simple establishment where the few bedrooms were over a popular café. It was managed by a Greek who spoke Italian, so we got on well together. My leisure moments after dark were spent in this crowded, lively café, where the noise was deafening, a canary bird's high notes adding to the racket. At small tables around the sides of the room sat Greeks and Arabs, Italians and Nubians, two Englishmen, a few Turks, several

15

Germans, and myself. Cards, checkers, and backgammon were games played by this mixture of races in a confusion of tongues.

I especially enjoyed Arabs with skins of a beautiful red-brown, like polished old Japanese bronze, and fine aristocratic features, who constantly gesticulated with long-fingered hands as they talked; and the Nubians were amusing, coal black, with flat noses and thick lips, and silver rings thrust into the upper part of the ear—not the lobe. It was a congenial atmosphere into which I fitted. My room was clean, the food sufficient, and I was to pay one dollar a day for bed and board, which included a sandwich lunch.

The day after my arrival I went to the lovely island of Philae. I found its situation unique, with trees and shrubs growing close to temples, in a wonderful state of preservation, with the colors on the sculptured reliefs, which must have been originally too bright, now delicate and exquisite. The main temple, dedicated to Isis, was built by Ptolemy II (285–247 B.C.), the second ptolemy to succeed Alexander the Great.

The Newmans' *dahabieh*, the *Hapi*, was moored close by. They gave me a cordial welcome, offered to take care of my painting equipment and pictures, and urged me to stay with them on board the *dahabieh*. I said I would be glad to do so occasionally, and we left it at that.

It was with a thrill of expectation that I walked up the steep sides of the island and into a beautiful temple dedicated to Isis. That morning I started on a magnificent doorway as a small boy sat beside me and brushed away flies. I enjoyed eating my lunch in the sun after having been in the shade all the morning. Little native children sat in front of me as I ate and, like hungry dogs, watched every motion of my hand to my mouth. I found it impossible with such wistful black eyes on me not to have food left over for those youngsters. In the afternoon I began a large picture of sculptured details on four columns in a bluish light.

When my light had gone, I joined Newman, who was a strange sight at work. He was not tall, but heavily built, with a sensitive, clean-shaven face and small, delicate hands. Both his face and hands were abnormally pallid, and he wore gloves without fingers. He seemed extremely nervous and obviously was disturbed by my unannounced

Joseph Lindon Smith painting in the tomb of Mereruka, 1907. Painting at left, original bas-relief at right: Mereruka and son.

Great Hall in the Temple of Isis, Island of Philae. Painting by Joseph Lindon Smith. Courtesy Fogg Museum of Art, Harvard University.

approach to him in his tent. In spite of the heat, he had on a heavy overcoat with the collar turned up, and a muffler. When he recognized me,
he smiled. Mrs. Newman, who was a large, imposing, handsome woman,
was beside him looking prepared to chase away flies and people, and was
doing something to protect him from imaginary draughts. She relaxed
at his reception of me, and we had tea in solemn state on the *dahabieh*.

I was familiar with Newman's water colors of Philae, painted with
a tightness of technique and lacking in clear tones, and with such minute
details that he frequently worked on the same study for several seasons.
Denman Ross told me that they had a great vogue and that he sold
them at large prices to clients who were lords and other rich people.

The Weir Mitchells and Philip Schuylers were on a *dahabieh* moored
behind "Pharoah's Bed," and they wined and dined me. They insisted
on having me go with them to the formal lunch at the hotel given in
honor of the Duke of Connaught, who was in Assuan in connection
with the great dam that was about to be built. But on this impressive
occasion I could only think that the additional water bottled up in a
huge reservoir, when released, would eventually submerge lovely Philae
and drown the attractive little town of Shellal.

Quite often I spent the night on the *Hapi* so I could wander about
among the monuments in the semidarkness. For more than two thousand years in the inner shrines of these temples the rushing bats had
shared the privacy with the Ptolemies and their protecting gods. But
shortly the first sound heard in the morning would be a shrill whistle
summoning the men of Shellal to work above Assuan, drilling in the
solid granite to make an irrigation system that would submerge these
temples for the greater part of the year. And when that same whistle
blew again at sunset, it would be a reminder to those same workmen
that by their day's toil their own homes and their date-bearing palm
trees were one day nearer to destruction.

I was vaguely beginning to consider my plans after Philae when in
the bazaars I happened to run across Roger Rich, a landscape painter
from Boston whom I had known pleasantly enough. He fired my
enthusiasm for a camping trip with him at the rock-hewn temple of Abu

Simbel. He said it was on the river bank not far from Wadi Halfa and the second cataract. We could get a small government post boat running from near-by Shellal into Nubia that would not be expensive, and he thought he could hire in Assuan a simple camp outfit. Luck came our way when, through one of my Greek friends, I met the sub-governor of the Sudan, an Egyptian living in Assuan. Through him and the local Greek postmaster, every difficulty was overcome and a fine tent was hired from the Chief of Police.

The Newmans found us a young Nubian named Dowe Mohamed to care for our simple needs. He was about twenty and spoke a fluent but rather strange English. He was dark-skinned but not a pronounced negroid type, with sparkling, responsive eyes, fine teeth, and a charming smile. He was so confident of his ability to give us complete satisfaction that I never doubted it.

Not only Dowe, but a younger brother of twelve named Abdullah, was waiting for us on the boat at Shellal. We had a day through rocky country, and occasionally the nose of the boat ran into the bank to leave mail and collect natives. About ten o'clock the following night, we neared a line of high cliffs, and soon thereafter there appeared in the mysterious light the huge seated figures guarding the temple of Abu Simbel and a great glacier of sand at one side that extended far up to the tall top of the cliff. Dowe bundled our things ashore on to a very narrow strip, whereat the custodian appeared from nowhere and helped put up our tent on the plateau close to the fragments of the head of the fourth statue, of which only the lower part remained. I heard an owl and later a wolf before going to sleep.

At dawn little Abdullah opened the flap of the tent a crack and slipped his thin little body inside and pulled out supplies from beneath my bed. I jumped up, and after a refreshing swim in the Nile, I saw the red sunlight creep down from the cliffs above until it lay like a warm blush over those impassive faces.

I squatted on my heels on the stone platform at the right distance to look at those seated figures to their best advantage. My complete absorption was interrupted by Dowe's summons to breakfast, which I ignored. I hurried to my tent to get a canvas and paints. I did not put down my brush until I had laid in with color the superb head of one of the Ramesses.

Immediately after the first rays of the rising sun reached the colossi, the brilliant sunlight flooded the interior of the temple, even reaching the holy of holies. The double line of statues and painted decorations on roofs and doorways were gorgeous. Ramesses in his chariot charged fiercely against enemies over long walls. All too soon, as the sun rose higher, the back part of the temple was again engulfed in blackness, and I was seated in the shadows. It was during this brief period that I worked on my first interior, a detail of reliefs carved on a column in warm, reflected sunlight and looking out through the great entrance door, a stretch of the river and hills on the farther shore showed in my picture—a view that was wonderful in the freshness of early morning. By breakfast time the light had changed, and I returned to paint on a large oil of the temple façade.

The nearest town was a small, straggling village of mud huts on the opposite shore, with beautiful tall palms waving over them. We heard the melancholy squeaking of numerous water wheels, and dogs barked all night. But in the early evening it was very quiet at Abu Simbel. I used to walk by the light of a single candle into the absolute stillness and the blackness of the holy of holies in the great temple.

My last waking thought would be of this Ramesses, who, during his long reign of forty-six years, had built more than a half of the existing temples in Egypt. I had seen his enormous court in the Luxor temple, admired his stupendous Hypostyle Hall at Karnak, and paid tribute to his Ramesseum, on the Theban Plain. None of these architectural masterpieces rivaled this Abu Simbel, where four seated figures with impassive faces kept a stony vigil.

It was here, at this temple, that Mrs. Phoebe A. Hearst caught me unaware and saw the work I was doing. The encounter led to all of the subsequent adventures recounted in this book.

SEARCHING FOR TOMBS

1904-1905

4. *Archaeologists as Neighbors*

THE NEXT SEASON (1899-1900) I began family life on the Nile. I hired a sailing *dahabieh* at Assuan, and with my wife, Corinna, whom I had married in September, 1899, and my parents, had two months in Nubia, spending most of our time moored to the bank in front of the Temple of Abu Simbel.

By the late fall of 1904 we were all back in Egypt, having added to the party by our two children, Rebecca and Frances. Again we took possession of a *dahabieh* at Assuan, but this time with the intention of going down river to Luxor.

The gigantic Assuan dam was now a *fait accompli* with sluices, canals, and navigation locks. The Nile was still rising, and the approach to the main court of the temple of Isis, on the island of Philae, had to be made in a rowboat. I was forced to paint sitting on a plank placed on a staging against the temple wall above the water line. The whole island was desolate with tottering masonry and bas-reliefs broken by wide, disfiguring cracks, and much of the beautiful vegetation was already destroyed by flood waters. The site of the attractive little town of Shellal could be identified by a fringe of tall date-bearing palms standing far out in the river. I was told that these trees would belong to their owners until they fell, and, ironically, the owners had to continue to pay taxes on a date crop they could no longer gather.

We were not tempted to linger in such depressing surroundings. Just before our departure for Luxor, Sir Colin Moncrieff, the chief engineer of the dam, turned up at our *dahabieh* with a letter of introduction. He stayed on for dinner and talked at length about the difficult construction problems that had to be overcome in the building of this large storage reservoir that was expected to revolutionize the economic life of Egypt. It was interesting to meet the man with the creative imagination to achieve the project of a dam a mile and a half in length. But Dowe, with many other natives, believed that the famine in Upper Egypt, coincident with the years of the building of the dam, was caused by the anger of *afreet* (evil spirits) living in the great granite boulders that had been blasted from place by dynamite, and he all but refused to serve food to that "bad man," as he termed Sir Colin.

On Christmas night a full moon made it possible for the boat to continue in motion until Luxor was in sight at dawn. We moored on the western shallow sandbank of Thebes, facing the vast plain with the Colossi of Memnon, the temples of Medinet Habu, the Ramesseum, Deir-el-Bahari, and also the tombs of the nobles of Sheikh Abd'-el-Qurna Necropolis. Behind these ancient monuments and extending the length of the western horizon were high, rocky cliffs. At once arrangements were made for a long stay, a permanent gangplank was put out, and a tent pitched on the sand.

A number of British and American travelers on sailing *dahabiehs* or private steamers often stopped for several weeks at a time. The simple-minded, happy-go-lucky crews made the evenings lively with song and dancing, and had a friendly community life of their own. One late afternoon father counted six such boats flying the American flag. We were very fortunate in the archaeologists who were river neighbors. Gaston Maspero, the French head of the Antiquities Service of the Egyptian government since 1881, would frequently arrive on official trips on a small steamer.

The Frenchman, Mariette Bey, had been director-general of Antiquities for the Egyptian government from 1858 to 1881. He had done a magnificent service in the preservation of Egyptian antiquities, protecting the sites of tombs, and in building a government museum in Cairo. Therefore, when the British occupied Egypt in 1882, an agreement was made between the British and French foreign offices that there would always be a Frenchman to head the Antiquities Service in Egypt, with English inspectors under him.

Maspero was short and stout and full of fun; he was very gallant with ladies in an archaeological party, and displayed the enthusiasm of a boy at each new "find." No one had the temerity to question Maspero's conclusions, since he was the acknowledged greatest living brain on Egyptology, and withal the charm of his personality was unforgettable.

The *Istar,* one of the largest sailing *dahabiehs* on the Nile, remained for a stay of several months. Its owner, Professor A. H. Sayce of Oxford, was, like Maspero, a world figure in scholarship. A small man with sunken, bespectacled eyes, thin hair, and a slight mustache and goatee, he had a sensitive face and hollow cheeks which gave an impression of the ill health he had fought successfully since boyhood. He told inimitable anecdotes and was very good to our children, who listened enthralled to an account of his having survived the bite of a horned asp and other adventures. At the opening of a tomb, Sayce was a familiar sight in the dust-covered, long black skirts of his clerical garments and a three-cornered hat, hopefully searching for the cuneiform tablets of the Hittites. At the rounded stern of the *Istar* was a comprehensive working library on Egyptology, and one usually found visitors there, many of them men of distinction.

Professor Somers Clarke often moored near us. He was agreeable and frequently brought guests with him on his luxurious boat. Directly in front of ours was the *dahabieh* belonging to an American, Theodore M. Davis of Newport, Rhode Island. He was an eccentric, brusque little man but a good friend to people he liked, and I was among them. This was his winter home while he was engaged in excavating a concession in the Valley of the Tombs of the Kings granted him by the Egyptian government. Robert Mond was financing excavations in the Sheikh Abd'-el-Qurna Necropolis, and stopped in fairly often when his day's work was finished, to chat before crossing the river to his own magnificent steamer, where he gave banquets to visiting dignitaries. He had a daughter about Rebecca's age whom the mother would bring to play on our sandbank. Mond was cordial in inviting me to "his" tombs, where I did some pictures of gay painted reliefs.

Georges Legrain found a most interesting drain at Karnak, between the Sacred Lake and recent excavations, which he considered a very important discovery. He proved that it went to the Nile and was used in ancient times. This energetic and amusing French director of works for the Egyptian government was as pleased with his canal as a child with a new toy. One day he persuaded me to descend with him into a damp, cold shaft to examine by torchlight a sluice and peculiar joints of well-laid masonry. I was left alone while Legrain was summoned to receive a distinguished guest. He soon returned and introduced me to Marquis Rudini, wearing patent leather boots and otherwise inappropriate attire for a dirty, dark pit. To say that the Marquis was not favorably impressed by the drain would be an understatement.

Those of us living on *dahabiehs* met frequently the staffs of French, Italian, and German archaeological expeditions in the vicinity. That season Professor Kurt Sethe of the University of Berlin was among the scholars at the "German" house. He was assistant to Professor Adolf Erman in the monumental task of compiling for the University of Berlin a dictionary of hieroglyphics based on a rechecking of the texts in tombs and temples. He was a small, thin man with a birdlike look accentuated by pinched features. And in great physical contrast to the solemn-faced Sethe was Edouard Naville of Geneva, Switzerland, a large, heavy-set man with an engaging manner and a pleasant smile. Naville was excavating the temple of Deir-el-Bahari for the Egypt Exploration Society. These two men, for some months on end near neighbors in a lonely desert area, were not on speaking terms because of a disagreement between them, carried on in print, concerned with events in the reign of Queen Hatshepsut, the builder of Deir-el-Bahari, and dead almost thirty-five hundred years.

Sethe had convictions about a confused period in Dynasty XVIII, after the death of Tuthmosis I in 1508 B.C., during the reigns of his son, Tuthmosis II, and Hatshepsut, his daughter by another Queen, who married her half-brother. Tuthmosis II, after a brief four years as king, was succeeded by Hatshepsut, who ruled jointly with her stepson, Tuthmosis III, until her death in 1483 B.C. Then Tuthmosis III, for the remainder of his long reign, which ended in 1450 B.C., became one of the great warrior kings of Egypt.

Sethe believed that family quarreling had interrupted the reigns, and that several times Hatshepsut had been driven from the throne and regained it. He considered that Hatshepsut, who always appeared on temple walls in male attire and referred to herself as "King," was the dominating factor in royal affairs throughout her life, aided and abetted by her architect, Senmut. Professor Naville considered that Sethe's conclusions were based on insufficient evidence and frankly said so. Sethe took offense. The feud was awkward in a small archaeological community, when carried to such an extent that Sethe would not remain in the same room with Naville. The kindly Maspero had failed in his attempts to heal the breach.

During Naville's excavations a great stone was suddenly loosened, and in falling brought down with it a mass of debris. Possibly a change in the position of long-settled debris caused the undermining of the foundations of the Naville's simple camp house, built near his excavations. In any case, Naville's kitchen collapsed into a tomb pit, with cook, utensils, and stove.

The rumor reached Sethe that Madame Naville was utterly discouraged at this housekeeping calamity, and insisted that her husband's excavations should be discontinued immediately and he return with her to Switzerland, whereupon Sethe invited the Navilles to stay with him—on condition that Hatshepsut's name was not to be mentioned. The invitation was accepted, and the German and Swiss scholars had a delightful time together exchanging ideas on learned subjects. After several weeks, when the kitchen had been rebuilt, the cook had recovered, and the utensils had been reclaimed or replaced, the Navilles returned to their camp house—and the feud over Hatshepsut was resumed.

5. *Discovery of the Tomb of Ouiya and Touiyou*

THE VALLEY of the Tombs of the Kings is on the west bank at Thebes. Very deep tombs were hewn in the living rock for kings of Dynasty XVIII (1570–1349 B.C.), Dynasty XIX (1349–1197 B.C.), and Dynasty XX (1197–1085 B.C.).

The following kings are mentioned in this incident:

Dynasty XVIII, Queen Hatshepsut (1504–1483 B.C.)
    Amenhotep II (1450–1423 B.C.)
    Tuthmosis IV (1423–1410 B.C.)
    Amenhotep III (1410–1372 B.C.)
    Amenhotep IV (Akhenaten) (1380–1363 B.C.)
Dynasty XX, Ramesses III (1195–1164 B.C.)
    Ramesses XI (last of Ramesses), whose reign ended in 1085 B.C.
The mummies found in this tomb were identified as:
        Ouiya, father of Queen Tiyi.
        Touiyou, mother of Queen Tiyi.

Both Ouiya and Touiyou had been connected with the court of Tuthmosis IV when the young prince was attracted by their daughter. When, on his father's death, the prince became king as Amenhotep III, he married the daughter, and she was known as Queen Tiyi.

The ages of Ouiya and Touiyou have not been determined, but both had white hair, and neither looked under fifty. Queen Tiyi was supposed to have married Amenhotep III the first year of his being king and was probably at least fourteen at the time.

Their son was a minor when, on the death of his father in 1372 B.C., he became king as Amenhotep IV, with Queen Tiyi, his mother, as regent. Later the son changed his name to "Akhenaten" and moved the court from Thebes to el-Amarna, where he died.

Queen Tiyi was known to have survived her son, but there is no record of how much longer she lived.

A "find" and the attendant excitement would temporarily interrupt my painting routine—as, for example, when Ernesto Schiaparelli, heading an Italian expedition for the Turin Museum in the Valley of the Tombs of the Queens and Deir-el-Medineh, found the tomb of Kha, a noble of the time of Amenhotep II (1450–1423 B.C.). The intact chamber was crowded with extremely well-preserved furniture. I was allowed to look inside and saw in the sandy surface over bedrock the footprints made in ancient times, probably by the last priest out, before he sealed the doorway. Another interesting discovery was that by Legrain at Karnak. He came upon a Greco-Roman shop, on the remains of wooden shelves of which were hundreds of miniature bronze figures of Egyptian gods and goddesses, with the price tags still in place on them. Corinna and I assisted all day in classifying the bronzes.

During January, 1905, we had seen a good deal of Mr. Davis and his party, including Mrs. Emma B. Andrews, a cousin of Mrs. Davis, and her two nieces, and he promised that if he found anything of importance he would be glad to have me among the first to see the discovery.

Maspero had earlier taken advantage of the interest of a wealthy American to have Davis agree to the clearing of the rubbish from the Valley of the Tombs of the Kings where the kings of Dynasty XVIII (1570–1340 B.C.) and Dynasty XIX (1349–1197 B.C.) were buried. According to the terms of his contract with the Egyptian government, Davis was to continue the concession as long as he wished as the sole "digger" in the royal valley. He was to pay all the bills, but the objects found were to belong to the Egyptian government.

During 1902 and 1903, in clearing the mouth of the valley, Davis had discovered the tombs of Tuthmosis IV and of Queen Hatshepsut, both of Dynasty XVIII. But now he had transferred his workmen to a small space between the Dynasty XX tombs of Ramesses III (1195–1164 B.C.) and Ramesses XI (1164–1085 B.C.). There was little likelihood of finding a royal tomb because of lack of space for the type of tomb that was very deep underground with long flights of stairs and endless corridors with chambers on both sides of them.

The digging had proceeded through an interminable heap of fragments of stone which had been taken out by the builders of these Ramesses tombs.

I kept in close touch with what was going on in the Valley of the Kings, where our friend, Arthur Weigall, was to superintend Mr. Davis's excavations for the Egyptian government. Maspero had appointed Weigall to be inspector of antiquities for Upper Egypt, a position Edward J. Quibell was to give up to be in charge of Saqqarah.

Most unexpectedly in the late afternoon of February 5, 1905, the top step of a tomb was uncovered. The second and third steps were found, but the rubbish above came down in an avalanche, making further progress difficult. On February 11, the top of the doorway was uncovered. It had originally been walled up, but the seals had been broken, therefore the tomb below was not an "untouched" one. The workmen were dismissed and they scrambled over the *gebel* to their Qurna homes, to spread the news. Weigall kept with him only the *reis* of the diggers and his small son, who was "captain" of the basket carriers.

Davis arrived posthaste from his *dahabieh.* A course of the walled-up doorway was taken down, the boy's turban was unwound and tied under his arms, and his father lowered him through the opening much against the boy's will, as he kept crying out that he was afraid of *afreet* (evil spirits) in the dark. Weigall's purpose was to have the boy discover whether the passageway was empty of rubbish and if there were inscriptions on the wall. The boy handed up into his father's hand the staff of a prince, a golden-handled and ferruled cane of a wood something like ebony, a large scarab, a pair of sandals, and the yoke of a chariot heavily gilded. It was obvious that these things had been dropped by a thief after reaching daylight and finding that the objects were not solid gold.

The heart-rending cries of the thoroughly scared little boy ended his ordeal. After he had said there were no inscriptions or reliefs on the wall and the entrance passage was clear, he was hauled out by his father.

Weigall helped the *reis* replace the stones in the wall and cover the entire entrance to the tomb with wooden planks. Davis tied his discoveries to the pommel of his saddle and concealed them with his overcoat. He mounted his donkey and rode out of the valley, across the plain to the river bank.

It was market day, and Davis met men of Qurna coming from Luxor without any possible way of having received information about his find, since no one except the *reis* and the boy had been present, and they were still in the valley. Nevertheless, several villagers accosted Davis and declared: "We know that you have under your coat the staff of a prince, a large scarab, and a pair of sandals."

Davis was too dumbfounded to speak, when another man added, "Also the yoke of a chariot of solid gold." This was indeed disconcerting!

It happened that Maspero was on his government steamer moored close to Davis's *dahabieh,* and a servant was sent to request Maspero to come over as soon as possible.

The great Egyptologist had seen hundreds of objects taken from tombs and showed no special excitement until he caught sight of the yoke of the chariot, then exclaimed enthusiastically: "This tomb will be a great discovery if a chariot awaits us, because, except for the one in the museum at Turin, no example of an early Egyptian chariot is known."

At that moment Weigall arrived, and Maspero, turning to him, asked: "Who is guarding the tomb through the night?"

Weigall explained that there were planks across the entrance and the door was walled up and sealed, and that in the valley were twelve *ghaffir* (tomb guards), all picked men who had fought under Kitchener at Khartoum, and who took turns on duty, six by day and six by night.

Maspero said emphatically that this was not enough in the way of protection.

"I have already heard in Luxor this afternoon that a tomb has been found in the valley filled with gold."

Weigall asked what further precautions should be taken, and Maspero replied, "You must yourself spend the night near the tomb."

Weigall had an engagement to have dinner with us that evening and came abroad our *dahabieh* to tell of the discovery of the tomb. He said that he had been ordered by Maspero to spend the night in the valley. He made a pretense of danger, and, pretended that he'd be "lonely."

Corinna said, jokingly: "Wouldn't you like company? Joe and I will gladly spend the night assisting you to guard the tomb."

To her surprise Weigall accepted the offer eagerly.

"Come as soon as you can, and bring something to eat," he suggested, "and blankets—there's nothing in the valley you know."

He got to the gangplank, then came back to repeat how pleased he was that we'd be over to join him. Then he disappeared on his donkey, for active night duty in a valley that he described to Corinna as "wonderful in the sunshine, but grim after nightfall."

All this I learned from her just before sunset, when I returned from "my" tomb. She was waiting for me on the sand and called out: "Keep your donkey. The tomb has been found and you and I are going there at once to spend the night guarding it with Arthur Weigall."

I told our faithful old donkey boy, Hassan Basouni, that, in addition to the donkey I was riding, we wanted another one immediately, and a camel to carry food and blankets.

Hassan went with the camel by the long route into the valley, and Corinna and I on the donkeys took a short cut across the fields, riding rapidly. At the temple of Deir-el-Bahari the donkey boys refused to go any farther. They were sure *afreet* were about. There was nothing to do but dismiss them with their animals, and Corinna and I walked unaccompanied up the steep workmen's trail, stumbling along a rough, narrow path, with a flickering candle to supplement the moonlight at doubtful turns.

It *was* rather scary, and the sudden mournful howling of a jackal made us both jump. A cold wind got colder as we climbed higher. At the top of the cliff, as our figures were silhouetted against the sky, we were challenged by a voice from the dark pit of the valley below. "Who are you?"

We shouted back, "Friends of the Inspector!" hoping that in all the excitement Weigall had remembered to tell the *ghaffir* we were expected.

We were greatly relieved on recognizing Weigall's voice. "Never thought you'd really turn up," he kept repeating, and said he was beginning to feel very hungry. Hassan had made good time, and our *dahabieh* cook, Abdul Rahman, had prepared a meal for us that only needed to be heated over a small burner he had packed.

We were all three pretty tired and decided to turn in early after our meal. We rolled ourselves in blankets and stretched out on the hard planks across the entrance to the tomb. Corinna was terrified of Weigall's pistol, so I got him to place it at a safe distance. But the six *ghaffir,* squatting over a small fire within a few feet of the tomb we were all guarding together, were armed, and we couldn't do anything about the long guns they flourished about with appalling carelessness as they chatted steadily.

Weigall's imagination in describing what might be in the tomb kept us wide awake, and several times when the *ghaffir* heard our voices they produced coffee! Before 3:00 A.M. we got up for good. We wandered over the *gebel,* one peak tempting us on to another, in the unearthly beauty of moonlight, and later, in the even greater loveliness of the coming of dawn. We were so enthralled by the show Nature was giving us that we actually *forgot the tomb* we were supposed to be guarding. And sunrise took us by surprise, on quite a high peak in the western valley.

We were eating a meager breakfast supplemented by coffee given us by the friendly *ghaffir* when we had visitors, two silent young English archaeologists and a good-looking young Italian, who was not silent. He had a long, distinguished name ending in "Medici," and informed us volubly about being a Coptic scholar, and that Bernard Berensen said about him he'd been "brought up by too many maiden aunts." The Italian's immaculate appearance in riding breeches and highly polished boots, and his recently shaved face, gave Weigall and me an inferiority complex, disheveled as we were, for we had not washed or shaved, nor even brushed our hair. The three of them hung about hoping to be asked to be present when the tomb was opened, but reluctantly departed when no invitation was forthcoming. The visit had delayed us in packing up our simple camp outfit.

Meanwhile word had come from Maspero that he and Davis would arrive shortly, and that Weigall was to have the planks removed and the stones in the doorway taken out. It was tantalizing to sit about and wait when all was in readiness for the discovery of what lay beneath that flight of steps.

Davis and Maspero arrived together at about nine o'clock. Maspero walked to the head step and, looking into the dark passageway, said, *"Bon!* I see the tomb is prepared for our entry." Then he turned to Davis, just behind him, who was trying to peer into *"his"* tomb over Maspero's shoulder. "I am getting pretty old for riding donkeys and I don't know how much longer I will be able to take the long trip to this valley." And added, "I shall take advantage of being here this morning to show you, Davis, in the near-by Western Wadi, a promising site I've wanted to excavate ever since my youth, when I first began working in this area."

And to Weigall's and my amazement, Maspero took Davis away with him, calling back to us: "Until we return, please continue to guard this tomb as you have done through the night."

If this was not enough delay, there was another. It was customary for the Duke of Connaught, uncle of the King of England and head of the Egyptian Army, to make a yearly official inspection trip of Upper Egypt. He was greatly interested in the ancient monuments and never missed a special archaeological experience that came his way. Weigall knew that the Duke was to be at Edfu that morning with Quibell in attendance and at an afternoon program arranged for Karnak, but Maspero had received a telegram from Lord Cromer stating that if the tomb in the valley turned out to be a fine one, the Duke was to be reached at once, and be present at the opening.

An hour passed, and Weigall, who was getting bothered, appealed to me: " Joe, don't you think I should get a message to Maspero, reminding him of the length of time it will take to reach the Duke at Edfu."

I did think so, and a *ghaffir* was sent to find Maspero.

Weigall and I became restless. We'd get up, look through the opened doorway that seemed inviting us to enter, then try to possess our souls in patience. Finally I burst out: "Weigall, if you feel that a message should go to the Duke at once, if the tomb is good, why don't you go down and find out what is in it?"

"Would you really?" he asked.

"Yes," I said, "but I can't let you go alone."

And we lit two candles and started down those tantalizing steps.

We walked down a passage cut out of solid rock at a sharp angle, and on a stone ledge to the left of us lay the first object we saw—a funeral wreath of onions, which, though it had become brown from age, was as perfect in shape as the day it was left there three thousand years before. Near the wreath was a large black wig that had managed to retain its "ceremonial" aspect. Some distance below the ledge we went down a second flight of very steep steps, but found our progress barred at the bottom by a second walled-up doorway. Thieves in ancient times had pulled down several courses of the stones. Thrusting our arms and candles through this opening into the darkness beyond, we peered at an extraordinary sight.

Directly in front of us was a great wooden box or case, the sides of which, towards us, had been broken and the top lifted up until it struck the roof of the tomb chamber. Within were three coffins, one inside the other, and their covers had been thrown against the far side of the box. In the innermost coffin, which was of wood richly carved and gilded, lay a mummy. The wrappings had been torn away from the face and hands of an old man of striking appearance and dignity. His splendid head and fine features bore a marked resemblance to Lincoln. The hands crossed on the breast were noticeably well formed.

To the left I saw a similar great box, the sides and lid of which had also been thrown aside. In it lay exposed the mummy of a woman, also in a rich gold coffin. The face was serene and interesting, a low brow and eyes wide apart, and a curiously expressive, sensitive mouth.

All about them was the gleam of gold and a wonderful blue in a bewildering number of boxes, and furniture showing little or no damage, and at the far end of the chamber resting on huge jars of pottery was a *perfect* chariot.

On hearing Maspero's voice at the mouth of the tomb talking to Davis, Weigall and I hastily blew out our candles and rushed up the long passageway to the entrance. I had paused a moment to examine two bowls of reddish pottery on either side of the walled-up doorway where finger marks were visible, doubtless belonging to the men whose hands had plastered the mud on the surface of the wall and stamped it all over with seals.

Temple of Abu Simbel, Nubia, with three portraits of Ramesses the Great. Painting by Joseph Lindon Smith. Courtesy Fogg Museum of Art, Harvard University.

Sketch of the mummy of Ouiya, father of Queen Tiyi, by Joseph Lindon Smith. Courtesy Museum of Fine Arts, Boston.

Chair presented to Queen Tiyi by her granddaughter Sat-Amen, occupied briefly by the Empress Eugénie, to the distress of Edward Quibell. Painting by Joseph Lindon Smith. Courtesy Museum of Fine Arts, Boston.

Maspero looked at Weigall and me holding smoking candles and obviously greatly excited, and with a twinkle in his eye said: "As far as you know, is the passageway clear of obstruction?"

We both agreed we thought it was. Then able to contain myself no longer, I blurted out: "There's everything down there—and a wonderful chariot."

Maspero told Weigall to get a message to the Duke of Connaught. Then he and Davis disappeared down the passage we had just come up. There was a moment of silence, and after that Maspero was calling for *ghaffir* to come at once. From the tone of his voice, it sounded as though something was wrong, so Weigall hurried into the tomb.

The excitement and lack of air had been too much for Davis, who had gone off into a dead faint. Weigall superintended getting his prostrate form to the surface, where he lay in the protecting shadow of a wall of rock close by, cared for by the nieces of Mrs. Andrews.

Again Maspero's voice was heard, this time saying that Mrs. Smith should come down and join him in the tomb. Corinna told me later that when she reached the second doorway she found that Maspero had widened the opening sufficiently to crawl over the wall. He was standing on the only open floor space in the tomb chamber not piled up with treasures. He assisted her over the wall and said: "Doubtless you are the first woman that's been in this tomb chamber alive—there's a dead one over there," and he pointed out the coffin containing the body of a woman."

"Who are these people?" Corinna had asked.

"Ouiya and Touiyou," was his answer. "They are the mother and father of Tiyi, a great queen of Egypt." He gave her a steady stream of information as he wheeled about waving a candle to read hieroglyphic inscriptions, but Corinna's eyes were too busy for her to listen to Maspero's descriptions, which he kept interrupting to rave about the chariot. She had tried to look everywhere at once at beautiful objects caught in flashes of Maspero's candle. Most of all, she looked at the wonderfully preserved old couple.

But to return to my story. While Davis was being cared for by the

33

nieces, Weigall and I sat in the sunlight on the top step of the entrance to the tomb. It must be remembered that we were a pretty unkempt-looking pair and in a nervous state of great excitement. Suddenly, around the corner from the road used by tourists, there came a *"kervass"* (a government dragoman who accompanies distinguished foreign visitors).

He was an imposing creature with a huge turban, wide trousers, high boots, sword, and a number of medals on his left breast. Altogether he looked like a character from the stage, as he stood above us, twirling his jet-black, long mustachios. He gave us a surly glance, and seeing no one else to speak to, said: "You know Monsieur Maspero?"

Incensed by the man's insolent manner, Weigall merely indicated that he did.

"And where is Maspero?"

To this question Weigall replied curtly, "He's down in that hole," pointing through the tomb door, and motioning the creature back.

Dissatisfied, the *kervass* repeated, "Where is Maspero?"

Weigall again pointed downwards with his thumb.

"Why does he not come out?" the *kervass* asked.

Weigall and I shrugged our shoulders and said we didn't know.

Whereupon, the *kervass,* with an imperious gesture, summoned a *ghaffir,* to whom he gave an order, and the *ghaffir* disappeared down the steps!

At this moment, around the corner came a long-legged Englishman on a donkey. He dismounted by straightening his legs, and the donkey walked away free. The Englishman beckoned to the *kervass* and in a commanding voice asked: "Where is Monsieur Maspero?"

The answers, which were those the *kervass* had gotten from Weigall, made the Englishman furious, all the more so because of Weigall's and my uncontrolled laughter. From my position I could dimly make out Maspero's figure, and he was still jumping about talking to Corinna.

The Englishman, ignoring our presence, scribbled a note, and we saw a second *ghaffir* go down the steps from which the first messenger had not emerged.

Now around the corner came a very important personage, a big man, red in the face, who, upon dismounting, mopped his forehead and the inside rim of his pith helmet and growled out, "Where is Maspero?"

The Englishman, echoed by the *kervass,* said, "He is down in that hole."

"Come, come, get Maspero out at once," the personage commanded.

In this dilemma the Englishman had to appeal to us, and Weigall, having recognized the red-faced man as the Duke of Devonshire, got to his feet. I did the same. Weigall, in Arabic, ordered a third *ghaffir* down into the dark depths with a note to Maspero, explaining the situation and asking for instructions.

The Duke sulked at a little distance. And now around the corner the characters were added to by another presence. No less a person than the Duchess, borne in state in a chair held up by poles on the shoulders of eight bearers. To keep out flies and dust, the Duchess had seen fit to wear a long green veil, but on the trip from the river to the valley she had been tossed about by her bearers, and a strong north wind had blown the veil until it encircled the lower part of her face and throat many times.

Her Ladyship's frantic attempts to pull the gag from her mouth had made the fabric all the tighter. She had breathed through the material so much that it was dripping with moisture. Even so, from her also we heard the phrase, already so memorable, but now in a voice strangely muffled. It sounded something like: "Wwwwhheerre iss Mossour Masszpuiro?"

The Duke, advancing towards the Duchess, said impatiently, "Get down, get down."

She was holding over her flapping hat a small black sunshade. She snapped it shut and, leaning forward, gave the naked backs of the front bearers a nasty poke, then screamed out through the veiling, "Down!"

They obeyed at once, but as no directions were given to the bearers behind, they remained upright and the Duchess was ignominiously poured out of the chair and fell at the Duke's feet. Whereupon an alert *kervass* stepped forward to help the Duchess up.

The Duke suggested going down himself to find Maspero; Weigall said in a feeble protest there was a "lack of air" in the tomb chamber. The Duke of Devonshire took this explanation in none too good grace, and advancing to the entrance, he stood leaning far over the steps as he peered into the darkness below, with his curiosity obviously whetted by being thwarted, and appeared about ready to take matters into his own hands in overcoming this unusual opposition to his wishes.

At this moment, when the Duke was hesitating with his foot on the first step, Corinna, deciding that the nieces should not longer miss the thrill she'd had, ran up the long dark passageway and emerging into the blinding sunlight, ran plumb into the ample stomach of the Duke of Devonshire. He glared at her and she heard him mutter angrily, "So it's a d—— American woman using up the air!"

Weigall hastily disappeared down the steps. He found the three *ghaffir* standing in a line in the passageway, not daring to deliver the messages because of orders given them by Maspero himself that he was "not to be disturbed." Weigall "retrieved" the polite French archaeologist, who was profuse in his apologies to the Duke for his seeming discourtesy. He admitted to a "great discovery" and stated firmly that until the Duke of Connaught, who was expected at noon, had formally opened the tomb, no visitors could enter. The Duke of Devonshire continued to glare at everyone in general and at Corinna in particular, but became sufficiently mollified by Maspero's graciousness to accept an invitation to come back for an improvised lunch and see the tomb immediately afterwards. But her Ladyship said she'd had "enough of the valley," and we saw the Devonshires move away engaged in a violent altercation.

A little later Professor Sayce arrived with Mrs. Andrews, who was to greet the Duke of Connaught. And Davis, walking a little shakily to meet her, gestured for silence in regard to his recent *contretemps*. Not Mrs. Andrews nor the nieces nor Professor Sayce went into the tomb that morning.

The Duke of Connaught, with Quibell as escort, appeared promptly at noon. Maspero took them into the tomb, where they stayed for almost an hour. After they had come up, a circle of important people, whom Corinna and I were permitted by Davis to join, stood waiting for the Duke to make a speech thanking Davis for his contribution to the world of archaeology.

We were supposed to pay our donkey boy Hassan about once a month. He kept tally of the number of our donkeys by tying a knot in a filthy old rope that he had around his waist. He and other natives were hanging around the edge of the circle, and just as the Duke got started on his oration, old Hassan saw Corinna standing on the far side of the group. In the presence of all these distinguished foreigners, he burst through the line, started towards Corinna, and, swinging his tally rope, shouted in Arabic: "It's not sixty but sixty-two donkeys you've had. Why not pay me now?"

The Duke of Connaught, who both understood and spoke the language well, stopped in the middle of a sentence, and advancing towards Hassan, asked: "Who is it, my good man, that owes you so much money?"

Hassan pointed to the embarrassed Corinna.

"Madame, you should settle your donkey debts," the Duke said, and went on with his tribute to Davis.

6. *Working the Tomb*

AFTER THE EXCITEMENT of the formal opening on February 13, Quibell took charge of the "working" of the tomb and asked me to be his assistant. For me it was a most interesting experience in an entirely new field. A sub-inspector and a squad of soldiers were installed in the valley, but a European had also to be on the spot day and night. Usually I slept in the valley with Quibell. Various celebrities delayed our progress. The Duke of Connaught and his Duchess were almost a whole day with us, bringing with them the Prince of Sweden, who was very intelligent. Maspero brought the Duke of Devonshire, but without his Duchess. He was most amiable and appeared to be really interested.

We had electric lights and used the adjacent large Ramesses III tomb as a workshop. I was responsible for the careful moving of the fragile objects, the packing of them for shipment to the Cairo Museum by *feluka,* and for getting the most valuable objects over to Davis's *dahabieh,* in which they were to make the trip.

Quibell gave me information about the objects he was recording with scientific detail and often called me over from my drawing and color sketches to examine something of special value. He told me the evidence furnished by the acts of the robber indicated that the entry had been made within the lifetime of a person who had exact knowledge of the location of the tomb. The thief had tunneled through the overlying debris which concealed the outer, blocked-up doorway. He had taken down just enough stones to allow him to crawl through, and had done the same with the second doorway leading into the tomb chamber.

Quibell had an amusing way of talking about people, and gave me a picture of this mother with a position at Court scheming successfully to bring about a marriage between her daughter and the King Amen-hotep III. The royal son-in-law had loaded his wife's parents with favors. Ouiya became "Divine Father of the Lord of Both Lands," and the mother was "Chantress of Amon" and "Mistress of the Robes." And he read off to me quite a list of other titles.

Until the discovery of this tomb, there had been a number of archaeol-ogists who believed Amenhotep's father-in-law was a foreigner. But Quibell considered that if this theory was correct, there would have been in the funerary furniture some trace of Ouiya's foreign origin instead of the tomb's being typically Egyptian.

He also told me that the beautiful chariot could not have been used with horses. It was too low, the gilt ornament was not adapted for rough usage, and showed no sign of wear. In his opinion, it must have been carried in the funeral procession to the valley. But, on the other hand, it was made of singular strength for a mere model of a tomb chariot.

Next in importance to the chariot was an alabaster vase bearing the names of Queen Tiyi and Amenhotep III. In the absolutely dry atmos-phere of this chamber, everything was in perfect condition. It looked as though a thorough parlor maid had recently dusted the furnishings and polished with a chamois skin gold- and silver-plated *shawabti* figures.

And what a display it was! Marvelous blue and black gesso with gold reliefs and inscriptions, beautiful workmanship in Osiris beds of fine matting fiber with strong legs and splendid head pieces, charming wig baskets, a cane chest for garments, and leather sandals with neat straps. There were a great number of mummified birds inside brightly painted wooden cases and some nice pottery. Also fine back boxes with gold designs for the canopic jars of Ouiya and Touiyou. Eight boxes of provisions and jewel cases of faïence work in exquisite turquoise blue were enchanting.

From one alabaster vase, the thief had torn off the cloth that had originally covered the mouth to look inside, and a few shreds still hung on the neck of the vase. There was still liquid at the bottom. A reporter stated in the press that he had seen a bee go to this vase when it was taken out of the tomb because it contained *honey*. This was newspaper "imagination." There was no one about when I carried the vase into the Ramesses III workshop. And it was I, not a bee, that tasted the liquid, which later was identified as natron.

After a week we had got out all the jars and outer coffins, and later unwrapped part of the mummy of Ouiya. Maspero lunched with us that day in our Ramesses III workshop, as did Sayce, who had not yet relinquished the hope of finding a stray cuneiform tablet lying about. The three of them, Maspero, Sayce, and Quibell, were in accord on the question of how far the great coffins were prepared outside the tomb chamber. Although Ouiya's three coffins could have been brought down, one inside the other, they were all certain that the outer canopy was set up in the tomb, since it was too broad to enter the door. And as there was no break in the horizontal bands of the text, the gilded plaster must have been finished in the burial chamber. The outer coffin of Touiyou must also have been set up and the decoration finished inside the tomb. I cataloged the objects for Quibell and made a plan diagram of the tomb showing the position of its contents, from notes of the way it had looked when first seen by me. Touiyou and Ouiya both had white hair. She wore a necklace of lapis lazuli and gold, which I removed, while coal-black eyes in a near-by cartonnage mask of her face were so alive as to seem to be blinking at me. I did pencil drawings of the old couple whose long privacy we had disturbed.

Nothing in the tomb equaled the three chairs, two of them gifts from the little Princess Sat-Amen to her grandmother. One chair had a delightful gazelle carved on the sides and a feather cushion in the seat in good condition. Another had the names of Queen Tiyi, Princess Sat-Amen, and her sister. On the back was a scene showing Queen Tiyi with the little girls in a papyrus canoe, and the dimensions proved this chair had been made for a child. In places the gold leaf had been patched where it had rubbed off, and the seat, originally of plaited string, had worn through and been cut out, and a rectangular board painted yellow inserted. Undoubtedly grandma had been given a chair that had been used in life!

But the great prize was the third chair, which was the largest, also a gift from the granddaughter, Sat-Amen. The back and the frame for the seat were of a wood, with a veneer of a rarer one, probably walnut, and the legs were carved out of solid blocks of walnut. The high back was curved to fit the body of the woman using it, and supports with bands of gold at the ends were attached to the frame beneath the seat to give extra strength. The designs on the front included two little princesses clad in close-fitting vests and skirts reaching to the ankles. They wore short wigs secured round the top of the head by a narrow fillet tied behind in a bow, a crown and earrings, and a broad necklace consisting of three bands of lotus petals. Each of these charming maidens was offering an elaborate necklace to grandma, who was seated.

After nearly three weeks the "working" of the tomb was finished, and a large number of heavy cases were ready for camel transport to the river. Over one hundred men were assembled for the difficult job that began at dawn. Unfortunately, the day was unusually hot. Quibell slept on the river bank that night, to be on hand for putting the cases on the train under a police guard. I had remained at the tomb to guard the last treasure still in the burial chamber. In the early afternoon he and I were kneeling on the floor of the tomb chamber, where nothing was left except this most wonderful of the three chairs, the distinctive feature being the arm supports that ended in exquisitely carved heads in the round. I was about to protect it for travel to Davis's *dahabieh* while Quibell was engaged in a final sifting of the sand on the floor of the chamber to make sure we had overlooked no small object.

Suddenly we heard voices from the outside entrance of the tomb. And from where we sat we could just see the skirt of a dress and the putteed legs of a man, and a woman said in French, "This is what I have come to see, Carlo, the tomb of the mother and father of the great Queen Tiyi."

"But your Highness, you've already seen more than was planned for the afternoon. I beg of you to postpone this visit till another day," her escort objected.

The woman's voice in answer said, "No, Carlo, I insist on going down."

"As you will, your Highness. Are you quite sure that we are expected?"

I turned to Quibell and asked if visitors were expected that afternoon, and he replied, "No. Lord Cromer has ceased issuing permits to distinguished people."

Then we saw that the passageway was being entered, and presently there stood before us on the threshold of the tomb chamber an old lady accompanied by a good-looking young Italian, she hanging on his arm with one hand and holding a cane with the other. By the strong electric light that we still had in the tomb, I noticed traces of great beauty in the face of the woman as we rose to receive her.

Without knowing who she was, Quibell said, "I am sorry your Highness has come at so late a date that nothing remains of the treasures that were found in the tomb when we opened it."

The woman replied, "Do tell me something of the discovery of the tomb."

Quibell said, "With pleasure, but I regret I cannot offer you a chair."

Quickly came her answer: "Why, there is a chair which will do for me nicely." And before our horrified eyes she stepped down onto the floor of the chamber and seated herself in a chair which had not been

41

sat in for over three thousand years! But the anticipated catastrophe did not take place.

The visitor turned to Carlo and said, "I see now where the Empire style came from. Behold these carved heads."

And then the identity of the visitor flashed across my mind. She was the old Empress Eugénie, the widow of Napoleon III, vigorously alive a lifetime after the disappearance of the French court in 1870.

THE LEGRAIN AND DAVIS "FINDS"

1905–1906

7. *Fishing for Statues at Karnak*

I N THE FALL of 1905, my family, including the children, were back in
Egypt living on a *dahabieh* moored to the same western sandbank
opposite the town of Luxor. A good deal of that winter I painted
at Karnak. The subject that took most of my time was a life-sized study
of a scene that included a long ceremonial barque of Amon, with huge
rams' heads at each end. It was in a high register on the exterior wall of
the temple of Ramesses III and represented the "feast of Opet." This
was the annual chief festival in honor of the Theban god, Amon, when
the ceremonial barque was carried in a river procession from Karnak to
Luxor and returned.

I often saw the French engineer, Legrain, who was still in charge of
the temple for the Egyptian government. He was straightening the tall
columns in the great Hypostyle Hall, and also excavating beyond the
third pylon to the right, near the Sacred Lake. He told me that he had
chosen this site on the conviction that Mariette Bey had been wrong.
The first great French director of Antiquities for the Egyptian government, after having excavated at Karnak for some years, made the statement in print, "Nothing more will be found here—Karnak is finished."

Legrain, in support of his own theory, said that the present level of
the Nile in this region was considerably higher than it had been at the
time of the eighteenth dynasty, and he had a feeling that there might

be a "cache" dating from ancient times at a much lower level. This "cache" was reached by walking through the Hypostyle Hall and then turning right. This kind of excavating meant that his workmen had to use a *shadoof* (bucket on a long pole) to get rid of flood water. For a short period only, during the late afternoon, the water would be sufficiently drawn off to permit searchers to feel about in the mud for possible objects before dark. And every day this same performance had to be repeated in a wide area.

Legrain was positive that he was on the right track when he made his first discovery of a part of a statue far below the level of the Nile today. This had been in 1903, and to date the yield had been rich and was still going on. He had found two statues of kings of Dynasty V (2565–2420 B.C.), one king's and over twenty other statues of the Middle Kingdom (2052–1786 B.C.), and nearly fifty statues of kings and queens of Dynasty XVIII (1570–1349 B.C.).

Maspero told me that this tremendous addition to the great body of sculpture in the round of the New Kingdom rivaled discoveries of the period in the Valley of the Kings, and was, in fact, of greater historical importance than funerary furniture.

One afternoon he sent for me when the head and shoulders of a large black granite statue were brought far enough out of the mud to be clearly seen. Large wooden beams were thrust beneath the statue for support. Legrain was jubilant. We spent much time down in the mud examining the fine head and face. Meanwhile a boy came with a telegram for Legrain, who read it and handed it to me. It was from Cromer saying that Lord and Lady X—— would be arriving at Luxor the following day and to show them something "particularly interesting."

We clambered out of the hole, and Legrain screamed to his workmen, "Pull out the beams and let the statue sink down."

The men looked puzzled and hesitant about obeying such an unexpected order. Legrain screamed at them again louder. And down into the mud disappeared the head that had taken so much effort to raise. He said to me with a broad grin, "I intend to 'discover' a statue for Cromer's distinguished guests. You must help me in creating an atmosphere of expectancy."

The next morning I found, commanding a view of the spot where we had seen the statue, two gilt, upholstered armchairs and over them a large sunshade. And a bit of red carpet had been spread to the chairs from the nearest point of entry. I was on hand to take part in the reception of the distinguished couple, who appeared towards the late afternoon with a dragoman, maid, and other attendants.

Legrain, looking doubtfully at her Ladyship's very high, narrow heels, asked how much walking they wished to do.

"Not much," she said. "Haven't you something unusual quite near at hand?"

I had my cue in Legrain's nod and asked, "How about your new excavations, Legrain?"

She took fire at once, and we all walked together through the Hypostyle Hall, while Legrain talked briefly about Karnak. Beyond the third pylon she caught sight of the red carpet and the armchairs beyond. In obvious relief, the visitors settled themselves comfortably. And Legrain explained, again briefly, what he was doing.

"Do you mean to say in that muddy water in which those half naked men are splashing about some object of value may be found?" she asked.

Legrain shrugged his shoulders, winked surreptitiously at me, and said, "One never knows."

"It's in the lap of the gods," I added, "and a wonderful moment when it happens."

"It must be," remarked his Lordship with the first spark of enthusiasm he had shown.

Legrain's timing was perfect. There was some desultory conversation before he gave a signal to his workmen submerged almost to their armpits. They at once redoubled their efforts, and louder and louder came their song, until it reached a crescendo, and their muscles strained as the head of a statue became visible. The visitors jumped from their chairs, their excited shouts mingling with the triumphant cries of the workmen as, leaning forward, they almost lost their balance and fell into the pit. Higher and higher the head was lifted until the shoulders and breast appeared out of the muddy depths.

Legrain gave orders to have the planks shoved beneath the statue to hold it in place. When he explained that unfortunately there was not time to get the statue up before dark, her Ladyship leaped down into the pit, followed by her husband.

Workmen emerged from the mud, their naked backs dripping, and stood about cheering the guests.

Legrain interpreted the rapid flow of words that accompanied the splashing of mud over the immaculate garments of the thrilled visitors.

"They are thanking you both for bringing good luck," he said.

Lord and Lady X—— were delighted, and she exclaimed exultantly, "To think I was actually present at a great discovery—weren't you surprised, Monsieur Legrain?"

He replied gallantly, "I was pleased to have Lord Cromer's guests see something particularly interesting."

8. *Siphtah and Other Tombs*

DAVIS, WITH HIS USUAL FRIENDLINESS, invited me to be present at the opening of a tomb in the Valley of the Kings that took place in late December. The tomb was that of Siphtah, a priest of Amon who, in Dynasty XIX, was king from 1222–1216 B.C. The tomb was built according to the general style of the late nineteenth and early twentieth dynasties. Two shallow flights of steps, with a sloping passageway between, led down to the entrance, the flanking rock being covered by white stucco but not decorated.

The entrance proper was a large doorway coated with stucco and ornamented in the usual way with the king's titles down each side. To the left inside the entrance passage was a scene of the Goddess Ma'at with wings outstretched. She was seated on a large basket supported on flowers of a papyrus plant, and was much finer than her counterpart opposite. And there was a standing figure of Siphtah himself, close to the entrance door, worshiping Horus. Both Ma'at and Siphtah were very brilliant in color and unexpectedly beautiful in details for so late a period. Davis was delighted by my enthusiasm at his find.

The ceiling in the main corridor with a design of spread wings was in a good state of preservation, and as brilliant in color as when originally made. Farther down the corridor there appeared to be nothing of special interest to an artist. During the winter I painted a picture of Siphtah, head and shoulders, and two other studies, one from a seated position at the top of the passageway with my subject the entrance door, and then sitting inside the tomb I did a detail looking out, which took in both sides of the entrance.

As Davis continued his excavations in the vicinity throughout the working season, I again saw a good deal of him, and also of Edward R. Ayrton, who was the archaeologist in charge.

I knew the temple at Abydos built by Seti I of Dynasty XIX. Its delicately carved white limestone reliefs were unique. Therefore, I enjoyed the opportunity to go frequently into his tomb, which was the outstanding one in the Royal Valley. It was tremendously deep, cut in the living rock, with long corridors entered down steep flights of steps, with an endless series of rooms, chambers, and antechambers opening off them.

King Seti's journey through the underworld in the company of gods was told on the walls in painted reliefs, extraordinarily well preserved and of high artistic merit. A particularly vivid scene in one of the antechambers described the "opening of the mouth ceremony" being performed for Seti by Osiris, king of the underworld, with the assistance of other gods of the dead.

The journey of the Sun through the underworld was related in detail, and an ancient myth on the walls of a small side room told of the rebellion of mankind against the Sun God, man's punishment, and the final rescue of the survivors. The text throughout the tomb was taken from the *Book of the Dead,* which was written on papyrus, and to date about twelve copies have been found. These inscriptions had a special interest for me from my familiarity with the various processes through which, by Dynasty XVIII, the prescribed ritual for the dead King had reached the walls of the Royal Valley tombs, adapted from pyramid texts used at Saqqarah in Dynasty V and Dynasty VI.

It was Maspero who, in 1881, discovered that the interior walls of the Pyramid of Pepy I, Dynasty VI, were inscribed. He deciphered the text in this and other pyramids of kings and queens of Dynasty VI which contained a number of magical formulas not recorded in the more famous pyramid texts of Unas, the last king of Dynasty V, which he also found in clearing the interior. Corinna and I were fortunate in having Maspero make a special trip from Cairo to Saqqarah in the spring of 1905 for the purpose of showing us the burial chamber of Unas.

We entered by a long corridor and from a square vestibule reached the burial chamber, which contained a large stone sarcophagus. At each end of it was an ornate panel design in alabaster with a carved and painted false door. A mass of inscriptions, both in the vestibule and burial chamber caught my eye. The hieroglyphs were deep-cut in long, vertical lines, and a filling of bright blue pigment made them conspicuous in white limestone. These pyramid texts were about the most dramatic examples of calligraphy I had ever seen.

Maspero explained that the texts did not give a continuous narrative but were merely a collection of "spells" arranged in no fixed order. The written word was a potent magic furnishing a guarantee that the idea expressed would be realized. During the King's journey to the other world situated in the sky beyond the eastern horizon, the power of these texts overcame by magic the dangers the dead King encountered. Among the texts, which numbered nearly seven hundred, with many variations in the different pyramids, were hymns to the gods and prayers on behalf of the dead King. Most of the ideas, but not the form, originated in early pre-dynastic times. The words of the text, usually on the north wall of the burial chamber, reproduced the ritual recited every day by the funerary priests in laying food on the altar in front of the false door.

Maspero talked at some length about the fact that certain signs in hieroglyphs were considered dangerous to be used in burial ritual and were represented by those of inanimate objects that had a similar hieroglyphic value. Also signs of human beings were rendered harmless by using only the heads and arms, and those of animals, by cutting their bodies in half. Serpents were preserved intact, but scorpions were without tails.

Akhenaten and Nefertete. From the original bas-relief in the Brooklyn Museum.

Mummy of Seti I, one of the "lost kings of the valley." Courtesy of the Egyptian government.

I commented to Maspero on the absence of any sign containing a fish, which the Copts of today had tattooed on the right forearm as a symbol of Christianity. He explained that fish were never on the walls of burial chambers, the reason being that although "innocuous to living people, they defiled the dead body."

During the Middle Kingdom, which lasted from 2052–1786 B.C. and included Dynasty XI and XII, pyramid texts ceased to be placed on the walls of tomb chambers. They were inscribed on the outside of wooden coffins used at that period and became known as coffin texts. They were found in burials of the nobility as well as in those of kings. At the beginning of the New Kingdom, with Dynasty XVIII, in 1570 B.C. and lasting through to the end of Dynasty XX in 1085 B.C., the texts, in a modified form, were written on papyrus and later referred to as the *Book of the Dead*.

The children never forgot their trip over to the Valley of the Kings and a visit to Davis's Animal Tomb. They were carried down the shaft of this pit tomb, into a chamber that was very low and extremely warm.

They both laughed in their delight at the sight of a yellow dog of ordinary life size, standing on its feet, his short tail curled over his back, and with eyes wide open. The animal looked alive.

We also took the children into a second pit tomb, where they saw an amazing display of mummified monkeys, dogs, birds, and ducks. These two pit tombs containing animals were so near the tomb of Amenhotep III as to warrant the assumption that some of the animals, at least, had originally been the King's pets.

The most bizarre spectacle was a perfect specimen of a large ape, completely without wrappings, and wearing a necklace of small blue disk beads.

When I was painting in the Tomb of Siphtah, on my way over the rocky gebel into the Valley of the Kings and back to the river, I would stop in for a word with Robert Mond, if I saw him in his excavations at the Sheikh Abd'-el-Qurna Necropolis.

One afternoon I stayed on when he told me he was about to open a tomb. The owner, named Neferonpet, was the head of the weavers, and one of the scenes in an upper register was rather effective and good in color. It represented the owner in adoration of Osiris, god of the underworld, accompanied by four women and a girl holding stems of papyrus. I made several studies for Mond in this tomb.

But even more frequently I visited Naville, who was working at the Temple of Deir-el-Bahari, and who, in the vicinity of his camp, was also doing a clearing job on a great hill of ancient debris. One morning I found him warning his head *reis* not to continue digging at this spot for fear that a loosened boulder would cause the whole mass to fall like an avalanche.

I started away and a moment later heard the tremendous roar of Naville's expected avalanche. I turned and was enveloped in clouds of dust. As the dust settled, I saw Naville and the *reis,* both uninjured, gazing at an opening in this hill of rubbish. And on the exact spot where Naville had given the warning to cease digging was the opening into a shrine with a vaulted roof. At the entrance was a life-sized stone statue of the Goddess Hathor, represented as a cow, in perfect condition, standing on a stone platform and led by a man. Hathor wore the customary disk and tall horns, and at either side of the headdress were lotus blossoms extending from the neck to the feet.

In later years, whenever I looked at this treasure in the Cairo Museum, I recalled Naville's expression of stunned amazement at his first sight of this enshrined Hathor cow.

Another experience connected with the Navilles occurred one day when Corinna was with me and we had accepted an invitation to lunch in their camp. Madame was very particular about her cuisine, for which she was quite famous, and she could be annoyed when her husband got so absorbed in showing guests some recent archaeological find that the food was spoiled.

We had arrived fairly early. Naville thought there would be time to show us a splendid statue that lay in a passage leading toward the temple.

"Perhaps you will be good enough, Joe, to make a sketch of it *in situ*," he said.

Madame took alarm at once and urged us to postpone visiting the excavations until after lunch. I told her this was impossible for me, as I must get back to Siphtah. Madame yielded and called after us a final request "not to be late to lunch."

Corinna and I followed Naville into a subterranean passage that twisted and turned toward the temple quite far underground, at a steep incline, and so low-studded that we could not stand upright. The air was stifling and the light of torches accentuated bad cracks where the rock ceiling looked about to fall. I liked the statue and painted a quick study of it which I gave Naville. He wanted us to make further explorations in another direction, but I, looking at my watch, said to him that it was getting late and Madame Naville would be expecting us. Therefore, we crawled out of the passage and at a rapid pace reached the camp. Madame was smiling as we sat down to an excellent meal. All of a sudden, there was a crash that reverberated and shook the adobe building we were in very much as if it were a rat being played with by a terrier. The sound came from the direction of the passage we had recently left.

Workmen appeared at a run to report to Naville that a great boulder had fallen from the rock ceiling between the statue and the exit. Had we been late to lunch we would have been caught in a passage from which escape would have been blocked for some days, even if the boulder itself had not struck us.

GREAT DISCOVERIES

1906–1907

9. *The Amarna Period of Heresy*

For a better understanding of the dim outlines of people living in a complicated period whom I came to know in tombs, I have jotted down briefly a few facts and premises of my own. First, however, let us look at the characters in the story and their chronology.

The kings to be mentioned in this chapter are as follows: in Dynasty XVIII, Tuthmosis III, 1504–1450 B.C.; Tuthmosis IV, 1423–1410 B.C.; Amenhotep III, 1410–1372 B.C.; Amenhotep IV (Akhenaten), 1380–1363 B.C.; Semenkhkara, 1364–1362 B.C.; Tutankhamen, 1362–1353 B.C.; Ai, 1353–1349 B.C. In Dynasty XIX, Horemheb, the first king of that dynasty, 1349–1314 B.C. In Dynasty XX, Ramesses III, 1195–1164 B.C.

The el-Amarna period, towards the end of Dynasty XVIII, was considered by Maspero and a number of other archaeologists primarily as a political struggle by the monarchy against the growing power of the priesthood of Amon at Thebes, rather than as a religious reformation by Akhenaten, the monotheist, as claimed by Breasted and his followers.

The situation had come to a climax when the priests made Tuthmosis III pharaoh, who, in order to fulfill his obligations, appointed the High Priest of Amon to be also his grand vizier. Here was church and state combined in one person! But Tuthmosis IV attempted to curtail the political power of the priests, and there were some traces of his leanings toward the cult of Aten. He was succeeded by his son, Amenhotep III, who married Queen Tiyi, daughter of Ouiya and Touiyou. Their son, as a child, became king as Amenhotep IV, under his mother as regent.

It has not yet been determined under what influences this young ruler left Thebes at about the sixth year of his reign and, taking the name of Akhenaten, lived with his court at el-Amarna, where he built the "City of the Rising Sun" dedicated to a new god, Aten, and forbade the worship of Amon and the multiple gods of Egypt, destroying every record of Amon on temple walls and persecuting his priests. Flinders Petrie's and other excavations have given much knowledge of the life of Akhenaten, his wife, Nefertete, and their six daughters in a city he was never to leave.

Queen Tiyi was supposed to have remained at Thebes and visited her son but rarely. But Nefertete's foster-father, Ai, formerly a priest of Amon, was known to have gone back and forth between Thebes and el-Amarna, and to have managed to be on good terms with both Akhenaten and the proscribed priests of the overthrown Amon.

Horemheb, the soldier-statesman, maintained his pledged allegiance to Akhenaten, even when Egypt's foreign possessions were lost through the King's policy as a pacifist. But Horemheb spent much of his time in Thebes waiting on events and planning to control them after the death of the visionary and fanatic Akhenaten.

Semenkhkara, a weakling and a favorite of Akhenaten's, had married his eldest daughter and succeeded Akhenaten as king at el-Amarna for a few years only, until he died or was murdered, possibly at the instigation of Horemheb. He in turn was succeeded by Tutankhamen, probably a younger brother of Semenkhkara's and married to Akhenaten's third daughter. Becoming king at the age of twelve, Tutankhamen abandoned el-Amarna, renounced the god Aten, and, returning to Thebes, restored the forbidden ritual of Amon and the power of the priesthood, and every trace of Akhenaten and his Aten was obliterated.

Horemheb, realizing that Ai, a priest of Amon, would be more acceptable than himself in a transition period, doubtless engineered Ai's selection as pharaoh after the convenient removal of the boy King Tutankhamen.

Ai did not reign long. He was an old man and his death might have been assisted. And now at last Horemheb came to the supreme power for which he had plotted long years, as the first king of Dynasty XIX. Although he was an able soldier and leader, it was too late for him to reconquer much of Egypt's lost foreign possessions.

Through the kings of Dynasty XIX, Amon remained the unchallenged supreme god. By Dynasty XX, the priests of Amon had become the pharaohs, thus ending a long political struggle between the monarchy and priesthood.

Norman de G. Davies, in his publication of *The Tomb of Ramose,* said, in summing up the el-Amarna period:

> Ramesses the Great was a much truer son of Egypt than even an idealized Akhenaten and the co-dominion of Amon and Osiris was better suited to its people than the less human rule of the sun disk. Kings and nations were incapable of "living in truth."
>
> It is a tribute to the rebels that they made even such a fleeting success and the brief revolt had such immediate and durable results, visibly in art and more subtly in religion.

10. *Discovery of the Tomb of Queen Tiyi*

THE WINTER of 1906–1907 Corinna and I spent in Egypt without the children or my parents. Our faithful dragoman, Dowe, was ill, but *dahabieh* life would have been difficult even with him. Professor Sayce was about to dispose of the *Istar*. Sailors could not be found, since steam had to a large extent replaced sails as the means of propulsion. The situation was further changed by the fact that foreign visitors no longer seemed to have time for a leisurely winter on the Nile. The rich chartered a private steamer to get a quick look at the important temples of Upper Egypt and be in Rome for Easter.

We were the guests of Arthur Weigall, now the English inspector of Antiquities for Upper Egypt, and his wife, Hortense. They lived in a delightful house belonging to the government in Luxor, close to the river.

Theodore M. Davis was as usual living on his *dahabieh* moored on the west bank of the river, as he continued his excavations in the Valley of the Kings. He had started his season's dig to the left of the path used by tourists on entering the valley. Had he chosen the right side, he, and not Lord Carnarvon, would have found Tutankhamen.

Early in January, Weigall and I stopped in one afternoon at Davis's excavations, and we found both him and Edward Ayrton, who was still the archaeologist in charge. A large gang of workmen, having commenced to clear on the apex of a hill covered with limestone chippings, had progressed quite a distance downwards and reached the level of the tomb of Ramesses IX without finding anything. To the east were known tombs of Dynasty XIX, and all of these had contributed to the debris being removed. Davis continued to sink pits through the rubbish to the left, and a few days later sent us word that the workmen had come to a walled-up doorway.

On the morning appointed for the formal opening, Maspero, Davis, and Weigall, as inspector of Antiquities for Upper Egypt, Howard Carter, who was working for the Egyptian government at Saqqarah, Corinna, and I were there. We had all arrived before nine o'clock. The doorway was closed by a loosely built wall of limestone fragments, resting not on the rock beneath but on rubbish. The original sealing, composed of rough blocks in a layer of a very hard cement, revealed the impressions of a jackal crouching over nine captives—the seal of the priestly college of Amon-Ra! At this sight hopes ran high, for here was a tomb apparently never rifled! After the intact seals had been photographed, they were removed with great care, and then the wall was taken down.

Rubbish filled the corridor to within about eighteen inches of the ceiling. Maspero peered inside and reported that, lying on top of the rubbish, there was a wide wooden door with the upper face covered with gold foil. This door almost filled the space between the walls, and obviously could not be moved for fear of damaging a figure and inscriptions. Weigall succeeded in getting a ten-inch plank against the south wall of the entrance corridor about on a level with the door. It was impossible at such an angle to take a photograph, and to my amazement and delight, Maspero asked me to crawl over this improvised bridge and make a drawing of what I saw.

In a position which had my head touching the ceiling, my nose almost on the door, and with stifling air coming up into my face from below, I set to work. Without injury to it, I sketched a scene in gold leaf of a queen worshiping the sun disk. I manipulated a torch so as to get most of a cartouche, which was partly concealed by a stone that had fallen on top of it. I wriggled backwards from my cramped position and was helped off the plank.

Maspero looked at my drawing, read the hieroglyphs, and said: "Excellent, Mr. Smith, yours is a document of the greatest importance, since this door may prove to be the only undamaged object in the tomb, and itself be destroyed in getting it out because of the fragile condition of gold designs loosened from gesso."

He then went on to say impressively: "To repay you for your great assistance on making it possible for me to read the name and titles of Queen Tiyi, I am going to permit you to slide along to the end of the plank and find out what are the conditions in the passage leading down into the tomb chamber."

I shared in the general excitement voiced on Maspero's identification of the name of Queen Tiyi, on a piece of the tomb furniture, and Davis was almost inarticulate in his joy. Maspero handed me his flashlight. The manner in which he had granted me permission was true to French gallantry, but on looking from Maspero to Quibell and then at Weigall and Carter, I realized that, with their physiques, none of them could have got over the plank, and I was glad that I was thin and agile.

I lost no time in getting back onto the plank again, and, on reaching the end, crawled over the rubbish beyond, which decreased in volume as I continued down the corridor to a second doorway, more or less clear, beyond which was a room about twenty feet square and fifteen feet high, with walls covered with stucco but not decorated. I stood motionless on the threshold, flashing my light back and forth and trying to get an idea of what had happened.

Great fragments of the ceiling had fallen and lay in confusion on top of a mass of wooden debris. Against the wall, opposite where I was standing at the threshold, leaned some great planks of the same fine cedar of Lebanon we had found in the tomb of Ouiya and Touiyou, with gold foil designs on gesso. My flashlight revealed on one of these planks fine low-relief figures of a queen standing behind a figure, the outlines of which were obliterated as though by an ax. I stepped inside. I had no doubt brought into that room a change in the atmospheric conditions, and while I was looking at this bas-relief, the gold foil parted from the wooden carving beneath and slid off to the ground with a loud, ominous sound which was heard at the mouth of the tomb. At this point Maspero shouted: "Hey, what are you doing down there, Mr. Smith—touch nothing!"

Lying beneath broken fragments of stone were doors like the one discovered at the mouth of the tomb, and on them were carvings of the Queen and other figures. Wherever the wood lay horizontally, as these did, the gesso and gold leaf still adhered, and the scenes and inscriptions were preserved.

I could distinguish some alabaster jars in one corner of a small recess on the southern wall, a few feet above the floor level, and directly beneath the recess on the floor was a coffin with the lid askew. It was inlaid with semiprecious stones and made a brilliant display there in the darkness, but it was partly open on one side, exposing the skull of a mummy.

Considering I had been down in that burial chamber quite a while, I returned to the surface and reported to Maspero. He immediately requested me to go down again and examine particularly for traces of the effect of water damage. The tomb was now lit by reflected sunlight cast by mirrors held by workmen at the surface. This method, used in remote antiquity for the same purpose, gave a steady and brilliant illumination that brought out details not visible by flashlight.

A crack in the roof a few feet from the entrance door looked to me as though the ineffective stopping up had been done in ancient times. And I thought that through this crack rain had entered the burial chamber and separated the thin coating of gilded designs from the wood on the cedar of Lebanon decorated panels. It was obvious that water had been responsible for the first confusion, by causing objects to float about promiscuously. But large-sized stones on top of, not under, the gilded beams on the floor seemed conclusive evidence that, after the water had dried, an earthquake had dislodged fragments of the stone ceiling, which, in falling, had broken wooden objects that had settled at random after the first water damage.

The position of the coffin with the side broken open and the lid askew seemed to indicate it had originally been on a higher level from which it had dropped, and that it also had floated about in the water. I noticed a block of stone inside the coffin that had separated the head from the rest of the mummy, and on the exposed skull was a crown of thick gold carved in the shape of a vulture. The coffin lid, which followed the lines of a human body, was dazzling as the increased light brought out exquisite details of a feathered design in semiprecious stones, but resembling the scales of a fish. The inscriptions on a band of gold down the center and on the gilded feet were very clear cut.

I made a rough sketch of the whole lid of the coffin. In the carved face, one black eye staring at me gave a startling effect to a visage which, except for the forehead and one eyebrow, had had the gold features violently torn from the wood beneath, and also from the wig and parts of the crossed hands. As I gazed from the gold uraeus on the forehead of the face on the lid to the crown worn by the skull at a jaunty angle, I thrilled at the realization of being alone in the presence of a king or queen last seen by priests of Amon who had left their seals on the entrance door in far-away antiquity.

I returned once more to the mouth of the tomb and gave my second report to Maspero. He complimented me on "close observation" and was delighted with another rough sketch I had taken time to make.

I had hardly joined the others before Ayrton showed up. He was a good sport about Maspero and Davis's not having waited for him for the "opening." Naturally enough, Davis was all eagerness to get into the tomb, and stared at the door covered with gold leaf that could only be passed over by means of the precarious improvised bridge, which

Maspero would not permit him to attempt. Ayrton, who was slight and, of course, experienced in tomb work, after a careful examination of the "golden door of Queen Tiyi," as Davis called it, promised him and Maspero that he would have them inside the tomb chamber soon after the early lunch that Davis's butler, Jones, was to bring over from the *Beduin,* the Davis *dahabieh.*

Ayrton told Maspero he had nothing to add to the information given in my drawing of the door, and as he tunneled through the rubbish at the tomb entrance, he busied himself in a careful underpinning of the decorated door with planks and beams. This was necessary to provide sufficient support to prevent disaster, both to those entering the tomb in a bent-over position and to the precious door. The tunneling and propping up was a ticklish performance which Ayrton carried out skillfully.

Everyone was too excited to eat much lunch. At about one o'clock all was in readiness for the formal entry. Maspero, Davis, Weigall, Carter, and I went in.

On reaching the tomb chamber, all of us held our breath as Maspero looked about him for some time before speaking. He pointed to the upright panel with the Queen standing behind a destroyed figure and said the inscriptions on this and other fragments of ornamented wood identified it as belonging to a dismantled shrine. He read impressively hieroglyphics which stated that "King Khuniatonu [Akhenaten] had made the shrine for the King's mother, great wife of the King, Tiyi." We gazed in awe at a shrine prepared by Akhenaten to carry his mother's body to her final resting place.

On the panel Queen Tiyi was charmingly dressed in a long, white, airy robe, wearing the headdress of the Goddess Hathor, with the Aten disk surmounted by two tall feathers. The Queen's features were characteristic of the portraits of the el-Amarna period, with a long face and prominent chin. The Aten disk, placed in one corner of the panel, emitted the customary numerous rays, each ray terminating in a hand, some of the hands receiving offerings and others protecting both the obliterated figure of Akhenaten and the resplendent Queen Mother.

The cartouches of the hated "heretic" King had been deliberately hacked out, but some of his titles remained, and a prayer to Aten the god of el-Amarna, as well. It flashed through my mind that only someone *friendly* to Akhenaten would have left intact a long text from the Aten creed and the rays still protecting his mutilated figure.

Maspero studied inscriptions on a number of small objects that bore the name of Amenhotep III and of his wife, Queen Tiyi, and said with conviction that the tray of cosmetics, boxes, tools, and offerings in enameled stone or glazed pottery were tomb furnishings belonging to the Queen. At this information Davis tried to get Maspero to identify the tomb positively as Queen Tiyi's, with her mummy in the coffin. But Maspero refused to commit himself; he declared it was unquestionably a "reburial" and conclusions should be "cautious."

He stopped a moment to study the niche in the southern wall that contained the canopic jars, but did not touch them, and then concentrated his full attention on the coffin. He thought it had originally been placed on a four-legged couch, and when the legs gave way, the coffin had dropped to the floor beneath. He also agreed with my inferences that water had disturbed the position of the tomb furniture and other objects and that an earthquake had come later. He thought no other sequence of events a tenable theory. He examined carefully the long crack in the beautiful mosaic coffin lid, close to the intact band of gold inscriptions, and said the lid was in a very fragile condition. He looked at the mummy forced out of the open side of the coffin and said that the stone which fell from above and landed on the lid, splitting it, had been caught by the tail of the vulture on the gold crown on the skull, thus preventing the latter from being completely crushed.

The fact that the crown was in place, and a sheet of gold lay over the part of the body visible, precluded the premise that thieves had been in the tomb chamber. Maspero cited, as further evidence in support of his theory, the unbroken seal on the walled-up entrance doorway. But, when pressed by Davis and Weigall, he refused to commit himself about the identity of the owner of the tomb.

He said emphatically, "I wish to repeat this is unquestionably a reburial, and therefore an archaeologist should avoid deductions that might prove to have been made without due consideration of all the relevant facts."

Ayrton, on his hands and knees in the vicinity of the coffin, found a gold-covered long boarding with lions' heads at both ends. This was confirmatory evidence that a raised couch had originally supported the coffin. The one canopic jar visible in the alcove niche had a head with a face like Queen Tiyi's as seen in the panel figure, and Davis was thrilled. He kept murmuring ecstatically, "We've got Queen Tiyi."

When Weigall submitted it as his opinion that, from the text on the coffin lid, the mummy was Akhenaten himself, Maspero frowned. He said he saw indications that certain parts of some of the inscriptions on the lid had been replaced by other words on patches of gold foil, which was puzzling, and several cartouches had been cut out deliberately. He said there was nothing inconsistent in finding the son's name in his mother's tomb, and that the furniture in the tomb unquestionably belonged to at least two persons. And he kept reiterating that the evidence would continue to be "conflicting and confusing and hasty conclusions are to be avoided." He added: "I believe in the end the identity of the owner of the coffin may prove a surprise."

This closed for the time being further comment from either Davis or Weigall.

Maspero peered inside the coffin itself, using his flashlight, and said he could not see much except that the skull was entirely free from the body and there seemed to be a "flash of gold." He emphasized again the very fragile condition of the inlaid feathered lid and warned Ayrton that it must be removed by an expert before the mummy was examined. He, therefore, instructed Weigall to telegraph for an Italian on the Cairo Museum staff, and also a photographer to take pictures of each object *in situ*. Nothing was handled by anyone, not even by Maspero, that first day. He promised to be back for the examination of the mummy. Davis invited me to be present, whereupon Maspero added, "and Mrs. Smith," to which Davis agreed.

When Weigall and I were left alone in the tomb chamber, I made notes of some of Maspero's statements about Queen Tiyi. He declared that the known facts about Queen Tiyi were meager. She was an Egyptian born of parents not high in rank, as was proved by the discovery of her parents' tomb, which had also dispelled the "myth" of a Mesopotamian origin. Her marriage to King Amenhotep III was recorded on several scarabs of the period, and her great influence with her royal husband was acknowledged. He had built for her enjoyment a palace with a near-by lake close to the Theban Plain.

In Maspero's expressed opinion, far from being the inspirer of the new creed of Aten, Queen Tiyi had preferred to keep out of it as far as was compatible with her position as mother of the religious reformer. He advanced (as a surmise) that she had remained in Thebes, died during her son's lifetime, and had been buried in the Valley of the Kings, or that Akhenaten might have had his mother taken to el-Amarna for burial. He also emphasized as a tenable theory that Akhenaten, as king, would expect members of his family to have their tombs near his royal one at el-Amarna, the city he had built and to which he had moved his court in an attempt to break the political power of the priests of Amon.

Maspero suggested as a possibility that the priests of Amon, who had nothing of a political nature against Tiyi, might have consented to her secret reburial in the valley after the death of the so-called "heretic" King and the desecration of his tomb at el-Amarna.

Ayrton at once began working the tomb under Weigall's supervision as inspector. I did not enter the tomb again until word was received of the morning set for the dismantling of "Queen Tiyi's" mummy, as Davis called it. For this second entrance Davis and Maspero came together, and Mrs. Andrews was with them. Weigall, Ayrton, Harold Jones, a dark-haired, small, pleasant young man assisting Ayrton, Corinna, and I were the others present.

I noticed that everything in the tomb chamber was in the same position that it had occupied on my first visit, except that the lid of the coffin had been removed. Ayrton explained to Maspero that the shifting of rubbish had so stirred up the dust as to obscure the outlines of objects and would have been fatal to photography. Therefore, the clearing of the corridor had been delayed until the photographing was completed. Thus the "golden door" was still suspended in midair, but there was a cleared space around the coffin. The condition of the mosaic lid was such that the Museum expert had skillfully cradled it in a padded tray before moving it to the floor where we saw it, split into two pieces because the lid had collapsed inwards on being touched. Also, the inlaid beard of the golden face on the lid was very fragile to handle.

As we all assembled around the open coffin, I could hardly believe my ears when Maspero, turning to me, said: "You have the delicate hands of an artist, please dismember the body." And he made way for me to be nearest the head of the mummy.

No one but an archaeologist who had had a similar experience would understand my sensations as, with hands I found hard to keep steady in my excitement, I approached the body which, from the neck to the feet, was covered with gold sheets about the size of sheets of foolscap, placed symmetrically from side to side, and, strangely enough, in spite of the collapse of the couch which had supported the coffin and the rock which had fallen into the latter from the roof, still were in their original positions. I lifted the first golden sheet that was sufficiently thick so as not to bend to the touch and handed it to Maspero. He examined it first on one side, then turned it over. "Not inscribed," he said. I removed the others as they lay in order, from left to right, and right to left. There were a dozen of them. The coffin apparently had been entirely lined with gold foil, now loosened from the wood. The interest of the archaeologists was focussed on the inscriptions on this gold foil, but Davis's eyes were almost popping out of his head as he stared at the amazing sight of a pile of sheets of pure and heavy gold glittering on the floor.

The outlines of a small-sized body were now clearly revealed. The left arm was bent with the hand on the breast, and around the upper arm were three broad bracelets of very thin, fragile gold. The right arm hung straight down at the side with the hand resting on the thigh, and on the wrist were remains of three similar gold bracelets; on one of them were *marks of teeth,* which did not excite Maspero when I pointed them out. There were no rings on either hand, nor other jewelry in sight. As I have said, the head had been found separated at least a foot from the body. Responding to Maspero's instructions, I stooped and gently raised the crown from the skull. It was a dramatic moment! The skull was badly damaged but there were two rows of good teeth in a jaw fairly well preserved. Maspero examined the skull intently and remarked that it was curiously flattened at the back and unusually wide. I placed it, together with pieces of bones that belonged to it, in a basket held by Ayrton.

Maspero asked me to feel through the mummy cloth around the neck for the necklace that should be there. But no sooner had my hand touched the surface of the mummy than it crumbled into ashes and sifted down through bones. So it was with the entire body until nothing remained except a pile of dust and disconnected bones with a few shreds of dried skin adhering to them. The water that had got into the tomb explained the cloth resembling the consistency of the ash of a cigar. In feeling around I found pieces of a broad necklace of gold pendants, inlaid plaques, lotus flowers of gold, and numerous minute beads. Some of the pieces gave indications of the original design.

Maspero several times warned Davis that there was insufficient evidence to warrant a definite conclusion about the identity of the body beyond the fact that it was royal, because of the uraeus. He said on a closer inspection that he thought the wigs of the heads on the canopic jars resembled those generally worn by men, and he felt this was also true of the shape of the wig on the coffin lid.

At this statement, Weigall got excited. "It must be Akhenaten himself!" he declared. And he was more confident than ever when Ayrton and Harold Jones found the series of four magical bricks that were placed in a tomb, toward the four cardinal points. These had on them the names of Akhenaten. But Maspero maintained they might have been taken from Akhenaten's own tomb and put in Queen Tiyi's. Several seals bearing Tutankhamen's name were discovered (one of them under the funerary couch) and some boxes containing various objects, the most beautiful being a small female figure holding a large vase.

Portrait head of Re-shep-ses, Saqqarah. Painting by Joseph Lindon Smith. Courtesy Museum of Fine Arts, Boston.

Portrait of Ti, the royal architect, Saqqarah. Painting by Joseph Lindon Smith. Courtesy Museum of Fine Arts, Boston.

Weigall, who was about to begin a life of Akhenaten and was much impressed by James Henry Breasted's interpretation in his recently published *History of Egypt,* began to talk along that line. Maspero rather heatedly insisted that but little was known of the el-Amarna period of "heresy." He considered the movement had been a protest against the power of the priesthood of Amon-Ra, therefore was a political rather than a religious revolution, and that Breasted's conception of Akhenaten as a "great religious reformer" had not been substantiated.

While this argument was going on, my hand touched something solid under the body in the small of the back which Maspero told me to raise. I did so. It was a golden sheet exactly like the others but with this important difference: from this gold sheet, which I took from the original mummy wrappings, a *cartouche had been cut.*

Then for the first time Maspero got excited as he examined the sheet very carefully and said, "This looks to me like traces of the name of Akhenaten—and the sheet being among the mummy wrappings is evidence of supreme importance." He turned to Davis, who looked crestfallen when Maspero warned him not to be too sure that the body was that of Queen Tiyi, and Weigall was jubilant.

I tried in vain to get Maspero to comment on the condition of the gold face of the cover lid, where, obviously, the damage had been done neither by water nor by a fallen stone. This was an act of violence, by the hand of man. I longed to know who had forcibly torn away so much of the beautiful golden features, and when.

Davis was astounded, as were the others, to see that my hands were wet from handling a gold sheet taken from under the body. Maspero explained this curious happening by pointing out a needle crack in the roof ceiling almost immediately above the coffin. He said that probably for many years water, having percolated through it, reached the stone floor of the chamber where the mummy lay. The tomb was absolutely airless, except for the air that was originally shut in or possibly came through the needle crack, which after some years was hermetically closed by dumpings from the many surrounding tombs. The air had absorbed all the dampness it could from objects in the tomb that had floated about in water, but it had not absorbed the water underneath the body. Davis recalled that, in the tomb of Ouiya and Touiyou, a large half-sealed alabaster jar had had liquid in it.

Meanwhile Quibell had unexpectedly appeared in the tomb. After listening to Davis declaring he had found Queen Tiyi and Weigall equally confident that the coffin contained Akhenaten's remains, he suggested to Maspero that, among the tourists of the day visiting the valley, there might be a surgeon who with authority could pronounce upon the sex of the mummy. Maspero approved the plan. An obstetrician was discovered by Quibell and brought into the tomb chamber. He examined the pelvic bones and said: "Without doubt this is the skeleton of a woman."

Davis was almost hysterical at this confirmation of his hopes and insisted he would telegraph to the head of the Expedition at el-Amarna, telling him to stop looking for Tiyi because he had found the Queen in the Valley of the Kings.

Once again Maspero warned Davis against "premature" conclusions.

In the presence of Maspero, I placed the remarkably well-preserved bones of the body in a basket, which was sealed and stamped by him. A number was put on a tag, and later on in the day a messenger took the basket to deliver it personally to the Cairo Museum. There was no indication of the tomb from which the bones had come, merely the number on the tag for identification at the Antiquities Service. When, a few weeks later, I saw Maspero in Cairo, he told me that he feared the Egyptian government intended to melt down the heavy uninscribed sheets of gold for bullion. I asked him about the sheet with the partially erased cartouche which I had taken from underneath the body. He looked perturbed and did not answer.

Some months passed, and then, as part of his routine work, G. Elliot Smith, the noted Scottish surgeon, who was professor of anatomy at the Cairo Egyptian School of Medicine, opened the basket containing the bones that I had placed in it. He had no way of knowing in which tomb they had been found. His duty was to make to Maspero an anatomical report on these bones, as he had done on dozens of other mummy remains.

Judge of the stunned amazement of archaeologists interested in the discovery of the great Queen Tiyi when Maspero announced that Elliot Smith's anatomical report stated the skeleton to be that of a *young man* of twenty-five or twenty-six years of age! And the report went on to say that the "cranium exhibited in an unmistakable manner the distortion characteristic of hydrocephalus."

Thus the physical description, including the shape of the skull, with its abnormal width and flattening, fitted the known facts about Akhenaten.

At the time it was generally accepted in archaeological circles that the body of the "heretic" King had been identified in a "cache" containing some of his mother's tomb furniture, and the three beautiful canopic jar heads in the Cairo Museum were labeled "Akhenaten." The fourth and loveliest of them all was given to Davis by Maspero.

How Akhenaten's body got into Queen Tiyi's tomb chamber was a matter for surmise. In Maspero's account (printed in 1908) he wrote that the evidence of the reburial was "both obscure and conflicting." But from the anatomical facts he accepted the conclusion that it was Akhenaten who had been found.

He offered (as a conjecture) that "wishing to prevent any harm being done to the King [Akhenaten] by some fanatical devotee of Amon, the hiders wanted the people to believe that the body they were burying was Tiyi's; accordingly they took with it Tiyi's catafalque and her small furniture." But this explanation he dismissed as being "too farfetched to hold good."

He accepted as an alternative the idea that a number of mummies of Akhenaten's family (including his own) had been brought from el-Amarna for safekeeping, with some of the furniture belonging to them, and that in a secret reburial done at night, the men in charge had mixed the coffins and put the son where the mother ought to have been. Maspero used as an argument for the possibility of such a mistake's having been made, the fact that the coffins of Ouiya and Touiyou were so much alike that they could easily have been confused, especially in a transfer that took place after dark.

In some temerity at disagreeing with the conclusions reached by one of the greatest archaeologists of all times, I decided to put on record certain of my own observations in the burial chamber that I found in conflict with the theory advanced by Maspero. I could not agree that it was a mistake made in ancient times which resulted in an exchange of coffins and put the son's where the mother's would have been expected.

I was firmly convinced there had been no mistake made but, rather, that what we found was the result of the successful carrying out of a carefully organized plan. It seemed to me incredible that priests of Amon would have deliberately hacked out Akhenaten's figure and cartouches on his mother's shrine and yet *not* obliterated the *prayer of Aten,* forbidden by the restored priesthood of Amon. And again, could it have been priests of Amon who raised the body to cut out a cartouche that identified to them the mummy as that of a king of whose reign they were determined to destroy every trace, then replaced the body in the coffin—*covered with gold?*

Who but faithful adherents of the dead Akhenaten could have done these acts in order to preserve his body through eternity by preventing identification? Adherents who knew that the priests of Amon, who had no quarrel with Queen Tiyi, had agreed to her reburial in this secret cache for safety, probably after her own tomb had been partially plundered. They had taken advantage of this knowledge and of the planned transfer (at night) to make the substitution of the coffins. They had brought the son's mummy to a place where no desecration need be feared —his mother's reburial chamber; and these followers of the hated Akhenaten must have had sufficient influence with the priests of Amon to secure the placing of the seal of the priestly college of Amon on the entrance door!

In my opinion, this theory accounted for the evidence in the burial chamber and inside the coffin. I realized, however, it did not explain why the forehead and one eyebrow were all that remained of the gold face on the coffin lid if no thief had entered the burial chamber.

11. *The So-called Akhenaten Mummy*

THIS WILL BE an account of how Maspero's prediction that the identity of the mummy found in the coffin in Queen Tiyi's tomb and of the beautiful alabaster head on the canopic jar might prove to be a "surprise" came to be realized.

Years passed and I was about to sail for Egypt just after Christmas in the year 1949. I noticed in the Metropolitan Museum that the canopic jar head presented to the Museum by Davis, and supposed to be Akhenaten, had been relabeled Semenkhkara.

Shortly after Corinna's and my arrival in Egypt, Dr. Douglas Derry, professor of anatomy at the University of Cairo, was dining with us one evening. He had succeeded Dr. Elliot Smith as "mummy anatomist," and through the years had examined more ancient mummies than anyone else. His findings were based therefore, not only on a thorough training in his profession but on great experience.

At this dinner I happened to remark on the change in attribution of the canopic jar head. When he asked me what my particular interest in the matter was, I told him that I had been the one, in the presence of Maspero and at his request, who had dismantled the mummy found in the tomb of Tiyi. Neither Derry nor Rex Engelbach of the Cairo Museum staff had seen the mummy *in situ,* in the identification of which years later both had made an extensive study, Derry from the anatomical standpoint and Engelbach in reviewing the archaeological evidence. And Corinna and I were the only two still alive who had been present on that exciting morning in Queen Tiyi's tomb, every detail of which I had recorded at the time.

The other guests listened while Derry and I discussed a fascinating puzzle of long ago, in a tomb where Maspero had described the evidence as "confused and conflicting." And now, more than forty years later, as Derry and I produced for each other's information my eye-witness account and his and Engelbach's re-examination of the facts, a different identification was to result.

Quibell, as "keeper" of the Museum, had asked Derry to attempt the restoration of the skull of the mummy in Queen Tiyi's tomb, with the intention of reviewing material in a period that had continued to be controversial among archaeologists. The request was acceded to. Apparently, from what Derry told me, the skull had been considerably further damaged since I had first handled it in the tomb, but fortunately he found the pieces and with a little trouble restored it. This led him to decide on a complete re-examination of the bones of the body, because the age of Akhenaten, at death, as determined by Elliot Smith, archaeologists had found difficult to adjust with the known facts of his reign.

Without going into the details of the process by which Derry reached his anatomical conclusions, he proved that Elliot Smith had made erroneous deductions about a skull of an unusual shape, flattened from above downwards and correspondingly widened. In the identification of the skeleton, Smith had been too much influenced by the fact that Akhenaten's portraits showed these same exaggerated characteristics. In addition, he had based the age of the skeleton on a premise in conflict with the anatomical facts, since the unusual shape of the cranium was not the result of the distortion characteristic of hydrocephalus, a disease of which the skeleton showed no signs.

From Derry's re-examination, he considered the bones to be those of a man not more than twenty-three years of age. If Derry's conclusions were correct, the body was far too young to be Akhenaten's, whereas, from the archaeologists' viewpoint, Elliot Smith's examination had not made him old enough.

Approaching the identification from another angle, Derry told me that when he had unwrapped the mummy of Tutankhamen, in the golden coffin in his tomb, he had noticed at once that the head of Tutankhamen resembled that of the so-called Akhenaten skeleton to a degree that could not be mere coincidence. The diameters of the two skulls approximated closely, and this was all the more remarkable because the shape of the skull of the Akhenaten skeleton was very unusual and in width exceeded any skull Derry had previously measured in Egypt. Such a similarity in the skulls of Tutankhamen and his father-in-law could only mean (anatomically) some close blood relationship between them, and that Tutankhamen might have been Akhenaten's son, probably by another wife.

But at this point Derry confessed to me that he had come up against a dead end. He had discovered a close blood connection between Tutankhamen and the skeleton in Queen Tiyi's tomb, which anatomically had proved to be too young to be Akhenaten. Who then was he? In this dilemma Derry appealed to Engelbach to re-examine the archaeological evidence of the coffin, as he himself had done with the physical facts of the skeleton, which had caused Derry to believe that the skeleton was an elder brother of Tutankhamen by the same mother.

What Engelbach discovered was also published in the *Annales* (1931) under the heading, "The So-Called Coffin of Akhenaten." After a brief résumé on the funerary furniture in the tomb, he summed up the statements by M. G. Daressy, who (in 1908) made the first complete study of the inscriptions on the coffin for Mr. Theodore Davis. Daressy observed that certain parts of all the inscriptions had been removed and other words or phrases inserted in their place on patches of gold foil. These alterations, which, according to Engelbach, were the key to the identity of the skeleton, had not been studied again until he, Engelbach, made his examination. Daressy had concluded, in brief, that the coffin was originally made for Queen Tiyi and later adapted for a man, and that man he accepted as Akhenaten on the same assumption Maspero had concurred in after the confirmation of Elliot Smith's anatomical report.

Engelbach noted, as Maspero had surmised, that the head of the coffin lid wore a wig instead of a royal headdress, the only emblem of royalty being the uraeus on the forehead, and that the wigs of the heads on the canopic jars were exactly like the wig on the coffin, and were of a type used by males. Guy Brunton of the Cairo Museum staff, assisting Engelbach, found some inaccuracies in Daressy's deciphering of the text on the coffin lid. He also made a most interesting discovery about the canopic jars, which was that the uraei had not formed part of the original scheme of the heads. This fact was evidence that the jars were prepared for someone not royal and later used by someone who was.

In various places on the coffin, alterations in words or phrases were inserted, and erased cartouches were preceded by titles. After a brilliant piece of work on a possible reconstruction of the text (which he described step by step), Engelbach found indications that the coffin, like the canopic jars, although used by someone royal, had been made for a person not royal. At this stage he wondered whether these two "somebodies" could be the same person. In other words, was there in the el-Amarna period some private person for whom a coffin could have been prepared who afterwards became royal?

The names of Tiyi, Akhenaten, and Nefertete, his Queen, did not fit into the spaces of the altered inscriptions, and the coffins of Tutankhamen were all accounted for. There remained in that el-Amarna Aten group, Semenkhkara, who had married the eldest daughter of Akhenaten and succeeded him.

The conclusion that the coffin had been made for Semenkhkara as a favorite of Akhenaten, and later altered so as to be used by him after he was king, Engelbach reached by much detailed data convincingly presented, and Semenkhkara's name fitted into the spaces of the altered text.

Then Engelbach, like the others before him, was at a loss to account for the sequence of events which had led to the finding of the mummy of Semenkhkara in a secret cache to which some, but obviously only a small part, of the funerary furniture of Queen Tiyi had been moved from her original tomb. Engelbach offered as a suggestion that Tutankhamen, when he became king, had intended to rebury Semenkhkara (his elder brother) in Queen Tiyi's tomb, to secure safety for his person as successor to the hated Akhenaten, but finding it plundered had taken Semenkhkara's coffin and the canopic jars and placed them in the "cache" which at that time contained the Queen's shrine and the few remaining objects of her original burial. Engelbach agreed that the corner bricks of Akhenaten might have been in Tiyi's original tomb.

Semenkhkara, when he became king, would be expected to have begun to prepare a royal funerary outfit, but his very short reign had not made his preparations sufficiently advanced to be of service at his burial, and some of his funerary objects were later adapted for use in Tutankhamen's tomb. What more likely than that Tutankhamen had altered the inscriptions on his elder brother's coffin given him by Akhenaten and which Semenkhkara had cherished for that reason?

The date of the alterations was, of course, an all-important factor, but it had not been possible to determine at what time the figure and cartouches of Akhenaten on Queen Tiyi's funerary shrine, and the cartouches of Semenkhkara on the coffin and on the canopic jars, were erased. A point to note was that the Aten prayer and the disk and Aten rays on the panel of the shrine with Queen Tiyi were untouched, although much pains had been taken to remove the offending figure and name of Akhenaten. Engelbach hazarded a guess that this might have occurred during the reign of Horemheb, and stated that Davis's description gave no indication of inspections subsequent to the sealing of the cache, as was the case in the tomb of Tutankhamen.

I told Derry, in this connection, that the only sealing on the blocked-up entrance to Queen Tiyi's tomb was that of the priests of Amon-Ra. Maspero, Ayrton, Weigall, and Carter, all had examined the evidence on that doorway and would not have missed the record of "subsequent inspections." Derry concurred.

I felt like a detective reopening a case, on new evidence, and I thrilled to the fact that the identification of the mummy as Semenkhkara cleared up some points I had personally never accepted in Maspero's conclusions, namely that the body had been placed in that tomb by "mistake" from the mixing of the coffins containing members of the Akhenaten family, in a transfer after dark, and that priests of Amon-Ra had hacked out the figure of Akhenaten and his cartouches.

Maspero had dismissed as "farfetched" the idea that the body of Akhenaten (as it was supposed to be) had been brought to this secret burial place for "protection," probably by Ai or Tutankhamen out of family consideration, a theory supported by the amount of gold in the coffin that no thief would have left. But I had always been confident that someone with kindly feelings toward the (by then) proscribed creed of Aten had raised the body in the coffin to remove the identifying cartouche under it, that no priest of Amon would have left intact the text of Aten prayers and the protecting rays of the sun disk, and that this must have been done by formerly friendly adherents to Akhenaten's doctrines.

In view of the likelihood that the body in that tomb was Semenkhkara's, the evidence of what happened ceased to be "obscure and conflicting." What more natural than for Tutankhamen, whose seal was found under the funerary couch, to have acted to safeguard through eternity the body of his elder brother? Associated as Semenkhkara had been as king with the Aten creed at el-Amarna, if his body had been in any known tomb, it would not have survived the wrath of a restored Amon-Ra.

Certainly no priest of Amon-Ra did the work in that secret burial cache, but Tutankhamen, who, after the death of Semenkhkara, had become king, did it. He had returned to Thebes and gone back to the official worship of Amon-Ra. But he had spent his early boyhood in el-Amarna and his wife was one of Akhenaten's daughters. The figure and name of his father-in-law had to be destroyed, but the boy king might well have stopped there and not damaged the text of the Aten prayers and the Aten disk, which had been a legacy from his own past which he had cast aside. And at the same time he altered the coffin of his brother to show that the owner at the time of his death had been royal and then erased the name wherever it occurred for protection against the priests of Amon. Unquestionably the lifting of the body to erase one final cartouche in the mummy wrappings showed knowledge of its identity.

No one had accounted to me for the act of violence in snatching from the coffin lid the gold wig, most of the face, and a part of both hands. It seemed to me this must have been done by a thief or thieves before the coffin, having collapsed, revealed the gold on the body. It was known that, after Tutankhamen's tomb was sealed, sixteen golden cups disappeared, and probably other valuables as well, but later the tomb was resealed. Engelbach had commented that little of Queen Tiyi's furniture was found, a fact suggesting the presence of robbers in the "cache" to which it had been moved in a reburial.

The placing of Semenkhkara's coffin in Queen Tiyi's cache and the burial of Tutankhamen could only have been a few years apart. The two tombs, both insignificant in appearance, were close together, with ancient workmen's huts between them on the same level. Therefore, since these burials must have been known to the same workmen, it seemed to me a tenable theory that the theft of Queen Tiyi's valuables and the gold from Semenkhkara's coffin lid might have been the act of the same thieves who had robbed the tomb of Tutankhamen, done at the same time, and undoubtedly discovered before they had secured much loot from either tomb chamber. Derry and I agreed that this must have occurred before the makers of the surrounding tombs treated the site as a barren spot on which to dump the rocks from various other tombs and thereby had preserved the deposits in the tombs of Tiyi and Tutankhamen for excavators of modern times to discover.

Derry, on leaving this eventful dinner party, picked up my hat instead of his own, and a similar episode in which I was concerned emerged in a startling flash of memory. Once again I imagined myself in the marble hall of Highclere, where I had put on Carnarvon's hat, which was the same color as mine. I remembered that it was not sufficiently large over my forehead but fell away behind and was very wide above my neck, a curious construction for a hat. Carnarvon laughingly had said, "Joe, I never lose my hats because no one else can wear them; they have to be made specially."

As I repeated this incident, Derry's eyes met mine, and I blurted out, "You said this evening that no other skull you ever measured was like those of Tutankhamen and the formerly 'so-called' Akhenaten mummy. Was there not a third?"

No words between us were needed after my story of the hat. He knew, I knew, that he had measured Carnarvon's skull when embalming his body for shipment back to England.

12. *The Lost Kings of the Valley*

MASPERO HAD MADE REFERENCE, at the time we were trying to reconstruct the secret reburial in the tomb of Queen Tiyi, to a series of events by which in ancient times, at royal command, the mummies of Queen Hatshepsut, Tuthmosis III, Tuthmosis IV, Seti I, Ramesses II, and Ramesses III, as well as many others, had been removed from their tombs in the Valley of the Kings and concealed in a "cache" for protection against thieves, over a period extending from 1504 to 1164 B.C.

An Austrian named Emil Brugsch Bey for many years held a position in the Antiquities Service of the Egyptian government, which administered the temples and tombs of Upper and Lower Egypt. The task of administration must have been a police job much of the time.

An inscription, found at the side of a doorway of a tomb in the Valley of the Kings, was made by a grand vizier in Dynasty XXII, in the reign of Sheshonq, between 950 and 929 B.C., who set down matter-of-factly that he had removed the royal bodies from their tombs and placed them in a secret resting place. In modern times, all of the tombs were found empty of the kingly bodies, except for Amenhotep II, who, alone of the royal personages, remained in his tomb, where I saw him in 1899.

It goes without saying that the search for the secret hiding place of these "lost" kings never ceased, and Brugsch Bey was always on the lookout for any indication that might reveal their whereabouts.

One day in his mail from Europe, a letter came from a collector in Austria, together with a photograph of part of a necklace, upon which was inscribed the name of one of the lost kings. The object had been bought from a dealer, who had obtained it from an agent, who had occasionally dealt with persons in Egypt of doubtful repute. Not long afterwards came another letter from an individual in England, who described an article, recently come into his hands, which was evidently part of the same necklace, of gold, with the King's name inscribed.

This led Brugsch Bey to believe that a modern thief had found the secret place of burial of one of the sequestered kings, and his guess was that the thief would be a man living not far from the valley. A thief obtaining rare material would receive a considerable sum of money from agents secretly handling such loot. At that time such agents would probably be found in Cairo and Alexandria.

With the co-operation of the chief of police of these two cities, both Englishmen, a watch was put on all natives from upriver who appeared in town and squandered large sums of money in riotous living. Those doing the watching were told to look out for the type of native who would not be expected to possess wealth. Meanwhile, when still a third piece of the same necklace had been purchased in Europe, Brugsch Bey determined to be personally connected with the recovery of treasures of antiquity belonging to the government.

One day he received from the chief of police in Alexandria a detailed account of the suspicious behavior in the previous six months of a native of Qurna. This man had made repeated visits to Alexandria and spent much money.

On the evidence, Brugsch Bey decided to have the local police of Luxor investigate the male inhabitants of Qurna. This was a delicate and difficult job, as the men, of course, would be suspicious and resentful at questioning by the police, and would protect one another. An unexpected family feud came to Brugsch Bey's aid. It appeared that three brothers looked with envy on their elder brother's sudden affluence. Through the careless talk of the wife, or wives, of the head of the family, the younger brothers became suspicious. One night they followed the elder brother to the cliff near the Temple of Deir-el-Bahari and watched him enter the cache, made their presence known, and demanded a share in the loot.

After a time, the brothers fell out among themselves over the division of the spoils. And through their quarreling the local police identified the family that was thieving. The head of the family was arrested and Brugsch Bey was summoned from Cairo.

I am afraid the poor wretch was subjected to the third degree before he confessed. At any rate, he took Brugsch Bey and the police to the place of concealment. It was a natural cave in a sheer wall of the cliffs, hidden from view by a great slab of stone that had been slid in front of the opening in remote times.

The thief said he had found it by accident, when a kid among his flock of goats had fallen through the opening.

Brugsch Bey gave a vivid description of the appearance of the missing kings, with the rich gleam of gold and precious stones on their royal persons.

The mummies were taken to the Cairo Museum and placed in coffins in a conspicuous gallery, with their faces exposed. There was always a crowd about them whose disrespectful comments about these once great rulers of ancient Egypt offended my sense of decency. Often in the early morning, before tourists arrived, or near closing time, when they had gone, if I was painting in the museum, I would pause to look at Seti I. The nobility and sensitiveness of his face made it easy to understand why the reliefs in the temples he built showed the feeling of an artist for sculpture.

Some time passed and the mummies of Queen Hatshepsut, Tuthmosis III, Tuthmosis IV, Seti I, Ramesses II, and Ramesses III remained on public view. In the early years of the 1930's, when the National party returned to power, Prime Minister Nahas spent many thousands of pounds of government funds to erect an enormous mausoleum in honor of the people's idol, Zaghlul, founder of the Nationalist movement, and, incidentally, an Egyptian statesman, which his successor Nahas, was not. Zaghlul's body was moved into the mausoleum with a great popular ceremony, and this building in a central square of Cairo became the scene of demonstrations and riots.

The Nationalist government fell, to be replaced by a coalition of conservatives. The new Prime Minister thought the emphasis on Zaghlul's personality would be lessened if this mausoleum included the bodies of the great kings in the Cairo Museum. The plan worked. The mummies (as always) made the newspapers in great headlines and feature stories, and the limelight was focused on them instead of Zaghlul.

But a few years later, Nahas was once again prime minister. He sent a curt message to the museum authorities that they must remove the royal mummies immediately. Rex Engelbach and an English colleague managed to find two ambulances, and in the dead of night, when Cairo was asleep, without attracting attention entered the mausoleum and collected the kings. The solemn cortege escorted by two Englishmen went through the deserted streets. Through a back court, the mummies were brought into the Museum, where they were deposited in an unused room in an upper gallery, placed together in dignified surroundings befitting their high rank. From that time on, permission to see the royal mummies had to be obtained personally from the Minister of Education, in whose department the Antiquity Service functioned, and a foreigner had to send an application through his own embassy or legation.

After the war, when I returned to Egypt in 1946, I had been asked to make a pencil drawing of King Seti, as I had done of the mummies of old Ouiya and Touiyou for the Egyptian government publication on their tomb.

I wrote a formal letter, addressed to H. E. Minister of Education, to be delivered by our cultural attaché. Very promptly, I received an "unofficial" summons from the under-secretary of Education, a good friend of mine. He explained with courtesy and tact that the government would be "distressed" to refuse anything I asked; therefore he was suggesting that I withdraw my proposal, and he handed me back my letter. I tore it up.

13. *A Dinner Party at Karnak*

THE EARL OF CARNARVON became a world figure in 1922 after the discovery of the tomb of Tutankhamen in the Valley of the Kings. But I had known him since 1906, when the Smith family were living on the *dahabieh Abu Simbel,* moored to the west bank at Thebes.

Cromer had personally requested Maspero to give the British peer a concession to excavate, accessible from the Winter Palace Hotel in Luxor. And Carnarvon was assigned an unimportant site on the Sheikh Abd'-el-Qurna Necropolis where nobles were buried during Dynasty XVIII (1570–1349 B.C.) and Dynasty XIX (1349–1197 B.C.) Several times, Corinna and I were invited to share a sandwich lunch with Carnarvon at Qurna in a large screened cage, protection from flies and dust, where he sat daily and watched his workmen dig. Frequently his Countess was with him. She seemed to me to be dressed for a garden party rather than the desert, with charming patent-leather, high-heeled shoes and a good deal of jewelry flashing in the sunlight, but she was a good sport in facing hardships connected with field excavations, and both she and Lord Carnarvon were delightful companions.

The discomfort of Qurna during the heat of the day, they faced without complaint. The evening meal was in great contrast. It was served in state in a private dining room of the hotel, and usually the manager himself appeared, to be sure everything was satisfactory. Food brought in from different parts of Europe was prepared by special chefs; Rothschild's cellars furnished vintage burgundies, ports, Madeiras, and old brandies. When we dined with Carnarvon, our fellow guests were archaeologists, who looked out of place and rather dazed in an atmosphere created by the style and elaborate details of the dinner. And Carnarvon himself seemed curiously detached from his surroundings.

He was of medium height and slight in build, with nondescript features and sparse hair. The shape of his head was abnormal, flattened on top, sloping abruptly downward, and widened, which gave a curious effect on a slender neck, an anatomical construction that led to the interesting secret which later I was to share with Derry. The unhealthy color of his complexion was made more conspicuous by the fact that his face was pitted from smallpox. But when he discussed Egyptology, his pale, lusterless eyes lit up with enthusiasm. He was a good listener, and, all in all, I found I liked him better each time I saw him.

Primarily, Carnarvon had been identified with sport. He owned a famous stable on his great English estate of Highclere, and his horses were successfully trained for the Derby and other races. From early youth, a series of severe illnesses had weakened his physique, and yet he was well known as a hunter of big game, with many daring exploits to his credit. He also had indulged in motor racing, was an excellent amateur photographer, and studied seriously spiritualistic manifestations. A terrible automobile accident ended Carnarvon's further participation in sports. When the doctors condemned him to quiet winters, spent out of doors in a good climate, he decided on Egypt. And he took up excavating with the same energy previously devoted to his other tastes.

Hunting scene from the tomb of Userhet, Thebes. Painting by Joseph Lindon Smith. Courtesy Museum of Fine Arts, Boston.

The golden hawk of Hierakonpolis, with "ladders of gold" at
the top. From a photograph of
the original in the Cairo Museum.
Courtesy of the Egyptian
government.

Bas-relief portrait of Khaemet, keeper of the royal granaries under Amenhotep III,
Thebes. Painting by Joseph Lindon Smith. Courtesy George Pierce Metcalf, Providence.

He was a rather pathetic figure in his determined fight against being an invalid. A continued semiactive life was in large part due to a Dr. Johnson, familiarly known as "Johnny," who was a permanent member of the Carnarvon household. "Johnny" was a red-faced little cockney who was a kindly man and made friends easily. Carnarvon was supposed to have a disease that "Johnny" alone knew how to keep in check, and he was always in attendance.

Before sailing from Egypt that spring, Corinna and I dined with the Carnarvons at Shepheard's. We met a large company of oddly assorted guests, mostly racing notables. Carnarvon kept explaining me to them as a "noted archaeologist." This did not seem to recommend me favorably to their attention. Corinna got on better than I did with men who talked about nothing except the stable.

In the winter of 1907, when we were with the Weigalls in Luxor, Carnarvon was back at his Qurna dig with unabated enthusiasm, even though the season before he had found practically nothing. Again we had seen more or less of him and had received generous gifts from the Rothschild cellar.

Carnarvon had been excavating for about a month when, one afternoon, he appeared at the Weigall's house, breathless with excitement. He had found a mummified cat! He personally superintended placing it in Weigall's government magazine for antiquities, and just before dinner came in to be sure the cat was "doing all right," as he put it. Carnarvon seemed fascinated with his first find, even though it was too "late" to be of value archaeologically, and was of no interest artistically.

That night the Weigalls and Smiths heard a loud explosion from the direction of the garden. We all rushed outside to find the door of the magazine opened from the shock of the blast. The change of atmosphere had adversely affected Carnarvon's cat. The case and the cat had been badly damaged, and Weigall was at a loss about how to break the bad news to Carnarvon. Later Carnarvon spent a large sum of money having the cat and case restored.

Indeed, spending large sums of money for more or less "trivial" things did not disturb Lord Carnarvon. Some weeks after this cat incident he gave a dinner party at Karnak. No one who was present will ever forget the occasion. Only those who had not been invited thought it a "desecration." It was full moon. The guests had been called for by carriages. We all arrived together at about seven o'clock and were received by the Carnarvons in the Temple of Ramesses, to the right of the large entrance gate to Karnak.

Most of the staff from the Winter Palace were there, costumed as for a performance of *Aïda*. It was as unreal as a scene from the *Arabian Nights* to look from the double line of standing figures of Ramesses to the very long table, perfectly appointed with glass, cutlery, china, and linen, as imposing as though it had been laid in a great banquet hall in England.

The food was hot and unbelievably good, and the service noiseless, as delicacies and choice wines appeared and disappeared. Maspero, the guest of honor, was in fine form as he led the conversation, which was mostly about Karnak. Many of the Egyptologists present had had some connection with Karnak during long careers in Egypt, and interesting and amusing anecdotes about excavations, conducted at various periods, flew back and forth among the guests. Maspero's comments were brilliant and to the point.

By a little after nine, the guests were in the great Hypostyle Hall, which was illuminated by artificial light in addition to the moon. No one before had attempted such a combination, which was extraordinarily successful in bringing out details on the tall columns.

The beauty of the night and the light of the full moon tempted us all to wander far afield, over the vast confines of the temple enclosure. Past the pylons and obelisks to the distant Bubastis Gate, then back to the entrance to Karnak, to climb to the top of the pylon and look across the Nile to the high gebel above the Theban Plain, with the dim outlines of temples visible, or on the Luxor side of the river, to see the bold peaks beyond the town. By mutual accord, the party got to the Sacred Lake and there stayed on in silent enjoyment until our host tactfully indicated it was time to go home.

Outside the Temple of Ramesses, a servant handed me my hat and

Corinna's wrap. Maspero happened to be at my side. We both looked at the great court and the standing figures of Ramesses where we had recently feasted. The table had vanished, so had the chairs. There was no sign of anyone's having been there.

Maspero rubbed his eyes: "An unexpected and a perfect climax!" he said.

14. The Cromer Legacy

THROUGH THE WINTER we Smiths, as guests of an English official, met a varied assortment of the "higher ups" in administrative positions who visited Luxor. The subject that found its way into all conversation was, What would happen after Cromer's departure from Egypt, which was scheduled for the early spring?

Those who had been in direct contact with the provinces expressed anxiety about the future of the *fellaheen* (peasants), an anxiety we found generally shared by the splendid young British inspectors who lived in the villages and spoke Arabic. Egyptian *mudir* (governors of provinces) knew to their cost that Cromer brooked no injustice to the patient tillers of the soil on whose ceaseless labor depended the prosperity of the entire population. He insisted that injustice done to them reached him personally, unless remedied when reported by the British adviser to the minister concerned.

Would a lesser Englishman than Cromer inspire the dread in Egyptian local authorities needed to protect the *fellaheen,* and to curb the national aspirations and self-assertiveness of a student class stirred up by politicians to demonstrate against controls imposed by the presence of British troops?

In retrospect, no one questioned the fact that foreign intervention had become inevitable, in order to restore internal order, re-establish a stable government, and guarantee protection of the Suez Canal after Ismail Pasha's misrule had brought the country to bankruptcy. And when a native fanatic Arabi, leading armed forces in open rebellion against the Egyptian government, had caused general unrest and political chaos!

The great powers were in agreement that England and France were to enter Egypt jointly in 1882, but at the last moment a change in foreign policy led France to withdraw. The British fleet then bombarded Alexandria, and after the Egyptians had set up brief resistance, the British restored order and assumed joint responsibility with the Khedive, Tewfik, for governing Egypt under the overlordship of the Sultan of Turkey.

By legal status, Cromer was only one of many accredited representatives of foreign powers. But he alone of the consular agents had an armed force in Egypt with the consent of the powers.

The Khedive governed through a council of ministers, but to each minister Cromer appointed a British "adviser." Even though the Egyptian ministers got most of the salary and all of the prestige, neither the Khedive nor the ministers were permitted to forget that, in a clash of opinion, the Egyptians must give way, since behind the Englishman's suggestions, offered tactfully as befitted a subordinate, was a British army, and force was something all races of all countries understood.

The situation was one that, not unnaturally, the Khedive and his ministers found increasingly irksome, especially when they heard so much talk from the English about the *fellaheen* and nothing they could turn to their own political advantage.

The question of capitulations was another cause for bitter controversy. Capitulations, originally established as a protection of European traders against arbitrary, unjust treatment by an oriental ruler, later were abused. Criminals of many nations, and large foreign business interests, unscrupulously sheltered themselves behind their consular courts, to the disadvantage of Turkish and Egyptian nationals, and became a source of constant irritation to the sensitive pride of the Egyptian government.

From the beginning, relations between the "occupying" British and the educated Egyptians in the government circles of Cairo and Alexandria had required the dominating will and ingenuity of a Cromer to keep them from being strained to the breaking point. Now the question was, What successor could be found with equal assets?

Everyone we saw was in accord about Cromer's greatness, marveled at his genius in putting the economy of the country on a sound financial basis, and applauded the stupendous engineering feats accomplished by British effort. But Cromer's most ardent admirers regretted that, during his long years of power, so little had been done toward the political education of the Egyptians, in order that they in turn, trained by Englishmen, would be qualified to carry on the future administration of their country for the benefit of their own people. It was well known that such a policy presented to Cromer by British colleagues had not received his approval.

After a generation of British control of Egypt, which London had repeatedly referred to as "temporary," Cromer gave no intimation of a date when British troops would be withdrawn. Many feared his failure to face both these issues threatened administrative disaster, sooner perhaps rather than later.

At a time when we were all reflecting upon these problems, we had a most enjoyable and unexpected visit from Maspero, who spent several days under the Weigalls' roof on a tour of inspection. I knocked off work and had a number of delightful hours with him and Weigall in tombs and temples, as they discussed the problems of the Antiquities Service. Maspero was frank in what he said to those whose discretion he trusted, and our talks covered a wide range of subjects in the quiet evenings at the Inspector's house.

His thoughts, like those of everyone else, were on the Cromer succession. He emphasized his genuine interest in antiquities, and reminisced about incidents, some of which I knew at the time they happened. After expressing high admiration for Cromer, he concluded his praise by saying that the great Englishman was "arbitrary at times in forcing his wishes without consulting the judgment of those with more experience in any given procedure he advocated." Of course, both Weigall and I knew Maspero had in mind the incident of the sacred boat, found in the Valley of the Kings, and its aftermath, an event that still rankled in Maspero's soul. Obviously, he enjoyed reviewing it in safe company. Cromer had personally "instructed" Maspero to have the boat left *in situ* so tourists could see it.

85

Maspero, with his usual tact in dealing with his British subordinates, had written Weigall for his opinion as to the advisability of such a procedure. Weigall had expressed himself strongly and adversely. The boat would be stolen with or without the connivance of *ghaffir*.

Maspero had seen Cromer personally and reminded us the interview had not been *"très agréable."* Cromer had insinuated it would be Maspero's fault if the boat was not adequately protected, and practically commanded it to be left in the valley. Maspero, in recalling the affair, shrugged his shoulders expressively. "You both know what happened," he said. We did. Within a week the sacred boat was gone, vanished without a trace.

Some months later, the Egyptian government had bought it back piecemeal from dealers abroad. Cromer was angry for having been thwarted in a plan he had at heart and continued to blame Weigall and Maspero. It was simply a case of Cromer's bad judgment. "The great Englishman does not always face reality," Maspero commented, and went on to indulge in surmise as to what would have been the outcome if his country, France, had occupied Egypt jointly with England. He considered the administrative system Cromer had introduced as too naïve for the more sophisticated French mind to accept, and he dismissed the topic abruptly by saying that, with the pressure from liberals in England and the "human" tendencies of Egyptian politicians, the British might soon find themselves in a position of responsibility without adequate authority in Egypt.

One of our best-informed English guests felt the prestige of Cromer could have changed, or modified, even the greed and self-interest of the Egyptian officials, and that would have been a legacy indeed, he declared. He summed up by saying earnestly about Cromer: "He's so magnificent and tireless in his efforts, but to him Egypt has been a *personal* responsibility and not something to share with Egyptians in authority. And within a few weeks he'll be gone from the scene, leaving behind no policy to meet the demands of a changing restless Egypt, resentful of British control. His successors have my sympathy. What a tragic harvest theirs to reap!"

Corinna and I were immensely honored to be invited by Lord and Lady Cromer to one of their final dinners, and felt well repaid for the night travel it entailed from Luxor to Cairo and back.

The dinner was a brilliant affair, but one tinged with sadness as we reflected that we were sharing in the end of the Cromer era. Except for our American minister, we were the only Americans present.

When someone had mentioned Corinna's study of the Koran to Cromer, he talked to her at some length about the importance of Islam in the life of a Moslem. He spoke with real feeling of the *fellaheen,* who, he said, had remained "deeply religious, and were neither interested in, nor fitted for, taking part in representative government, in their daily routine concerned with the realities of village life."

I joined Corinna to take her home just as he made the above remark. I thought he looked older, there was a slight stoop in his erect carriage, and he had tired eyes. His nobility of character impressed me afresh as on every glimpse I had had of him through my years in Egypt. He towered above me, smiling as he shook my hand in a firm grip. I thought of the attitude of the *fellaheen* towards Cromer's government. In him they knew they had a friend and to the customary oath sworn on the Koran they added the *Kalam inglisi* ("word of an Englishman").

What better monument could he have left?

ANCIENT SITES AND MODERN THIEVES

1907–1908

15. *The Tomb of Horemheb*

I N THE SPRING of 1908 Theodore Davis found another tomb in the Valley of the Kings. I was at Assuan when I received a telegram inviting me to the opening. I was unable to accept, but immediately upon my return to Luxor my first question to Weigall was for a detailed account of the new Davis tomb. Weigall said at once that the opening was not dramatic. He took Lady Carnarvon and me to view Horemheb, the dynamic general and great statesman in whom I had been interested because of his connection with Akhenaten. The tomb was a very deep one of the usual type. It had been entered repeatedly in ancient times and horribly knocked about. The wall decorations of the corridors were paintings of the King in the company of gods and, although comparatively uninjured, were coarse and crude in workmanship and color. This seemed strange when the Horemheb chariot scene in the Feast of Opet in Luxor Temple was notably good art, as were his Karnak reliefs.

Lady Carnarvon was greatly intrigued by a small room about ten feet square. In it was a painting of Osiris, the lord of the underworld, somewhat larger than life size. It was quite unique and really remarkable, although uninteresting from an artistic standpoint. In the Osiris room we saw bones that Weigall told us had been identified as belonging to two different female skeletons. The last and largest room contained a splendid red granite sarcophagus of the King in perfect condition. And in this there were some scattered bones, probably those of Horemheb himself.

During a reign of thirty-five years, from 1349–1314 B.C., Horemheb, after the failure of Akhenaten's cult of Aten, re-established the strength of kingship, and both Seti I and Ramesses II maintained it. But after them the political power of the priesthood of Amon was completely entrenched. A long list of consecutive "priest-kings," appointed by the priesthood of Amon, ruled Egypt in a period of decline.

I thoroughly enjoyed Randall-MacIver as a fellow guest at the Weigalls'. Randall-MacIver, curator of the Egyptian Department at the University of Pennsylvania Museum in Philadelphia, had brought all his treasures with him, excavated that season for an expedition financed by Eckley B. Coxe. There were five hundred or more pots and jugs, countless beads, bracelets, and rings, and splendid stone statues and bronzes. A most important lot of things. I helped in packing them. Weigall took very little for the Cairo Museum, and from this generosity on the part of the Egyptian government, 90 per cent of the objects went to America.

The Carnarvons were driven away by three successive days of dust blown about by a *khamseen* (hot wind from the south) in the offing, and I telegraphed Quibell to expect me any day at Saqqarah.

16. *Saqqarah Tombs*

EVERYONE, INCLUDING MYSELF, who intended to travel north when the good weather broke, attempted to get on the train for Cairo the next night. When the storm came, I had to sit up in a third-class compartment hideously overcrowded. In Cairo I was present at a dinner Maspero gave in honor of Davis. Guests, for the most part, were British and French officials of the Egyptian government Antiquities service. Quite a collection of brains, with Maspero in a class by himself.

The dinner was a tribute well deserved by Davis, who made an excellent speech. He said he would always remember with pride that he had never searched for loot on a "likely" spot. And he explained at some length that, in his excavating experiences in the Royal Valley, the most difficult, tiresome, and expensive job was finding a "dump" for the debris. Generally he had had to move the debris a number of times, as the first dump might cover a tomb. If no tomb was found under any given spot from which the debris was removed in the search, the latter had to be returned to the same spot. This was dull routine, but it did have the advantage of exhausting the possibilities of hidden tombs in a given area. He declared he had never regretted the procedure he had agreed to, and after all, he had been amply rewarded. Both the tombs of Ouiya and Touiyou and Queen Tiyi were discovered at "unlikely" sites.

I had a quiet morning in the museum with Maspero, at his request, and I was flattered by his saying that he had learned much from my evaluation of ancient treasures from the viewpoint of an artist. He showed me Davis's recent find of jewels, necklaces, and bracelets belonging to Queen Tauoserit found in the tomb of Horemheb. I was decidedly disappointed in them. The designs and settings of the stones were poor, and the metal looked thin and tinny. A tawdry exhibit, I thought. Maspero concurred, then together we admired the Dashuhr jewelry, unrivaled for perfection in execution.

Quibell had come from Saqqarah for the occasion and took me back with him. Saqqarah was situated in the desert about fifteen miles from the modern city of Cairo. It had been the burial place of kings of Dynasty I (3200–2980 B.C.), Dynasty II (2980–2780 B.C.), and Dynasty III (2780–2680 B.C.). After the collapse of Dynasty IV (2565 B.C.) at Giza, Dynasty V was established at Saqqarah with Weserkaf as the first king who reigned seven years. The dynasty lasted from 2565–2420 B.C. and Dynasty VI from 2420 to 2258 B.C. Quibell declared I brought good luck when a small find was made right under my eyes as we approached the big Egyptian government house which he occupied as chief inspector of Antiquities for the district. Scholars turned up almost daily, among them, Arthur C. Mace, a cousin of Flinders Petrie, with whom he had started his archaeological career. And Petrie himself came and spent several days "tombing" with Quibell. He discussed with him many interesting sites they had known together, such as Hierakonpolis, Abydos, and el-Amarna, and I listened to all the grand old archaeologist had to say with bated breath.

During his stay, Percy Newberry happened to come to Saqqarah, and as Newberry had started his archaeological career with Petrie in 1888, because of the special botanical information he could supply, this fact put Petrie in a reminiscent mood, and his mind focussed on his early days in Egypt. He said laughingly, believe it or not, that he had first come to Egypt to measure the Giza Pyramids at the request of a relative, who was a pyramid mystic. That was in 1880, the final year of Mariette Bey's long directorship. He thought that he (Petrie) had traveled quite a distance scientifically after such a poor start, and said he expected to be in Egypt and Palestine long enough to write a book entitled, "Seventy Years in Archaeology."

"Why limit it to seventy?" Quibell commented.

I felt this was a real opportunity to get to know Petrie, whom I had previously only seen casually. Maspero had told me that Flinders Petrie was the founder of archaeological research in Egypt and the first scientific excavator. He said, not without awe, that the list of sites at which Petrie had worked was a most impressive one, and that he expected the record to stand for many years to come. Petrie's most notable contribution had been at Abydos.

John Garstang also came, and I went to the top of the Step Pyramid with Quibell and him. Of all the dirty ascents in Egypt, this was by far the dirtiest. Garstang arrived looking immaculate in breeches and high riding boots, very much polished. And when he came down from Zoser's Pyramid, he was just as immaculate—boots and all. Quibell told me jokingly it would not be for fine scholarship and excavations in Egypt, the Sudan, and Palestine, or for his writings on the Hittites and Bible history that Garstang would be remembered, but for the perfection of his desert appearance.

Quibell was working the tomb of Re-shepses he had discovered only a few weeks back, northeast of the Step Pyramid. It consisted of a small chamber which had never been opened in our time. The painted sculptures on the narrow little doorway were the brightest in color of any

I had seen, as well as being beautifully modeled and drawn. The subject was a procession of young men leading deer, gazelles, and antelopes. Like the loyal friend he was, Quibell had waited for me to be with him when he opened a shaft in the tomb chamber. With the usual thrill of anticipation, he and I watched the workmen remove the debris. At the very bottom of the shaft, Quibell found a large-sized wooden head, which was a portrait of the owner of the tomb. It was wonderfully life-like, with a face full of expression. I was glad to make a study of this head with its vigorous characterization of the fifth dynasty. I also painted in the tomb chamber a full-sized detail on the highly decorated door-way. He asked me to make a cast of a death mask in plaster found in the debris of the Pyramid of Tety II. This was a most important dis-covery, since from its position the mask must have been one of the royal family. Quibell at first thought it the face of a man. But my confidence that it was a woman finally convinced him, and later Maspero agreed with me.

The continuity of agricultural Egypt was strong upon me as I walked up the steep desert slope to the Step Pyramid and went beyond it to enter the tomb of Ti, a high court official who lived at the beginning of Dynasty V. Scenes on the walls showed the daily existence on earth of the owner, who seemed to be thoroughly enjoying himself as he watched every process from the sowing of crops to the reaping of the harvest. These sculptured and painted men were portrayed first as caring for the growing crops, then cutting and binding the sheaves together and piling the grain high, the same sequence that I had observed time and time again up and down the Nile Valley. The modern *fellah,* like his prototype in stone, has square shoulders, a straight back, and narrow hips. He wears the same kind of closely fitting round cap, uses the same small, curved adze and primitive plow. Up to 1908, resemblances be-tween the two could not have ended with outward appearances. No highly industrialized centers had yet changed habits, method of work, and outlook on life in the population along the river banks. Even thoughts of the toilers could not have differed much. As seen in stone, or in the village life of today, the faces were much alike, dignified and cheerful in expression, and have the same shrewd eye for calculations connected with crops. Then, as now, the wants of the worker were simple, merely enough water for fields and livestock and the privilege of being let alone to cultivate the rich black earth, making the most of the all-prevailing sunshine.

To make two portrait sketches of the owner of this famous tomb, I had to stand on a high scaffold Quibell had put up for me. Outside, the wind blew savagely, banging things about in wild fury—the driven sand crashed against doors, sounding like hail and sleet, but it was the south wind, always very hot. The tomb was deliciously cool, and I experienced the violence of the storm only on my way to and from the house on a donkey that staggered along bravely.

As I painted in Ti and wandered about the tombs of Ptahhotep, an official and priest of Dynasty V, Kagemni, a courtier and grand vizier of Tety and overseer of his pyramid, and Mereruka, an official and priest, both of Dynasty VI, I found myself swept off my feet by the art of the fifth and sixth dynasties and wondered why I had devoted all my time on previous trips to painting sculptured reliefs in eighteenth and nineteenth dynasty tombs and temples in Upper Egypt. I had made fleeting visits to Saqqarah but never stayed long enough to get the "feel" of this greatest period of Egyptian art. And Saqqarah made me wish to know something about the fourth dynasty of Cheops and his successors at the pyramids of Giza, where George A. Reisner was in charge of the joint field expedition of the Boston Museum and Harvard.

The Saqqarah tombs were cheery abodes, planned comfortably for eternity, and in this ancient period they were mansions with many rooms. Glass in the roofs, put in by archaeologists, brought an agreeable lighting to the reliefs. I found Kagemni a delightful host. Apparently he did not concern himself too much with affairs of state since his predilections were shown, more than in others of these tombs of Dynasty VI, to be those of a sportsman. He was depicted catching birds in the same kind of nets that are used in this region today, and in the marshes he floated about easily in a papyrus skiff spearing a hippopotamus or fish and generally enjoying himself. He owned a vast property in livestock, and dancing girls in extraordinary postures enlivened for him the monotony of eternity. Carpenters were building for him, and he watched the harvesting of grain.

Quibell wanted to see how Reisner was progressing with his excavations of part of the Valley Temple of Mycerinus, and although Reisner was temporarily away in Palestine, we made a trip to the Giza Pyramid plateau. It was rather late in the afternoon when we arrived at Harvard Camp, where I had been only once before, for a casual, brief call. We reached the high top of a rocky plateau over a straggling, steep road. The camp consisted of simple, low mud buildings around a cement court, and beyond, from a small terrace, was a breathtaking view. In the foreground was the mighty pyramid of Cheops (2656–2633 b.c.), and the smaller ones built by his son Chephren (2625–2600? b.c.) and Mycerinus (2599–2571? b.c.), his grandson. Vast desert stretches lay between the camp and a number of pyramids visible on the far horizon. I saw a seemingly endless expanse of sky with heavy clouds, sombre in tone. But at the approach of sunset there was a dramatic change. A brilliance of color that no artist's palette could reproduce inflamed the clouds. Quibell took me over the tombs excavated by Reisner which were not open to the public. Again, as at Saqqarah, I was completely astonished by these sculptured reliefs. It was hard to realize that such magnificent, virile works of art had been done more than five thousand years ago. What people they were then!

17. The Story of the Golden Hawk

DURING THIS VISIT to Saqqarah, Quibell told me of one of his recent experiences as a government inspector. In all districts near ancient monuments when a modern building was to be put up, an official from the Antiquities Service had to be present when the foundations were being dug, in case historical material was unearthed. In the vicinity of Hierakonpolis, the capital of Upper Egypt before Dynasty I, situated on the west bank of the Nile opposite the modern town of el-Kab, a sugar mill was to be built. Quibell had a special interest in the ancient site because he had excavated it (1897–99), and his finds included such treasures as the slate palette of Narmer (Menes, the first king of Dynasty I), a huge ceremonial mace, heads of limestone in relief, and a mass of small but interesting objects of faïence and stone. Therefore he decided to go personally. He arrived at the designated spot to discover it was in the compound, or front yard, of an Egyptian whom he had put in prison several times for his thefts of antiquities found in the vicinity.

Quibell, on being warmly greeted by this old scamp, said to him, "You have not recently been in difficulty with the authorities!"

"No," replied the well-known thief, "I'm still living well from my last sale—what do you come here to seek?"

Quibell explained his mission.

"It is true," the old man said, "they propose to build one of the piers for the mill here, but no men are available to do the digging today because it is market day."

Quibell went out into the high road near the house and there found an old professional beggar who appeared fairly strong. Quibell offered him a good wage to come into the thief's yard for this work, but the digger needed a boy to carry off the baskets filled with debris loosened by the pick that a workman used. Therefore, leaving the old man at the door of the thief's house, Quibell went towards the town and found a small street urchin and engaged him for the job of basket carrier. The boy was a stranger and unknown to the beggar, who was a rather disreputable citizen of el-Kab.

The thief obligingly lent his short hoe and shovel, and he and Quibell sat and smoked cigarettes together as the old beggar and the boy began digging in his front yard. Quibell had left his name at the police station so that the authorities might know where he was. After a little while a message came from the police, saying that a native had been caught in the village with some antiquities hidden in his clothes, and asking Quibell to come at once to look into the matter.

The old thief said to him: "I will superintend the digging. You needn't come back. If there were any antiquities near my home I would have found them long ago."

Quibell went off and returned in a couple of hours. As he approached the high mud brick wall surrounding the thief's residence, he heard the anguished voice of the owner, and on entering the grounds saw a surprising sight. The professional beggar and the boy were standing at either side of the old thief, whose hands were tied to the chair back, and who was gnashing his teeth in rage.

Quibell asked why the old thief was tied.

The beggar and the boy both said, "He is a bad man. He asked us to steal 'ladders of gold.' "

They pointed down into the shallow hole they had dug, where there was visible a golden gleam from some object.

Quibell knew at once that the "ladders of gold" represented the royal feather of a crown or diadem, and jumping down into the pit, he rubbed away the clinging soil from a magnificent head of a hawk in rich, soft gold. The eyes were a single shaft of onyx running through the head. He was told by the beggar that the old thief-owner of the property kept insisting that the object was his, being dug upon his land, and offered him and the boy forty pounds if they would go away and let him inform the Inspector that nothing had been found. Instead of yielding to this offer, the beggar and the boy had tied up the thief.

Quibell determined to make a public example of the honesty which had preserved a great treasure for the Cairo Museum, and to have the government richly reward the beggar, and also do something for the boy. Because of a beggar's dread of the "law" and all officials, Quibell knew his hero would at once become suspicious if told to return to el-Kab on the next market day, and that the only way to insure his appearance and that of the boy, was to have them both kept at the police station in protective custody until the appointed day.

The poor old beggar believed he was under arrest and reproached Quibell bitterly, shrieking out as the police led him away that never again would he be "honest."

The thief egged him on.

The director-general of the Antiquities Service furnished a generous purse for the beggar and a smaller one for the boy for a presentation at

Bas-relief portrait of Ramose, vizier to Amenhotep IV, and his wife, at Thebes. Painting by Joseph Lindon Smith. Courtesy Museum of Fine Arts, Boston.

Funeral scene, tomb of Ramose. Painting by Joseph Lindon Smith. Courtesy Museum of Fine Arts, Boston.

The Pyramid of Cheops, Giza, with buildings of Harvard Camp in foreground

The Ramesseum, Thebes.

el-Kab, just after the noon prayer on market day, when there would be a large number of people about.

During the week spent in the local police station the "honest" beggar had been utterly wretched, in spite of a new *gelabieh* and good food, but the urchin felt himself fortunate in being in a place where he was given all he could possibly eat and where everyone treated him kindly.

On the following market day the beggar and the boy were taken to the market under police escort. Quibell got the attention of the crowd, who seemed to sense that something interesting was about to happen. In dramatic, well-phrased Arabic, he told of the finding of the hawk and of the splendid behavior of their fellow townsmen when sorely tempted by an offer of money, and then he said:

"Because of this good action which saved a great treasure to be enjoyed by all Egyptians in the museum at Cairo, the government has entrusted me with this purse of gold, which I hereby give to an honest citizen of el-Kab."

The old beggar reached out his hand to take the gift, but his eyes were fastened on Quibell's left hand, which held the second, smaller purse. And at once turning to the urchin, who he knew was about to be rewarded, he said, "Little boy, I give you my only daughter in marriage."

But the boy replied, "I had rather have a *gamus* [water buffalo] for my family."

THE CURSE OF AMON

1908 – 1909

18. *A Submerged Area*

MASPERO had interested me in inundations from the point of view of the villagers in ancient Egypt. He explained that these people had used the same word for "field" and "marsh," because, during the summer months and until late autumn, the fields were submerged by water from the Nile in flood.

This annual experience of villages' becoming floating islands led to the Egyptians' concept of a world after death as a "field of reeds and field of offerings," where islands appeared in a heavenly inundation for the repose of the dead.

When a young Englishman suggested that I go with him, in 1908, in a minute canvas canoe for a sail in the inundation that came close to the Pyramid of Cheops, I accepted with enthusiasm. I was told it would be quite an experience. It was! The young man was decidedly inexpert in handling a boat under sail in a stiff breeze, and tacking was for him and me a perilous performance. Several times we all but upset. Water poured in until I was soaking wet.

We hurtled towards the half-sunken wall of a village, had narrow escapes from collisions with houses barely above the water level, and skittered through the upper branches of submerged trees. When we were almost wrecked on an island rising out of the inundation, I lost my romantic feeling for Maspero's floating islands in eternity. In spite of the marvelous effect of looking from the reflections of the pyramids of Cheops and Chephren just below the canoe, and up to the tops of the pyramids themselves, I was thankful to set foot on *terra firma.*

Just before Corinna and I left Cairo for Luxor, a secretary in our American Embassy offered us mounts in order that on horseback we might see the extraordinary sight of the flooded basins along the edge of the desert between Mena and Saqqarah, which the Irrigation Department had been late in emptying this season. Soon after sunrise, we were hastening on swift English thoroughbreds through the streets of the modern part of Cairo, a city of cafés and Levantines, of Coptic clerks and bedraggled tourists. But once we had passed the island of Ghezireh, we were headed towards the "real Egypt."

Just below the Pyramid of Cheops, the region of flooded basins began, and near the ancient quarry, houses emerged above the water, isolated from customary village surroundings except for a fringe of trees, with nothing showing but their tops, and in them could be heard the flapping wings of birds that had taken refuge. We rode for miles and miles along a high embankment looking over a wide lake, reminiscent of submerged areas in the tropics during the rainy seasons. At a little distance, with the high, narrow trails invisible, a continuous procession of animals and humans appeared to be moving along on the surface of the water— a curious effect!

Egypt has been called the "land of light." That day it was a very special kind of light, which did wonderful things to reflections of greens of varied crops on high ground, to animals and men, to white clouds and a deep blue sky, and to pyramids even more perfect when seen in the clear depths of still water than on a skyline where they belonged. There were pyramids everywhere, those of Abousir and Saqqarah facing us, the Giza ones behind, but frequently reappearing as our route twisted and turned to avoid the flood—and always on the far horizon those of Medum and Dashuhr.

After we had passed through the region of the flooded basins, the Bible became current history. At a crossroad where we had drawn up to let a funeral go by, Moslem women were wailing and throwing dust over their heads, just as their forebears were described in the Old Testament. A little farther on, any one in a group of women could have posed for a Ruth or a Rachel. They wore the same jangling silver anklets and carried on their heads the type of heavy jars and baskets responsible for the erect carriage and firm tread of barefooted women in Biblical times. In the fields a man who might have been the patriarch Abraham was working the black earth with a plow as unchanged as his features in all these years. And near by, long, wooden rolls were being turned by man power, the same kind that had been used in this district to irrigate the same kinds of crops long before Cheops built his great pyramid; and all around us *fellaheen* were breaking hardened cakes of earth with short hoes similar to those on the walls of the tombs in Saqqarah.

19. *The Tombs of Officials at Thebes*

LATE IN THE FALL of 1908 and early in the following spring, we were back at the Sheikh Abd'-el-Qurna Necropolis, with its tombs scattered among the rubbish mounds below the tall cliffs that hemmed in the Theban Plain. Here, beyond the Colossi of Memnon, near the Ramesseum and to the west of the road leading to Deir-el-Bahri, were the burial places of ancient officials of Egypt. From them I was to gain much new insight into both the art and the general culture of earlier times.

These tombs covered the same period as those in the Valley of the Kings, but structurally there was no resemblance between them. The Qurna tombs were entered by a short flight of steps, with several connecting low-ceilinged chambers cut into the rock, and the burial pit, usually about thirty-odd feet in depth, was at the end of a short passage. The walls of the chambers were decorated, but not those of the passage.

Painted reliefs on the walls of tombs in the valley represented the king in company with the gods of the underworld, going through a complicated religious ritual, not yet fully understood by Egyptologists. But these tombs of government officials on the other side of the cliff depicted intimate scenes of the owner's life on earth which he carried with him into eternity.

For instance, in the tomb of Userhet, a royal scribe of the period of Amenhotep II (Dynasty XVIII), the murals afforded an excellent idea of the owner's main interest in life, which was unquestionably sport. He dutifully offered gifts to his king, saw to it that storerooms were well stocked with bread (in ancient Egypt the staff of *death* as well as life); the vintage was not neglected, and he kept barbers employed. But when seen in a chariot, every line of Userhet's body and expression of his face, in a series of spirited scenes full of color, showed his keen enjoyment in shooting gazelles, hunting in the marshes, and fishing.

The tomb of Nakht, beautifully published by Norman de Garis Davies and his wife, Nina, in a book for the Metropolitan Museum, gave a very comprehensive view of life in Dynasty XVIII. Nakht was a priest of Amon who was continued on in some official capacity into the reign of Akhenaten. This was evidenced by the obliteration of the word "Amon" in several places. Nothing could be more domestic than the sight of Nakht and his wife seated at a table, with an attendant serving geese and bunches of grapes, while a son offered flowers. A cat near by was eating fish. Relatives were seated stiffly on benches, women on the floor were conversing with a blind harpist, and music was being performed.

Outdoor scenes were equally realistic. Nakht was supervising laborers in the plowing and sowing of seed; others were breaking hard lumps of earth with short hammers; and a tree was being cut down. Reaping and winnowing was going on, and women were plucking flax or measuring corn. All suggested farm existence anywhere, as it was carried on by primitive implements before the tractor took over.

Interesting and significant as were the painted tombs of this city of the dead in giving a detailed account of provincial life, to me they lacked the grandeur of the early Saqqarah tombs of the Old Kingdom, telling the same story in sculptured reliefs at the great period of Egyptian art one thousand years earlier (2680–2258 B.C.).

It was the delicately carved reliefs in the tombs of Khaemhet and Ramose that made a strong appeal to me as an artist, as well as for their connection with the transition period of Akhenaten's revolution against the established order of Amon and a conventional, stylized art. They were of the Akhenaten period (1380–1363 B.C.), but they had the same delicacy as the reliefs of the Old Kingdom, mentioned above.

Khaemhet, keeper of the royal granaries under Amenhotep III, was known to have followed the son to el-Amarna. In the beautifully modeled reliefs in his tomb, however, there, were *no* signs of the art "exaggerations" introduced by Akhenaten. A superb figure of Khaemhet at the entrance door of his tomb offered a prayer to the sun god with upraised hand. Agricultural activities were gracefully suggested, but less realistically than in the tomb of Nakht, as was a record of crops Khaemhet was reporting to his king. The unusual beauty in the reliefs was perhaps best expressed by exquisite figures of youths, their hair sharply cut, wearing effective short garments, and holding geese in their hands. A soft patina on the stone of these scenes, which were executed with the skill of an expert draftsman, made a visit to this royal keeper of granaries something to remember.

Both artistic and historical importance were combined in the tomb of Ramose, "governor of the metropolis" and vizier to Amenhotep IV, at the beginning of the latter's reign and before he became Akhenaten and renounced Thebes. This was one of the few remaining monuments that, in art, showed the transition from the ancient religion to worship of Aten. On near-by walls were striking contrasts. At the entrance door leading to the pit was an unfinished detail of the King (as Akhenaten) giving audience to foreign ambassadors. A few masterly strokes had drawn in black pigment the exaggerated position of the King's body, the distorted, elongated head, with its abnormal jaw and prominent chin, not an agreeable characterization to an artist. I preferred Akhenaten's realism in art, in terms of scenes from nature, with flowers and other details quite modern-French in feeling and altogether charming.

The composition and expressiveness of the funeral scene was the most dramatic I have seen on a painted wall of an Egyptian tomb. The mourners appeared actually to be wailing, and the illusion of real tears was an incredible creation through the medium of pigments on a stone surface.

102

Eventually I was to spend many hours on Ramose, painting him and members of his household, delicately modeled with a firm line in very low relief on white limestone that gave a luminous quality to sculptured figures and faces. This was to happen after Walter B. Emery had completely restored the tomb of Ramose, replacing the original round columns and (obligingly for the artist) putting in windows in the roof that furnished a studio "top light."

He did the work between the years 1924 and 1926, for Sir Robert Mond's expedition of the University of Liverpool. On my first visit in 1907, it was thanks to Arthur Weigall's thoughtfulness that a further bit of the tomb wall was cleared for my benefit.

The pleated garments of attendants with offerings and the voluminous wigs worn by more important people had a style that was curiously modern in effect and very *"chic."* This led to an amusing incident. Once I came down a ladder from a high scaffold holding a finished picture of a head with a very elaborate "hair-do." A Frenchman turned from examination of a painting I had done of an attendant with a most complicated skirt to look at the head in my hand.

He remarked with enthusiasm, "What style! And how perfect for the Paris trade today."

He introduced himself as "M. Doucet" and said he was a Paris dressmaker. The card he gave me showed he was also a high-up official in *Les Amis du Louvre.*

I took it for granted, therefore, that he would not commercialize the "exclusive garment" and "hair-do" of members of Ramose's entourage which he took away with him in the form of my pictures.

It was to me a very interesting experience to study the bas-reliefs in the tombs of these two officials who had followed Akhenaten into retreat. Here was a form of art expression and a delicacy in execution not known before the Amarna period, entirely unlike it, and never seen again.

20. *The Curse of Amon*

WE GOT TO LUXOR for Christmas. The Weigalls, with whom we were to spend the winter, gave us a new roof bedroom with a glorious view over the Theban Plain. Sayce, on the *Istar,* was greatly missed, as were other archaeologists of whom we had seen so much during former days of our own river life. But even with changes I found the same Egypt of amusing natives, camels, donkeys, sunshine, starlight, the noble old river, the well-known temples, and the thrill of a "find."

The news of the dreadful earthquake at Messina shocked Egypt, with the rest of the world, and as the weeks passed, it became obvious that the tourist season would be dull, since visitors were afraid of passing through the straits. There was much resulting gloom on the part of natives because of the expected loss of their trade. Corinna and I several times stayed with Harold Jones over in the western part of the Valley of the Kings, in Theodore Davis's house, which he occupied during the excavating season. While we were with Jones, Petrie and his wife welcomed us in their camp, near the site where Petrie was digging in the gebel at the mouth of the valley, finding little or nothing but retaining his enthusiasm.

Late one afternoon in January, 1909, the Weigalls and Smiths were scampering over the steep paths into the Valley of the Kings to assist in guarding what looked very much like a Dynasty XVIII tomb. As before, we slept right on the spot, and next morning Davis appeared and the tomb was opened. We discovered a plundered chamber filled with rich brown mud, which obviously had been there for many centuries, but the chamber was empty of treasure as far as a first sight disclosed. Through the day, we dug out the mud and rubbish in the bottom of the shaft (it was a pit tomb without steps) and found some historically very important objects in gold leaf and alabaster. That evening Jones and I straightened out the crumpled gold sheets, and in the process discovered the names of two kings, together with pictures of one of them in his war chariot shooting enemies with bow and arrow, a very spirited scene. Later we found in the debris a most exquisite small alabaster figure, as fine in its way as the canopic jar heads in the tomb of Tiyi. Davis let me make a study of this figure.

Weigall discussed the idea of taking a holiday for a desert trip of two weeks on camels from Keneh to Kosseir on the Red Sea, across an ancient historic route between Arabia and Egypt, used later, in Roman times, in quarry operations for porphyry and semiprecious stones. This would be an experience for us that tourists never had, but Corinna was afraid that, after an attack of typhoid fever, I was not yet physically ready for a strenuous camel ride, so we decided to postpone the Red Sea adventure and instead establish a camp in the Valley of the Kings.

We had almost too many camp guests who loved the experience of sleeping under the stars on army cots placed in a row and using near-by late Ramesses tombs for dressing rooms. In one of them Arthur Weigall was revising his book on Akhenaten and his times, and I was using the same Ramesses tomb as a studio. Many of the younger Egyptologists would join us for a few days at a time, when their work took them to these royal tombs of the eighteenth and nineteenth dynasties. Ayrton, who turned up from Abydos, was not popular at night; by a consensus, his cot was placed a long distance away from the rest of us. He had dreadful nightmares in which he shrieked in fluent Chinese. He had been born in China, but left, never to return, at the age of three. Most curiously, he had retained no knowledge of the language when awake.

Howard Carter was another frequent guest. He was rather inclined to be moody but told amusing anecdotes well. One early morning Tom Russell, an English inspector, (later, as Russell Pasha, to be commandant of Cairo police), stationed at Sohag, turned up in the valley, and we persuaded him to stay with us. After lunch, when we were sitting about, an idea forming in my mind for some days suddenly crystallized, and I said to no one in particular: "I think the curse is a shame and I am going to remove it." My outburst aroused general attention.

"What curse?" I was asked by Tom.

"The curse of Amon-Ra against Akhenaten," I told him. And in response to his questions on a subject with which the young inspector was unfamiliar, I explained, as I have done earlier in this book, how Akhenaten, when he became king, had moved from Thebes and built a city of his own at el-Amarna; how the name of the established god of Thebes, Amon-Ra, was obliterated from every temple wall and replaced by the Aten rays and sun disk of Akhenaten's "new" religion; and how the priests of Amon were persecuted.

Then the story of Akhenaten's death, the return of the court to Thebes, and the restored worship of Amon-Ra. El-Amarna was completely destroyed, and in revenge for Akhenaten's action in denying the power of Amon-Ra, the restored priesthood had pronounced a curse on the so-called heretic king. Akhenaten's body and soul were condemned to wander through eternity as fugitives in space and never join together like those of other pharaohs.

Weigall and I reminisced about the finding of the tomb of Tiyi and the dramatic climax of the mummy's having turned out to be that of a man. This brought the conversation back to my plan for removing the curse. I said it would be in a play acted in this Valley of the Kings.

The scene would be the night when Akhenaten received the pardon of Amon-Ra and was restored to his prerogatives in eternity as a king. This would be accomplished through the intercession of the mother, Queen Tiyi, and the gods of the underworld represented by the hawk-headed Horus.

I made my selections for the cast then and there. I chose Hortense Weigall for the role of Akhenaten. She said she had never acted, but all agreed she could be made to look exactly like him. Corinna was to be Queen Tiyi, and I the symbolized gods of the underworld.

Next day I had my plans ready for presentation to Maspero, whose permission was necessary if an audience was expected to come into the valley at night. Weigall thought a show after dark in the valley would be difficult because of getting people from Luxor and back again. And Hortense and Corinna pointed out to me the housekeeping problems involved in putting up overnight in the valley, and feeding, an audience of about thirty which I had in mind.

I was adamant. The play must be given at the head of the valley, and my enthusiasm so fired Weigall that together we wrote a letter to Maspero, who answered by return mail. He had no objections, he said, since he realized that I intended to make it a serious occasion, with an

106

audience composed of Egyptologists. He simply requested that he and Madame Maspero be included in the invitations.

I set to work on the simple book of the play, and Weigall helped me in the wording of a dialog based upon archaeological data. The date was decided for the evening of the next full moon, about three weeks off.

Corinna and Hortense went to Luxor next day, but returned to the valley tired and rather discouraged over the prospect of providing beds for our guests. We seemed to have exhausted the local supply of cots in filling out our camping equipment, and beds from the hotel would cost quite a fortune to transport by camels. But they found the Weigalls' cook confident that he could attend to the food. In fact, while they were at the house, he had started off on a foraging expedition for turkeys and had returned with four live ones.

Both Corinna and Hortense were obviously bothered about the tremendous amount of work involved, so they were delighted, a day later, to find my plans under consideration for a complete change. Tom Russell suggested to me having the play in the Valley of the Tombs of the Queens, as being much nearer to Luxor, and with a good road from the river. He offered to have part of a Sudanese camel corps sent from Assuan on the day of the show to escort the guests from the river bank to the stage and back, and to have the entire route lighted by flares. I was also assured by officials that the Antiquities Service, with a house near the temple of Medinet Habu, built by Ramesses III, would be glad to have the supper served there.

All of this sounded convenient, but I reserved my decision about changing the scene until I could personally examine the possibilities from the producer's standpoint. Next morning, soon after sunrise, we went in a body over the cliffs and down into the Valley of the Queens. I found a wonderful site for the stage and the audience, in a natural amphitheater with near-by crags that I intended to use for Akhenaten's first appearance.

I made headdresses of papier-mâché for myself as the hawk-headed god, and another for Hortense as Akhenaten. We bought all the black worsted Luxor had for a ceremonial wig for Corinna as Queen Tiyi. Her figure was to be swathed in flame-colored silk from shoulder to ankle, making her look like a *shawabti* figure (servant of the dead). She kept pointing out to me that, thus tightly bound, any movement would be difficult for her.

There was also great activity in the sewing of costumes for Akhenaten and for mine as Horus, from designs I copied from temple walls. Russell sent to Cairo for red fire, to be used in the deep pit from which Horus was to appear from the underworld.

During the final preparations, we decided to live in Wilkinson's tomb above Sheikh Abd'-el-Qurna Necropolis, which was not visited by tourists, and supposed by natives to be haunted. The headdresses and costumes were deposited there in a great government chest, together with our simple camp outfit. It was a week before the date set for the play that we moved over from the Valley of the Kings. And after my working day was over, I wrote the invitations in longhand by flickering candlelight.

The text, prepared by Weigall, told of strange phenomena observed in the tombs of the Valley of the Queens, on one night in each year. It was a lengthy and most learned document, beginning with a quotation from a demotic inscription and mentioning a scribe who had seen, about an hour after sunset, the figure of a pharaoh pass before him, accompanied by the very "fearsome image" of a man with the head of a bird. The second reference was in Greek, and mentioned a night when the soul of a dead king of Egypt was seen hovering near a special tomb in the Valley of the Queens. A third record of the same nature was given by a Moslem historian, who stated that this valley was said to be visited once a year (on or about January 26 of our reckoning) by the ghost of a heathen king and his daemon companion, "very awful in appearance and like to a hawk."

And in the tomb of Akhenaten at el-Amarna an offering had been placed in the form of a prayer, asking the gods to pardon the King and permit his spirit to rest in peace. This inscription was dated the seventh day after the eclipse of the sun in the reign of Ramesses II and referred to the observation of a spirit (presumably that of Akhenaten) wandering in distress. The Pharaoh Akhenaten died in the year 1363 B.C. on January 26, according to well-assured astronomical data (verified by the record of this eclipse), which was the exact date given by the Moslem historian.

And the document ended by saying: "You, among a few persons, all experienced in Egyptological and psychological matters, are invited to come to said valley on January 26 at six o'clock in the evening, in order to observe whatever phenomena that may take place. And after a supper served at the Government House, guests will be escorted back to the river."

We asked all the distinguished archaeologists in Egypt at the time. Among those who accepted the invitations were: the Masperos, Petries, Carnarvons, Navilles, Legrain, the Quibells, Mr. Davis, Mrs. Andrews, G. Elliot Smith, the Newberrys, Garstang, Howard Carter, Schiaparelli, and members of the expeditions from Ermant, from el-Amarna, and from other archaeological centers.

As soon as the invitations were out, Weigall and I were pestered by innumerable requests from Cairo and elsewhere for "tickets to the show." We referred the matter to Maspero and heard no more on the subject.

Not long after our arrival at Wilkinson's tomb, Weigall had got into conversation in the Ramesseum with a man who introduced himself as Beerbohm Tree. Weigall had such a good time with this great English actor, who asked intelligent questions about Egypt, that he brought him back to camp for lunch. When Tree heard of the coming play, he insisted upon having it read to him. He was overgenerous in his comments, said the whole conception was dramatic and unique in stage production, and thought both the text and the wording of the invitation were happy. He examined the costumes and papier-mâché headdresses and declared my hawk-face was a masterpiece. When we asked him to come to the performance, he told us he would change his plans accordingly, and could he bring his manager?

There was to be one rehearsal, scheduled to take place three days before the performance. Fritz Ogilvie, a semi-invalid from Helouan, a health resort near Cairo, had arrived with his guitar to play the music he had written in a minor key and skillfully adapted to the theme of the play. He was to stay at a pension in Luxor, but the Hibbards and Eunice Follansbee, from Chicago, were to be our guests at Wilkinson's tomb from the rehearsal until after the performance.

It was Billie Hibbard's birthday when, in high spirits, the "cast" assembled on the site selected to rehearse a play that was to defy the power of Amon-Ra, the mighty god of Thebes.

The rehearsal started off well. The play opened with a god of the underworld (myself) coming up from a deep pit pursued by fire that worked beautifully as handled by Ogilvie. The hawk-face and head-dress received a burst of applause from the audience. Weigall was almost inarticulate in his excitement. The god bawled a few notes and was realistically answered by the echo from encircling cliffs. He shivered, danced a step or two, and complained that Akhenaten was always late in keeping these yearly trysts. Then he called for a musician to play the "dance of the white hawks." Ogilvie's music was superb, and I gave an encore at Billie Hibbard's insistence.

As the god was finishing the dance, Akhenaten was supposed to walk slowly on to the scene from a crag above. As Akhenaten (Hortense) approached in costume, it was as though the King himself had stepped down from the temple wall. But the lack of the dramatic in her acting made me, as stage director, intervene to coach her.

I had started to do the part myself, repeating the lines, when without warning a terrific peal of thunder, flashes of lightning, and a sudden gale of wind brought the rehearsal to a halt by drowning out my voice. After a few moments the elements subsided and the rehearsal continued.

Akhenaten and the god exchanged greetings, and after some conversation the god informed the King that on this night of nights it was his privilege to ask for anything he wished. Akhenaten replied by asking to have his mother, Queen Tiyi, brought from the land of nothingness. At this request the hawk-headed god made a spell above the pit leading into the underworld. Out of the flames and enveloped in a cloud of smoke Tiyi emerged with her slight figure swathed in flame-colored silk from shoulder to ankle, and her head surmounted by an enormous ceremonial black wig.

Mother and son stared at each other. Then, after exchanging greetings, she sympathized with him for his long years of suffering and reminded him that tonight his prerogatives as a king would be restored to him in eternity, and briefly referred to the glories of his court in the city he had built.

Akhenaten interrupted Tiyi to say that, in the last earthly moments before his soul found peace, his thoughts were on the great love of God, "the rising sun," which after his death had become only withered dreams because of the restored power of Amon-Ra. And he asked his mother to repeat his own great psalm, the chant of praise to Aten the divine.

The hawk spirit had left the stage after Tiyi's entrance, which gave me a chance to move to a higher level of the amphitheater and get the audience's view of this scene, which was the climax of my play. From where I now stood, my eye took in the wide sweep of the Theban Plain with temples built to honor Amon-Ra still standing, despite the passage of time.

Tiyi's voice began to repeat Akhenaten's praise to the rising sun, in the actual words of long ago, defying the mighty god of Thebes, and the cliffs gave back her voice clear and triumphant.

Weigall cried out excitedly, "I don't believe the Aten hymn was ever before heard here on the Theban Plain!"

Hardly were the words out of his mouth when a sharp rain squall, including hail falling in sizable pebbles, and masses of dust from the desert swept over actors and audience alike. The storm was so violent that I shouted to Akhenaten to protect his headdress, and I hastened to salvage that of the god and his papier-mâché face. The audience fled to cover, the donkeys panicked, and the donkey boys' shrill cries of terror rose high. Tiyi alone stood firm. Her figure was drenched and the silk clung even more tightly to her body; the hail struck her face, her great wig looked bedraggled, but her voice never faltered. She repeated to the end the very long hymn.

I refused to admit even to myself that nature was deliberately abetting

111

an enraged Amon-Ra. With the final words of Tiyi's speech, the rain and hail ceased, although the wind continued to howl dismally.

As stage director, I resumed command and said: "That's all for today. Everyone knows the lines and the simple stage business was satisfactory."

"How about rehearsing the rest of my music?" asked Ogilvie, with difficulty making himself heard.

"It's sure to go all right," I told him.

Ogilvie had protected sufficient fire for the performance itself, and Tiyi said cheerfully that her wig could be dried out and the silk of her costume was not injured by the thorough wetting. Fortunately Akhenaten's and the god's headdresses would need only slight repairs. The donkeys had been calmed and the donkey boys stopped talking together about the "rain of stones," unheard of on the Theban Plain. The little party of cast and audience, although enthusiastic about the play, were still somewhat subdued.

The road from the amphitheater to the Government House, recently sanded, would have to be done over again, but both sand and labor were easy to get in Egypt. Fortunately, the decorations at the river bank and at the entrance to the amphitheater had not yet been put up, and cushions, made in Luxor from gay cloth for the audience to sit on, were still at the Medinet Habu house. The turkeys had arrived and were strutting about, and the other food and serving arrangements were well in hand. We left our stage properties and rode on.

Altogether, when we got off our donkeys to climb the steep height to Wilkinson's tomb in the glorious sunset glow, our spirits had fully revived. At camp we found Sir Flinders and Lady Petrie waiting for Weigall to show them some of the tombs in the near-by Necropolis. They stayed on for supper, and when they left, we all settled down for the night.

Corinna and Hortense had given their beds to our guests and shared a single mattress. They had gone to bed early but not to sleep apparently. I heard Corinna mention a pain in her eyes, which she diagnosed as probably an eyelash or dust from the storm. And Hortense said she had violent cramps in her stomach.

By daybreak I awoke to see Corinna and Hortense sitting bolt up-

Mycerinus and Queen Kha-merer-nebty I. Photograph of the original slate pair in the Museum of Fine Arts, Boston.

The Sphinx, Giza, actually a portrait of Chephren, which may be compared with the portrait head of Mycerinus below. Note similarity of headdress the clue to the identification of the Sphinx. Upper courtesy Ray Garner for the American Research Center in Egypt; lower, courtesy of the Egyptian government.

right and looking ghastly. Both seemed completely unnerved. I managed to get from them the fact they had been scared by bad dreams. It was rather uncanny to me to discover from each of them separately, before they had spoken together, that their dreams had been identical. They had seemingly been aroused from a troubled slumber to find themselves in the Ramesses II temple of the Ramesseum, in front of the standing figures in the court. One of these Ramesses statues, in a temple dedicated to Amon-Ra, had come to life, slowly opened his crossed arms, and with the flail in his right hand had struck both women. But with this difference: Corinna had received a blow in her eyes and Hortense in her stomach. And even more horrible had been the triumphant vindictiveness in Ramesses' eyes as he looked at each of them in turn.

By breakfast one of Corinna's eyes was half-closed, and Hortense seemed in bad pain. Corinna went to Luxor alone to lunch with Mr. Theodore Ely, a vice-president of the Pennsylvania Railroad, and his two daughters, Gertrude and Henrietta, to invite them to the play. Also to give final orders to the Weigall servants about the party. And, incidentally, to see an oculist to have the supposed sand removed from her eye. The oculist could find nothing wrong and she returned to Wilkinson's tomb rather depressed.

The play was not given. The curse of Amon-Ra (if it were that) was widespread. Forty-eight hours after the rehearsal every actor and member of the rehearsal audience had been removed from Luxor by a severe attack of illness.

The day on which archaeologists had been invited to the Valley of the Tombs of the Queens, to watch with the Weigalls and the Smiths phenomena expected an hour after sunset, Corinna was about to go to a Cairo hospital with so virulent a case of trachoma that her sight was despaired of. Hortense, a few days later, was in the next room having an abdominal operation that proved all but fatal. I had a sudden bad attack of jaundice, and Weigall a complete nervous breakdown.

Ogilvie himself was spared illness, possibly because so little of his music had been played. But his old mother, who had come to see the play, on stepping from the train at the Luxor station, fell and broke her leg, and he returned immediately to Cairo with her. Even the audience did not escape the god's anger. Billie Hibbard had an abscessed tooth, and his wife and Eunice came down with the flu. The three of them decided to get back to the treatment of a Cairo doctor.

The Egyptologists whom we could reach took no chances, and one and all tore up their invitations. I had the temerity to keep the original text of it and the play itself.

The worst details of that hideous final night in the "haunted" tomb fixed themselves in my mind for all time. There was no sleep for Corinna nor the rest of us, and at about midnight, from the agony of darting pains, she went out of her head. Weigall managed to get a stretcher and guards, and it was decided that the Hibbards would stay in camp with Hortense until daylight, while he and I, holding Corinna on the mattress, walked all the way to the river by lantern light (it happened to be cloudy). We roused the *reis* of the *Beduin* who rowed us across the river, whence we went directly to a German doctor. His diagnosis was that this was the most virulent case of trachoma he had ever seen in a European and that he was puzzled by it.

A grim day followed until we boarded the evening train for Cairo. The natives of the staff stood about the court of the house wailing without a stop and wringing their hands. An even more difficult situation to cope with was the arrival at the house of a steady stream of archaeologists expected for the play whom we had not been able to reach. Also Beerbohm Tree and his manager. Through all the ghastly happenings Billie was a tower of strength. It was he who got in touch with Elliot Smith in Cairo and through him arrangements were made for a room in an English nursing home and for Dr. Edward Fischer to meet us there on our arrival the next morning. He was considered the best oculist for this eye disease that was the curse of Egyptians of the poorer classes. Fischer concurred in the German doctor's opinion that the violence of the attack was difficult to understand in a European. This diagnosis almost made me accept the curse of Amon-Ra theory.

The day I received the wonderful news that Corinna's eyes would not be permanently scarred, I took my determination in both hands, went to the Government House at Medinet Habu and collected the headdresses, costumes, and other stage properties. With my donkey boys' assistance I brought them up to Wilkinson's tomb and placed the lot carefully in the government chest. I sat and watched the sunset, looking down on temples dedicated to Amon-Ra far below, and then and there I renewed my pledge to Akhenaten that some day I would give the play and remove the curse.

THE GREAT PYRAMID SITES

1912–1913

21. *The Pyramid Field of Giza*

Reisner became curator of the Egyptian Department of the Boston Museum in 1911, and soon after I saw him on one of his rare visits home to give a series of lectures at Harvard University on Egyptology. He had started a collection of my paintings of the tombs and temples of Egypt by persuading numerous friends who owned them, to give or loan them to the museum as a study series, thus carrying out a purpose he had outlined to me at our first meeting.

A fund was raised, and I agreed to spend part of my time at Harvard Camp as a member of Reisner's staff, painting the subjects he selected. He told me they would for the most part be Giza tombs of Dynasty IV. He reminded me that I had taken Egypt in the reverse order chronologically. I had started with the late period of a Ptolemy (285–247 B.C.) and had devoted the next ten years of my work in Egypt to subjects of the New Kingdom (1570–1085 B.C.). In 1908, I had painted the splendid reliefs of Dynasty V (2565–2420 B.C.) and Dynasty VI (2420–2258 B.C.) in Saqqarah tombs. Reisner considered that, artistically, I had arrived at the greatest period of Egyptian art, that of Dynasty IV (2680–2565 B.C.)

My engagements kept me in other parts of the world and I did not arrive in Egypt again until the early winter of 1912. I would have liked making a sketch of Reisner as we sat together on the terrace after tea

116

on the afternoon of my arrival at Harvard Camp. His ruffled gray hair made an attractive setting for a face that showed eager interest in the fact of being alive with work to do. I had a strong feeling that his mind was seeing rather than his deteriorating eyes, and that he was undefeatable. He seemed to belong to that pyramid scene, and his word pictures, given with an air of authority, recreated for me the Egypt of the Pyramid Age as vividly as a movie "flash-back."

From the start we were on an intimate basis of friendship that was to last until his death in 1942. He treated me not as an artist painting for the expedition but rather as a colleague, and more and more a sympathetic counselor. He considered it important for me to familiarize myself with the Giza Pyramid Field. Daily we tramped from one "funerary complex" to another, he giving me invaluable archaeological data while we concentrated on a search for subjects. In our few leisure hours together, he continued to talk about the excavations he had done and about future plans.

Reisner, like Maspero, was one of the very few great archaeologists who had genuine appreciation for the artistic value of ancient Egyptian portraiture and reliefs, aside from their archaeological importance. He told me he intended to emphasize this art aspect by having it dealt with in a separate volume by someone more qualified than himself in that special field.

That first evening, after dinner, he took me into his small study, reached by crossing a court, where we had difficulty in avoiding a rather confused group of dogs and cats not getting on too well together. In the dim light of a flickering candle, he told me briefly how he had got from cuneiform to excavating in Egypt. The first step had been three years devoted to a study of Egyptology at Harvard with no definite purpose. In the spring of 1897, the Egyptian government appointed him a member of the International Commission for Cataloging Objects in the Cairo Museum. He had gone for a year and had stayed on for a second; then he had accepted the responsibility of organizing an Egyptian expedition to excavate for the University of California, believing this was an opportunity to develop scientific methods in excavating and recordings.

He went on to explain that in 1903, under a permit issued by the Antiquities Service of the Egyptian government, the Giza Pyramid Field was divided into three concessions. One was given to a German expedition; the Italians got another; and he, Reisner, applied for and received the third, which he was to excavate concurrently with Naga-ed-Der, where he was digging for the University of California Hearst Expedition. He gave a dramatic picture of expectancy when lots were drawn by the three parties concerned to determine the choice of Giza sites, and the delight of the Germans and Italians at the result of the draw. Reisner said with a chuckle that, although he lost out in the choice, he got the concession that included the two temples of the Pyramid of Mycerinus, which was what he wanted.

After two seasons, an unexpected crisis in Mrs. Hearst's financial situation caused her to withdraw her support in archaeological work in Egypt. The Egyptian government was entirely agreeable to Reisner's continuing the excavations under other auspices, and Reisner immediately proposed to President Eliot of Harvard and to Gardiner Lane, president of the Board of Trustees of the Boston Museum, a joint Harvard-Boston expedition. Both men were Reisner's personal friends and admirers of his scholarship, and they accepted his plan whereby the museum was to supply funds needed for excavations, and in return would secure the objects given by the Egyptian government in "divisions." The cost of the publications was to be paid by Harvard, and the resulting prestige belong to the university. This arrangement, which was an informal gentleman's agreement and not a written contract, was later to be confirmed, in turn, by President Lowell and President Conant.

When, after a few years, the Italians relinquished their site (which they had not worked), the Egyptian government, with Selim Hassan in charge, took over the part of the Italian concession in the vicinity of the Pyramid of Chephren, while Reisner undertook the Western Cemetery, where he had begun excavations at the time of my visit.

I found nothing more amusing as a diversion from painting than being with Reisner when he escorted distinguished guests on a tour through these ancient cemeteries. From his anecdotes and running comments, the personalities of Cheops' family emerged from the shadows of the past with their human frailties, ambitions, and intrigues. They were made to seem like people I had actually known. To me, it was a unique and thrilling experience to have a *Who's Who* of long ago become live men and women. His descriptions made equally vivid the manners and customs of the period.

What I learned about architecture was similarly revealing. Only kings and queens were buried in pyramids; queens, incidentally, in smaller ones; children and court favorites were buried in less pretentious *mastabas*. These had a flat top and a deep, vertical pit leading to the burial chamber, while the pyramid was pointed and had a sloping entrance. But both had an offering chapel on the valley side. Reisner said that when Cheops came to the throne (about 2656 B.C.) on the death of his father, Sneferu, the great plateau was a bare domelike rock of limestone, and the cemetery of the royal family of Dynasty IV at Giza was unique in Egypt. During the construction of his own tomb, the Great Pyramid of Giza, he laid out the royal cemetery directly east of it. This consisted of three small pyramids for his three chief queens and eight enormous twin *mastabas* for his favorite sons and daughters. One of them was for his eldest son, Prince Ka'wab (who was murdered before his reign began). The broad stone plateau boulevard, by which one reached the pyramids of Cheops' chief queens, was always referred to in the expedition as "Queen Street." Cheops also began to lay out cemeteries of *mastabas* to the west of his pyramid for three separate branches of his family and members of his court. The vast area covered by the ruins, in rows, and regularly spaced as to distance between them, suggested to me the town planning of today.

Lord Kitchener, then high commissioner, had personally asked Reisner to explain ancient stone construction to his chief engineer. I went along. Reisner took us first to some of the *mastabas* in the vicinity of the Sphinx. The three of us climbed a *mastaba* by precarious footholds to examine some of the individual blocks on which were identified both the name of the foreman and the length of time in transit from the quarries in the Mokattam Hills across the Nile. We returned to camp by the Pyramid of Cheops. Here, again, we did a lot of scrambling about above the square base. Save for the courses near the top of the pyramid, the limestone "casing" from the Turah quarries had long since disappeared, and, therefore, the rough "core" boulders were clearly visible. They had come from local quarries in the Giza Cemetery and had been evened by cutting off the long edges and fitting in shorter ones. Reisner explained the method by which the massive granite blocks of the casing were taken from the quarries. This was done by cutting trenches (about one foot wide) with copper chisels and wooden hammers. When a trench was finished, long levers of heavy wood were used to pry a stone block loose, then water was thrown in, the wood swelled, and the block was freed from the surrounding mass of stone and ready to be moved. It was dragged on a sledge to the river and, when the latter was in flood, floated across on a huge raft. These heavy blocks were turned over only twice, once in the quarry on being loaded, and again when fitted into the place prepared to receive them.

In laying the granite blocks for the first course, engineers had their workers draw the sledge across the smooth surface of the foundation platform, where planes of rubble packed with limestone were set against the construction already in place, and the new blocks rolled up this incline over the "core" boulders which had been raised in the same way. Reisner then described the last phase of the work as being that of dressing the granite casing, beginning at the top of the pyramid. This was done in three processes: first, by hammering; second, by rubbing; and, finally, by dressing by means of a flat-faced stone.

He summed up by saying that pyramid building had been accomplished by means of endless man power, and the Great Pyramid was a visible proof of an efficient organization of works, and an amazing progress in stone-cutting since the first use of stone in tombs of Dynasty I. Also, as engineers, the Egyptians had overcome difficulties that engineers of today deemed impossible with the simple tools known in the time of Cheops.

Reisner was greatly surprised when Kitchener appeared at Harvard Camp at about five o'clock, accompanied by two juniors among his subordinates. He was a tall, powerfully built man, with an aggressive manner and an arrogance in his speech that did not appeal to me.

As Reisner had started a scouting expedition in the Sudan before excavating a site at Kerma, he was anxious to talk about the Sudan with Kitchener, who certainly knew that region. But the soldier preferred to hold forth at length on the topic of village life in Egypt. The juniors were merely an echo of praise to whatever statements their chief made.

Once when the engineer asked Reisner how many men had been engaged in constructing the great monuments of the Pyramid Age, Reisner replied, "I believe never less than twenty thousand at a time and probably generally as many as fifty thousand during the lifetime of Cheops." Whereupon Kitchener burst out, "They should have spent their time in developing agriculture," and then went on to tell again all *he* was doing for Egypt in that direction.

I saw Reisner was getting restless at some of Kitchener's statements about the ways of *fellaheen* he *knew* to be wrong, and finally he said with his frank bluntness: "I've lived in villages, which gives me a certain advantage over those who haven't."

The young men looked startled but the remark was not taken personally by Kitchener. He was too sure of himself. After a brief stay, he made an impressive exit, taking the nice engineer with him.

That night from my bed, I looked out of the window towards the east where a huge triangle of darkness soared into the heavens. Half awake, half asleep, I pictured to myself the wonderful pageant of the Pyramid of Cheops, the greatest monument of all time, rising tier above tier from the desert plateau. And then I saw the price of the achievement in terms of human beings, who in the pitiless heat and glare of the sun were moving through clouds of dust. In my imagination I also saw the operation in full swing at the time of the annual flood, and thousands of men were poling heavily loaded rafts across the river, with other thousands dragging the huge blocks of stone on sledges through inundated fields. Long lines of slaves were harnessed and chained together pulling on long ropes attached to the sledges; miserable, wretched creatures, spoils of war, driven unmercifully by the lash, and those who fell exhausted were dragged along dying, chained to the others. Every now and then a halt was made and the dead men unshackled and thrown aside, and the toil and the lashing and exhaustion went on.

The lot of the slaves in the quarries was hardly less grim. The blinding glare on the dazzling rock, the intense heat, the suffocating dust filling the air! All this added to the hardest of labor and cruelty of overseers and guards.

22. *Sensational Treasures*

REISNER'S EXCAVATIONS at the two temples of Mycerinus, the grandson of Cheops, which had been completed during the previous season, had yielded sensational treasures. He devoted several hours in describing to me on the site the particulars of the finding of nine important pieces of sculpture of Dynasty IV, from one of the temples of Mycerinus (2599–2571 B.C.). He had a beaming smile in rehearsing for my benefit the slow, methodical clearing that made possible the reconstruction of the various structures surrounding the Pyramid of Mycerinus.

I relived with him the excitement of the opening of room after room filled with amazing sculpture in the round. Two alabaster portrait heads of the King, five complete statues, and the slate triad. He could hardly contain himself in talking about this triad, in an amazing state of preservation, with the Goddess Hathor in the center between Mycerinus and a personification of the Hare Nome. It was now in the Boston Museum, as were several of the alabaster statues of the King and one of the heads.

And when he referred to the slate pair of Mycerinus and his Queen, Kha-merer-nebty I, his enthusiasm knew no bounds. He mentioned Boston's good fortune in securing this piece of sculpture, *the first of its kind,* and one that influenced the fashion for similar compositions in later dynasties in showing husband and wife of equal size and in an intimate pose of family life.

Suddenly, he interrupted himself by saying that the scientific knowledge obtained from solving the identity of the Sphinx by evidence found

122

in this valley temple was of far greater value than the wonderful objects for museum display. His clue, he told me, was the fact that, in the portrait head of Mycerinus, he wore the same kind of pleated headdress as the Sphinx. Up to that time (1907), this headgear had been thought to be of a much later origin than Dynasty IV (2680–2565 B.C.). Reisner's conclusion, based on this clue, that the Sphinx was a portrait of Chephren (father of Mycerinus), had been accepted by other Egyptologists.

One late afternoon, when I was in Reisner's office looking through some of his early publications, he remarked abruptly, as was his habit in introducing an idea that meant something to him, "Joe, tomorrow, knock off work early; I want to take you to the Sphinx and explain it in terms of being a part of Chephren's 'funerary complex.' "

Restorations had destroyed the charm I had felt when I first saw, on the crest of a rocky ledge, the weather-beaten, inscrutable face appearing above a mass of desert sand. Today the great head had beneath it an uncovered, outstretched, massive lion body and awkward paws. Romance was gone, and it was now a part of a "funerary complex" and dissected as such by Egyptologists.

Reisner paused to point out a stela between the paws of the Sphinx, with the text on it recording a picturesque story, told by Tuthmosis IV (1423–1410 B.C.), to the effect that, as a young prince on a hunting trip, he had fallen asleep in the heat of the day under the shadow of the Sphinx. In a dream the sun god appeared and promised him he would become king if he cleared the sand from his (the god's) body.

Reisner commented that the significance of this legend was that, for over a thousand years after Chephren had carved the Sphinx, its identity had been lost by the ancient Egyptians themselves, who had worshiped the image as the sun god.

This huge head, Chephren's sculptors had carved from a high rock ledge left by the quarrymen of his father, Cheops. Reisner considered it was Chephren who first put into execution the "Sphinx-idea" as guardian of a temple precinct, with the portrait head of the king on the body of a lion to symbolize power. And without doubt, the great Sphinx of Giza was the first of all sphinxes to be carved in stone, and the largest.

123

The Valley Temple of Chephren, over which the Sphinx had watched through the ages, had recently been excavated (1909–1910), and Reisner wanted to examine it in some detail. This was the Sanctuary erected as the valley entrance to the causeway which ascended from the valley to the Mortuary Temple and Pyramid of Chephren. The whole was a perfect visible example of the component parts of a "funerary complex."

The Sanctuary was a huge building with square granite columns, and beyond were a number of the rooms opening from it where some royal statues had been found. In a shaft leading off one of the corridors, Mariette Bey discovered his famous seated figure in black basalt of Chephren with a hawk on his shoulder.

There was just time before returning to Harvard Camp for me to take him to the high spot in the desert I had selected as the site for a painting—a large study of the Giza Pyramid Field Reisner had urged me to do. We made the short but rather stiff climb over rough ground without stumbling and stood together in a high wind that blew us about, watching great clouds of dust swirling over the pyramids built respectively by Cheops, Chephren, and Mycerinus that were to pose for me.

When we had caught our breaths, it was I who broke the silence. "A versatile and imaginative family of kings," I said. "Cheops with the simplest of tools constructed a pyramid that, for size and an engineering feat, astonishes the world today; his son Chephren introduced the Sphinx-idea that was to become very popular with later Egyptian rulers; and Mycerinus, grandson of Cheops, created a marvel in slate that set the fashion for a different type of portrait sculpture."

"Yes," concurred Reisner. *"My* people of the Pyramid Age," and to him they were *his* people, "had grand ideas and the genius to carry them out—are there families today with such a record for three generations?" he asked, looking confident about my reply, as well he might.

In the spirit world, in which the deceased of Dynasty IV lived on, according to Reisner's account, nothing seemed to have been overlooked. As in the tombs of Saqqarah, the owner was shown as an overseer of the manifold operations carried out on Egyptian agricultural estates. There were also pictures of him watching dancing girls, fencing, wrestling, and playing board games with his friends, listening to music, and traveling up and down the Nile in his boats. These scenes repeated for the spirit-man not only his daily bread and drink, but all those phases of his life which he had enjoyed. They were supposed to be visible in spirit form to the *Ka*, the soul of the deceased. At first, statues of the buried man or woman were placed in the outer chambers of his, or her, tomb. In them, the spirit was supposed to reside and receive the visitors who brought offerings. At a later period, the figures were placed behind the walls of the offering chambers and a hole was cut through the walls so that the *Ka* could watch the arrival of the people with the offerings.

A false door in the tomb, in form, a heritage from the reed matting "palace façade," permitted the spirit to come and go at will. Repeated carvings were found in wood and stone of the buried man seated at a table before the false door. In front of him were drawings, or a list in writing, of all the food, clothing, and games that he would require during his journey after life. These lists were a guide to successive funerary priests concerning the *Ka's* requirements.

The great Cemetery of Giza was supposed to be a city of the living dead, whose material needs continued to be supplied by live servants. The silent statues of thousands of men and women sat behind the walls of their offering rooms in the spirit world. Every day hundreds of live servants of the *Ka* came up from the valley to place their offerings and to recite the magic formulas. On the great festivals of the dead, the whole population of the near-by villages appeared to pay respects.

Reisner explained that the plural marriages of Cheops had resulted in a vast number of descendants buried in eighty-nine *mastabas*. Funerary endowments had to be established for each one of them for all the things they had enjoyed on earth. The funerary priest was a *living* civil functionary who, by a contract, became the servant of the *Ka*. He and his heirs, forever, were given specified land properties, were exempted from taxation and forced labor, and, in return, were to maintain the offerings in the chapel of the tomb.

The royal income was dissipated in supporting an ever growing

125

body of funerary priests, who performed no productive service and eventually controlled most of the land originally owned by Cheops and the members of his family.

Funerary endowments continued unabated through Dynasty V and Dynasty VI at Saqqarah and were the principal factor in the economic collapse of the Egyptian state, which was to last until the Middle Kingdom, when, between the years of 2052 and 1786 B.C., there were once again kings of a united Egypt.

Incidentally, this same losing battle with priests was to be waged unsuccessfully by Akhenaten nine hundred years later.

TUTANKHAMEN AND NEFERTETE

1922–1923

23. The Tomb of Tutankhamen

IN 1914 I MADE a short trip to Egypt to be with Reisner. Below the Pyramid of Mycerinus, tents stretched over a vast extent of desert. They were occupied by a large contingent of Australians being trained for service in France. Reisner's was the only archaeological expedition that had continued to excavate during the war. In the Sudan he was keeping about two hundred natives employed, and the sight of Americans working as usual did much to strengthen the general morale.

At Luxor, as elsewhere, no archaeological work was being done, but across the river at Thebes, the Burtons continued to have Metropolitan House an active center, Norman de Garis Davies and his wife were living in their house near by, and Howard Carter was living in his. Their presence did much to protect the tombs of the Theban Necropolis from vandalism. Both Minnie Burton and Nina Davies were indefatigable in looking after visitors who turned up. I stayed with the Burtons briefly, and again in 1916, when I spent a few weeks at Harvard Camp, which had been difficult to reach after the sinking of the passenger ship *Ancona* in the Mediterranean.

After 1916, my time was fully occupied with war activities in France, but in 1921, I returned to Egypt, this time bringing my daughter Rebecca with me. We were for a number of weeks in the Sudan with Reisner and his expedition excavating at Meroe.

By the fall of 1922, excavations interrupted by the war in the Valley of the Kings had been resumed, with Howard Carter in charge. By a contract with the Egyptian government held jointly by Lord Carnarvon and Carter and signed in 1914, two veteran searchers after antiquities took over the concession Theodore Davis had relinquished.

Among broken jars and an unbroken one containing the entrails of the body not preserved in a canopic jar, and seals and fragments of all kinds discarded by Davis as worthless and given to the Metropolitan Museum, Herbert Winlock had found materials used in funeral processions, and these indications of a possible burial were found near the "cache" of Queen Tiyi. Also in the same vicinity, Davis had made a chance discovery of a blue glaze vase, hidden under a rock, inscribed with the cartouche of Tutankhamen (1362–1353 B.C.). And close by, about twenty-five feet underground, he had happened upon a small room filled with dried mud almost to the ceiling, but the contents also included a box containing several pieces of gold with the cartouche of Tutankhamen and his wife's name on them, and a lovely alabaster funerary statue. Other objects bore the names of Ai and Tiyi, the foster-parents of Nefertete. This was the same Ai, a priest of Amon, who, after the young Tutankhamen's death, became king. The dates of the reigns of Semenkhkara, Tutankhamen, and Ai fell in the period between the years 1362 and 1349 B.C.

Maspero, at the time of the discovery in 1906 of the cache containing Queen Tiyi's furniture, had supposed that Tutankhamen's tomb had been in the western part of the valley, possibly near Ai's tomb or that of Amenhotep III. He considered it likely that, when the reaction against Akhenaten and his followers was general, Tutankhamen's mummy and his tomb furniture were taken to a secret hiding place, just as those of Queen Tiyi had been. And Maspero stated in print (1908) that Davis had probably found all that remained of Tutankhamen's tomb furnishings after many transfers and much plundering. He, however, qualified his opinion by saying, "But this is mere hypothesis, the truth of which we have no means of proving or disproving as yet." Carter had begun a systematic clearing of the area across the modern tourist

False door from a tomb of Dynasty VI, Saqqarah. Courtesy of the Egyptian government.

View in the antechamber of the tomb of Tutankhamen, Valley of the Kings. Photograph courtesy Metropolitan Museum of Art, New York. From Howard Carter, Tomb of Tut-ankh-Amen, *London, 1930.*

The golden mask of Tutankhamen. Photograph courtesy Metropolitan Museum of Art, New York. From Howard Carter, Tomb of Tut-ankh-Amen, *London, 1930.*

path from Queen Tiyi's tomb, between the *ghaffir* house above and the much visited tomb of Ramesses VI. When, at the level of the bottom step of Ramesses' tomb, he came upon a series of ancient workmen's huts that extended under the present-day path to Queen Tiyi's tomb, Carter knew he had possible evidence of another tomb or "cache" of an earlier period. His deductions proved to be correct, and just below the entrance to Ramesses' tomb he found the lintel of a doorway, and on it were seals of the Necropolis Cemetery, with signs of entry in ancient times. Steps led to a second doorway, which bore the seals of Tutankhamen and of the cemetery priests. Carter immediately cabled to Carnarvon, who was still in England, that an untouched tomb awaited his arrival. Carnarvon came posthaste.

Meanwhile Albert Lythgoe, head of the Egyptian Department of the Metropolitan Museum, who was at sea on his way to Egypt, read a ship's bulletin about the tomb, and by cable offered the services of Harry Burton as photographer and the services of the other members of his field staff. The offer, of course, was gratefully accepted. The discovery of King "Tut's" tomb, as it was familiarly called, fired the imagination and excited the romantic interest of the public throughout the world. The London *Times* distributed telegrams to a chain of newspapers all over the Anglo-Saxon world about the greatest quantity of objects ever found in a practically untouched tomb, formally opened on November 29, 1922.

Everyone who was permitted to enter the tomb those first few months caught the thrill and spread the news. "Riches beyond the dreams of avarice," Carter had telegraphed to a Cairo friend after his first sight of a chamber piled high with objects of every description. And as time went on, a series of four shrines ablaze with gold, one inside the other, was opened. The outer one showed signs of having had the seals on closed doors broken in ancient times. But when the sarcophagus itself was reached, the pall lay over it as it had been placed there by the priests after the final funeral rites. Two more years were to pass before the lid of the coffin was raised, and those privileged to be present at that dramatic moment looked at last upon the face of a pharaoh exactly as he had been laid to rest thirty-three hundred years before. But even before that event the first excitement of the public never died down, and anything about King Tut was news and has remained so to the present day.

That first season, literally thousands of visitors to Egypt, and those living in the country, took the trip to Luxor merely to gaze on the "site" of the discovery. They would appear in the valley in the early morning and sit quietly in groups, as near the mouth of the tomb as the police permitted, in the hopes of seeing some object brought to the surface, to be photographed or taken to an improvised laboratory in a neighboring tomb.

Women brought their knitting or sewing, others reading matter, and waited patiently, hour after hour—a strange spectacle in that royal valley that went on day after day. Those who produced introductions from people too important to be ignored had to be admitted into the tomb. They held up work in the very narrow space and threatened injury unwittingly to fragile objects. And the numbers of these visitors ran into some thousands.

When Carter took me in, some of the alabaster vases did not appeal to me as an artist, and many of the elaborately carved gold objects and the jewelry were of an art already decadent. Even so, I could understand why spectators were overwhelmed by the general magnificence, and would be for years to come. There was no gainsaying that King Tut's tomb was the most remarkable find since, in ancient times, robbers had had their choice of the treasures in many other such burials. The golden head with the jeweled face mask of the young King was very striking. Among the objects that were less ornate was an alabaster cup with simpler handles than those of some of the other alabaster vessels, and I liked a box of fine proportions. A number of objects I saw *in situ* gave an idea of the mass of material found in this small tomb chamber.

I thoroughly enjoyed dropping in on Harry Burton in the tomb of Queen Tiyi, which he was using as a photographic studio. Alfred Lucas, the Englishman who was chief chemist for the Egyptian government, was a distinguished chemist noted for several brilliant discoveries in his field in England. He cleverly adapted a near-by tomb for a laboratory, and he never seemed to be too busy to explain something unusual he was doing. Professor Percy Newberry recorded the botanical specimens found, and Mrs. Newberry's repairing of the pall over the sarcophagus was an amazing achievement in needle work, as was her mending of other textiles, some of which were very fine.

Some years later, Corinna and I had a memorable morning in the Cairo Museum with Lucas, who showed us a number of textiles from this tomb that were not on public view. He gave high praise to the work of both the Newberrys.

Everyone agreed that Carter's skill was outstanding in overcoming the many problems presented in handling such a mass of material in a very restricted space. But everyone also agreed that he was "difficult." Poor Engelbach, who was inspector of Antiquities for Upper Egypt at the time, certainly found him so. Doubtless some (but not all)) of the controversies over the tomb that arose were the result of Carter's inability to get on with people. Burton's contribution in photography was magnificent, and Lucas did a splendid job in the preservation and repairing of damaged objects in fragile condition which needed his expert services to be saved. The staff of the Metropolitan Museum continued their assistance in the "working" of the tomb, until the final clearing of the chambers in 1929.

Lord Carnarvon did not have the thrill of seeing the mummy unwrapped, since he died in April, 1923. He had been taken desperately ill in Cairo, and his attending physicians were unfamiliar with his past medical history. In a semiconscious state, Carnarvon kept calling for "Johnny." No one knew who Johnny was until some friend connected with Carnarvon in his early visits to Egypt remembered the little cockney doctor who, in the past, was always in attendance on Carnarvon medically. I, myself, had seen Johnny's prompt and effective treatment of an angry-looking, swollen mosquito bite, preventing the infection from getting into the blood stream—a dangerous matter in that area.

A cable was sent to England and a frantic search made for Johnny. Finally he was located and put on a plane for Egypt. He reached Carnarvon's bedside half an hour after he had died.

Many visitors to the tomb yielded to the influence of the uncanny atmosphere created by the sight of the sarcophagus with the pall over it, and at the end, towards the entrance to the main chamber, long carved arms and hands seemed to be actually waving away the intruder from a nearer approach. Those hands carved on the sarcophagus increased a feeling of something threatening and mysterious. They were not easily forgotten. After Carnarvon's death, the story of the "curse" spread widely in the press, in spite of the determined efforts of those who were working the tomb to prevent articles' being circulated with little regard for facts.

I have always remembered Douglas Derry's account of his examination of this, the only royal mummy of a king of ancient Egypt found intact in the funeral chamber in a golden coffin, just as it had been left by the priests who had mummified the body, and with the jewels and other objects in the mummy wrappings.

Unfortunately, the head and skeleton of Tutankhamen were in an unexpectedly poor state of preservation. This, Derry explained, was due to the fact that the large quantity of fluids used in the embalming had caused the body to disintegrate in a tightly sealed coffin. On the other hand, the many royal mummies found in the Deir-el-Bahari cache were well preserved, since they had been saved from disintegration by robbers' having removed them from sealed containers flooded by embalming fluids that would have resulted in the same conditions that Derry found in the body of Tutankhamen. According to Derry's conclusions, this fact proved that the embalming process was not for the preservation of the body but for some ceremonial purpose not yet understood by archaeologists.

Too many people forget that the importance of the discovery of Tutankhamen's tomb, from the historical and artistic standpoints, was not commensurate with the continued public attention given the mass of objects, showy and magnificent from the flash of gold, but for the most part of a very decadent art, on permanent exhibition in the Cairo

Museum. At the entrance rotunda arrows on inescapable signs now point the way to "Tutankhamen." Except for archaeologists and other scholars, visitors, for the most part, spend their available museum time wandering through the enormous galleries devoted to the contents of King Tut's world-famous tomb. In doing so, they have missed the statue of Renofer, the diorite head of Chephren, the golden hawk, the jewelry found at Dashuhr, and the furniture of Queen Hetepheres, to mention but a few among the great art masterpieces of ancient Egypt.

24. Near Death in Pharaoh's Tomb

CARNARVON, thinking to avoid trouble for himself and Carter, had sold the exclusive rights of publicity on the Tutankhamen tomb to the London *Times,* for which I understood at the time he received fifty thousand pounds. The sensational nature of the find made King Tut a "newspaper" tomb, and, incidentally, publicity about any incident connected with any other tomb became news, always linked up in some way with King Tut.

The *Times* delegated to Arthur S. Merton, its Cairo correspondent, the handling of the distribution of news, a task which he carried out in a most efficient way and in a spirit of fairness to the press. But other newspapers sent out correspondents who were refused admission into the tomb. They remained in Luxor writing stories that were good copy from the news editor's point of view but not too accurate. And the real damage to the cause of foreign concessions to excavate in Egypt came from having the Egyptian press excluded from the tomb. Not unnaturally, this was resented and the Arabic newspaper representatives brought pressure upon the Egyptian government.

The situation had reached a climax when I arrived in Egypt in October, 1923. Rex Engelbach told me a clause was about to be included in the concession form which would require expeditions to issue all news about their finds through the Egyptian Press Bureau. The gossip reached me that Engelbach and Quibell, representing the Antiquities Service of the Egyptian government, had had heated interviews with Carter

133

about the continuance of newspaper notoriety which the Antiquities Service considered deplorable and undignified. It was generally understood that a movie was to be made of Carter discovering the tomb. This plan had been stopped.

In addition, disagreements between the Carnarvon-Carter expedition and the Antiquities Service reached the courts. According to the contract previously made, if the tomb was "untouched," all the objects would belong to the Egyptian government. But evidence of entry in ancient times was the basis of the Carnarvon-Carter claim for a division. The views of the Egyptians won out, with the result that the whole of the find was to remain in Cairo. The administrators of the Carnarvon estate decided that, in this situation, they would no longer stand the expense of working a tomb from which the estate was to receive nothing —a not unreasonable stand. The tomb was closed pending a reconsideration, but an agreement was reached which was satisfactory to both parties concerned. Lady Carnarvon consented to continue to pay the bills, and, in return, the estate was to receive some duplicates and objects already well represented in the museum. With this understanding, Carter worked the tomb until it was completed six years later. The sale of some of these antiquities at a later date accounted for the baseless rumor that they had been stolen from Tut's tomb and not acquired legally.

Carter arrived in Luxor about the same time I did in 1923, and looked me up at the Luxor Hotel, where I was staying. He was affable and amusing and told me he was about ready to open the door into the inner of the four shrines. He did not mention any of the difficulties he was having with government authorities, but when I had to excuse myself, as I was dining with Engelbach, he walked down the river front with me to the Inspector's house but did not come in.

The intense excitement associated with the King Tut find gradually spread, as I have suggested, to practically everything connected with Egyptian archaeology. What happened to me—or did not happen, to be more accurate—at this time is perhaps typical.

Reisner was anxious for me to make a study of the seated diorite statue of Chephren with a hawk on his shoulder which was in the

Cairo Museum. He had decided that the same sculptor who did the slate pair had done this Chephren. I wrote to Reisner that I would do this painting before sailing. I finished my work in Ramose and was about to leave the hotel to take the night train for Cairo, when I was accosted by a young reporter for the *Times* syndicate with whom I had had several agreeable conversations. He asked me if I had heard about a great mass of rock that had fallen from the roof of the Tomb of Ramose near the second doorway.

I said, "No," and added facetiously, "It's too bad I wasn't there at the time, which would have been good copy for the American press." I thought no more about the matter and was settled in Cairo painting in the museum when, on November 15, I was handed a cable which read:

FAMILY ANXIOUS ACCIDENT TO YOU IN A TOMB REPORTED IN BOSTON
AND NEW YORK NEWSPAPERS. PLEASE CABLE. SMITH

I cabled back:

REPORTED ACCIDENT UNTRUE, AM PERFECTLY WELL. ARRIVED
CAIRO YESTERDAY MORNING. WIRE ME NAMES OF NEWSPAPERS.

There had been a delay in my reply, since Corinna's message had been sent to Harvard Camp, and I was living at a small hotel near the museum so as to get Chephren done as quickly as possible. On not hearing from me at once, Corinna got excited and sent cable inquiries to Carter, Engelbach, Brunton, and Quibell.

All these men (Carter excepted) were Antiquities Service officials with definite ideas on the subject of ill-founded items appearing in the press sent from Luxor. Their replies to Corinna were as follows:

Brunton: RUMOR UNFOUNDED. JOE IN CAIRO IN GOOD HEALTH.
Quibell: JOE PERFECTLY WELL IN CAIRO, REPORTER LIAR.
Engelbach: JOE'S WORK RAMOSE COMPLETED BEFORE ROCK FELL. RE-
PORTING SHOULD BE LIMITED TO FACTS. SAW HIM OFF FOR CAIRO.
Carter: NO ONE IN TOMB OF RAMOSE WHEN ROCK FELL. JOE IN CAIRO.
REGRET YOUR ANXIETY.

135

Quibell created quite an uproar in Cairo, and as a result the *Times* correspondent in Egypt (no longer Reisner's friend Merton) came to see me and rather truculently insisted the news had not reached America through the *Times* syndicate. As soon as Corinna's second message came, I sent for this confident representative of the great London newspaper and gave him her cable, which read:

ITEM IN NEW YORK TIMES AND BOSTON HERALD, UNDER HEADING
ROCK FALLS IN LUXOR TOMB, NEARLY CRUSHED JOSEPH LINDON
SMITH AN AMERICAN ARTIST PAINTING THERE AT THE TIME!
COPYRIGHT 1923 BY THE NEW YORK TIMES COMPANY. SPECIAL
CABLE TO THE NEW YORK TIMES LUXOR NOVEMBER 14.

The representative, after a moment of silence, said, "No comment." I later heard from Corinna that the Boston *Herald* had given the information a conspicuous news spread on the front page with my photograph and the caption "Near Death in Pharaoh's Tomb," and, of course, the story was linked up with King Tut. She had called up the editor and read him the cables from Egypt and asked him to do something toward contradicting the press articles in the many cities where Joseph Lindon Smith was well known, since she was bombarded by a steady flow of telegrams and telephone calls from anxious friends. The editor was very sympathetic in his regrets and, although frankly admitting that a newspaper did not like to give publicity in correcting an error, told her that, under the circumstances, he was glad to make a "correction" on the editorial page.

I thus survived both rumor and the tomb crash at a time when "anything could happen" in Egypt.

25. *The Germans and Nefertete*

CONCESSIONS FOR DIGGING in Egypt were obtained, as I have noted earlier, by foreign archaeological expeditions from the Egyptian government through its Antiquities Service. The German expedition of distinguished scholars and diggers was given the important site of Akhenaten's city of el-Amarna, and between 1909 and World War I they made many important discoveries.

The procedure at the end of a season's dig was to have the excavator report to the director-general of Antiquities of the Egyptian government what had been discovered in the way of objects, so that the director-general, who was always a Frenchman, could decide after a personal inspection of the finds what was needed for the Cairo Museum, and the remainder of the objects was allotted to the expedition concerned.

Pierre Lacau, who had replaced Maspero as head of the Antiquities Service in 1914, received an official request from the German expedition to come down to el-Amarna to examine the material found. It was announced that the objects were insignificant but would be most acceptable for a study series in the Berlin Museum.

Lacau, believing this statement made by a well-known German archaeologist about the quality of the objects to be investigated, decided that it was not necessary for him to be present at the division and sent one of the younger Frenchmen of his museum staff.

The material that was displayed on long tables in the magazines of the expedition at el-Amarna fully justified the description of its insignificance as reported to Lacau. On the tables in baskets were broken bits of pottery, pieces of statues of stone, plaster, or wood, and an ear, half of a nose, a bit of a neck, and other parts of a head, all imbedded in mud, and scattered widely in the display. It was a jumble of poor-looking stuff from the Cairo Museum point of view.

The German head of the expedition assured the young Frenchman that he had seen all the results of the season's dig, and the latter, in turn, told the German that the Cairo Museum wished none of the objects. This apparently unimportant material was then boxed and sealed with the stamp of the Egyptian Antiquities Service, which permitted exit from the country. And in due time this study series was received at the Berlin Museum.

Some years later the artistic and archaeological world was thrilled and amazed on seeing photographs of a recent treasure added to the Egyptian collection in the Berlin Museum. It was a magnificent portrait bust c'

Queen Nefertete and was immediately recognized as a rare el-Amarna piece. Very persistent queries were made to the director of the Berlin Museum as to when and how this great treasure had been acquired. The answers were so evasive as to arouse suspicions, but finally the Germans admitted that the Nefertete bust had been found by their expedition at el-Amarna, and they stated bluntly that they had received the bust in a division and gave the date of the transaction.

The young Frenchman was believed by the director-general of Antiquities when he said he had not passed the portrait bust of Nefertete but a confused mass of broken objects, which apparently had included this great treasure, unrecognizable when shown to him in its several fragments. The Germans countered this statement by declaring that it was not until the Berlin Museum staff, with great skill, fitted together the broken pieces of a head and face that they themselves had realized its importance.

For a just estimation of the facts, it must be reiterated that the Germans concerned were well-trained archaeologists and would instantly have realized the importance of the piece, even in fragments. And if Lacau, instead of an inexperienced young French colleague, had been at the division, the bust would not have been passed.

Soon the lovely Nefertete displayed in the Berlin Museum became a *cause célèbre,* and a formal request was made to the German government by King Fuad himself to have Nefertete returned to Egypt, as it was obvious from the evidence that the bust had left the country through design on the part of the German expedition at el-Amarna.

The German government flatly refused to give up Akhenaten's beautiful queen. Several more attempts were made by the Egyptian government to have the matter settled amicably and without further notoriety, but the Germans persisted in their refusal. The Egyptian government then sent an official notice to the German government that until Nefertete was returned to the Cairo Museum, where it belonged by right, a concession for excavating would not be given to a German expedition.

Nefertete remained in Berlin and no German concession has since been renewed.

This was the account I heard personally from official sources at the time the negotiations for the return of Nefertete were going on, and I have no reason to doubt its accuracy.

Incidentally, a most remarkable series of models (facial masks) and unfinished sculpture was found at el-Amarna in the earlier years of the German excavations. The importance of this material that gave scholars a new angle from which to view the sculptured art of the New Kingdom was lost sight of in the postwar excitement and controversy over the Nefertete bust.

Probably even without the controversies connected with Tutankhamen's tomb and the Nefertete incident, the Egyptian government would have changed its policy governing the conditions under which permits for excavations were issued to foreign expeditions. But, unquestionably, the bad feeling, engendered by disagreeable publicity with both the Tutankhamen and Nefertete finds hastened regulations that foreigners found disconcerting.

Under Maspero, who was the first director-general I knew in 1898, the Antiquities Service included in its staff foreign archaeologists as inspectors of antiquities and "keepers" of the museum, most of them Englishmen. For a time, Maspero gave permits to excavate to private persons as well as to museums. Contracts and a fifty-fifty division of the objects found, with the director-general having the decision as to which half of the finds the Egyptian government wished to keep, were not onerous conditions. Maspero saw the museums of the world as one family, and in his divisions managed to see to it that each museum excavating in Egypt was rewarded by a representative collection of fine objects, although, naturally, unique pieces were reserved for the Cairo Museum. During Maspero's regime, many countries were permitted expeditions: England, the United States, Switzerland, Germany, Italy, and France.

Private excavators were required to obtain the services of a trained archaeologist, and Davis and Carnarvon were the last individuals to receive concessions.

But in 1924 the Egyptian government, through Lacau, announced a change in the conditions for issuing permits, under which foreign expeditions were to receive no *guarantee* of being given *any* of the objects found. This condition was qualified, however, by the statement that duplicates found, even though they were "capital" pieces, could be assigned to the excavator.

The new method did not appeal to trustees of interested museums, and a general protest was made. In all fairness to the Egyptian government, it must be said that, if divisions under these regulations were executed reasonably, which could be expected under Lacau's wise administration, foreign expeditions would still have continued to consider it worth while to excavate, but unfortunately several of them withdrew.

SCHEMING WOMEN AND SCHEMERS

1925-1928

26. Descendants of Cheops

E DWARD JACKSON HOLMES, the president of the Boston Museum, had a special interest in the work of Reisner's expedition. Although it was more than a decade later than the events which are to be related in the present chapter, the trip that he and Mrs. Holmes made to Egypt in 1937, to spend several months at Harvard Camp, helped to consolidate information which will explain much that follows for the earlier period of excavation in 1925-28.

Holmes told Reisner that the relationships between members of the Cheops family, owing to plural marriages and the resulting numerous descendants of chief and secondary queens, might be clear to a person of Reisner's learning but were only confusing to him. Would Reisner provide an explanatory note about complicated events and the personalities concerned, covering a period of over one hundred years beginning with Sneferu, the first king of Dynasty IV (2680–2565 B.C.), and lasting through the reign of Cheops' grandson, Mycerinus?

The following information was given by Reisner (with a few minor changes made later). He said it must be remembered that in ancient Egypt inheritance was from the mother's side, and frequently a king married his full or half-sister of royal blood, or a "commoner" obtained the throne through the claim of his wife as being the daughter of a king. By way of introduction to the great ladies in the family, he referred to the blood royal's having been brought into Dynasty IV by Hetepheres I. She, the daughter of Huni, the last king of Dynasty III, by his chief queen, had married Sneferu, a son by a minor wife, and their son, Cheops, was king because of her royal blood.

Cheops, who succeeded his father, married, as his chief queen, his full sister, Merytyetes. Their children were Ka'wab (the eldest), two other sons, one being the famous "magician," Dedef-hor, whose wisdom has been preserved on papyrus, and Min-khaf, and two daughters, Meresankh II and Hetepheres II.

Cheops was probably in his early twenties when he ascended the throne, and probably outlived his eldest son, Ka'wab, whose tomb shows him as a portly man beyond youth. Ka'wab had married his full sister, Hetepheres II, and their daughter, Meresankh III, later was to marry a king.

Radedef, a son of Cheops by an unknown queen, succeeded him, thus setting aside the claims of the descendants of Merytyetes (Cheops' chief queen and full sister). This unquestionably aroused resentment in what was thereafter known as the Giza legitimate branch of the family. By marriage with his half-sister, Hetepheres II, Radedef (who apparently had murdered Ka'wab) sought to strengthen his position as king by her royal blood. But indications of a family feud were shown in his building his pyramid at Abu Roash, some distance away. During the eight years of his reign no royal assistance was given apparently to any project at Giza that remained incomplete at the death of Cheops, including work on the family *mastabas* in the eastern and western Giza cemeteries. Furthermore, malicious destruction of the family inscriptions cut by the famous wise man, Dedef-hor, was evidence that his half-brother, as king, had taken drastic action against the descendants of Merytyetes, their father's chief queen.

In retaliation, Radedef's pyramid at Abu Roash was wrecked under the new king, Chephren, who immediately restored to power the legitimate Giza branch of the family. Although not a son of Cheops by his chief queen, he brought to himself, as king, the royal blood of Hetepheres I, by marrying Meresankh III, the daughter of the great lady's grandchildren, Ka'wab and the second Hetepheres, who, herself, returned to the court at Giza and there built her tomb.

By this time many of Cheops' original family must have reached an advanced age and died, and Chephren and Min-khaf may well have been the only surviving sons of Cheops. Chephren in his reign probably had been materially aided by Prince Ankh-haf, of the older generation, and by Nefermaat, a grandson of Sneferu, who was the third vizier in turn after Ankh-haf and Min-khaf.

Hetepheres I, herself the daughter of a king, the wife of a king, and the mother of a king was the ancestress of the great men of Dynasty IV. Not only were the kings her direct descendants, but she was the grandmother of Dedef-hor, whose masterly intellectual achievements were only surpassed by Imhotep, the inspired genius of the reign of Zoser in Saqqarah, later to be deified by the Greeks.

She was also related to all the viziers who served from the creation of that office in the reign of her husband, Sneferu, until the beginning of Dynasty V. Viziers were a part of the system of keeping all government control in the hands of the royal family, and often were the eldest sons of minor queens.

Behind names recorded on tomb walls there was contributory evidence of persistent family strife. Chephren's reign had been definitely and adversely affected. He had built no pyramids for his queens, and very few members of his family were buried even in cased *mastabas*. He managed to complete his own pyramid, which was almost as large as that of his father's, Cheops', but Mycerinus had a much smaller pyramid, and that of Shep-ses-kaf was so insignificant as to be barely visible, built in a brief reign that terminated in a state of chaos.

The most picturesque career in the family was that of the colorful Hetepheres II. When she failed in becoming chief queen from the death of Ka'wab, her husband and brother and heir to the throne, she laid her plans with the success of a brilliant opportunist by allying herself temporarily with her half-brother, Radedef, as king. At his death, however, she threw in her fortunes with the legitimate branch of the family, and promptly established herself at court by the marriage of her daughter to Chephren.

143

This extraordinary woman lived through the reigns of Chephren and Mycerinus, and was last heard of in the first year of Shep-ses-kaf, having entrenched herself at court for a period of over sixty years.

27. Secret Reburial of Queen Hetepheres I

DURING THE WINTER OF 1925, I took my second daughter, Frances, to Egypt for a short painting trip. After living on a *dahabieh* at Luxor and camping out at Abu Simbel, I telegraphed Allan Rowe, in charge of Harvard Camp during Reisner's absence in America, to expect us. Late in March, we arrived, and Rowe took us to the site of the recent discovery of a tomb chamber at the bottom of a deep shaft, in which the name of Sneferu had been deciphered. This was sensational news that made headlines in the American press, which went so far as to state that "Sneferu himself had been found." Rowe showed me a characteristic cable received from Reisner, which said the burial was *not* Sneferu's and to close the tomb at once. This, of course, had been done, so all we could do was to look down into a long shaft from which blocks resembling paving stones, and set in plaster, completely filling it to the ground level, had been removed. Soldiers and government guards were on duty, day and night, and our Harvard Camp guards as well. It was safe to say that no robbers of today would get into this doubtless royal tomb. And none had entered it in the past, after the burial, according to the evidence.

The discovery was one of pure accident. The expedition photographer was taking pictures on the plateau near the Pyramid of Cheops, when one of the legs of the camera tripod slipped and it collapsed. In stooping to set it up again, the photographer noticed on the leg of the tripod a patch of white plaster. This white stuff was also on the scarp of the rock surface. *Reis* Ahmad Said, Reisner's head man, was summoned and at once reported to Rowe. The plaster had been stained the color of the scarp and thereby had remained unnoticed through the ages. After stone packing under the plaster was removed, a secret stairway was found. After more plaster and nine courses of Turah limestone blocks

Bas-relief from the tomb of Meresankh III at Giza, showing the Queen and her mother, Queen Hetepheres II, in a papyrus boat. Painting by Joseph Lindon Smith. Courtesy of the Museum of Fine Arts, Boston.

The family of Queen Meresankh III, from her tomb at Giza.

were removed, and still more laborious digging through a shaft, a tomb chamber was reached one hundred feet below the surface.

Reisner had wanted me to return to Egypt and be with him when, in January, 1926, he reopened the chamber. This I was unable to do, because of commitments to paint in Central America. He resumed work without knowing whose tomb it was that had escaped being pillaged during almost five thousand years of ceaseless plundering of the family *mastabas* and small pyramids built by Cheops for his wives. In the following April, he learned that the tomb was that of Hetepheres I, who was, indeed, a royal personage, being the daughter of a king, married to King Sneferu, and the mother of Cheops.

Early in February, 1927, I made a special trip to Harvard Camp to represent the trustees of the Boston Museum on the occasion of lifting the lid of the alabaster sarcophagus in the tomb chamber, from which everything else had been cleared. During a number of delays, I kept busy painting in Giza tombs, and I also assisted in the reconstruction of the Hetepheres beds, chairs, and other furniture. Three days a week Alfred Lucas, the chief chemist of the Egyptian government, came out to Harvard Camp. I had last seen him in his improvised laboratory in the tomb of Seti II in the Valley of the Kings, busied with the objects from King Tut's tomb. I watched him mix up terrible smelling baths of acids, in which he dabbled about with copper objects. He treated fragile wood with preservatives, damaged gold foil with skill, and generally seemed to be giving himself a wonderful time. Reisner's staff learned a lot from him.

Both Dows Dunham from the Boston Museum and Lieutenant Commander Noel Wheeler of the field staff were working with Reisner at the time of my visit. Reisner wanted me to make an oil painting of the tomb chamber as originally found. I had a water-color sketch and excellent photographs of the objects *in situ,* and Reisner's vivid word pictures recreated the scene obtained by looking through a small opening at the top of the doorway leading into the burial chamber. In it was a beautiful, uninscribed alabaster sarcophagus with its lid in place, and on it, or fallen close by, were a number of gold-covered poles and beams of a large canopy. On the floor in a confused mass lay pieces of gold-cased chairs, lion legs, palm capitals, bars, and beams, all showing a glitter of gold. There were also copper and alabaster vessels. Sheets of inlaid gold formed an inscription with the cartouche of Sneferu, and had been responsible for the excitement when the tomb was first opened by Rowe.

Much of the wood on the furniture had shriveled or disintegrated. Reisner told me that, at his first sight of the tomb chamber, he realized that the confusion of objects was the result of something more than decay. A good deal of the damage had been caused by the falling of heavy alabaster vessels from wooden shelves, placed along the walls, that had rotted. The evidence showed clearly this was a reburial, transferred from the original tomb. The removal of the funerary deposit from the chamber had begun in early February, 1926, and was entirely completed ten months later. The process of clearing the objects as they lay seemed to me like playing a game of jackstraws, because of the entanglement of material, broken, bent, or disintegrated. It took a steady hand, skillful manipulation, and infinite patience. Dows Dunham had done the major part of this work of salvaging.

Early in the proceedings, a horizontal row of gold hieroglyphics on a bar of gold-covered wood over gold casing revealed the title "Mother of the King of Upper and Lower Egypt." The position of the king's mother was the most important one that a woman could hold in the Pyramid Age, and Reisner, with this fact in mind, started in to try to find out why the mother of Cheops had been reburied in a secret tomb that had not been seen again by human eyes until the expedition discovered it.

At the time I made my sketch, it took Reisner's practiced eye, vivid imagination, and graphic power of description to bring realization to me that the loose gold rods and sheets of metal among the debris belonged to furniture. The ancient wood, which was probably cedar of Lebanon, had crumbled away. It was little short of magic to watch the process of reconstruction, for which Dows Dunham must be given the largest share of credit. In the course of it, flattened sheets of gold casing, a mass of inlays which had fallen out of decayed wood panels, copper staples, and gold hieroglyphs were restored to their original condition and position on foundations of new wood that were facsimiles of the wood that had held them together in Dynasty IV.

The reconstruction of the objects gave an idea of the culture and luxury attained at the time of Cheops. But the gold-covered pieces of furniture were in perfect taste, with a simplicity in line and exquisite quality of design. No more beautiful hieroglyphs in any age were ever hammered into wood carvings than were placed on the gold-cased door-jambs of the Queen's bedchamber, which contained her royal bed and canopy. And also unrivaled for delicacy in workmanship were tiny gold hieroglyphs set into the small ebony panels of her carrying chair, probably used by Hetepheres when she was alive.

An armchair exhibited a striking design, below the arms, of three papyrus flowers with their stems held together by bands of metal. Reisner told me that this papyrus-flower decoration was the first evidence that the tomb did not belong to a king, whose chair would have had the flower of Upper Egypt entwined with the papyrus of Lower Egypt, about the hieroglyphic sign for union.

Several times when Reisner and I were alone in the tomb chamber with the unopened sarcophagus, I marveled at his lack of curiosity (to use an attribute common to all human beings) in waiting two years before lifting the lid to settle, once and for all, what *was* inside.

The date for the great event was set for February 26, then was postponed again until March 3, when it actually took place. There was an air of pleasurable expectancy among the distinguished officials assembled at the wooden shanty that protected the mouth of the tomb shaft. The under-secretary of State and the minister of Public Works represented the Egyptian government. Lacau was there as director-general of Antiquities, and our American minister, Morton Howell came, too. One by one, they got into a modern armchair to be lowered down the shaft by a pulley. On entering the tomb chamber, they sat or stood near the alabaster sarcophagus.

Wheeler and Dunham were at either end of the sarcophagus, to operate two short projectors, which were to serve as handles for lifting the lid. Fitted under the handles was a frame of wooden beams resting on three jack screws. Reisner sat on a small box, and I was next to him, kneeling, and closest to the sarcophagus.

In a breathless silence, the lid began to be lifted. When it was sufficiently raised for me to peer inside, I saw to my dismay that the queen was not there—the sarcophagus was empty! Turning to Reisner, I said in a voice louder than I had intended, "George, she's a dud!"

Whereupon, the minister of Public Works asked, "What is a dud?"

Reisner rose from his box and said, "Gentlemen, I regret Queen Hetepheres is not receiving." And added, "Mrs. Reisner will serve refreshments at the camp."

The guests, looked amazed and somewhat annoyed, left the tomb chamber and were taken to the surface. Reisner and the rest of us pulled ourselves together and joined the party. Later in the day, he and I went back into the tomb chamber, where the contents of the sarcophagus were no longer a matter for conjecture.

He had previously mentioned to me, as somewhat of a shock, the discovery of a flake of alabaster that fitted corresponding chipped places in the sarcophagus and lid, possibly indicating that the lid had been pried open in ancient times. But even so, in many talks with him on the subject, I formed the definite impression of his confidence that the mummy was inside the sarcophagus.

As we sat together, he acknowledged his disappointment, but with his usual philosophy, he at once turned his thoughts to solving the problem of why the sarcophagus was empty in an "intact" burial chamber. He first drew my attention to a faint discoloration on the bottom of the sarcophagus, which, he asserted, showed it had been used for an actual burial.

Reisner accepted as a likely premise that Hetepheres had originally been buried at Dashuhr, in a tomb beside the pyramid of her husband Sneferu. He suggested that filial piety might have induced the son to bring his mother's body and funerary equipment near the great tomb he was preparing for himself. But the alternative and, to me, the more probable explanation was that Cheops had heard of plundering going on in the royal cemetery at Dashuhr, and to forestall a threatened attack on his mother's tomb, he had had her body and funerary deposit placed for protection where no thieves of antiquity would find them. This theory accounted for the extraordinary precautions taken for conceal-ment in an insignificant pit chamber at Giza.

It was not possible, however, that the King had thus acted, knowing the sarcophagus did not contain his mother's body. Granted the fact that the King himself had commanded the transfer, how had the truth of the destruction of her body prior to the reburial been kept from him?

To explain this fact, Reisner and I reconstructed a crime of long ago. It had happened at a time when the attention of the court was con-centrated on the new royal cemetery at Giza, where Cheops was build-ing his pyramid. The old royal cemetery of Sneferu at Dashuhr had been left to the care of funerary priests, police guards, and workmen in the necropolis. A conspiracy was formed, doubtless with the connivance of the keeper of the cemetery and the priests, to loot the tomb of Queen Hetepheres. The thieves pried open the alabaster sarcophagus and, removing the mummy, dragged the latter to the surface, since light was necessary for a quick search of the mummy wrappings. They had found the customary jewelry and rich gold ornaments and, leaving the body exposed in the desert, fled.

Some member of the conspiracy had turned informer. The Vizier knew the desecration of the Royal Mother's body could not for long be concealed, and should this terrible news reach the King's ears, it would mean instant death to himself. He had, therefore, immediately reported to the King that the royal cemetery at Dashuhr was being plundered, but, thanks to his (the Vizier's) vigilance, the thieves had been caught as they had reached the outer doorway of his mother's tomb. They had been tortured and put to death. But others in the conspiracy might still be at large, and the Queen's body was no longer safe. She must be moved at once!

The Vizier was in the complete confidence of the King, and was ordered to prepare with all speed a secret burial place on the plateau near the middle of the Great Pyramid of Giza, consisting of a small chamber devoid of ornamentation or inscription.

The King instructed his Vizier that the Queen Mother was to be transferred to this secret tomb at Giza, and told his Vizier it was not sufficient to bring the body in the alabaster sarcophagus, but the essentials of the funerary equipment as well, including the customary food offerings left for the dead. He may even have planned to go to the royal cemetery at Dashuhr to superintend the arrangements. This the Vizier must have prevented by pointing out to his royal master that a sign of the King's interest in the tombs there, or in the insignificant shaft selected for the reburial, might prove fatal to the utmost secrecy necessary for the success of the difficult undertaking. The King agreed.

The Vizier had to depend on the co-operation of the keeper of the royal cemetery at Dashuhr and some of the priests. With them he had entered the tomb of the royal mother, together they had gazed in horror at the opened and empty sarcophagus, sealed it, and brought it and the essentials of the funerary equipment out on to a quiet spot in the desert. The canopy, the great carrying chair, other chairs, beds, alabaster and copper vessels, a box of anklets, toilet articles of pure gold, all were there. Near the empty sarcophagus was an alabaster chest, and in it four canopic packets wrapped in linen, containing what was left of the mortal remains of the queen. And in the darkness, as the bright gold of the furniture glittered, trusted men of the Vizier's had killed the priests and keeper of the Dashuhr cemetery.

Two days later, the Vizier, aided by these men whom he trusted, had got the sarcophagus and other tomb equipment to Giza. The sarcophagus had had to be lowered on end down the shaft. It was carried into the burial chamber and the objects placed around it. Food was left in a niche in the shaft, and all was ready for the filling of the shaft with stones, which the King's foresight had caused to be placed near by. Should the King himself decide to appear in that chamber at this hollow mockery of a reburial, when the body had already been torn to pieces by jackals in the desert wastes, the Vizier was indeed undone.

Urged on by promises of rich reward, men who might have suspected the truth quickly put in place stone after stone, set in plaster, until the shaft was filled to the surface and the entrance cut in the rock face was disguised by plaster. Then the men, who had been under the eye of the Vizier since joining him in the desert at Dashuhr, started to move away from the pyramid plateau. At a little distance they were set upon and murdered. At last the Vizier felt safe. And well he might, for his secret was destined to be kept for almost five thousand years!

Reisner and I sat in that tomb chamber in the semidarkness, each of us engaged in our thoughts, then he said:

"Joe, no other explanation fits the known facts."

28. Offering Chapel of Queen Meresankh III

REISNER HAD FOUND the painted offering chapel of Queen Meresankh III soon after the excitement of the empty sarcophagus. My artist's brush was attracted by the reliefs on the walls of the large chambers, vivid in color and very gay, showing Meresankh and her mother, Hetepheres II, together, standing in a reed boat pulling papyrus in a swamp, and other scenes equally charming. The daughter was demure and conventional, but the mother, whom we already knew for a trouble-maker and a successful opportunist, was shown with short red hair, instead of the usual black ceremonial wig, and the smile of an individualist who had dared to defy convention and blazoned the fact on the living rock.

The fact of the mother's having survived her daughter was confirmed by a record above the outside doorjamb of the tomb which stated that, she, Hetepheres, was giving to her daughter the tomb she had started to prepare for her own use.

The lists of a vast number of funerary endowments were recorded in detail on the walls of this tomb chapel, in sharp contrast with the mutilated and imperfect lists previously found in *mastabas* in which other descendants of Cheops were buried. For instance, the funerary estates had been bequeathed by Cheops to his daughter, Hetepheres, by a secondary queen from Lybia. Hetepheres, in turn, bequeathed them to her daughter, Meresankh. Since inheritance in ancient Egypt was through the mother, this kind of information was of the utmost importance in determining family relationships. The interior of the chapel composed itself charmingly, and I enjoyed making several studies of it.

Reisner believed that Yankaf sculptured the reliefs and Rahay laid in the brilliant colors that had faded so little in this delightful tomb of Meresankh, so full of reminders of a pleasant family life. He told me that the son of Chephren and Queen Meresankh III followed the precedent set by his mother, and in his own tomb, inscriptions were cut stating that the overseer of works, Yankaf, made the tomb and Semerka painted it. Reisner considered that this was probably the same Yankaf referred to as a sculptor in this tomb of Meresankh. As an artist, I was pleased that the name of a sculptor and painter had actually been recorded—a rare event in an Egyptian tomb. Another interesting family tie-up was disclosed in connection with the chief priest, who was shown on a doorjamb reading a papyrus roll to Meresankh. His name was given as Khemten. The tomb of Ka'wab contained a well-known inscription stating that Khemten was the steward of Ka'wab and Hetepheres. This family steward, therefore, appeared quite naturally as a funerary priest in the tomb of their daughter, Meresankh. And Khemten the younger, son of the Khemten reading a papyrus, was carved on the back of the pillar of a doorway. Also, a group of four figures, which were inset (not cut), were identified by Reisner as children of the younger Khemten, and registered as heirs of the chief priest of the family funerary estate.

This tomb was a very human document, to become even more so for me when one day I was let into an ancient secret. A member of Reisner's staff, who had joined me to do some copying of the inscriptions on a wall in the main chamber, noticed a piece of loosened plaster. On touching it, he caused the plaster to fall out, revealing in a niche a small statue of Yankaf which the sculptor himself had placed there, unquestionably with the connivance of one of the family. It seemed to me a shame to remove the statue of a sculptor after so careful a plan had been made to keep him concealed through eternity, in a tomb in which he had no legal place.

The importance attributed to a sculptor in this tomb of Meresankh recalled to my mind a scene from which emerged the equally vivid personality of an artist, who, although nameless, was as definitely individualistic as the sculptor, Yankaf. In this more recent instance, occurring some sixteen hundred years later in a different part of the Nile Valley, the reliefs were the "narrator" instead of the text.

The key to the onlooker's understanding of a confused mêlée of ships and chariots, with water and land episodes intermingled, and making of it a great epic, lay in the genius of the artist. He treated his subject with an original and entirely successful technique not tried before or since in ancient Egypt.

The naval battle, which took place about 1190 B.C., was recorded on a long outer wall of Ramesses III's Temple of Medinet Habu on the Theban Plain. It was considered by scholars to be a valuable document for two reasons: as relating the naval triumph of Egypt's last great warrior king, and, even more essential, it was unique in being the only *sea* battle shown in an Egyptian temple.

Professor Harold H. Nelson, as field director of the Oriental Institute of the University of Chicago, with headquarters at Luxor, had administrative responsibility for a series of volumes of copies produced by the Institute's epigraphic and architectural surveys from the temples of Medinet Habu and Karnak.

On the many occasions when I was a guest of the expedition, I became familiar with the details of this naval battle from his lucid interpretation. The story was one of barbarian tribes from the North dislodged from their northern homelands, turning southward into Syria and Palestine, eventually to encroach on the shrunken boundaries of the Asiatic empire of Egypt.

The artist showed the progress of the fight by the simplest of means, land being indicated by a base line, whereas water was represented by green with zigzag black or blue lines across it. Enemy land forces were separated from the naval units by a lion hunt skillfully interposed. The foreigners in the boats wear both horned helmets and feathered head-dress, but in the campaign on land only the feathered headdress is shown. The beginning of the naval battle was represented by Egyptian ships shown at the mouth of a river, probably in the Nile Delta, attacking in an orderly fashion, with their prows all turned toward enemy boats clearly unprepared to maneuver, their oars not in position and their sails furled. The artist vividly expressed the heightening confusion of an enemy caught by surprise and at anchor, many of his ships still afloat but faced in the opposite direction from the rest of the squadron.

All land battles depicted on temple walls followed the same pattern. The colossal figure of the Pharaoh Ramesses III stood in his huge chariot with drawn bow and arrow poised, as he drove into the mass of his enemy being crushed between the horses' hoofs and wheels of his chariot. By this means, the artist rendered a graphic presentation of the theory of kingship, with the Pharaoh exercising godlike powers in defense of his people and in divine solicitude for their welfare. But the artist who designed this naval battle was confronted with a very difficult problem. To have reduced the size of the King to anywhere near the proportions of vessels in the space allowed would have dwarfed his figure, and like-wise the enemies on the decks or in the water would have been no longer distinguishable from being so small.

This dilemma the artist's skill overcame in a most convincing man-ner. The Pharaoh was symbolized standing with the dead bodies of his enemies washed up on the shore in front of him, corresponding to the masses of slain beneath the horses' feet and the wheels of the Pharaoh's chariot appearing in the usual land battle scenes. Although the actual area of the sea battle was at quite a distance from the part of the shore where the Pharaoh stood, the terror of enemies on the boats was real-istically expressed in faces all turned in the direction of the Pharaoh across the intervening stretch of water. With the same symbolic em-phasis, the arrows protruding from the bodies of the land forces also pointed back to the Pharaoh and carried the eye inevitably to his mighty bow, which alone was capable of discharging them. The unity of the theme was secured by having the Pharaoh remain the central figure of the scene, as he was, in fact, the central figure in the institution of the absolute monarchy.

EGYPTIAN PORTRAITURE

1 9 2 8 – 1 9 2 9

29. *Sculpture in the Pyramid Age*

I HAD SEEN, in 1925, the most remarkable portrait bust ever found at Giza, in Reisner's excavations, or in any others, while Reisner was away on a short trip to America. It was of a man named Ankhhaf, and the head, with its curiously modern appearance, came as near to realism as convention permitted in portraiture in the greatest period of Egyptian sculpture in the round, during the fourth dynasty.

I wrote Reisner of the appreciation of Lord and Lady Allenby, who made several visits to Harvard Camp particularly to pay homage to Ankh-haf. Professor Newberry was very enthusiastic over the bust, as were many other Egyptologists, including Capart, the Belgian. But it was Georg Steindorff of Leipzig University, Reisner's old friend, who was the most thoroughly satisfactory in his criticism. He said what I had felt, that the bust of Ankh-haf was like some of the splendid Florentine portrait busts of the Medicis. James H. Breasted, whom every American high-school student of ancient history had come to know by this time, was equally impressed.

The bust was assigned to the Boston expedition in a division (April, 1927) in which Pierre Lacau, the director-general of the Antiquities Service (who had succeeded Maspero in 1914), took for the Cairo Museum the entire contents of the secret reburial of Queen Hetepheres I. Certainly no finer example of ancient portraiture than Ankh-haf ever left its place of origin to come to an American museum. This was a well-deserved recognition of the brilliant reconstruction by Reisner and his staff of the only household furniture of the Pyramid Age ever recovered by excavators.

The bust bore the titles of "Prince" and "Eldest Son of the King's Body." Unquestionably, moreover, Ankh-haf, as vizier and overseer of all the King's works, was very influential with the royal family of Dynasty IV, because his was the largest *mastaba* in the eastern or royal cemetery, in which the major tombs belonged to sons and daughters of Cheops and their immediate relatives. Reisner took me into the room of the *mastaba* where the bust was found lying on its back in front of a white-plastered pedestal of mud-brick. He explained his reconstruction of the probable arrangements as follows:

The bust stood on a pedestal facing out into the room to the east. Below it were ninety-four plaster models, placed on a low offering bench at the north. Some of these depicted food offerings. One or two stands carrying bowls were on the floor near by. This group consisting of bust and objects constituted an unusual offering place in the westernmost of a series of rooms of the exterior chapel of Ankh-haf's tomb.

The base of the bust was finished off flat and, therefore was never a part of a statue. It seemed to have been used only in the room in which it had been found. From a technical point of view, the bust was of considerable interest, since, although it was of white limestone, of which the ancient sculpture at Giza was generally made, it differed from other figures of the period in being covered with a light coating of gypsum plaster. Finally, the entire bust was painted red, of the tone normally used to represent the flesh of men, the body color of women being yellow. Ankh-haf wore no wig, but the outlines of sparse hair were clearly indicated, revealing an unmistakable tendency to baldness. The eyes were originally white with dark pupils, but the color had faded until now it was only faintly visible.

The preservation left much to be desired. The most obvious blemish was a large abrasion on the forehead, which must have come from an ancient blow. The end of the nose was missing, also both ears, which had been made separately. The point of the chin was somewhat damaged but showed that the head originally had a beard, probably of the very short type frequently seen in relief representations of men of high rank.

There was no way of telling the exact date of the bust, since it was not known when Ankh-haf died, but it must have been made during the first half of Dynasty IV (2680–2565 B.C.). In spite of the mutilations suffered, the features were sufficiently intact to reveal the personality and character of a man who, nearly five thousand years ago, held high rank in the government of what was then the most civilized country on earth.

Cheops and his immediate descendants had at their royal command sculptors who were master craftsmen, reminiscent of the painters whom the Medicis as great patrons of art assembled at their courts. Unfortunately, the wonderful statues these ancient sculptors produced for early Giza chapels have not survived. But a series of amazing examples of portraiture were preserved in what Reisner described to me as "reserve heads."

These heads were not part of a statue, as was evidenced by the fact that they were rounded at the neck, as the bust of Ankh-haf was further down. They were placed in the burial chamber with the mummy, to serve as a substitute for the head of the mummy, should it be destroyed during the journey through eternity.

These white limestone, unpainted portraits were the climax of perfection in the sculptor's art, never surpassed in later ages, not even by the Greeks. In them all unnecessary details were eliminated, but every essential was there, in the modeling of the features, which brought out the individuality and strength of personalities clearly belonging to living men and women personally known to the sculptors.

Several unfinished heads found by Reisner in a Giza workshop dating to Dynasty IV interested me greatly in showing the processes of workmanship. The rough outlines of features in alabaster or limestone were done by an assistant with a stone hammer. Then the master sculptor took over and completed the modeling of the face and gave the final texture to the surface.

Immense material prosperity marked the Pyramid Age of Giza, initiated by the genius of the mighty Cheops, builder of the Great Pyramid. His fantastic extravagances, followed by those of his son Chephren, and his grandson Mycerinus, left a legacy in sculpture for which the modern world is the richer. But during the process, the royal wealth was redistributed.

The great Dynasty IV ended abruptly in 2565 B.C., only a few years after Shep-ses-kaf came to the throne. Among the many treasures discovered by Reisner in the Pyramid Temple of Mycerinus was an alabaster head that has been identified as Shep-ses-kaf, who became king through his marriage with Khent-kus, a daughter of Mycerinus. This head, a very fine example of the sculptor's skill, was a present reminder of a royal family that, during a period of one hundred years, created a glorious era in Giza.

30. *The Head of Weserkaf*

I HAD LEFT EGYPT in the spring of 1927, just after the wonderful news that the Ankh-haf bust was to come to the Boston Museum. I was kept busy at home until January, 1928, when Corinna accompanied me on her first trip to Egypt since 1909. She settled down to a routine life at Harvard Camp, working with Reisner in his office on archaeological records and his manuscript, sometimes accompanying me in the Giza tombs. Later Reisner made arrangements through Lacau for Corinna and me to have the loan of a small house at Saqqarah, just below the large house belonging to the Antiquities Service. Our simple wants were cared for by two of Reisner's men from the village of Quft in Upper Egypt, which supplied his large native staff of about two hundred from one family group. Neither of these Qufti spoke English, and Corinna enjoyed housekeeping again in Arabic, as on our early trips together. From a small terrace we got intimate glimpses of village life in the valley below. Also a view of vast extent; on a clear day the Citadel stood out from the long stretch of the Mokattam hills, as a reminder of Moslem Egypt in the midst of pyramids that were all around us.

In the morning, soon after dawn, we watched the village come to life and the movement of men and livestock toward the fields. At dusk, it was equally interesting to see men slowly separate themselves and their livestock from the green fields and move toward the village. A signal that this was about to happen occurred when flocks of birds began their flight in the direction of certain large sycamore trees, where they spent the night. Voices rose in the still air from women in trailing black, carrying on their heads water jars, loads of fodder, or wide corn-stalks, usually with a child slung across the shoulders. Men followed with heavier, broader loads on their backs, or carried by donkeys and camels. A dog trailed the procession of family groups hastening to the evening meal, and thin smoke curled upwards with an agreeable smell of fragrant burning wood in small fires, where the outlines of women were just visible from our height above. Children rushed out to meet their returning fathers; dogs barked. Simple scenes, but ones we never willingly missed!

Cecil Firth was the English inspector in charge of Saqqarah who had succeeded Quibell. His wife was a delightful woman and an excellent artist, and Diana, their daughter, was with them. They were all three very pleasant companions to find in a desert solitude. Since my previous visit, Firth had uncovered more of the "beautiful temples of Zoser." This he told me was the way Egyptian pilgrims in the annals of antiquity referred to these buildings made by the architect, Imhotep, for Zoser, the first king of Dynasty III, who began his reign in 2780 B.C. and ruled for nineteen years. No one believed that any trace of them existed until Firth's excavations in 1924 had revealed them.

He said that the clue to the early date of the building lay in the doors of chapels. They were made of masonry, but carved to represent the type of wooden door used by very ancient Egyptians, and left standing open so that the soul of the king might pass back and forth easily. And, in turn, the wooden door was an adaptation of the earliest known door made of reed mats.

Firth said excavations had already proved that, but by the end of Dynasty II, architecture had been well developed in the use of molded

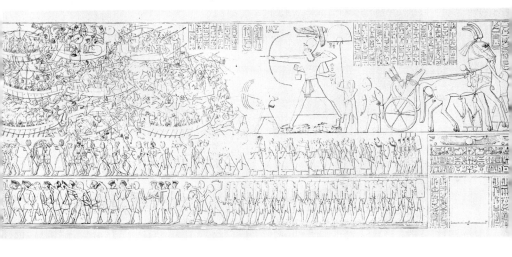

Two bas-reliefs of the great naval battle of Ramesses III in the Temple of Medinet Habu at Thebes. Courtesy Oriental Institute of the University of Chicago.

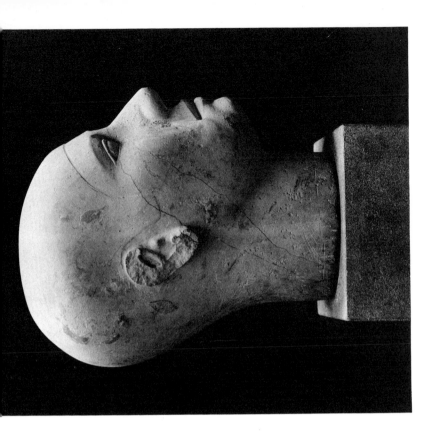

Portrait head of the husband of a Negroid princess, Giza. Photograph courtesy Museum of Fine Arts, Boston.

Portrait bust of Ankh-haf, Giza. Painting by Joseph Lindon Smith. Courtesy Museum of Fine Arts, Boston.

mud brick and wood, from which the stone forms of the Pyramid Age were derived. Stone construction was found as early as Dynasty I (3200–2980 B.C.). But these buildings in the great enclosure surrounding Zoser's Step Pyramid were the earliest known in Egypt using *dressed* stone. He showed me a chapel built of masonry in small blocks, with lovely surfaces and details of great beauty. The door frames, roof, moldings, and niches were all obviously derived from an architecture using crude brick and wood.

One order of column was very tall semiattached to the walls, and had a capital. Another type had a fluted stem. This was twenty-three hundred years earlier than the first examples of Greek fluted columns. He indicated the significance of the find by saying that Imhotep had originated a form in building technique that meant rewriting the history of architecture in ancient Egypt.

One day, Firth took us through an amazing colonnade to reach the southern enclosing wall where an enormous tomb shaft was contemporary in date with Zoser's Step Pyramid. From the surface, we went down a long flight of steps to reach the entrance to underground chambers. We entered a very narrow, winding passageway and made a descent that was difficult because of the steepness of the incline and shallow steps that were badly broken or, at times, missing altogether. Down and down we plunged, in a stooping position from the lowness of the roof. The flickering light of the candle I carried served to accentuate jagged and none too secure rocks overhead or on the sides of the passage. Several times in the darkness, we came to rock platforms to the left that led "into space," Firth warned us. "Follow me closely," he kept calling out, which was not too easy, for, in spite of his bulk, he moved as lightly on his feet as a cat.

The air was stifling at the bottom of the stairs. Firth stopped to light an acetylene lamp, and then we went into a long, very narrow corridor where we could stand erect. I got a general idea of blue faïence tiles lining the walls, and on a small false door or niche, under the outspread wings of a vulture, and with blue tiles on either side of him, was a small-sized, spirited figure of King Zoser, shown at a run and carved in low relief on rather poor stone, with the surface in bad condition. Firth urged me to paint this figure, since he was afraid the original might not be long preserved. The plaster holding the tiles in place had loosened in many places, and the floor was strewn with them. He said there was so little air in the corridor that it would be better for me to be alone while I worked. I started in the very next morning.

This season Firth had stopped work on the Zoser buildings to excavate the Temple of Weserkaf, the traditional founder of Dynasty V (2565–2420 B.C.) at Saqqarah. After the death of Shep-ses-kaf that brought Dynasty IV to an end at Giza, possibly his widow, Khent-kus, married Weserkaf. If this was the case, then once again, as with Hetepheres I, the blood royal was carried into the next dynasty through a king's daughter.

It has been accepted as a likely premise that Sahura and Neferir-ka-re, the second and third kings of Dynasty V, were issue of this marriage.

In the southwest corner of the court of Weserkaf's Funerary Temple, scattered over the basalt pavement, fragments of small statues of the King in diorite and red granite, all with his cartouche, had been found. Early that morning, in a deep hole under the pavement, Firth's workmen had come upon some large stone object, and in the early afternoon we assembled in Weserkaf's Temple. After a good deal of effort, since it was very heavy, a magnificent red granite portrait head of the King was got to the surface. The face was caked in mud, but Firth made out at once that the forehead, nose, mouth, and chin were all unbroken, a condition true also of the back of the head and the ears. He was jubilant, since this head of Weserkaf, over three times life size, was the first colossal head to be found dating to the Old Kingdom.

It was at once taken to the small storeroom just inside the entrance court of the big house. The larger cakes of mud were removed, and by dinnertime the face had sufficiently emerged to suggest the greatest care in completing the cleaning of the features, especially so since traces of color were discernible on the eyes, nostrils, and mouth. Two days after this important discovery, Herbert E. Winlock, former head of the Egyptian Department of the Metropolitan Museum, and Helen his wife,

162

were to spend the day with us. Both Mrs. Firth and Corinna wanted Weserkaf to be looking his best. They worked hard in a small, stuffy room all the next day, and late into the night by electric light. The head of Weserkaf was impressive not only from its size but also from the technique employed on hard stone. The features and eyes had the simplified, strong modeling characteristic of the finest heads of Dynasty IV. I felt that it was unquestionably a portrait from life. Mrs. Firth put a long, black velvet scarf behind Weserkaf, a background that suited him. The Winlocks both were quite overcome by the charm of the head and kept going into the storeroom to get another look at it.

For years, now, this unique portrait head of Dynasty V has been facing the door at the entrance rotunda of the Cairo Museum on a high pedestal. All trace of color has faded from the features, but Corinna and I can point out each place where there *was* color at the time of the discovery.

Winlock got to reminiscing about his excavating days and told of a practically intact female burial of early Dynasty XII (1991–1786 B.C.). His account was so vivid and clear-cut, it seemed a pity he was no longer able, for reasons of health, to find these delightful ladies of long ago. This was about the discovery of Senebtisy by him and Arthur Mace, in 1907 at el-Lisht. She was not of royal blood, but undoubtedly was someone high at court, judging by the similarity between her jewelry and other funerary equipment and that in the Dashuhr burials.

He told of the appearance of the offering chamber, with jars and dishes and food and drink, and then gave a dramatic description of the series of coffins covered with gold foil, with neatly arranged linen sheets over the outermost-coffin. He did full justice to the mummy herself, a small woman of about fifty, with a lovely circlet of twisted gold wire on her head, her long hair sparkling with gold rosettes entwined around separate locks of hair, all indicated even before later restoration.

She was wearing three necklaces with pendants and amulets and beads of carnelian and other material, and the clasp to her girdle was effective and characteristic of the period. He ended, as he began, by saying how fortunate it was that robbers who had entered the chamber, apparently soon after the burial, had been interrupted before getting much.

One late afternoon, not long before we were to leave Saqqarah, the Firths were to come to tea. The ladies turned up promptly, but we ultimately finished tea without Firth. It was a mild evening of full moon and we had lingered on the terrace. Firth finally appeared, looking rather exhausted, and said he had been delayed by an experience that only a small dog that had "all but talked" prevented from being a tragedy.

This was the story:

Firth was about to leave the Weserkaf Temple when the distant barking of a dog in the direction of the Step Pyramid held his attention. The Firths had as a pet one of the village watchdogs which was always with him at the dig. He had noticed his dog's ears go up as the barking became louder, then a small, brownish dog not belonging at Saqqarah came into view. He ran a bit, then stopped, as though looking for someone. When he got fairly near, Firth, fearing that his desert-grown dog would attack a stray, called his own dog to heel and began to walk toward the little brown animal.

When he reached the dog, Firth stooped and patted his head and then turned back, believing the dog would follow him. Instead, the little animal gave a series of barks that Firth described as "desperate" and went a little distance back in the direction of the Step Pyramid, whence he had come. When he saw Firth was not following, he rushed to him and caught hold of his trouser leg. Still thinking the dog was lost and hungry, Firth picked him up in his arms and took a few steps again in the direction of his house. At this the strange dog seemed absolutely frantic, and, wriggling free, rushed off a little distance toward the Step Pyramid again, then stopped and looked back at Firth.

The dog for the second time returned to clutch at Firth's trousers and tried to drag him along in the direction of the pyramid. When Firth, shaking off the dog's hold, took a few steps in the direction indicated, the dog was apparently satisfied. But each time Firth turned and headed toward home, the dog howled as though in agony. Finally, Firth was persuaded that the dog was trying to tell him to come to the Step Pyramid. He was fond of animals, but found himself feeling rather foolish at the end of a long day's work, when he wanted his tea, yet he followed the dog's lead for almost a mile, until he reached the iron-locked gate at the entrance to the Step Pyramid. The dog, crawling through the bars, ran down into the dark passageway, barking loudly. When he saw Firth was not following, he came back to the entrance and tried to drag him inside by his trouser leg. Firth by now was thoroughly convinced that the dog was telling him he must come into the passage. He saw a *ghaffir* at a distance, hailed him, and told him to bring the key to the gate and a lantern.

When the dog saw that Firth was remaining at the entrance, he came to him and licked his hand. The *ghaffir* arrived with the key and the lantern, and, preceded by the dog, Firth and the *ghaffir* crawled down the main passageway for a short distance. Then the dog, returning to Firth's side, barked and rushed off on a left turn, looking back to see if Firth was behind. Then, after a bit, the dog indicated in all but the spoken word that Firth was to go right. On their knees, the two men penetrated far into the depths of the Step Pyramid, when, suddenly, they heard a groan. Firth shouted; the dog barked; and as they went forward, the groaning sounded nearer. Finally, they came upon two sailors of the British Navy, lying in pitch blackness on the edge of a deep pit.

When the sailors had pulled themselves together, they told Firth what had happened. They had crawled over the top of the gate, taking the dog with them, just for a lark to see what was down the passage. They had no candles, but each thought the other had plenty of matches. However, they had only a small supply between them that was soon exhausted. They lost their sense of direction and crawled about for several hours searching for the entrance. Finally, completely exhausted, badly bruised, and terrified, they had given up hope and, fortunately, had stopped moving on the edge of the pit.

The dog, a stray that had adopted them, stayed with them until they had ceased their efforts to save themselves. Then, in the pitch blackness, the dog had taken all the correct turns to reach the surface, and, once there, had started off to find help.

Firth said that, to him, the most amazing thing in the whole episode was that his own dog seemed to have sensed an emergency in which the strange dog was involved, and had let the dog clutch his master without a protest.

31. *Reisner's Excavations in the Sudan*

I WAS PARTICULARLY INTERESTED in Reisner's work in the Sudan from my desert caravan trip to Semna with the Bayard Cuttings in 1908. This was long before Reisner began his excavations of the Egyptian forts at Semna and Uronarti in the season of 1923–24. He had started with exposing the underlying buildings of the West Semna Fort, stage by stage, and the following season he had continued at Semna and also worked at Uronarti.

His first site in the Sudan had been Kerma, where in 1914–15 he had excavated the fort buildings and tombs of the Egyptian colony of Kerma. After that he had excavated the Ethiopian temples at Barkal and the pyramids of kings and queens at Napata, but I did not have a chance to visit any of these sites.

It was in 1921, when Reisner was excavating at Meroe, that I stayed with him at the expedition camp, established at the modern village of Kabushiyeh, and my eldest daughter, Rebecca, was with me. Everything thrilled her, from the early morning rides far over the desert to long painting hours and walks among great mounds and groups of pyramids and cemeteries, both in the plain and on the hills of the higher desert about three miles from camp. Reisner's young daughter, Mary, was an excellent scholar in languages, including hieroglyphics, and was of constant assistance to him in his work. Mrs. Reisner devoted many hours to patient and skillful reconstruction of objects found, and particularly to putting bead patterns together, in itself a very laborious task.

I had quite a time doing a view Reisner wanted of fourteen pyramids and a splendid mountain in the distance. To paint it, I sat on the very top of a pyramid. Several times, both my picture and I almost blew away from the buffeting of the strong winds.

In one ruined pyramid, Reisner took us down a cleared stairway of ten steps and into a chamber that contained a badly decayed wooden coffin. The mummy had been removed by plunderers, who had left only a few broken bones in the debris, a mummy eye, and beads scattered about.

On another occasion, in a partly cleared rectangular pit, Reisner showed us a skeleton of a woman lying on her back, with the head and all the body complete, but much decayed. These scenes of ancient burials stirred Rebecca's imagination. "I never thought of Ethiopians before coming to Kabushiyeh," she would say, laughing at her own excitement, "and now I can't hear enough about them."

Reisner gave, as a background of Ethiopia, a brief outline of Egypt's control through Egyptian viceroys. He mentioned Hepzefa, who was appointed by Sesostris I, Dynasty XII, who dated back to 1971–1928 B.C. He died at Kerma and was buried there, a long way from Assiut, his home in Egypt. It was not to be expected that his *Ka* would remain in this savage land exposed to dangers of an unknown spirit world. He had provided for himself a large tomb at Assiut, and in it magic formulas which supposedly would transport his soul there after death. Sandals found on the feet of Egyptian officials who died in the Sudan, Reisner considered evidence of the intention of the *Ka* to return to Egypt.

The continued existence of the deceased under the accustomed habits of life was an accepted fact. Therefore, the deceased took his family with him, and the *sati* burials should not be considered inhuman. Many instances of this type of burial were found in the Kerma cemeteries, with the position of the skeletons showing that the surviving members of families had been interred when still alive—instead of being burned as in India.

By the time of the New Kingdom (1570–1085 B.C.) Kush (Ethiopia) had become thoroughly Egyptianized, including the Lybian family, which became the royal family of Ethiopia in 900 B.C. and imported Egyptian craftsmen.

Reisner, who found their burials, reconstructed for us the fascinating episode of the royal Lybian family. About 900 B.C., this family established itself at Napata (Barkal) and seized the roads from Egypt to the gold mines and southern markets. These Lybians found Ethiopia a province of Egypt, made it a kingdom, and Egypt a province of Ethiopia. They developed no culture, for the power of these kings of Ethiopia had been founded on the profits of caravan traffic.

Reisner declared impressively, "Our expedition has traced the history of this Lybian royal family through twelve centuries, from Napata (900–750 B.C.) and two periods at Meroe beginning in 538 B.C. and ending in 350 A.D." He said that Francis L. Griffith of Oxford had determined the alphabetic character of the Meroitic hieroglyphic writing, as well as of the cursive, an unidentified language. He had found the sound values of the letters in the two scripts without a bilingual text to assist in establishing a vocabulary. Griffith's decipherment, although far from complete, had made it possible for almost any scholar to understand about fifty words in the Meroitic script.

Reisner said that the great significance of this contribution to knowledge was that it had enabled him (Reisner) to read the names and titles of about 130 Ethiopian kings and queens.

He gave a splendid tribute to Griffith by saying that, without his brilliant language interpretation, the results of the archaeological excavations in the Sudan would have been defeated in large part by the inability of the excavators to identify the kings and queens found. I was able to remind Reisner that the reverse was also true, and I had heard it expressed by Griffith. Griffith's second wife, when a young woman studying Egyptology, had been our guest in a *dahabieh* on the Nile for a month. This began a friendship that lasted.

After their marriage, Corinna and I were with the Griffiths at Oxford. I happened to ask him what stood out in his memory as a unique achievement in his distinguished career as a philologist. Without a moment's hesitation, he replied it was the opportunity afforded him by Reisner's archaeological data to decipher, in part, an unknown language without a bilingual clue. Here was a pleasant example of an archaeologist and a philologist acknowledging a debt each owed to the other.

The first reference to an expedition into Nubia from Egypt appeared in a record made during the reign of Sneferu, who set down as notable the year in which ships had been built for the devastation of the land of Negroes. He reported bringing back 7,000 men and women captives and 200,000 head of cattle.

There was no evidence of active relations between Egypt and Ethiopia until Dynasty XII, when the policy of establishing agencies as fortified posts, not for conquest of the people but for the caravan trade, was adopted. The kings of Egypt in transit left behind them beautiful temples instead of devastated land and an abject conquered people.

At Meroe, Reisner dug up a number of objects imported from Alexandria into the Meroitic kingdom; the earliest were two silver vessels dating from the first half of the third century B.C. The day before Rebecca and I reached camp, a gang of his men clearing the debris from an Ethiopian tomb came across an exquisite piece of pottery that was unquestionably of Attic Greek manufacture. It was of a helmeted warrior on a prancing horse mounted on a pedestal. At the back of the warrior was a cup of red figured design with a handle. Rebecca made a charming drawing of it.

Several days later, a splendid bronze warrior was brought into camp. At Meroe, jewelers had practiced ancient Egyptian traditions with skill, as was shown in earrings and bracelets; also, a new use was made of enameled detail in bracelets and in ornamented gold disks.

On February 2, 1930, Commander Noel Wheeler, then in charge of Reisner's work at Semna, Phelps Clauson, his assistant, and I left Cairo by train for Shellal. From there we were to take a post boat into the Nubia I knew well from having seen often, on other government boats, sailing *dahabiehs,* and for a time on a luxurious private steamer.

Something fundamental had gone wrong with the engine of the boat bound for Wadi Halfa, our destination, and as a result we were much delayed. This afforded me an opportunity to see more of the country through which we passed than on previous trips. There was less cultivation than on the lower river and no unbroken line of distant mountain ranges. The landscape was varied and bold in character, with rocky heights in darker colors often close to the water's edge, as in the dramatic black gorge of Kalabsheh.

Since time immemorial, scenes above the river banks have remained the same and have always been enlivened by a refrain of shrill, raised voices and by the echo of laughter and song as people worked at their tasks—such as the husking of maize in flat baskets, the threshing of *dhoura* (corn), the grinding of grain, the thud of the *shadoof* raising water to the level of the crops.

The Negroid element in Lower Nubia was pronounced in the noticeably poverty-stricken inhabitants living an isolated, primitive agricultural life, producing little beyond poorly made bowls of Nile mud almost exclusively red with black tops, similar to those found in the early pre-dynastic period, relying on the sale of dates, goats, and baskets for the few luxuries imported from Egypt.

A group of unnaturally silent men near a dilapidated *feluka* attracted my passing attention on account of the abject misery indicated by tattered rags that showed pitiably thin legs and arms and by hollow eyes in sad, flat-featured, broad faces. They looked underfed and helpless to meet the needs of modern existence. And the livestock they had unloaded was in no better condition, some goats and a bedraggled cow with a calf scarcely able to stand because of weakness.

I preferred to let my thoughts dwell on the prosperity of Nubia in the ancient period beginning in Dynasty XII (1991–1786 B.C.) and lasting through the New Kingdom (1570–1085 B.C.), when Egyptian kings gained political control of Ethiopia. The Egyptians became great merchants, importing into Egypt for the royal treasury, from regions south of the second cataract, ebony, ivory, gold, panther skins (worn by priests), ostrich feathers, resins, and black slaves. Their expeditions, comprising a fleet of ships in constant river traffic, furnished employment to the villages of Nubia which lay in a protected area behind the massive forts of Semna and those farther south built by the Egyptians in late Dynasty XII. The trade brought a significant change in the economic condition of Nubia, and the people shared in an era of wealth that made it possible for them to import Egyptian-made goods. It seemed strange to me that, even under such favorable conditions, the ancient Nubians had remained backward in cultural development, even their pottery being crude, although the potter's wheel had been in use among Egyptians since very early times.

From Wadi Halfa we were to continue the trip to Semna in a Ford that was famous in archaeological circles as having been the first car to reach the Anglo-Egyptian Sudan. This was in 1924, and it was taken by George Vaillant, who was excavating for Reisner.

I regarded the Ford with respect, even though it did not seem to have much to go on except its reputation. The runningboards, which were broken in several places, were held together by wire and rope, and the same kind of repairs had been performed on the badly cracked hood. The most ingenious mending was a piece of narrow wood inserted where a vital part of the brake was missing. The engine creaked and groaned as we started off along an abandoned railway embankment, now used as a road. I told them I wondered if on this trip it could maintain its record of shortening the journey from Halfa to Semna by camel. About two hours out, my doubts apparently seemed about to be confirmed when the engine jerked ominously and then came to a full stop. But I underestimated the mechanical ability of an alert old Sudani in Reisner's employ. He crawled underneath the car, then reappeared, greasy but smiling, and motioned us to get inside again. After a few uncertain sputterings, the engine picked up and the car began to run smoothly at a slow pace. Our canvas bags of personal belongings fastened on behind at a rather precarious angle beat a steady tattoo as they flapped in a high wind that sprang up against us, hindering our crab-like motions forward.

Soon we were at Abousir. In the distance were mountains and the desert, and near by the pylons of a temple, the minaret of a mosque in a charming little village, and, above all, the beauty of the second cataract with quantities of small islands formed by rocks and rushing water. The blackness of the rocks and the greenness of tamarisk trees made enchanting contrasts. Beyond the cataract we rode into the desert, and after several hours the route brought us back to the Nile, before we were confronted by a great fortress of the Middle Empire built on a high rock rising sheer from the river level. Close by was a small temple erected by Sesostris III in Dynasty XII, who reigned from 1878 to 1842 b.c.

From thence our route twisted, going away from the Nile and then returned to it through a picturesque gorge. We had a combination of ancient fortresses, ruins of temples and remains of tombs dating to the early Christian era. Later on we saw a chapel built by Tuthmosis III of Dynasty XVIII. On the final lap of the trip we were in the midst of desert heights that camels had taken in their stride, but on the rising levels the Sudani, still smiling, spent more and more time under the car, trying to make disgruntled parts co-operate. After twelve hours of struggle, hungry and exhausted, our party found the expedition camp at Semna a welcome sight.

Here, the current of the Nile was broken by a series of cataracts or rapids, extending for a distance of about sixty miles. On the shore, a large fleet of boats with cargoes of dates had gathered to pass upstream through the middle channel of rocky islands. It was as though we were back in the days of Sesostris III, nearly two thousand years before Christ, when the river route as far as the third and fourth cataracts had similar trading fleets.

The caravans, where they were exposed to attack, as at Semna, were protected by forts within signaling distance by smoke or by calls across the river. This was the situation here. On the east bank, built at the top of the last of a line of rocky hills and separated from the river by a wind-swept ravine, was an impressive fort. Below the raging cataract waters and almost directly opposite on the west bank was another fort, equally impressive. Both of them were of the same kind of masonry, with massive walls of thick brick-work, strengthened by layers of horizontal wooden beams, and resting on a foundation platform of rock or granite rubble.

After three years of Reisner's excavations, it was a very much more interesting Semna than I had seen before. It was quite a scramble to the flat top of Semna West, but it was worth the effort in gaining an idea of the general topography of the region near the present boundary of the Anglo-Egyptian Sudan. The main idea in the construction of all these forts was to force enemy attacks to be directed against troops lining the ramparts. The outside walls could be scaled only by ladders, and the water supply was protected by an inner stairway of ninety-five steps to a pool at the ground level in the center of the fortifications. After a personal inspection I was not surprised to hear that none of these forts had been captured.

I went with Wheeler to the rocky island of Uronarti, three miles to the north, where there was another fort. Several times we almost capsized, but the Sudani sailors were skillful in handling the boat. When I was asked if I would like to visit some of the eleven forts fifty miles south of Semna, my answer was an emphatic "no."

Semna had yielded rich finds. In addition to informative rock inscriptions of Tuthmosis II and Tuthmosis III and the ruins of a temple, there were statuettes and stelae dating back to the Middle Kingdom, and for the New Kingdom, royal edicts, inscriptions of Egyptian viceroys, and ornamental weapons. Complete plans of the forts had given Reisner the greatest satisfaction.

On my return to Giza and Harvard Camp, Reisner summarized for me what his expeditions to the Sudan had accomplished from the first reconnoitering trip in 1914 until the close of this 1930 season. The fort buildings and tombs of the Egyptian colony at Kerma had been excavated. So had the Ethiopian temples at Barkal, as well as the pyramids of five kings of Ethiopia and Egypt. In addition, the tombs of twenty kings of Ethiopia and seventy-two queens at Napata, and the pyramids of forty-three kings and reigning queens at Meroe had been excavated.

"The examination of the tombs of the kings of Ethiopia has recovered the outline of the history of the Sudan for eleven centuries, from 750 B.C. to 350 A.D.," Reisner said.

THE CONTINUITY OF EGYPT

1931-1932

32. The Beiram Festival

RAMADAN WAS THE MONTH in which the Koran was sent down to the Prophet Muhammad from God, and fasting was prescribed during the entire month for all Moslems. No food or water was allowed between the hours of sunrise and sunset. On my arrival at Harvard Camp in 1931, there was still one more week of Ramadan, and Reisner was preoccupied with the physical hardship on his men.

That same day, soon after a late lunch, Reisner took me to the current dig. Strained faces, ragged nerves, and a tendency to be quarrelsome were very noticeable among the crews of our usually cheerful Qufti, who were moving some heavy boulders. As we lingered in the eastern cemetery, I saw Reisner's eyes follow those of the men raised to watch the sun about to disappear behind the western horizon. The instant the sunset gun was fired from the citadel, with one accord all dropped whatever they were doing and rushed to the nearest water. Reisner, on hearing the gun, repeated several times with satisfaction, "One more day of the fast is finished."

During the final two days of Ramadan the weather cooled off, and, with it, the tension of the men. Reisner shared the holiday mood of old and young busily preparing for *Beiram,* often referred to as the "feast of sweets," from the quantities of them consumed during the celebrations after the fast. Much to my amazement, he decided to take me into Cairo himself to watch the excitement as, after what was termed "a day of waiting," Ramadan was over at the first sight of the new moon.

We motored past the tombs of the Caliphs, that spectacular city of the dead below the Mokattam Hills, which we reached from the Citadel by dropping down through winding streets. The approaching sunset cast a glow over endless shrines and domes and minarets. And then we entered the *Muski,* where we got out and walked through dense crowds.

Overhead banners and the crescent of Egypt waved in the midst of the rustling leaves of crossed palms. Women and children were seated in carts, the wheels ornamented with pink and green paper. Butcher shops were doing a brisk trade in meats painted in bright colors, fish and fowl amusingly decorated with paper flowers, and whole animals with an apple in the mouth. Live sheep sold at auction were bringing high prices, and glittering trinkets were exposed for sale on all sides. The clink of silver exchanging hands was audible above the hum of the voices of men and women buying fast and furiously. Laughter and good will were contagious. Everyone was talking at once and exhibiting their purchases even to strangers like Reisner and me. We saw many of our Qufti men getting new garments and scarfs for themselves and dresses for their girls.

The atmosphere of expectancy reached a climax when someone shouted: "I see the new moon!" The sound of excited voices was lost in the roar of exploding cannon.

Ramadan was over!

We stayed well after the evening prayer, wandering casually through brilliantly lighted streets where Moslems crowded the cafés. On the way home, we stopped the car to watch Moslems feasting in groups in a large open space near Giza, and a great mass of people enjoying native music and story telling.

Next morning, I waited to have breakfast with Reisner, as I was expected to exchange *Beiram* greetings with our men in his office. It was well towards nine when they began to turn up, all freshly dressed and in the best of holiday spirits. Reisner spoke a few words in Arabic to each man, calling him by name and referring to some intimate details of his personal life. When, after a general handshaking, they disappeared down the hill for a day of celebration in town, Reisner did not seem inclined to settle down to the customary office routine. I had found their obvious worship of the *Mudir* and the laughter and jokes an agreeable interlude from tombs, and I listened with pleasure to his comments on the important village of Quft, two hours by motor to the north of Luxor, that had produced such "Quftis," as his native staff were called.

It was Petrie, as far back as the early 1880's, when he began to excavate for the Egypt Exploration Fund, who had discovered the superior quality of the inhabitants of this village as "diggers." And Reisner, in two years of uncovering Coptos, an ancient site in the vicinity of Quft, had become a part of the community life of the modern village. From that time on, for all his expeditions, the natives employed (including those who were house servants) were exclusively men from Quft. He further restricted the selection to members of families that were interrelated by marriage and formed a closely knit, clannish group. He made it clearly understood that if anything disappeared from a dig, the entire native staff would be dismissed. He told me that he attributed to this system the fact that his expeditions were considered unique in having absolutely no thefts.

Reisner got to talking, as he frequently did to me, of his long-time head *reis,* Ahmad Said, as an example of what an intelligent peasant of a good village family could accomplish when given highly specialized training by an interested foreigner. He referred to Ahmad's having come to him at the age of twelve and staying on until as head *reis,* he was in complete charge of the native staff, which averaged about two hundred at an important site. Ahmad was responsible for engaging the men, planning their work, checking the results, and personally keeping a duplicate record in Arabic which, at the end of each excavating day, was compared with the English one made by the Egyptologist in charge.

"The records never failed to tally," Reisner told me with obvious pride. This close association with his head *reis* had meant much to

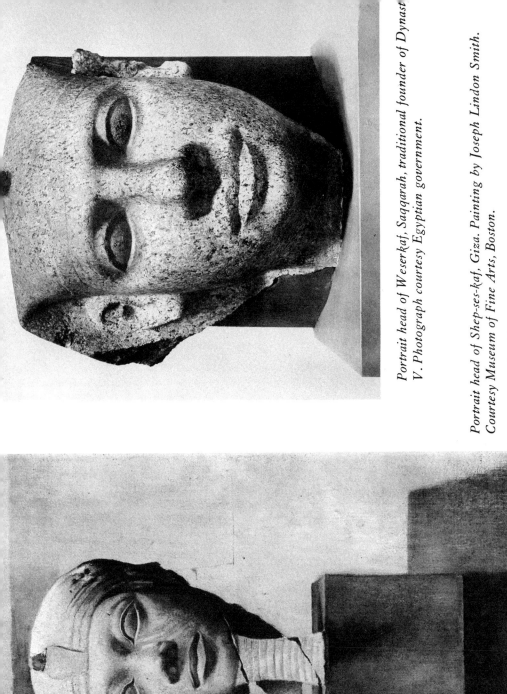

Portrait head of Weserkaf, Saqqarah, traditional founder of Dynasty V. Photograph courtesy Egyptian government.

Portrait head of Shep-ses-kaf, Giza. Painting by Joseph Lindon Smith. Courtesy Museum of Fine Arts, Boston.

Zoser's Temple, the first building of dressed stone, Saqqarah, designed by the architect Imhotep. Note fluted columns. Photograph courtesy the Egyptian government.

him, and he pointed out with satisfaction that many of the Quftis who had their experience under Ahmad were now themselves head *reis* in numberless excavations elsewhere. He was telling of one of the older sons, who was getting on well as a *reis* at Harvard Camp, and the youngest, who was being educated at a school to become one of Reisner's office secretaries, with the job of making reference cards of data to be used in publications, when one of the staff arrived by motor from Cairo and reported that he had passed an impressive line of camels with handsome trappings, each beast carrying two wide boxes balanced over the middle of its back. Reisner remarked that they were on their way to the Moslem cemetery situated on the edge of the ancient quarry beyond the Pyramid of Cheops. "Joe," he said, "let's go and watch the *rahma,* the offering of bread ceremony, at the individual graves." I nodded acceptance, and he ordered the car.

We arrived at the cemetery well in advance of the slowly approaching camels. Behind them were black-draped women and men in dignified attire on foot, while in the rear straggled the "needy" in the hope of later supplementing their customary meager diet from the ceremonial offerings. Many in this group looked hungry.

The Moslem at the head of the procession of mourners, having noticed Reisner and me seated inconspicuously at a distance, courteously invited us to a point of vantage close to the entrance of the cemetery. There were many Sheikhs present. We watched a number of mothers or wives perform the prescribed ritual of repeating the *Sura* declaring the unity of God before leaving a ceremonial bread offering, and in many instances an entire family, including solemn-eyed children, sat in a group around a grave. But the poor at the gates stood in silence and appeared too timid to pass inside the cemetery to take from the individual graves the food that was their perquisite from an age-old tradition on this very site.

Reisner reminded me I was witnessing living scenes re-enacted from those I had painted from the walls of the tomb of Idut, a priest of Dynasty VI, close by, where bread offerings were being given to the dead at some festival of long ago. Even the shapes of the loaves I had seen being taken from the boxes on the camels' backs were similar to the painted ones in this priest's tomb dating back forty-five centuries.

I felt the continuity of events in Egypt in realizing that, before the building of Cheops' Pyramid was started, with masses of rock for the core taken from the quarry near where Reisner and I sat, the dead were honored by the same kind of loaves of bread placed on graves in this *Beiram* ceremony of the Moslems, and that probably a forlorn group of the poor of the ancient Empire had patiently waited near by, looking exactly like the present-day pathetic creatures for whom I now felt sorry.

Reisner and I were so absorbed that our usual lunch hour came and went, and we returned to camp just as the staff was about to leave the table. Reisner called out, "Atito, bring us anything." When Busheer, the second *safragi,* entered, Reisner remarked, "I forgot Atito is back in his home village; it is the first *Beiram* after his little girl's death, and he must perform the rites at her grave."

Here was the ancient past, Moslem tradition, and our own household doing the same thing.

33. *Influence of Ancient Religion and Tradition*

I HAD LEFT HARVARD CAMP and the Old Kingdom art to come up river to Luxor to paint some of the splendid reliefs at Karnak of Dynasty XVIII (1570–1085 B.C.), thus moving chronologically through a period of more than one thousand years. And in Luxor Temple I had just finished pictures of Amenhotep III, the father of Akhenaten, a fine head of Ramesses II in one of his chapels, and a portrait of his charming Queen, Nefertari. In looking around for my next subject, I saw that the light was particularly good on a superb figure of the great conqueror, Alexander (332–323 B.C.), on the outside wall of a chapel. As I started to paint him, it intrigued me to realize how each conqueror in turn was conquered by Egypt's ancient traditions. For instance, here was Alexander with the magnificence of his Egyptian headdress as a "king-god" outdoing the Egyptians themselves. While I was at work, my thoughts frequently lingered casually and pleasantly on something connected with my chosen subject, and as I sat hour after hour in front of Alexander, I was glad that the cult of the divinity of the ruler appealed to his imagination and that he had joined, with great artistic success, the imposing processions of the Egyptian "king-gods" carved on the walls of the temples up and down the Nile.

I wondered whether it was the Oracle of Siwa that prevented him from making the mistake of the Persians, whose public insults to the animal gods of Egypt earned the resentment of the entire population. But the Greek conqueror, by accepting their local and national gods and goddesses *in toto,* caused the Egyptians to voluntarily become a part of the Hellenic Empire of Alexander's dreams. Therefore, although the advent of Alexander and his successors created a modern world in embryo, the Greek conqueror adopted much of the form and sub-stance of an ancient pagan religion. Several times my brush had yielded to the charms of Isis, and it was easy for me to understand how, when Egypt was a province of Rome, the worship of Isis as the mother-goddess and of her son Horus had become popular among the sophisticated Roman governors. The cult of Isis found its way to Rome, but a great though ultimately abortive reversal of this trend occurred when a new faith was preached by Saint Mark on his first visit to Egypt early in the Christian era. The Virgin Mary and the infant Jesus were a more inti-mate conception of a mother and child than Isis and Horus, and there was the added claim of the Holy Family in flight having taken sanctuary on the soil of Egypt, thereby invoking the desert law of hospitality.

Naturally, a future life presented no difficulty of credence to a people familiar with the death and rebirth of Osiris, the mighty god of the underworld.

I remembered an explanation given me by an archaeologist of a scene I had admired on the outer enclosure of a temple. It was a series of standing birds, and in addition to claws, they were provided with hands upraised in praise. The ancient sculptor had depicted an amazing humility in the expression of the eyes fixed on the cartouche containing the king's name. This was the *rhakyt* bird, symbolizing the people not

179

permitted to look into the face of the king or to approach the many gods of ancient Egypt in inner shrines of temples, accessible only to the king and priests. Small wonder that, with their own gods remote and indifferent, the doctrine of *one* Supreme God personally interested in each one of them, down to the humblest, spread like wildfire among the people in the land of the pharaohs.

In the fourth century after Christ, these indigenous inhabitants, who were descendants of the ancient Egyptians, became Christians and were later to be known by their Arab conquerors as Copts. Annie Quibell had taken Corinna and me to see their first church built in old Cairo on the site of the spot where, according to Christian tradition, the Holy Family had rested. She told us that when Egypt was under the Byzantine Empire and ruled from Constantinople, many of the early schisms within the church were fought out at Alexandria, the Egyptian city founded by Alexander. Theological decisions made there were not to the liking of the Christianized inhabitants of Egypt, who adhered with a blind faith to the simple doctrines preached by Saint Mark, and the Copts suffered persecution during their constant religious conflicts with the decadent Byzantine Romans, and the "Era of Martyrs" was recorded in the annals of the Coptic church.

The Arab hordes that swept over Egypt in A.D. 640 were welcomed by the Christian Copts as far preferable to their Roman oppressors. The wild desert tribes brought with them a fiercely fanatical religion based on the worship of one god alone, as believed in by the Copts, and an inherited taste for poetry. In their nomad existence, they knew but little of government, and at first were satisfied to leave the machinery of political administration very largely to the conquered population. For several generations, all official documents of the Arabs in Egypt were written in Greek or Coptic. And they continued to carry on an organization in the villages and provinces similar to that of the ancient Egyptians. Here again was a legacy of a past that has remained to the present time.

But later Moslem rulers began to persecute the Coptic minority who had refused to embrace Islam. These Copts were made to wear a distinctive dress and were restricted in the trades they might take up. But the Copts, in turn, conquered their conquerors, by bequeathing to them their own inheritance of the practice of magic, which was the foundation of the religion of the ancient Egyptians. Magic was forbidden in Islam, but proved irresistible to the imaginative Arabs, and was adopted as passed on to them by the Copts. Perhaps the most absurd examples of a belief in magic have persisted among the Moslems living in towns as well as villages, and Corinna and I frequently encountered them long after the Lord Cromer era.

Moreover, the pastoral Arab tribes knew nothing of agriculture, but the heritage of the indigenous Copts, whose ancestors had filled the granaries of Egypt to overflowing, taught their Moslem conquerors how to till the rich soil of the Nile Valley. The simple Arabs were caught in the toils of an ancient tradition, and the *fellaheen,* who are the vast majority of the Moslem population today, are the victims of a political system handed down by the pharaohs to the rich modern Egyptian landlord, keeping the tillers of the soil in the Nile Valley in a condition hardly above that of slaves.

It often amused Corinna and me, in talking to a *fellah* working in his fields, when, in reply to a question about when his crop would ripen, he would give his answer after calculating, not by his own Moslem calendar of the lunar month, but by the Coptic calendar taken from that in use among the ancient Egyptians. By this calendar, the Moslem agriculturist prepares his ground and sows and reaps his crops, using the same processes and primitive tools as those employed by his prototypes on the walls of ancient tombs.

In Egypt, the past is never dead, but very much alive. Religious forms have changed, but the life of man is guided by customs and practices which developed millenia ago. That this is true of other societies, even the most advanced, only the most observing and scientific of students can be fully aware.

An example of ancient tradition which continues to influence ceremonial procedure in the Egypt of today occurred during the "Feast of Opet." I became interested rather early in this annual chief festival in honor of Amon lasting twenty-four days, and had painted at Karnak in 1906 a long detail in which the ceremonial barque containing the enshrined god was the center of the ancient river procession between Karnak and Luxor.

Some years later, I had painted a series of highly colored river barques of Amon in a Theban tomb at the suggestion of Harry Burton. The tomb scene showed the god Amon's journey during the "Feast of the Valley," to visit the temples on the west bank of the Nile. The sacred barques were arriving at quays to be carried on men's shoulders to individual shrines in temples.

Also, in Queen Hatshepsut's chapel at Karnak, I did a study representing the final stages of this river feast. As late as in some of the Greco-Roman temples in Egypt, a feast of Amon, considered a "visitation" festival, was concerned with a river trip.

One afternoon in 1931, I was putting the finishing touches to a picture of reliefs on an end wall of the court of Ramesses II in Luxor Temple. My subject was a line of sacrificial fatted oxen, with gaily ornamented horns and necks, branded "Feast of Opet," in solemn procession, with the King leading them and priests following behind. I turned, on being greeted by an old native friend, Hajji Mohamed Abdalla, who spoke English. With him was Sheikh Hofni, *wakeel* (custodian) of the tomb of the Moslem saint, Sheikh Ab'l'Haggag, which was inside the "intrusive" mosque dating to A.D. 800 and a conspicuous landmark in the Luxor Temple.

Through Abdalla as interpreter, Sheikh Hofni explained that I might be interested to learn that Moslems of today had "borrowed" this ancient ceremony (of which I was painting the oxen), in honor of their Sheikh Ab'l'Haggag. He mentioned similarities between the Moslem celebration and that of the Feast of Opet, such as an annual procession featuring a sacred boat. In the Moslem ceremony the boat contained the coffin of their saint and was placed in a cart dragged through the streets by men, instead of the boat's being on the river with an Egyptian god in it. But the oxen in the Moslem procession were much decorated around their necks and horns, exactly like the ones in stone, and just as fat and large.

On observing my genuine interest in what he was saying, he invited me to see the sacred boat belonging to Sheikh Ab'l'Haggag. The three of us walked through the huge pylons, with the sunset glow giving emphasis to the gilded crescent above the dome of the mosque. We scrambled up a steep, rough hillside and through a narrow alley with the middle distance dominated by the ruins of a mud minaret, supposed to date from the time of the Moslem saint.

From here we went into an inner court facing the main door to the mosque. The chatter of women flitting about instantly ceased, and they stared at me through slits in their head veils as Sheikh Hofni took me to the boat made for the Saint's procession long centuries ago. Curiously, it had not become "old in its wood."

It was a simple scene, but one of extreme drama, as the procession of the Feast of Opet I had known on walls of temples lived again in Sheikh Hofni's description. He told me that the modern procession no longer had a double line of sphinxes to pass through from a gate in Karnak to the pylons of Luxor Temple. But, he assured me, I would not miss the sphinxes when I could see the Moslem procession along that same route, and after it, through the night, rich and poor alike eating buffalo meat, listening to the Koran, and watching dancing girls.

It all came from an intermingling of religious rites, feasting and entertainment, recorded in hieroglyphic inscriptions which described what happened when the sacred barque of Amon rested each night at a different station during the Feast of Opet.

During a brief stay at Luxor, in the days when one still rode a donkey over the Theban Plain, I was painting across the river in the Ramesseum when, one afternoon after my work for the day was finished, an archaeologist friend living near Medinet Habu took me into a number of the tombs with painted reliefs in the Sheikh Abd'-el-Qurna Necropolis, some of which I had not previously visited.

My departure was delayed until it was a race with darkness to arrive at the boat waiting to ferry me across the river to the Luxor side. This happened because I was held up for quite an appreciable length of time by the passing of a funeral procession. The deceased was a local *omda* (mayor) and a large crowd had collected.

Many professional female mourners preceded the coffin. The way they were grouped, their draperies, position of the bodies, movement of the feet, upraised arms, and also the expression of their faces, as shrill cries issued from their mouths, was reminiscent of long ago. I had just been in a tomb where, on a wall, there was a painted scene of a funeral procession for which these female mourners might have posed.

In the tomb I had been attracted by a little girl depicted among the women mourners being taught the funeral rite young so that the tradition would not die out. Now over three thousand years later, in the same locality, my fascinated eyes watched a small female child of today going through the same performance as her elders, so that she in turn could pass it on, as the child of long ago had been taught to do.

There was one difference between the women mourners of then and now. These I was watching each had a strip of blue cloth about the size of a large handkerchief, which she was either twisting in her raised hands or stretching back of the neck, then over the forehead, the emphasis of the accompanying wailing being at the end of each stretching motion. And the child was outdoing the others with her strip of blue cloth. Certainly she would be able to pass on this part of the rite!

There were so many customs and ceremonies of modern Egyptians I identified as being based upon ancient tradition that I thought I might, in some tomb or other, discover the origin of the stretching of the blue cloth as part of the rhythm of the *zagareet* shrieks of female funeral mourners of today.

The power of laughter, like that of grief, has survived in every age from the earliest known pre-dynastic period of Egypt down through the period of foreign domination which began with the Persians. There are many well-known examples of caricatures of ancient court life existing in papyri owned by several museums. One of the most amusing is a papyrus of animals in which the vizier and other high court dignitaries can be identified in hippopotami, crocodiles, and other animals standing erect and looking pompous and pleased with themselves. It

184

is impossible not to burst into laughter at their absurd antics which are similar to modern dance steps. Some of the papyri of this nature probably illustrated popular fables.

Limestone flakes, called ostraca, have been found that were obviously caricatures and used as illustrations. Incidentally, they were sketched by artists in a very free spirit, but observing the conventions of classical Egyptian art, which made them all the more laughable.

Maspero showed me several of these ostraca, scratched in black pigment on limestone flakes that he said were discovered in the Valley of the Kings among the vast mass of chips lying about everywhere from excavations of tombs. He believed they were jokes in stone made by the men working long ago on the royal tombs. He also mentioned an ostracon that had been picked up in one of the small rooms off the burial chamber of the tomb of Tuthmosis IV, who had a short reign. His tomb was unfinished, entrance being achieved today by sliding down the face of the rock because steps normally leading to a tomb door had not been cut. This ostracon Maspero believed was an amusing caricature of the King himself, made by a workman and tossed aside at random.

And even tomb robbers had their fun. In one deep pit, their point of entry was clearly visible. Also there was evidence that the robbers had removed the mummy wrappings from a dog and a monkey. They had taken a fragment of the monkey's coffin and propped him up on it, standing upright. Then they had put the dog on his hind feet beside the monkey, with the noses of the dog and monkey touching.

This was a very old joke that was still funny.

And even today I discovered in my archaeological work that laughter once saved a situation in which I was involved.

In the early spring of 1936, the signing of the Anglo-Egyptian treaty seemed to be imminent and feeling ran high. Regrettable incidents were frequent when nerves were made tense by the strain of the fast of Ramadan, and in the reaction of the feast that ended it. Reisner and I had unwisely chosen the afternoon to call on a fellow archaeologist friend in Cairo about to sail. The dense crowds were orderly until, on the return trip, we found ourselves in the midst of a riot and realized that we had happened on to a "float" decorated to attract native attention, with accusations against the British written in large Arabic script on high boards placed against its sides. An agitator standing on the float had begun a provocative speech which was greeted by shouts of glee from rioters already elated by their successful attack on a tram.

At a particularly tense moment, there came into view a small cart drawn by a diminutive donkey. On the front end sat a large group of boys, and at the rear end of the planks was a very stout Egyptian female. In their eagerness to view the float, all of the boys jumped off the cart at the same moment, so that the donkey was overbalanced by the woman's immense weight and was bodily lifted into the air, where he hung limply with his feet madly struggling to regain the road. The terrified woman never budged. It was an absurd spectacle! The men nearest began to laugh immoderately. Others looked and saw the plight of the small donkey and the heavy woman. They, too, laughed. It did not take long for all eyes to turn in the direction of the cart, and a good-natured roar of amusement rose above the agitator's voice. Even the police burst into hearty laughter. From his position on the float, the agitator could not see the cart. He thought that the ridicule was directed against him. As his voice faltered, a quick-witted policeman managed to get to him while the general attention of the crowd was focussed on the donkey's dilemma. Unnoticed, the agitator was led off under arrest.

When someone had the presence of mind to remove the woman's bulky form from the cart, forcibly, thus allowing the donkey's feet to reach the ground, a great sigh of relief went up from what had been a raging mob. The crowd, by now thoroughly good-natured and having completely forgotten the agitator and his harangue against the British, melted away.

REISNER AND
THE LENGTHENING SHADOW

1932–1933

34. *The Enduring Mind of a Scholar*

I N LATE NOVEMBER, 1932, after a brief stay in the United States, Corinna and I sailed for Egypt on an Italian steamer. At Port Said, I encountered difficulty with the police passport officials on board, owing to my having written "artist" as my profession, which in Egypt meant "artiste," a cabaret performer. These performers had been giving the authorities so much trouble in Cairo that they were ranked next to drug traffickers as undesirables. And when I wrote down our proposed destination as Harvard *Camp,* the police repeated to one another Harvard *"Café,"* their suspicions confirmed. Corinna managed to extricate me from a situation that contained a threat of being denied entry into the country by further explaining I was an archaeologist on my way to join an American expedition at the Pyramids of Giza, a combination known to them. The passport was stamped and landing cards issued.

At the Cairo railroad station, we were told that Dr. Max Meyerhoff had operated successfully on Reisner for a cataract of the left eye, and that Reisner was back at Harvard Camp. He met us at the entrance to the familiar court, and his joy at having the Smiths back was apparent through his dark glasses. Reisner had left the hospital December 15, and the steady improvement in the vision of his left eye continued until after New Year's Day. Then I noticed he began holding his hand up

187

at a little distance from his left eye, wriggling his fingers, then lowering his hand again and looking sad. The day after this performance, Reisner admitted to me that the shadow over his left eye had returned and that he had decided to consult Dr. Meyerhoff. He wanted both Corinna and me to be with him. I knew, from Meyerhoff's expression after a cursory examination, that the news was bad, but I believed Reisner had realized it from his calm acceptance of the verdict. The retina of the left eye was detached, which meant a second operation in a hospital, and time was a factor in saving the sight. I heard Reisner murmur, as though speaking to himself, "And the left was my *good* eye."

I exchanged cable messages with the trustees of the Museum, who suggested that Reisner be brought to America immediately to have the benefit of Dr. William Wilmer's expert care. But as sea travel was out of the question while Reisner was in serious condition, there was no alternative; the operation must be performed in Cairo by the Egyptian oculist who had been trained in Vienna. By January 3, Reisner was back in the Anglo-American Hospital which he had left so recently in high hopes. Corinna was in the room next to his to be available for night calls, as well as to stay with him most of the day, as did Evelyn Perkins, his devoted secretary. Mrs. Reisner was too far from well herself to help in his illness. Two days later, the second operation took place, done under a local anesthetic and lasting two hours. Reisner's courage never faltered. Alas! the detached-retina operation failed of its purpose, and within a short time it was obvious that vision in the left eye would thereafter be limited to distinguishing light from darkness. Almost at once, his life in the sick room became that of his office regime. He was serene and cheerful and never referred to his condition.

He took tremendous satisfaction in the fact that William Stevenson Smith from the Boston Museum, now on his field staff at Giza, had made an excellent start in collecting his material for writing the history of the art of the Old Kingdom for the expedition.

The way Reisner faced the tragedy of approaching loss of sight had made it turn into a thing of little account. His mental faculties remained unimpaired by a grueling experience that would have destroyed all

188

initiative and activity in a man of a lesser intellectual stature. Nothing distracted his attention from the manuscript, on which he was doing what he called the final "tidying up." It was a comprehensive study of the structural development of the tomb from pre-dynastic times. He seemed so happy and triumphant that I could not feel sorry for him.

"It's going quickly, Joe, and well," he once interrupted his dictation to remark to me, then went on, speaking to Evelyn, "Have you got that?" She nodded and read aloud in a sing-song voice: "Man standing, left hand on breast, right one grasping a goose and below something else. I can't quite make out what, Doctor."

Reisner completely forgot my presence as he was mentally figuring out what that "something else below the goose" could be.

I contrasted this example of Spartan fortitude with what I saw had happened to poor Davis when I made a brief visit to him on his *dahabieh* during his final season of excavating twenty years earlier, in 1912. Although younger than Reisner, Davis had visibly become an old man, even more so mentally than physically.

He seemed to want me to be near him, but most of the time he just sat with a lack of animation in his face and in a silence I could not break down by attempts to arouse his interest in his own notable record as an excavator. He listened as though my words were meaningless. It was a pathetic ending to an active business career as a copper magnate, followed by ten years of personal participation in excavations.

His interest in archaeology was that of a hobbyist; therefore, at the first test, it was quick to go. But with Reisner, archaeology was his whole life. Sightless eyes and increasingly impaired health would never prevent his keen brain from functioning and, with the enduring interest of the scholar, passing on to others his vast fund of scientific knowledge.

Just before Reisner left Harvard Camp for the hospital, he had summoned the head natives and members of the staff and told them I was to be in charge of the expedition during his absence. The next week we did a little successful excavating in our dig and found an untouched burial in the northern chamber of a *mastaba* shaft in the western cemetery. It was of a man who lay in an uninscribed wooden

189

coffin. There was nothing else in the chamber. We got the coffin to the surface intact. A much more interesting discovery was an "intrusive burial" in a Dynasty IV pit in the great necropolis of court officials to the west of the Pyramid of Cheops. I had been down into the pit with Lieutenant Commander Noel Wheeler of the expedition, and on tapping the wall behind a shelf, we found an opening in which lay a small body, in mummy wrappings, but no evidence of a coffin. The wrappings did not crumble to the touch, so we got the body into one of the magazines without damage. As Derry was expected to come out to the camp shortly, I sent a message to him that there was a mummy to be examined. Corinna arrived for the event.

It proved to be the body of a small woman lying within an outer layer of beautiful linen wrappings, pieces of which Derry unrolled intact. There were no ornaments, but on a bandage on the right thigh was an inscription in ink in perfect condition. The head was bandaged in the shape of the conventional wig over a neat, well-formed skull. Eyes and eyebrows were outlined in paint, and a dainty nose and lips were so realistically represented in the linen that I thought I was looking at the actual features of a young and lovely girl. I was amazed when the removal of head draperies, firm to the touch, disclosed straggling gray hair. A mask over the face came away intact in Derry's hand. A moment later, he had laid aside girlish round breasts with pink nipples, so charmingly modeled and colored in the linen garment in which the mummy was clad as to have the appearance of the original organs, and next he removed beautifully shaped hips. Beneath further layers of linen, the tissues of the body exposed to view were nothing more than fragments of skin.

Derry's only interest in that pathetic undraped skeleton was the clue to the dating of this "intrusive burial," made possible from this procedure of layers of linen wrappings molded to represent the actual organs of a body. All these examples, he said belonged to the ancient empire, at a time when Egyptians had not yet perfected embalming techniques, which at a later date preserved the face and entire body, thus making linen effigies of the organs unnecessary.

But science meant nothing to me when I was miserable from having been a party to the destruction of the handiwork of someone in ancient times who had fixed up a grandmother of the family to appear as a young girl. He had done more: he had managed somehow to get the body laid away in the burial pit of an important person of the same period. I heartily wished that I had not by chance tapped the wall behind an alcove, thereby revealing a deception that injured no one but guaranteed perpetual youth to a little old lady of long ago.

AT SAQQARAH AND ABYDOS

1933–1938

35. Quibell's Alabaster

Dows DUNHAM, curator of the Department of Egyptian Art in the Boston Museum, Corinna, and I arrived in Egypt together in early November, 1933. Reisner was so cheerful about the *very little* that was encouraging in the present condition of his sight that I admired his courage even more than in those tragic days in the hospital.

One afternoon when my painting had detained me until almost dark, I found Reisner still in his office and in a mood to discuss his work. With a quiet satisfaction of achievement he mentioned his coming publication on the history of the development of the Egyptian tomb. He traced it from the stage of the simple pit, with the body laid in gravel and a superstructure of twigs and matting, to the climax of the magnificence of burials in the Pyramid Age, with enormous *mastabas* or pyramids marking the graves.

He explained in detail how he had followed the logical development of offering places and two types of chapels, those of the palace façade and the plain type. Also, he had been able to separate the later modified cruciform chapels into two kinds, and so on to the two types of false doors known in Dynasty VI.

He paused for breath after his long sentence of explanation, and,

Pyramids of the Northern Royal Cemetery, Meroe, Kabushiyah, Sudan. Painting by Joseph Lindon Smith. Courtesy Museum of Fine Arts,

A young prince shown throwing a bull with the assistance of his father, Ramesses II. Painted from the bas-relief in the Temple of Seti I at Abydos by Joseph Lindon Smith. Courtesy Museum of Fine Arts, Boston.

Bas-relief portrait of Seti I in his temple at Abydos. Painting by Joseph Lindon Smith. Courtesy Mrs. Robert D. Sterling, New York.

noticing my bewilderment, he jumped up, grabbed my arm affectionately, and said, "Now you may laugh, Joe!"

I went almost at once to Saqqarah to paint again in the tomb of Ptahhotep of Dynasty V. There I stayed with Quibell in a small house he had built near the Dynasty I cemetery of North Saqqarah when he resumed his excavations for the Egyptian government in 1932 after a lapse of some years. Quibell had originated the excavations (1919) in this cemetery, which dated from the beginning of the Archaic Period, Dynasty I (3200–2980 B.C.); Firth had continued the work (1930), and after his death, which occurred a year later, Quibell had returned to Saqqarah in 1932 to resume the excavations in this cemetery, but, as it turned out, alabaster found in the passages of the Step Pyramid occupied his full time.

He started this season's work in early November, inside Zoser's Pyramid, by cutting a trial passage southward from the middle of the gallery he and Lauer, a French engineer in the employ of the Egyptian government, had opened the previous year. On the first day, a complete alabaster jug with a handle was found, and pieces of sixteen other vases in porphyry and diorite, and an alabaster shard with an ink inscription. At the time of my arrival, the end of this gallery had been reached. There was no sarcophagus in it, but a quantity of packets of fragments taken from the gallery were all over the yard, and bowls and dishes and vases everywhere in the rooms of the passages, and with them plenty of inscribed bits. Quibell told me, with a comical expression on his face, that the situation was becoming "awkward" as an endless number of shards came from the passages daily. Worse still, the clearing process alone would take several seasons of steady work, and classifying, photography, and publishing many more.

Pierre Lacau, who had replaced Maspero as director-general of the Antiquities Service in 1914, showed up on December 6 to live in the big government house where I had previously been the guest of the Quibells and the Firths. Lacau met the immediate problem of the oversupply of alabaster promptly by ordering the construction of a large and well-lighted magazine with adequate shelves to hold the material, and tables for sorting and putting together the pieces of vases crushed by the collapse of the roof. I accepted with alacrity Lacau's cordial invitation to accompany him and Quibell on a tour of inspection of the new galleries. Lacau was wildly enthusiastic about some short inscriptions in ink, repeated in several instances, and presumably of Zoser's time. One was certainly of Dynasty I and gave the name of Az-ib, a king of that dynasty, and also the name of a temple or palace and the sign of the *Sed* festival (commemorating the length of a king's reign), all incised on a shard from a cylindrical vase of alabaster. Other first dynasty inscriptions had been found, and one of Dynasty II.

In every particular, Lacau confirmed the accuracy of Quibell's deductions and concurred in his theory that the vases must have come from the office of a *garde meuble* at Memphis. When a royal personage died, a definite number of thousands of vases was issued. Most would be of *recent* make (comparatively speaking), but sometimes an old, forgotten store of earlier reigns than Zoser's was opened. Incidentally, this suggested both to Lacau and to Quibell that the history of the first three dynasties that comprised the Archaic period (3200–2680 B.C.) was of a moderately peaceful character, or at least that this government office was never raided. The completely absorbed Egyptologists spent an interminable length of time in a warm, unpleasant atmosphere studying sections of what they referred to as "nests of bowls," in places as many as several dozen to a nest. Some were inverted, others right side up, and among them were stout cylinders and other heavy vases. Most of them were near the floor, and practically all of the bowls, even when broken into small pieces, had remained in contact.

The conversation consisted of an attempt to develop a better system than the one devised by the *reis* of Quibell's workmen for dealing with the problem of removing the fragments without losing their relations each to the other, for the purposes of reconstruction in the magazine. The idea of a number for each vase, penciled on all the fragments after they had been embedded in molten paraffin, was one of the many propositions thought of, only to be abandoned as too expensive in time and money.

Quibell mentioned that, in a pile of spheres such as a bucketful of marbles, each one was in contact with at least twelve others. This fact, he felt, accounted for the solidarity of these alabaster fragments; if one was removed, many others would be disturbed. Therefore, it was not feasible for the men to take the shards in layers from above, since, while extracting the pieces of one vase, ten others would be broken from treading on them. The final decision agreed on by both was to continue the old way of having the *reis* or some other experienced native pick out as many of the pieces of one vase as he could, while fragments from three or four others were loosened from each side and above, and had to be handled with extreme care to keep them from falling. This description reminded me of the game of jackstraws played in retrieving the scattered bits in the tomb of Hetepheres. When I referred to it, Lacau said there never would be a better job of salvage in any tomb, and that no one except Reisner could have done it. Quibell concurred and put in a word about Dunham's skill in disentangling and reassembling the parts of an object which produced the marvelous results now on view in the Hetepheres Room of the Cairo Museum.

The *reis'* explanation of the process used in handling the fragments, given in Arabic, was translated into French by Quibell for the benefit of Lacau. His accompanying pantomime was so expressive, as he and the men with him acted out the entire performance, that an interpreter was hardly needed for one to visualize a sheet of packing paper spread over the face of the little cliff below the vase being worked on, while the men to the right and left caught loosened stray pieces and, in removing them, made a mental note of where they came from. The fragments of each vase were wrapped separately in soft paper and placed in one of the uncovered boxes, eighteen inches long and three in width, made of cheap, thin wood, not planed, brought from the house each morning, later to be taken back to the magazine and marked in blue pencil with the date it was filled.

Quibell told Lacau that this procedure would be invaluable when the mending of the vases began, for missing pieces were most likely to be found in boxes of nearly the same date; whereas it would be hopeless

195

to search for them in the hundreds of boxes already filled, or, next season, several thousands.

Lacau made a nice little speech to the *reis,* which lost nothing by Quibell's Arabic translation.

There was great variety in the stone used in vases and bowls, the commonest being alabaster, and some of the shades of coloring were particularly lovely. Quibell pointed out stone that had been cut so as to bring out vertical stripes, and several bowls of plain yellow alabaster painted red. Another had holes or imperfections in the stone filled with a paste, probably made, he said, of plaster and stone dust. I was stiff from having stayed so long squatting in one position, but Lacau was as nimble as a gazelle as he kept pace with Quibell, hurrying to get to the magazine to gloat over the more important finds.

On one shelf, a few vases bore incised inscriptions. Lacau read off excitedly the names of Zet, the third king of Dynasty I, the length of whose reign is not known, and Az-ib, fifth king (twenty-plus years). There was also a new king, with a name he could not decipher, who greatly excited him for his potentialities. There were numerous short hieratic inscriptions in ink, with the name of a man, probably the donor, he thought, an office, a place name, or the name of the quarry from which the stone came. A current script was evidently well developed, with the forms of the signs simplified and fixed. When Quibell said that already they had more than one hundred texts, many incomplete, but often recurring, and, that undoubtedly, therefore, there would be better examples for study before the digging season was much further advanced, Lacau remarked with a twinkle in his eyes that his stay in Saqqarah would be lengthy.

The gem of the collection to date was the only vase with a decoration in relief, consisting of a *sed* platform that had stairs on each side and a figure below, also two shrines with thrones inside them, and a large beetle above, a truly remarkable object in an excellent state of preservation and with an unbroken handle.

I carried away with me from that Saqqarah visit the memory of eager-eyed workmen carefully moving about in the galleries to retrieve pieces of vases. And in the magazines of natives, experienced in handling tomb material from training given them by foreign archaeologists, I saw expertly fitted together whole vases from the fragments taken from boxes approximating in date, laid out on a long table.

The most vivid of all my recollections were of the indefatigable Quibell flitting about hither and yon with a word of encouragement to the men, and of Lacau's handsome, long-bearded face, his flashing black eyes and clear-cut features, as his tall, erect body bent over an inscribed piece, his notebook in hand.

By next season, Quibell's enthusiasm for alabaster had not waned, and the extraction of the fragments from the galleries and putting them on the shelves of the magazine built for the purpose was approaching completion. Three thousand boxes, eighteen inches long and three inches wide, had been filled during the past two seasons, each containing four or five vases in fragments, which meant about fifteen thousand pieces in all that awaited reconstruction. Quibell said that, when work was shut down during the summer months, he had set aside on the tables an assortment of huge stacks of alabaster fragments for four of his best men, on the chance that they might be able to assemble a few whole vases from this discouraging mass of shards. He had been agreeably surprised by the results. More than one hundred vases had been made presentable for museum exhibition, only a few pieces missing from each.

He remarked on the extraordinary sense several of the workers had shown for form and matching colors, and said it frequently happened that a man mending a vase would recall a shard he had seen the previous year which might fit a still vacant place. He would get it and find that his memory had been correct. Each such achievement stimulated the other men to renewed effort for a successful search for a missing fragment. He told me that the method first established by the *reis* had not been changed. Four diggers were at the working face of the "nests" in the galleries, while eight others were kept busy carrying the boxes out. The boxes, after being marked with the date and a sequence number, were placed on the shelves in the magazine, where they were examined for inscriptions. When an inscription was found, no matter how meager, the neighboring boxes were searched for another inscribed fragment belonging to it, and the vase or dish was then reassembled as far as was possible.

Uninscribed dishes, when broken into only a few pieces, if they were of a rare shape or of striking ornamental stone, were also mended; but the vast mass of uninscribed stone vessels of a common variety, which would have taken an endless amount of time to mend, were left in their boxes stacked on the shelves and readily accessible for further study. Most of the fragments were from shallow bowls or dishes of alabaster. Among them were some of schist or red and white conglomerate, and some were of even harder stone. In what Quibell referred to humorously as an enormous "pantry," nothing very expensive had been stored in ancient times.

Quibell was pleased with a bowl made of rock crystal that must have entailed many months of steady effort, since the stone worker had no harder material than the crystal to use as an abrasive in shaping it. It seemed to him unlikely that the bowl was made on a wheel or turntable. In this connection, he stated that, even though no part of a turntable had ever been found, nevertheless evidence indicated that such devices were in current use at this early period. Another process he described was the dressing of the outer surface; to do this, the worker embedded the vase in pitch or clay. He said also that cylindrical drills were used in the manufacture of a vase, a fact proved by the cores of diorite and granite which have been found, as well as by the ends of drill holes in alabaster. When I held in my hand a vase and asked him by what device the first cylindrical hole in its narrow neck had been enlarged into the shoulder, he laughed and replied, "That has me stumped, Joe, but I still hope to find the answer."

Another question that had remained unanswered, Quibell asserted, was whether the vases had been broken deliberately for a ritualistic purpose, or through the carelessness of the early workmen who stacked them. Certainly many were already broken when the gallery was originally closed, since the fall of rocks from the roof, or movements of the earth through the ages, would not explain the contact between the broken edges of a heavy tubular vase and the fragile dishes leaning against it. What was very puzzling was broken piles of dishes nested in one another, with the individual pieces in contact. Quibell thought this might be explained by a very heavy pressure on the dishes by the heavier vase through a long period of time.

One of the surprising objects to find among thousands of shards was a copper dagger in good condition, with traces of cloth wrapping, which was possibly the lining of a scabbard. Human remains also had their story to tell in another part of these same underground passages. There was always an interest in watching the examination by an anatomist of bones and skin that had lain through the ages concealed from sight, and especially so when the remains were *in situ,* as in the present case, inside the granite sarcophagus chamber of the Pyramid of Zoser. Quibell and I stood near Derry, who was to make the examination, as with a skillful touch he began to handle the skeleton, which had nothing to identify it beyond the period of the burial in the place where it was found. There was the upper half of the right shoulder, with traces of skin and tissues; a first left rib, with cartilage attached to it; and a smaller fragment of a rib on the right side. He recalled to me that here was the method of "effigy" used as in the little old lady of long ago at Giza, but in this body without drama. To emphasize his premise, he pointed to a foot that I had failed to notice. It was complete as to joints and was in linen wrappings, including all the toes. In order to give the appearance of tendons in relief, the linen used for this purpose had been soaked in some substance (not yet identified) and it was obvious that, while still wet, the linen must have been molded into shape by pressing it down at intervals.

As Derry talked, I could all but see the undertaker, with the lugubrious expression of the present-day ones, waiting for the liquid applied for the purpose of modeling joints and toes to dry before wrapping the entire foot in outer linen bandages.

"The skeleton in this chamber of Zoser's Pyramid is another confirmation of a method of preserving organs used in the time of the Ancient Empire, later to be abandoned in favor of embalming," Derry commented to Quibell.

Both of them, one an anatomist, the other an archaeologist, looked completely satisfied that a few scattered bones and a bit of linen had, to their trained eyes, yielded significant evidence.

To date, more than two hundred different texts had been deciphered on a thousand separate fragments, a few among them incised, the rest in ink. Lacau had devoted himself religiously and enthusiastically to the deciphering of these inscriptions. His results, subsequently to be published, would justify the time and money spent on this unique dig, according to Quibell. When I remarked, "It was *your* work that furnished Lacau with the material to make this discovery one of primary importance to archaeologists," Quibell's face lit up with the quick smile that gave his personality so much charm.

Archaeology, as all those participating in field work will tell you, demands intelligence of a high order, study, and concentrated effort, hours at a stretch. A "find" keeps all concerned full speed ahead, a characteristic that makes many archaeologists old before their time. Still other scholars must synthesize from the painstaking recording of the evidence made available by field workers. Their deductions and conclusions provide the end-product for the enlightenment of mankind about his ancient heritage in Egypt and elsewhere.

On coming back into the sunlight after a particularly difficult climb through intricate passages, I noticed with a definite sense of alarm a purple flush on Quibell's face and a shortness of breath. He placed an arm affectionately across my shoulders, his eyes turned downwards into the passage from which we had just emerged. As he started to walk away, in a silence that was unusual with him, I felt a sudden pang at the realization that he knew from his physical condition that this would be his final season with "more alabaster."

36. *The Archaic Cemetery of North Saqqarah*

QUIBELL DIED in the summer of 1935. That fall Walter B. Emery took over his house and excavations in Saqqarah for the Egyptian government. Emery was an Englishman whose distinguished career in Egypt

as an excavator began in 1923 at el-Amarna as a young member of the
Egypt Exploration Society. It had continued at Thebes for the University of Liverpool, and in 1929 he had joined the Egyptian government
service as director of the Archaeological Survey of Nubia, an undertaking which was completed six years later.

Reisner's earlier survey had recovered the history of Lower Nubia,
and Emery acknowledged with gratitude what he had learned from
studying the methods and thoroughness of the much older and more
experienced archaeologist. A close association between these two men
was to become intensified through a mutual interest in the Archaic
Cemetery of North Saqqarah. Reisner had consistently stated that there
must be a systematic examination of the *mastabas* of this cemetery in
order to reach a solution of the great problems connected with Egypt's
dynastic history. It was not only the most important site for the early
period, but possibly the only one of its kind. Moreover, it was of peculiar interest from being near Memphis, the city founded by Menes, the
first king of Dynasty I.

Emery had technical and administrative qualifications of a high
order, an amazing power of concentration, and imagination in his interpretation of data, combined with common sense. He had also rare ability
in winning the loyal co-operation of his subordinates, both European and
Egyptian, and he endeared himself to his archaeological colleagues by
his prompt, concise, and accurate publications. Reisner was delighted to
have him responsible for a thorough examination of this cemetery.

Firth had excavated the paneled façade of a large *mastaba* corridor
and enclosure walls, where many intact wine jars were found. But it
was Emery who, in continuing the clearing of this same *mastaba,* discovered subsidiary rooms. Emery showed me two of these north rooms
with seals bearing the names of King Udimu, the fourth king of Dynasty
I, which lasted from 3200–2980 B.C., and Ankh-ka, a noble. These rooms
had contained pottery, stone vessels, cylindrical jars and bowls, and
flint instruments.

During the winter of 1936, I made a long visit to the Emerys. No
one could have taken better care of me than did Molly, Emery's attrac-

tive, red-haired wife. He was making fine progress. His first find of the season was an intact burial, located at the foot of a group of small niches under the superstructure of the *mastaba* first rediscovered by Firth. It was a rectangular pit faced with thick mud plaster and covered with white stucco. The body of a male lay in the remains of a wooden coffin in a contracted position on its left side. Near the body was a schist bowl, and another bowl and a cylindrical jar, both of alabaster. Also there were endless jars of red ware in every direction.

In another *mastaba* discovered at about the same time, revealing a superstructure with terraces, was a granary with sealed doors and the name of Nebet-ka on the grain bins. Emery considered that architecturally this find was his most interesting to date in Saqqarah.

One of Emery's finds that I saw had for me the same kind of human element in it as that of our little old lady of long ago at Giza. This was a first dynasty burial of a woman. She was not mummified, merely wrapped in a roll of linen that was twenty yards in length and still in perfect condition. The funeral meal spread about her could be identified as consisting of grain, bread, lentils, quail, chicken, and beef. When Derry examined the body, he discovered cancer of the throat as the cause of her death.

By March, Emery's efforts were richly repaid when, after clearing the superstructures and digging down farther, he found, in magazines built of crude brick like the *mastaba,* an intact group of pottery wine jars bearing the names of Udimu and Hemaka. The fact that Hemaka was probably the owner of the *mastaba* was confirmed by the finding of his name on a wooden sickle and two ivory labels. His title, translated by Griffith, read, "Ruling in the King's Heart." He was already known as the "King's Sealer Hemaka" from tablets found by Petrie at Abydos, in a tomb in which the name of Udimu was mentioned. Up to this time, Petrie's excavations at Abydos had seemed to prove that the cemetery for kings of Dynasty I, including Menes himself, was at Abydos.

In other magazines there were large deposits of very important objects wrapped in matting. Included among them were several reed arrows with bone and flint tips which had been in quivers made of panther hides. Unfortunately only one quiver was sufficiently well preserved to be removed. There was also a collection of great ceremonial flint knives of the same general type Petrie had found at Abydos and Reisner at Naga-ed-Der, a provincial cemetery of the Pyramid Age. In addition, there were copper tools and an adze handle in excellent condition. But a wooden sickle, with flint teeth set in the cutting edge, was a prize over which the archaeologists waxed enthusiastic. It was, they said, the best example of this implement ever found and centuries earlier than others of record.

A label tablet of King Zer, second king of Dynasty I, with the year name, was of special interest, as was one of Udimu. Textiles were well represented in fragments of woven fabrics of a coarse, irregular weave; then there was a fiber of flax, a big coil of rope, and a leather bag. But the most dramatic of the finds were small disks made of a variety of material, such as stone, horn, wood, and ivory, all placed together in an inlaid box. In size, they were between twelve and fifteen centimeters, and were pierced through the center with a stick of wood or bone. Some of the disks had decorated upper surfaces, one with a beautifully drawn scene of two dogs pulling down a gazelle or an oryx; another showed large birds caught in a bird trap; and many of them had less sensational patterns done in color. No archaeologist had an explanation to offer concerning the use of these disks placed carefully in a box.

Reisner declared that Hemaka contained the most important deposits of funerary furniture found, not only in a tomb of Dynasty I, but in any of those of the first three dynasties. Emery told me that the general plan was similar to that of a brick *mastaba,* with a palace façade paneled on four sides, surrounded by two enclosure walls. The magazines were within the superstructure, and probably contained originally the more precious and intimate possessions of the owner. The rooms had floors raised above the ground level by fillings of rubble and sand, and were probably roofed over with wooden beams and planks. Each magazine was entirely separate, without communicating doors between it and any other magazine. There was a shallow pit which barely penetrated the hard rock strata of the plateau, and the pit was divided into a series of rooms by brick walls; the one in the center, used for the burial, was longer than the other rooms in the pit.

A view of the cemetery from an airplane indicated sites of at least eight or ten such *mastabas,* and since they were only a very short distance below the surface, the danger of their being discovered by thieves and plundered was a very real one.

37. *Emery's Sensational Find*

EMERY RESUMED HIS EXCAVATIONS in the Archaic Cemetery of North Saqqarah in late December, 1937. During the following spring, when I was again a guest of the Emerys for several weeks, his work was often interrupted by visiting archaeologists who came to discuss with him recent discoveries that were proving to be even more sensational than those of the previous season.

Emery had begun by excavating the south side of a large *mastaba* of Dynasty II, which Firth had discovered in 1931. He soon came to a large brick construction which he decided had been the casing of a funerary solar barque. The fact that a part of the structure of Firth's Dynasty II *mastaba* was over this "boat grave," which was of a similar type to the "boat grave" Emery had found the season before in this same cemetery to the north of the Dynasty I tomb of Ankh-ka, warranted the premise of the existence of a Dynasty I *mastaba* in the vicinity. Further excavation in the area resulted in the discovery of a large Dynasty I tomb of the type Reisner had excavated in the provincial cemetery of Naga-ed-Der. The tomb had the construction expected of this period, a superstructure divided into a series of twenty-seven magazines built above the original ground level, and below, five subterranean rooms, originally roofed with wooden beams and planks. The exterior of the superstructure was decorated on all four sides with "palace façade" paneling lined with thick white stucco in a fairly good state of preservation.

I had previously known the "palace façade" construction in the chapel of the tomb of Hesy-re, which was to the west of Emery's house, in the Archaic Cemetery, and was dated to the reign of Zoser in Dynasty III.

The walls of the corridor in Hesy-re's chapel had carved wooden panels fitted into the back of the "gateway," and some of the smaller niches were painted in gay patterns to simulate strips of reed matting.

Emery told me that these fragments, still extant, and also impressions on the mud facing, indicated that the mats were arranged in pattern form. This was the origin of the painted "mat" decoration in the tomb of Hesy-re and elsewhere. The development of the same design in different mediums was to me another example of the persistence and continuity of tradition in Egypt—this time in architecture.

Calligraphy through the ages has been a special interest of mine, to own as a collector or to examine. I had shared with Lacau and Quibell the thrill of the inscribed alabaster fragments inside the Step Pyramid, and now I examined with joy in Emery's magazines the hundreds of broken pottery vessels found in three of the subterranean rooms, all inscribed in black ink in bold, cursive hieroglyphs, with great variations in the style of writing. These inscriptions appealed to me as an artist and on account of their being among the oldest dynastic inscriptions known, antedating the Step Pyramid finds by some centuries. I never tired of looking at the details on a large collection of clay jar seals, which bore the name of Aha. The state of their preservation was amazing. The designs were clearly discernible and showed hunting scenes with dogs, gazelles, crocodiles, and lions in profusion.

The central subterranean chamber contained an immense quantity of stone vessels; many of them were broken, but when repaired would be a valuable contribution to knowledge of designs in objects of this character in use at the beginning of Dynasty I. A number of slate palettes were unfortunately not inscribed. In this same chamber were the scattered bones of two adult males, the copper feet of a large wooden bed, and four ivory bull's legs from a casket or gaming board. The magazines within the superstructure were built with false doors like those in the tomb of Hemaka, but very little was found in them beyond scattered pieces of ivory and wooden furniture.

The question of the identity of the owner of this huge tomb led to endless discussion, and long after I had gone to bed I would hear lengthy arguments on the subject drifting in to me from Emery's near-by office. These conversations between him and other archaeologists would linger on in my thoughts and become a part of my dreams. Although Emery kept repeating that "definite evidence of the ownership of the tomb is lacking at the present time," he would say that, taking into consideration the great size of the tomb, its similarity to the tomb of Naga-ed-Der now attributed to Queen Neith-hetep, the wife of King Aha, and the hundreds of examples of Aha's name in the Saqqarah tomb, the evidence suggested the possibility of its being the tomb of King Aha or of one of his family.

But the arguments, I felt, had convinced Emery personally that it *was* Aha's tomb. They were impressive as I listened to him citing them many times over. This premise assumed identification of Hor Aha with Menes, the first king of a united Egypt. "What is more probable," he would continue, "than that he should be buried near Memphis, the city he, Menes, had founded?" This statement led to the logical conclusion that, at Abydos, the "so-called" tomb of Aha was a cenotaph and that the tomb itself was in this Archaic Cemetery at Saqqarah.

In support of this theory Emery summarized the following facts: The tomb attributed to Aha at Abydos was considerably smaller and less elaborate than either the Naga-ed-Der tomb or the Saqqarah one. Furthermore, the evidence of labels and clay jar seals on which the identification of the Abydos tomb had been based by Petrie was far from conclusive. Whereas at North Saqqarah, in the course of the past two years, five tombs of great nobles had been cleared, and in each one the name of the owner of the tomb had been more prominently displayed than that of the king in whose reign he was an official. Moreover, in this Saqqarah tomb, remains of seven hundred pottery jars bore the name of Hor Aha *and no other name*. Finally, many jar seals bore his name and *mentioned no other person*. It must be remembered that the usual procedure in sealing wine jars was to impress the clay with two seals, (a) of the owner and (b) of the king. But in this tomb only King Aha's name appeared on seals, inscribed jars, and other materials.

German archaeologists had expressed doubts, but Emery was encouraged by the acceptance of his tentative identification by several British archaeologists, and most of all by Lacau's conviction that he (Emery) was the fortunate discoverer of Menes, the first known king of a united, dynastic Egypt, known in this tomb under the name of Aha.

38. Housekeeping at Abydos, 1937

IN MY EARLY YEARS in Egypt, after that first trip when the majesty of Abu Simbel had swept me off my feet, I had been back there intermittently, and also at Abydos to Seti's great temple. Sculptured reliefs of Ramesses II covered so much area in so many temples of this period that much of the work was hastily conceived and slovenly executed as to details.

On the other hand, although the work executed under Seti I, the father, was seen almost as frequently in temples up and down the Nile Valley, it was recognizable at a glance from the exquisite rendering of its sculptured reliefs and sensitiveness in the cutting of its hieroglyph inscriptions. These points of distinction stood out even when in juxtaposition with the best pieces of the great period of the art of the New Kingdom, that of the immediately preceding Dynasty XVIII. It seemed as though Seti must have had special craftsmen and sculptors at his royal command, as happened at Giza during the reign of Cheops. I felt in both instances as though I could pick out individually, in the workmanship of unknown artists, particular details—and there was no careless mass-production element.

Seti's own temple at Abydos was an artistic triumph for its masterly execution of low relief on white limestone, with some of the same characteristics as those appearing on the white walls of Ramose's tomb at Qurna one hundred years earlier. I first painted at Abydos in 1905, when I had a tent pitched in an outer court leading into Seti's great hall and was cared for by a camp servant. I was at it again in 1907.

In the early twenties, Quibell invited me to go to Abydos with him and Petrie, an invitation I accepted with alacrity. Abydos was Petrie's old stamping ground, since he had excavated the early royal burials there over a period of years for the Egypt Exploration Fund. I enjoyed the trip with them to the former excavations. It was a hard donkey ride of about five miles, over very rough ground, but when reached, the site was dramatic, situated, as it was, on a rocky slope under superb cliffs. There were but few traces left of the cemeteries of Dynasty I and Dynasty II, but Petrie told me it had yielded important information on the earliest known dynastic period, including evidence of luxury, at the time when Narmer (Menes) from his capital of Memphis had united Egypt.

Petrie emphasized the fact that the discovery of the use of hardened copper for tools several centuries before dynastic Egypt emerged had given an impetus to culture that was reflected in his finds here. There were fragments of furniture already sophisticated in workmanship, with ivory legs to couches beautifully carved; elaborate stone vessels, ivory labels, portions of a gold scepter; and gold bracelets, copper bowls, and Aegean pottery that could be identified as Cretan. There were seals of the kings Narmer, Zer, and Zet, a stela of Zer, and many other rare specimens.

During Dynasty XVIII, the middle of the tomb of Zer, with its burial chamber built of wood and brick cells around it, had been cleared for the construction of a shrine of Osiris. Now nothing remained to mark it except a few fragmentary pieces of sculpture in limestone. Pottery found by Petrie, as offerings laid on the shrine, was dated to the reign of Amenhotep III, and scattered specimens continued as late as Dynasty XXVI.

The structures of Zer, like those of Zet, had several of the same architectural features that Emery subsequently uncovered in tombs in the Archaic Cemetery at Saqqarah, such as shallow recesses in the brick walls. There were also similar vases of alabaster, quartz crystal, and porphyry; and pottery bore certain marks characteristic of Dynasty I.

In my early stays at Abydos, it was generally accepted that the Dynasty XIX building called the "Osireion" was a sanctuary dedicated to the god of the underworld. According to legend, Osiris was buried at Abydos, and the Egyptian kings wanted to have a cenotaph in the vicinity. Weigall and Ayrton thus interpreted the structure of Sesostris III they discovered at Abydos when excavating for the Egypt Exploration Fund in 1905.

I had had an interesting visit with Henri Frankfort in 1928, when he was excavating the Osireion for the same organization and proved it was the cenotaph of Seti I. In taking me into it, he pointed out a fact I had already realized; namely, that the plan was like Seti's tomb at Thebes. It had the same long, sloping entrance passage, a few antechambers, and a central hall with square pillars. In the tomb, one room contained the sarcophagus, but in Abydos, the room itself was an enormous sarcophagus, and the ceiling had great figures of Nut, goddess of the sky. The texts in both structures resembled those in the sarcophagus chamber of the Saqqarah pyramids of Dynasty V and Dynasty VI which I had seen with Maspero. The entrance into the hall of the so-called Osireion (with Nun, the goddess of the waters, in the corridor) led us on to a ledge with the water below, and we stood closed in by projecting piers, unable to reach the "island" in the middle of the hall. From the "island" a double flight of steps went to a canal.

A papyrus, owned by the British Museum, reflected the same idea that was expressed both in Seti's tomb and in his cenotaph. On the papyrus, a "Primeval Hill" and surrounding waters was represented at Abydos by the rise and fall of water around an island in a stone building. This conception was supposedly connected with Osiris' being drowned every year at the time of the inundation of the Nile.

The text in the *Book of the Dead* in the New Kingdom described the island where the blessed "rested" as being at Abydos. This brought to my mind Maspero's comments on the fields of the blessed that had led to my adventure some years before in an unseaworthy small boat in the submerged area around the Pyramid of Cheops. Meanwhile, Frankfort was saying that, furthermore, there was a reference to the "famous steps of Osiris at Abydos," where the kings prayed to be buried because of the burial of Osiris on the "Primeval Hill."

In Egypt, the setting and rising of the sun was symbolic of death and resurrection; therefore the "Primeval Hill" where death was vanquished and life renewed became the appropriate place of burial for Osiris, whose most essential characteristic was that he had died and been resurrected and reached immortality through his burial. Several German archaeologists collected conclusive evidence to show that the "Primeval Hill" was represented by a double flight of steps. An ostracon found during the clearing of the entrance passage made evident Seti's personal interest in the buildings at Abydos, and indicated that he had a palace there so he could personally supervise the work.

Frankfort was holding forth at length on the subject of Seti's attempt in his cenotaph to bring about a revival of old beliefs connected with the burial of Osiris, vindicated by the collapse of the el-Amarna movement. He mentioned the dreariness of the texts which covered the walls of the cenotaph and the inconsistencies in them. He was saying how artificial and involved funerary ritual had become, hopelessly entangled as it was with meaningless tradition and demonology. It was unworthy of a great king like Seti, and from a religious point of view the reforms of Akhenaten were justified. In the excitement of his harangue he caught my arm; the action threw me off balance; I slipped, causing Frankfort to do the same; and we both rolled over several times on the double flight of steps, symbolic of the "Primeval Hill," before we fell into the water below. The stunned surprise of his expression as we scrambled onto the rocks made me roar with laughter. I don't think Frankfort ever quite forgave me for taking as a joke a mishap which upset his dignity and interrupted a fine oration on theology in ancient Egypt.

When Reisner, in 1937, wished me to paint more of Seti's great reliefs in his temple of Abydos for the Smith Collection of Egyptian Paintings in the Boston Museum, I was returning to surroundings full of pleasant associations. He had written to Alan Gardiner asking for the use of the Expedition House of the Egypt Exploration Fund for a six-week stay for Corinna and me. We came by train from Cairo.

The Expedition House had been closed for several years but the Society retained in its employ *Reis* Sadek, who had been in charge for the varied groups of well-known Egyptologists who had excavated the many ruins in the vicinity. The immediate previous occupant of the house was a talented young Canadian woman, Amice Calverley, who for a number of seasons had recorded the temple reliefs for important publications under the auspices of the Oriental Institute of the University of Chicago.

Reisner had sent two of his men for personal servants, and we Smiths took over *Reis* Sadek and his staff.

A welcome sight in a near-by magazine were wooden horses, planks, and a mass of staging necessary for my painting of some of the reliefs in very high registers on the walls of Seti's great hall. We also explored dark passages leading off the dining room of our temporary home, to find on the shelves of gloomy, dust-covered alcoves parts of pottery jars, uninscribed fragments of stone, and bits of glassware that recalled the presence of the many archaeologists who had handled them, a number of whom I had known. Most vividly of all, Petrie's eccentric personality remained as a living entity, particularly so from my having just come from being with Emery during the recent excitement in determining whether *he* had discovered Menes, the first king of Dynasty I, who had united Egypt, or whether Menes had been buried, as Petrie believed, in his cemetery at Abydos.

Petrie's way of life in the field fascinated me. He ignored physical comforts for himself and, therefore, neglected to provide the ordinary amenities for his staff. Even so, every member both respected and loved him. Corinna and I searched in vain through black passages and magazines for a serving table, used instead of ordinary equipment for meals, described by Reisner. It stood in the dining room, lighted by a few very small apertures on the wall just below the ceiling. In a trough down the center of the table stood a double row of tins containing various kinds of food, and near by a can opener.

His idea of satisfying the pangs of hunger, when they became intense, was to eat from several tins at random until they were empty. He took for granted that his staff would do the same, and this in a hot climate! Prior to their marriage, Annie and Edward Quibell, as fellow members of one of Petrie's expeditions, became engaged while nursing each other through ptomaine poisoning. Frequently Petrie did not bother to go to bed at night, merely dropping asleep in his clothes wherever he happened to be, waiting for the coming of dawn to resume the work interrupted by darkness.

But his amazing achievements in establishing sound principles of archaeology will be remembered, and not his eccentricities. His establishing of "sequence dates" was a stroke of genius. He had found fragments of unidentified pottery scattered in ancient settlements of the Fayum and at other places in Upper Egypt. For the purpose of classification, he divided them into early predynastic with the arbitrary numbers, S.D. 30–39, middle predynastic (S.D. 40–52), and late predynastic (S. D. 53–79). This system proved very helpful in determining periods in which definite types belonged, such as cylinder alabaster jars (not found after Dynasty I, I understood). Again, he placed large pottery jars, brownish in color with a wavy edge handle and a ledge that fingers fitted under, which was at first functional, later merely ornamental, in early predynastic (S.D. 38). The red pottery with a black top that was known in very early predynastic times has persisted in Nubia. The history that pottery has to tell of a people has fascinated me throughout my career, equally with that of calligraphy.

A vivid impression I have retained of Petrie was his conversation as we jogged back to Abydos on donkeys side by side. He told me, with flashing eyes, about the unnecessary amount of work and the infinite patience and ingenuity that had been required of him to salvage and piece together the many rare objects in this early dynastic cemetery, because, after the Frenchman, M. Amélineau, had uncovered the cemetery in 1897, they had been *deliberately destroyed.*

The afternoon of our arrival for housekeeping in 1937, I rode to that desert cemetery outside of Abydos, and although there was now nothing to see in it, the mere being on the site gave me a thrill. Early next morning, we went to Seti's temple dedicated to Osiris, plodding through deep sand and up and down steep grades. Underfoot were shards, mud bricks, and other old fragments, each bit casually loosened by the foot, a reminder of the great civilizations that once covered what was now desert waste.

Modern village life was mostly to the north and east, and above bright fields and palm trees was visible a faint trace of the cliffs on the Lybian side of the Nile. Beyond a sharp left turn, where many footprints showed the route taken to a series of villages, were the walled-in ruins of the temple of Seti's son, Ramesses II. And directly in front we saw, conspicuous in its glaring whiteness, the roof put on by the Antiquities Service to protect the almost intact walls of the main part of Seti's temple. We entered by a side gate down a flight of worn steps and paused to admire a spirited scene of a young prince throwing a bull, with his father's assistance. This son of Ramesses II and the grandson of Seti, wearing the side lock to denote immaturity, was a charming-looking boy. The quality of this portraiture can only be regarded as superb, the figures charged with movement, grace, and, above all, realism. Then we walked through the corridor with the famous list of kings on the left wall, and a second sharp turn brought into view the long line of columns in the great Hypostyle Hall.

Men employed by the Antiquities Service to clean and repair the great Hypostyle Hall were on ladders, or on platforms, and their grunts resounded as huge beams were raised or lowered, a scene that was reminiscent of their forebears', many centuries ago, performing the same service with probably the same grunts. I was attracted by the very white figures on the west-end wall of the great Hypostyle Hall, unpainted, in very low relief. I particularly liked standing, slender figures of two girls holding hands; one, Ma'at, goddess of truth, the other Renpet, goddess of the years. They were offering King Seti millions and millions of happy years in eternity.

39. Forgeries

THERE WAS, in the prewar years, a lively trading of small antiques "made in Germany" all over Egypt, but on such ancient sites as Saqqarah and the Theban Plain forgers became expert in producing scarabs that were frequently mistaken for genuine ones. Even the hieroglyphs and other markings were "authentic." These modern workers produced their forgeries from ancient bits of ceramics, mainly from varieties of glazed ware, but also from red carnelian and amethyst.

A favorite trick with donkey boys was to permit their clients to discover, on their own, in a ruin, a scarab or some other object that had been carefully planted in advance. An amazingly good fake in scarabs and other diminutive sacred objects was often produced by copying a genuine one, usually stolen but sometimes borrowed from a dealer friend. It took an archaeologist to find something wrong with the markings. I saw several small heads of limestone, alabaster, and basalt which showed real artistic ability on the part of their perpetrator.

Fakes that flooded the tourist market were usually of insignificant objects, such as blue beads that had been used by the thousands for burials. On the other hand, blue beads found near tomb pits or in the debris of mounds were frequently genuine, and a persistent tourist could pick up a sufficient number to make himself a necklace of old beads, instead of buying the modern manufactured ones.

The artisans of Qurna carried on what was, to them, an important industry in making small figures of blue glaze. In order to do this it was necessary to use as a model a genuine *shawabti* figure stolen from a near-by dig.

One day, a persistent boy had followed Corinna's donkey many miles over the Theban Plain, offering her one of these blue figures, an imitation she thought particularly good in color. Finally, to get rid of the nagging voice, she had bought it for the large price of ten cents in our money. That evening, I was surprised to find the children playing with a genuine Dynasty XVIII (1570–1349 B.C.) blue *shawabti*. When I took possession of it, loud shrieks of woe brought Corinna rushing in to their *dahabieh* nursery. She explained to me that this was her purchase from the boy of which she had already told me.

Maspero happened to drop in for dinner, and, of course, he instantly noticed the lovely little figure on the sideboard. He remarked severely that he did not think *I* would buy an antiquity stolen from the dig of a neighboring archaeologist. Whereupon I related the story of how we had acquired it.

The next afternoon, when Corinna and I dismounted at the river, there was an array of natives gathered near our *dahabieh,* all in their best clothes. Our donkey boy, Hasan Basouni, explained that the delegation consisted of citizens of Qurna who had important business to transact with me. Dowe ushered them into our quarters and coffee was served. Not until after a courteous exchange of greetings did Hasan, as spokesman, make a speech. He told us that the sale of the blue figures was the most profitable industry of Qurna and benefited the many families living there, since every tourist wished to possess a figure "just found in an eighteenth dynasty tomb," as the imitation ones were advertised.

By mistake Corinna had been sold, by the boy who had followed her donkey, the original figure stolen from a dig and used as a model. Without it to copy, no more new ones could be made. If she decided to keep the figure, it was hers by right of purchase and no one starving in Qurna as a result of the loss of this trade would blame her. On the other hand, if she gave it back, the "hearts in the village would be glad." Otherwise our tourist friends would have to buy blue figures with "Made in Germany" stamped on them, and these friends would be unhappy in knowing the purchases were not genuine.

At this point in the discussion, another servant came in to say that Maspero was waiting on the upper deck to find out if Corinna and I could lunch with him the next day, to meet some English scholars. I accepted the invitation and then told him the reason for the visit of this delegation from Qurna and asked his advice.

He said, with a twinkle in his eyes, "It would be unfortunate for tourists to be reduced to the trade in German-made blue glaze figures on the Theban Plain. I suggest you return the original for a model."

Corinna handed over to Hasan the lovely little genuine Dynasty XVIII *shawabti,* and, in return, was given the equivalent of the ten cents she had paid for it.

The real problem for government officials of the Antiquities Service, and for archaeologists, occurred when a native dug up among his crops an antiquity that was an important piece. Usually, instead of its reaching a government inspector, as had happened with Quibell in the find of the Golden Hawk, it got into the hands of an unscrupulous dealer, or even a dishonest petty official, who gave the finder a few pounds for an

Egyptian antiquity later to be sold to some foreign museum for thousands of pounds. In such instance, not only did Egypt lose treasure that belonged to her, but the provenance of the find was not known, which, to archaeologists, was more serious from a scientific point of view.

On the other hand, antiquities frequently represented to have been dug up by a native were merely clever fakes to catch the gullible traveler, who bought them in great secrecy and then paid bribes to get out of the country absolutely worthless objects made yesterday. More than once, my archaeologist friends told me of their failures in preventing such frauds. The purchaser, perfectly satisfied, would retort that his dragoman had vouched to him for the genuineness of the canopic jar. This would be sufficient authentication for the buyer to pay two hundred pounds for a canopic jar worth only the price of the modern alabaster used in making it.

On one such occasion I mentioned to an annoyed archaeologist a similar kind of incident told me by Frank Lowell, the judge of a circuit court in Boston. Judge Lowell had tried to get some men who had been duped into buying large blocks of stock in a nonexistent mine to prosecute the man who had been caught in perpetrating this fraud. The consensus of those duped had been to give the man a little more time and the mine would be all right. "People seem to want to be fooled," the Judge had commented.

Another complication that harassed an archaeologist was when a clever forger managed to bury a fake in the debris of the archaeologist's own dig, where he would sooner or later discover it and believe it belonged to the period he was excavating. This was particularly true of the el-Amarna heads, which were easy to imitate. On a visit I made to an excavation at el-Amarna, I was shown two beautiful heads that had been planted in debris recently removed from a tomb, to give the appearance that, in sifting, they had been overlooked. The heads were so good that the archaeologist in charge began to question the genuineness of his real finds.

This particular excavator was not the only one to be puzzled by fakes of the period, since whenever a "new" el-Amarna piece turned up at a dealer's, archaeologists and government officials would groan, "Is it genuine or another clever fake?" Opinions of experts sometimes differed, and acrimonious disputes then ensued. Lacau once said to me that the Brooklyn Museum was fortunate in its el-Amarna collection, since the museum had acquired it from a historical society in New York that had bought the pieces long before forgeries had started. "Therefore, *they*, at least, are genuine," he said.

By a series of coincidences, I saw, soon after my arrival in Egypt in the fall of 1920, in the home of an Egyptian, under conditions of some secrecy, a seated scribe of dark stone. It was about three feet in height with the face intact and apparently dated from the Old Kingdom and, therefore, from somewhere between 2680 and 2258 B.C.

I found the Egyptian was willing to dispose of the statue, but there were several puzzling factors. I believed from his reputation that he was the actual owner when he so stated. He made no objection to my suggestion of showing it to both Lacau and Reisner. He disclaimed any idea of its origin. The price he quoted was far too low for a genuine piece of that early period and too high for a fake.

In certain particulars it was similar to some standing statues in the Cairo Museum labeled Dynasty V, all of them varying slightly in the conventional details. In my opinion, this seated scribe was unquestionably genuine. It was like the figures in the museum, and though it may have belonged to the same group, it appealed to me more as an artist. I got Lacau to see it. He declared it "splendid," but said there was something wrong with the details. He felt the wig was too short for the period in which the inscription might belong, and he pointed out an error in the hieroglyphs giving the name of the scribe. Reisner also came in at my request. "Looks *almost* all right," was what he said. He, too, mentioned the mistake in the hieroglyphs. I had suggested, without success, to both these experts that, after all, an artisan of long ago was a human being and might have inadvertently made an error in carving that had not been noticed at the time. Neither of them would accept my theory. With Reisner and Lacau dubious, a sale to a museum was at that time out of the question. The next season the scribe had gone. The

217

Egyptian told me he had sold it, but mentioned neither the purchaser nor the price paid. I still believed the scribe was genuine and felt that some day I would see it again in some important museum.

Nahman was a dealer, who, like old Mohamed Muhassib in Luxor, was never in difficulties with the Egyptian government. My rare trips to Cairo usually included half an hour at his shop, where I was always rewarded by being shown something of value.

There had been much talk of a clever Greek forger living in Alexandria who was flooding the market with fakes, mostly el-Amarna pieces, but also a few of the Old Kingdom and the Saitic periods (663–525 B.C.). The forger specialized in rich American suckers, and never knowingly showed his collection to anyone with a knowledge of antiques.

One day Nahman said to me, "Joe, would you like to see that collection? If so, I can arrange it."

"It would give me great satisfaction," I replied.

I was warned to pose as a rich American nonentity. I thought I could. A few days later I received a message that Nahman had made an appointment for me to go to Shepheard's to see the forgeries at 3:00 o'clock promptly. He warned me again that I must be very careful, as the forger was shrewd.

I was shown into a large suite where an apparently marvelous collection was on view and well displayed. I took an instant dislike to the Greek, which, however, I managed to conceal. I was dressed for the part: a loud checked coat, a necktie in keeping, and a straw hat borrowed from a Texan gave the right note. The pieces were certainly amazing. If I had not been an artist and very familiar with all the periods of Egyptian art from having painted them, I believe I would have been fooled, but as the Greek kept up a steady patter while leading me from one object to another, I would notice something that gave the show away. In the el-Amarna heads, an eye not in character, or the modeling of the cheek, or the line of the hair. It was the same for the Old Kingdom and for the Saitic period.

I considered I had done pretty well in preserving my assumed identity and in my comments on the "remarkable" specimens which the Greek hoped to sell to me. But suddenly in a reaction to the fakes I had looked at with inward disgust, my eye fell upon a very charming small head of the el-Amarna period that was unquestionably genuine. I picked it up, and the quick eye of the Greek saw from my expression that I knew the difference. For a second he looked dazed, then he became furiously angry. He shouted to me, "I have been deceived. You are an expert."

Before I had had a chance to say a word, he pushed me into the hall and locked the door. It was not until I reached the hotel lobby that I realized I was still holding the splendid little Amarna head. I went directly to Nahman and confessed I had given myself away. I showed him the head. "Do you want to own it?" he asked.

"I certainly do," I replied.

Nahman assured me he could get it reasonably.

My conscience caused me to ask whether "reasonably" meant my silence about the fakes.

"No," Nahman told me. "I'll buy it and give it to you because you are my friend."

THE EGYPTIANS TAKE OVER

1 9 4 6 – 1 9 5 0

40. *Aftermath of the War*

ALL ARCHAEOLOGICAL ACTIVITIES had closed down in Egypt during World War II, but Reisner had refused to leave the Giza Plateau where he had lived and carried on scientific research for more than forty years. If an enemy plane appeared above Cheops' Pyramid, he joined the voluminous records covering the Harvard Expedition's excavations, which had been placed in a pit tomb for safekeeping, and there resumed his interrupted daily routine of work.

The Metropolitan Museum's headquarters on the Theban Plain near the temple of Deir-el-Bahari had been occupied by Harry Burton and his wife. He, as the expedition photographer, had continued to compile the most comprehensive and valuable photographic collection in tombs and temples ever made. Mrs. Burton was an intelligent and charming hostess.

But both Reisner and Burton were dead before Corinna and I returned to Egypt in the late fall of 1946. The Boston Museum had given up its concession and some of the staff were dismantling Harvard Camp before turning the property back to the Egyptian government, which had indicated its intention of using Reisner's offices and some of the living quarters for their own archaeologists. The Metropolitan Museum Expedition was going through the same process.

In spite of these and many other sad changes, I did not feel that this

220

was the end of an era dominated by foreign Egyptologists. Most of them were gone, but their memories were being kept alive by the unique collection of antiquities in the Cairo Museum representing every period of Egypt's ancient past. This was the result of collaboration, over the years, between the French, Germans, British, Americans, and Italians either in the employ of the Egyptian government or on expeditions staffed and financed by museums. Publications in a number of languages would continue to interpret for future generations the immensely important knowledge gained in excavations.

I recalled with pleasure a charming episode connected with the first great scholar to devote the active years of his life to work in Egypt, the Frenchman, Mariette Bey. In 1858, he was appointed by the Khedive to preserve the ancient monuments of Egypt, under the title of *Directeur Général* of a *Service des Antiquités*. So loyal was he to the trust placed in him that when Eugénie, as Empress of the French, was in Egypt on an official visit and the Khedive personally presented her with several of the most important statues in the museum, Mariette refused to let them leave the country.

In the early days, there was harmony between nationalities later to be in conflict. Mariette Bey was actively assisted in his difficult task by Heinrich Brugsch, a Prussian Egyptologist sent to Egypt by his government. Similarly, Maspero was to receive later the same effective kind of co-operation from both Adolf Erman and Kurt H. Sethe of the Berlin Museum. Two Americans benefited from training in German thoroughness: James Henry Breasted from Erman instruction, which qualified him to organize the most monumental epigraphic survey—specifically, the details of the Temple of Medinet Habu—ever undertaken in Egypt; and also George A. Reisner, who continued his collaboration with Sethe, became pre-eminent among excavators. Flinders Petrie, on the other hand, had his preparation for becoming an acknowledged leader in modern scientific excavation in his own England.

For the past fifty-odd years, the British School of Archaeology and the Egypt Exploration Fund, mostly under Petrie's stimulus, had attracted some of the best-known Egyptologists. The University of Liverpool had

221

been on the scene at an early date. James Edward Quibell and Cecil M. Firth were among the great Englishmen in the employ of the Egyptian government, and during most of their long years of service had been in charge of excavations.

Ludwig Borchardt was the founder of the powerful German Institute in Cairo, and Georg Steindorff, among his many other scholarly activities, revised what was to be the final edition of the Baedeker guide to Egypt and the Sudan. Maspero was responsible for the creation of the French Institute that continued to be supported by an impressive list of distinguished French Egyptologists whose record in excavations was not short of brilliant. The Italians also had done good work, under the auspices of the Turin Museum.

America had been effectively represented by the Metropolitan Museum of Art through its expedition headquarters on the Theban Plain, with notable excavations directed by such outstanding men as Albert Lythgoe, Arthur Mace, and Herbert E. Winlock. Other American museums had contributed through field expeditions.

And for forty years Reisner had been in residence at Harvard Camp for more months consecutively, winter and summer, than any other foreign scholar in Egypt. This joint expedition of Harvard University and the Boston Museum, situated on the top of a dramatic plateau overlooking the pyramids of Giza, early became an informal cultural center developed around the personality of Reisner, as has been seen. Visiting scholars passing through Egypt knew they would find him in his office, as did resident Egyptologists, men engaged in varied scientific research of allied character, and leading Egyptians.

After our arrival at Alexandria in the fall of 1946, Corinna and I went directly to Saqqarah to be with the Emerys. It had been helpful to me to have my thoughts dwell on the lasting foundations laid to insure the future success of Egyptological research, but I was not prepared for the disconcerting news that Emery had just resigned from the service of the Egyptian government to be head of British security in Egypt. No one regretted more than he did that circumstances made it necessary for him to give up his excavations at the Archaic Cemetery at North Saqqarah.

His final find in the preceding September had been the Dynasty I tomb of Queen Merneith. Its significance lay in the intact slave burials in the vicinity of the Queen's, with the implements used in the performance of slave's duties beside the skeleton. This had made possible the identification of a number of strange-looking objects, the purpose of which previously had not been known. In one intact burial was a large supply of long, absolutely smooth copper needles, with beautiful eyelets. Emery demonstrated by a thread and piece of cloth that they could be used today, but there was nothing to show *how* the eyelet had been bored.

When Emery's responsibilities kept him in Cairo on my subsequent visits to Egypt, the Antiquities Service gave Corinna and me the use of the little house where we had stayed so often, first with Quibell and then with the Emerys. Our nearest neighbor was Abd'es-Salam, an engineer of international reputation as well as an architect. He was directing the government work both at Saqqarah and at Dashuhr, and under him was a group of well-trained young Egyptologists. His attractive house, built on the high ledge overlooking the cultivated areas below, had become the same kind of cultural center that Harvard Camp had. English and Americans met here with Egyptian officials interested in archaeology.

Corinna and I became a part of the working regime of the Egyptians and were treated with the utmost cordiality. Really, my Egypt had remained the same—a land of tombs and temples, of brilliant sunshine, and of simple existence, which I shared with villagers, rising with the sun, working long hours, and going to bed soon after darkness fell.

I painted many of the recent Saqqarah finds made by Egyptians during 1945 and 1946. One was a lovely, long stone slab, with low-cut, delicate reliefs in color of gazelles, antelope, and other animals that Abd'es-Salam had uncovered in clearing a part of the causeway leading to the Unas Pyramid of Dynasty VI. Then there were two very fine wooden statues made of cedar of Lebanon signed Akhethotep found in a Dynasty V tomb. Unfortunately, the king was not identified. The faces looked as though they might have been portraits. I also painted fragments of charming, small limestone reliefs and heads, all of Dynasty V.

I worked in the Dynasty V *mastaba* of Neferherptah, a recent discovery of Abd'es-Salam's. The reliefs were in the upper story, high on the wall, and my staging in the width available could be only two extremely narrow planks placed across a very deep, black, open pit. The *mastaba* was difficult of access up a steep ladder, several rungs of which were missing, and at the top I had to crawl along a narrow ledge of a cliff to a low entrance door, where I could not stand erect. I had refused to use artificial illumination as being too harsh for the delicacy of the subject, which was a marsh scene with birds flying about, and, as in similar cases, solved the problem by the use of mirrors reflecting natural light from a level far below.

Abd'es-Salam asked me to make a study of a 1945 find from a Saqqarah tomb which showed the owner seated at the entrance. An inscription read that he was a "lessee" of a funerary estate. This tomb was dated from the latter part of Dynasty VI (2420–2258 B.C.), and provided evidence that priests were still landlords.

But two discoveries made on my 1948 trip to Saqqarah were of an upsetting nature. No trace of color remained on the charming funerary animals I had painted only the year before. Another and even worse blow was to find that King Zoser's small figure, which was surrounded by gay blue tiles in a room of his pyramid far underground, had broken loose from the plaster that held it to the wall. The figure was in a sad state of deterioration. I was only thankful that I had painted it twenty years ago at Firth's request.

Egyptian officials, like the rest of the world, always had time for a mummy. Our Saqqarah mummy excitement came about in the following manner. Under the direction of Abd'es-Salam, men were clearing a mass of debris that had lain for years at the top of the desert plateau near the Pyramid of Unas. Unexpectedly, the workmen's short hoes uncovered the opening of a wide shaft sunk through the living rock. The fact that it was filled with hard, caked sand, obviously untouched through the centuries, gave promise that the contents of the pit were intact. The clearing went on for several days, before, at a depth of about one hundred feet, they came to the rock bottom. Four men holding a pulley lowered Abd'es-Salam and me into the blackness as we clung to a makeshift seat

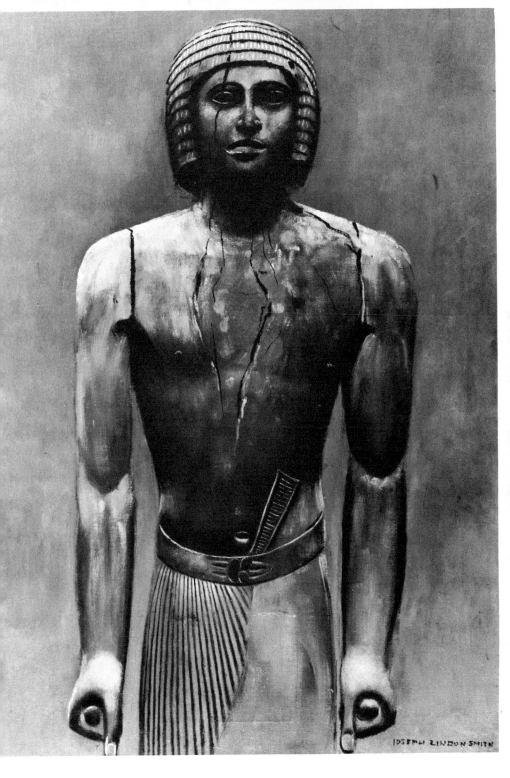

Cedar of Lebanon statue of Akhet-hotep, Saqqarah. Painting by Joseph Lindon Smith. Courtesy Egyptian government.

Amenhotep I, the upper portion only of his bas-relief portrait in the Alabaster Chapel, Karnak. Painting by Joseph Lindon Smith. Courtesy the Egyptian government.

Dancing girls from depiction of the Feast of Opet, Queen Hatshepsut's Red Sandstone Shrine, Karnak. Painting by Joseph Lindon Smith. Courtesy the Egyptian government.

made of a few boards fastened together hastily and without sides. The descent was a little too fast for pleasure, with the creaking boards swaying perilously back and forth. (I had recently turned eighty-three and liked the notion of continued activity without foolhardy stunts.) We crawled through a gap in a stone wall into a gloomy chamber about five feet high, where the flickering light of our torches disclosed, in the distance beyond, cavelike openings cut into the rock and filled with crude brick. There was no sign of entry either by ancient thieves or by modern archaeologists.

We peered into the room adjoining the chamber we were in. The torches illuminated three wooden coffins flat on the rock floor. In front of them was a great number of tiny statuettes made of blue glaze. A parchment scroll had been laid on the lid of a coffin. Without disturbing an intact burial, we signaled the men above to take us to the surface. Again above ground, Abd'es-Salam rushed to the telephone and called Etienne Drioton, who had succeeded Lacau in 1935 as head of the Antiquities Service. He turned up promptly, and shortly thereafter Abd'es-Salam and I were close at his heels in crawling through the same hole in the wall by which we had entered the main chamber before. Drioton motioned us inside the room with the three coffins, which turned out to have three others behind them. He picked up the inscribed statuette I had noticed and read the name on it, "Kanefer," adding, "a scribe of the temple of Ptah," and dating the burial to Dynasty XXVI (663–525 B.C. Meantime, I had counted over three hundred of these blue glaze figures. Drioton thought that this might turn out to be one of the large cemeteries of Dynasty XXVI, and felt that the find rated an official opening, with all the fuss and fanfare of such an occasion. This was arranged, and by the next morning at eleven o'clock an array of cars was visible on the horizon. When the caravan arrived, several ministers and other high officials of the Egyptian government got out. To my amazement, all were garbed in the black European gear of ceremony. Havoc was about to be produced by that dirty hole in the ground, where standing erect was impossible. Immaculate long coats and well-creased trousers could not survive here. Abd'es-Salam, Drioton, and I were suitably dressed for tombing, but above ground looked shabby in contrast to the ministerial splendor.

The ropes creaked noisily as the chair successfully deposited at the bottom of the shaft one distinguished guest after another. They had one advantage over those of us who had entered earlier—electric lights had been brought in. They were all good sports, however, and looked definitely interested when, on hands and knees, they crawled into the room containing the coffins, their garments revealing severe casualties, some having been torn in vital parts. The party crawled into one cavelike room after another with very low ceilings. In one of them, a minister discovered on a coffin an inscription. In pointing it out to Drioton, he got a bad blow on his head from a projecting rock. He was oblivious to the blow in his eagerness to listen to Drioton read the name of the owner of the coffin.

By now, they were a sorry-looking group, disheveled and perspiring freely beneath their red fezes, as once again they squatted on their heels in the outer room, mopping their brows and breathing heavily, their coats in tatters and trousers a wreck. Several persons had bleeding knees.

The ministers did full justice to a meal served them later, when they went above ground. Their garments had miraculously recovered some of their elegance, thanks to the ministrations of Abd'es-Salam's versatile staff, which included a man skillful with a needle. In high good humor, the ministers then got into their motors and returned to Cairo.

As an interlude to my Saqqarah regime, I went to Luxor at the suggestion of Lacau. He, like me, was an old-timer who could not keep away from Egypt's ancient graves and temples. The particular attractions that brought him back after an absence of ten years were the texts on some monuments that had recently been found. He urged me to paint some of the reliefs from these same monuments.

Corinna and I thoroughly enjoyed being back at "Chicago House," as the Oriental Institute of the University of Chicago was called locally. And it was an impressive sight to see the large number of young Egyptian archaeologists making use of a library for scholars at the headquarters of the only American expedition still functioning in Egypt. The staff, which was doing a splendid job in co-operating with Egyptian scholars, included men of varied interests. Richard A. Parker was an authority on the astronomy and calendars of Egypt. He was later to leave field work on being called to the first chair of Egyptology established in the United States, at Brown University, Providence. George Hughes was a specialist in the demotic characters used in Egyptian writing after the fifth century B.C. Charles Nims was an expert trained for the exacting recording of monuments by photography. Their wives, Gladys Parker, Maureen Hughes, and Myrtle Nims, at all times made visiting Egyptians welcome at Chicago House.

John A. Wilson, author and administrator since his first working trip to Egypt in 1926, had added greatly to the prestige of Breasted's Oriental Institute of the University of Chicago. He and his wife, Mary, had a wide circle of Egyptian friends among his many colleagues in Egyptology, and their return to Luxor in 1950 for a season was fortunate as an American contact at a critical period.

Mustafa Amer was an able director-general of the Antiquities Service for the Egyptian government. Labib Habashi, whose outstanding archae-ological work at the first cataract on Elephantine Island was recog-nized by all foreign scholars, had followed this by equal achievements in other parts of Egypt. Another Egyptian who had a close association in his work with archaeologists of other countries was Ahmad Fakhri, who made an important survey of the western desert and oases. Some of his other notable contributions were an archaeological trip to the Yemen and a special study of some of the texts at Dashuhr.

Zakaria Ghoneim, inspector of Antiquities, was excavating at Luxor some of the Sphinxes at the Luxor Temple end that once had lined the entire route from Karnak to Luxor. On the Theban Plain another Egyp-tian excavator, Khalid Bey Darwish, chief government architect for temples, had come from Port Said to restore the second pylon of the Ramesseum, and also to carry on excavations in the arable land on the desert side of the Colossi of Memnon. Corinna and I went to see his discovery.

To reach the site, we had to scramble down a hole about nine meters below the surface level. But it was like the good old days of foreign excavations in this district to hear workmen singing as, from the vicinity of a huge object *in situ,* they carried baskets of loosened debris to deposit on a near-by dump. We stood at the head of a colossal statue lying on its side and facing north. I assisted Khalid Bey in gently clearing wet mud from the head and features, which were very fine. The figure had originally been carved from a single block of stone, roughly speaking, some thirty feet high, but it was now in three pieces, with the lower part of the legs and feet missing.

We moved along it to a square base, which was inscribed with the name and title of Amenhotep III (1410–1372 B.C.), the same Pharaoh who had built the near-by seated Colossi. There was much interesting information in hieroglyphic inscriptions. This find of a standing statue, with a magnificent head and face intact, when set up, would make a sensation in archaeological circles. We were delighted with Khalid Bey's good fortune.

The material that had interested Lacau was a series of inscribed blocks with reliefs, some of alabaster, others of white limestone, and a third group consisting of a vast number of blocks of red sandstone. The history of the find is as follows: From the west entrance to Karnak facing the Nile, Pylon I was just beyond the avenue of Sphinxes, and Pylon II led into the great Hypostyle Hall. A few years before the recent war, Pylon III, which was at the far end of the hall, collapsed. Henri Chevrier, the French government engineer in charge of restorations at Karnak, had to take this pylon entirely down before rebuilding it. He had found these blocks inside the pylon among huge boulders, all in an excellent state of preservation from having been used as foundation stones by the unknown builder of Pylon III, very late in date.

Chevrier assembled and set up in the vast enclosure of Karnak the alabaster chapel and the white limestone shrine, even though there was no archaeological data found to determine where they originally stood. Inscriptions, however, indicated that both of them were "way stations" in which rested the sacred barque of Amon during ceremonies connected with some festival, probably the Feast of Opet.

These were the postwar days when Corinna and I would be up before six, and by seven, in the delicious freshness of early morning, we were speeding along the river bank headed for Karnak. The Nile was like a beautiful vision, with the surface barely stirred by a light breeze, and reflected in its depths were black hulls and tall sails, and from across the river, green fields, and on the horizon, pink cliffs. *Fellaheen* with livestock were on their way to the fields, carrying short hoes similar to those used in predynastic times. Other men were making bricks according to the old-time method. When we approached the entrance to Karnak, a *ghaffir* jumped to attention from a bedroll spread on the hard ground, saluting with a smile as he opened the iron gate. We paused briefly to look down the long line of tall columns in the Hypostyle Hall, where sounds of workmen's songs echoed delightfully. The alabaster blocks we saw before us belonged to a chapel built within the colonnades of a roofed-over temple. They had given the name to this structure, the Alabaster Chapel of Ahmose I. The roof slabs and also the closed-in sides were intact. The entrance was through a rather wide opening. Reliefs on the walls in the lower register depicted various scenes showing Ahmose, the first king of Dynasty XVIII, making offerings to the god Amon. On the upper register was a sacred ceremonial barque of Amon rather badly broken. I selected as my first subject figures of the King and the god standing together.

I uncovered my canvas just as the sunlight was giving a dramatic effect of radiance to my beautifully garbed and bejeweled slim King. It needed the sunlight directly on him to bring out the beauty of details of his wig, ornaments, and stiff ceremonial skirt carved in the difficult medium of alabaster. Similar light was needed on the tall headdress of the god. I seated myself on a high stool and painted rapidly. In a brief half-hour, the sun, which soon after rising penetrated through the opening of the doorless chapel, had disappeared for the day, making the figures all but invisible.

On leaving, I noticed on the outside wall of the doorless opening that places for hinges were still visible and an ancient inscription read, "the like of this gold door has never been seen." Hieroglyphs also gave the name of the quarries from which the alabaster had come, a site later to be identified by archaeologists as Akhenaten's city at el-Amarna.

Still other limestone blocks belonged to the Shrine of Sesostris I that was practically intact and unique, moreover, in being of the splendid Middle Kingdom period of Egyptian art hitherto known by remnants of buildings and scattered statues and inscriptions.

The wide, carved casing stones to the shrine platform were about four feet above the ground level. Entrance was at both ends, east and west, by a ramp of easy tread, with a flight of steps in the center. The shrine was about square, with two columns, also square, in a double row, covered with reliefs and inscriptions. Unpainted delicate figures were a little over twenty-four inches in height. Everything else was in proportion. On the floor down the middle of the inside columns was an altar of red granite. The roofing blocks were intact, and only a little of the architrave had to be restored. The outside walls had no carvings.

The reliefs showed the King being honored by Amon, who, in my first subject, was wearing a feathered garment with a headdress of tall plumes. The King was equally magnificent with just as beautiful clothes and necklaces. Amon was presenting the key of life to the King, and Horus, the hawk-headed god, stood behind him. There were no doors, and from where I sat, the very blue sky, seen through wide openings between the columns, was a wonderful sight. The reliefs in reflected sunlight gave a warm glow to the small figures, bringing out lovely details. After about a week of long hours of painting, in preparation for obtaining the desired effect of bringing out the cameo-like figures, which, in certain lights, merged into the background, of a sudden one afternoon, as though by a mirage, these people of long ago lived again on the painted surface of my canvas.

In the same large enclosure containing the Alabaster Chapel and Sesostris Shrine, a vast quantity of huge, red sandstone blocks, also discovered inside Pylon III, had been set up in long rows (not in order) available for study. The texts and reliefs identified them as belonging to a large shrine built by Hatshepsut during the period she had built the Temple of Deir el-Bahari and ruled in her own right. On one of these blocks was a very spirited figure of her in the male attire and crown of a king she wore on temple walls, showing her straddling a young bull. In another she was laying out the confines of her shrine with the goddess of writing. A variety of scenes on about ten of these blocks showed Hatshepsut's participation, as king, in ceremonies connected with the ancient Feast of Opet. Lacau thought that this would probably be the most complete description of what happened at the stations at which the sacred barque of Amon rested at stated periods during the visit. To date, information about the specialized rites performed were lacking. After Hatshepsut's death in 1483 B.C., Tuthmosis III, until the end of his long reign, did his utmost to erase all trace of her reign by hacking out her figure and name, not only throughout Karnak, but even on her own temple of Deir el-Bahari. Now, by the irony of fate, after the publication of this shrine, Hatshepsut's name will become associated with the most important festival of the New Kingdom. Woman *will* have the last word!

The record of this archaeological comeback was encouraging. We had seen the successful excavations by Egyptians, and I had been privileged to paint in shrines that Lacau and other archaeologists considered the most important discoveries in recent times.

As early as 1947, something happened to me that seemed to give that note of recognition which justifies the long commitment of a lifetime. Before we left Egypt in the spring, soon after getting back to Saqqarah from painting in Lacau's shrines, I received a message from H. E. Sanhoury Pasha, the minister of Education. He wished me to bring some of my pictures to the big Antiquity Service House where he was spending the night.

I hung a standing life-size figure of Mereruka on the wall of the room in which the Minister was to receive me. Without noticing my presence, he walked directly to Mereruka and touched one of the hands.

231

Then, turning, he said, "I can't believe it isn't stone." He asked if I would be willing to teach my painting technique to several specially selected Egyptian graduates of the Government School of Higher Art in Zamalek, Cairo. He would like them trained by me, to paint a government-owned study series of their own traditional art.

I said I would be delighted to have the opportunity. When he next asked me whether I would be willing to exhibit my collection of this season's paintings in the great entrance rotunda of the Cairo Museum, primarily for the benefit of Egyptian students and artists, I almost fell off my chair.

Being invited to show my pictures of sculptured reliefs by the side of the great treasures of ancient Egypt was an honor I knew had never been accorded any other painter.

This museum exhibition of my pictures, after a formal opening, was to be held for four consecutive years. Reisner had enjoyed having all Cairo come to Harvard Camp annually by invitation to see my paintings. But he thought they should also be on public view at the Cairo Museum. Now his wish had been realized after his death. The dean of Arabic inspectors, of the Ministry of Education, wrote a pamphlet about me, illustrated with some of my paintings. It was entitled: *The Artist and the Man.* Thousands of copies were distributed in Arabic and in English, in Near East cultural displays done with the active assistance of our cultural attaché at the American Embassy in Cairo. I was invited to meet members of the Arabic press at a conference; feature articles appeared about my work.

One such was in a small-town Arabic newspaper under the heading in large type: "Joseph Lindon Smith—Egypt's Cultural Project." What pleased me very much in the text was the statement that Mr. Smith's paintings had stimulated the interest of many Egyptians to go and see for themselves the wonderful monuments of their own country and to take pride in their great traditional art.

41. *Half a Century in Retrospect*

IN MY EXTREME YOUTH, a decision confronted me about a future career that no one could make for me. I made it when I came face to face with one of the great monuments of the Nile Valley. I realized instantly that I preferred portrait sitters to be of stone, and it was Reisner who persuaded me that my paintings of sculptured reliefs in the tombs and temples of Egypt would serve a useful purpose.

As a result of my decision, no living man has spent more consecutive hours in ancient graves during the past fifty years. My reason for doing this was that the kings, their families, and the court dignitaries who lay buried in these graves lived at great periods of art. I have covered hundreds of yards of canvas with the sculptured reliefs appearing on the walls of these tombs and in temples.

Now, after half a century of work in a highly specialized field of painting, it is logical for people to ask, as I have asked myself, about the value of my replicas, which reproduce on canvas the size, form, and color of ancient sculptured reliefs. What purpose are they serving?

I will try to define a useful purpose served by my pictures in museums and elsewhere. This is not easy for me to do, since I am personally involved. I shall not start by contending that in these years of visiting and revisiting ancient sites in the Near East, the Far East, and in the land of our Maya, I saw things that countless scholars have not studied and written about. To me, it comes down to this: the observing eye of an artist of my experience, from being constantly in ancient countries with a great traditional art, gains something that is at once worth conveying to others, and that is outside the sphere of the scholar. I can add, not incidentally, that it is impossible for the highly perfected modern camera to record these art objects even in color.

If my pictures did no more than reflect, as in a mirror, reliefs and other ancient art treasures, I should deserve the classification of copyist given me by critics of my early exhibitions. I like to think, on the contrary, that the poet Whittier was correct in his premise that my type of painting was creative. This would not be justified, however, merely

233

from my development of a technique that reproduced on canvas the exact details, in outward appearance, of my subjects—even to the patina of ancient bronze and the textures of marble and wood surfaces. I must do far more and give my pictures qualities which another human eye can catch in looking at them—not in a flash, but in contemplation. In other words, my interpretation must convey both the spirit of the original and my own appreciation of its beauty, to make it understandable to someone else.

The late Royal Cortissoz, the leading art critic of his time, was more than kind when he told me that an exhibition of my paintings put him in a mood of awed wonder at the majesty of the monuments of ancient Egypt. He then went on to say that, to him, my canvases bore witness to my sympathy for the art of these ancient peoples. He felt that whatever values my work may have achieved lay in my ability to recreate, through my own self-effacement, the work of a genius who had lived long ago.

Through the years, my paintings have been fairly widely scattered and seen by many and varied groups. I feel confident that they have been of service in arousing interest among art lovers, and even more important, potential art lovers, for the great traditional art in many countries, of which these pictures of mine are only a few examples. And this, I consider, is an adequate *apologia pro vita sua.*

THE ANCIENT NEAR EAST

42. *The Long Influence of Egypt*

COUNTRIES in the Near East were, even in ancient times, easily accessible to one another. We may not, therefore, place their respective traditions and cultures in air-tight compartments and consider them separately. In my own frequent wanderings through what might be termed the Art Belt of the Ancient World, I have personally come across many interlocking traditions and influences as I have exchanged ideas with the peoples now occupying these countries. On such trips it has always been of special interest to me to meet archaeologists and historians who were uncovering, through scientific research, similarities in ancient cultural centers. But to prove by these similarities the direct influence of one civilization upon another, and to account for time sequences, were difficult matters.

Take, for example, the relations between Egypt and the Sumerians, which have remained of a more tenuous nature than those of Egypt with the Semitic nations of Palestine and Syria. In the Nile Delta, during the pre-dynastic period, when Egypt was known to have direct cultural contact with her Semitic neighbors, it would seem likely that she was also in touch with the civilizations growing up in the valleys of the lower Tigris and Euphrates valleys.

For instance, both cultures had the expected sequence of the use of reed-matting and wood and brick in building. In Mesopotamia, mud-brick blocks, made in wooden molds, went back to very ancient times. Many scholars considered that Egypt adopted this method from Mesopotamia and did not develop it independently. In the latter part of the pre-dynastic era, Egypt had brick buildings, and the wood employed in construction, generally cedar of Lebanon, came from Syria. By Dynasty I, as excavations in the Archaic Cemetery of North Saqqarah disclosed, brick architecture had become impressive.

Before the dynastic period, certain types of pottery in the graves of Lower Egypt came from Palestine and Syria. Some of the animal forms in decorations were found in Sumerian designs of about the same date. Lapis lazuli must have been imported from Mesopotamia just as obsidian was from Abyssinia and Arabia.

Probable links between Egyptians in the Delta and the Sumerians were suggested in discoveries by Quibell in his excavations at Hierakonpolis in a cemetery dating from Dynasty I (3200–2980 B.C.). One was the commemorative carved slate palette belonging to Narmer. This find was of primary importance in showing the King, the Horus Narmer (Menes), wearing the tall crown of Upper Egypt, celebrating his conquest of Lower Egypt. That crown was added on the reverse side of the palette, as evidence of his being head of a united Egypt. Narmer was the first of a long line of dynastic rulers in Egypt.

There were other significant features in the designs on this commemorative palette. The archaic animals, including the lion, and certain symbols were similar to those appearing contemporaneously on cylinder seals in Mesopotamia, Syria, and Egypt. In addition, on the palette was a very early example of a "palace façade," in this instance, surmounted by a royal falcon.

Furthermore, Quibell discovered in the same Hierakonpolis cemetery pear-shaped mace heads that had their counterparts in the work of the Sumerians. These similarities indicated at least a trading connection at a period when Egypt was sending expeditions to the Syrian coasts to bring back huge beams needed for construction.

By the time of Dynasty IV at Giza (2680–2565 B.C.), Cheops and his successors were importing oil from Syria and Palestine, and the trade with Syria for cedar remained active throughout Dynasty V (2565–2420 B.C.) and Dynasty VI (2420–2258 B.C.), as evidenced by the number of statues discovered made of that special wood.

Egypt's documents of all sorts were written on papyrus and long since were eaten by white ants. On the other hand the cuneiform clay tablets of the Sumerians have been preserved and some hundreds of thousands deciphered. Apparently, among the vast numbers, recording business transactions varied in kind, not one of them mentioned any contact with Egypt.

The Persian domination of Egypt began in the reign of Cambyses (525–522 B.C.) and lasted nominally about two hundred years. The lost army of Cambyses has become legendary history, telling of an invading army which vanished in Egypt's desert sands, leaving no trace beyond a few broken water jars—a fitting symbol of Persian rule in the Valley of the Nile. Persian rule was strictly military in character, assailed by constant revolts of a people outraged at the open ridicule of their en-shrined animal gods. No Persian ruler had his name or image carved on a temple wall in Egypt!

Alexander's brief career there was in striking contrast. Egypt cap-tured his imagination, and he appeared as a companion in the pantheon of Egyptian gods in temples up and down the Nile Valley. Even his half-brother, Philip Arrhidaeus, who was never in Egypt, had a large red shrine built in his name at Karnak, still extant.

The appreciation of things Egyptian inaugurated by Alexander was carried on by a long line of Ptolemies, the first descended from one of Alexander's generals. It lasted through the domination of Egypt by Rome, beginning in the early part of the Christian era, and there were no features distinguishing these temples from those built during Egyp-tian dynasties many centuries earlier.

The Museum of Alexandria, the city built by Alexander, is filled with objects of the "transition" between ancient Egypt and classical and later Greece. There are to be seen many evidences as surprising as that of the fluted column, so prevalent in Greece, which was used in Egypt by Zoser's inspired architect, Imhotep, twenty-three hundred years before the time of Pericles. These museum objects are eloquent of the debt owed by Greek sculptors to Egyptians, who handed down great ideas of form to the workers in Greece's archaic period.

However great Egypt's tradition in art, she had nothing of a religious character to pass on. In Egypt, religion consisted of magic formulas and a complicated ritual, performed by priests for the benefit of kings, in which the people had no part. There was neither spirituality nor intellectual depth in the Egyptian conception of an eternal life dedicated to the possessions and pleasures the deceased had enjoyed on earth. The real development of the mind and spirit of Egypt occurred when Alexander brought to Alexandria the most complete library of the ancient world.

The Romans in Egypt continued in the path defined by the Greeks, but with less success. As a consequence, the people of Egypt welcomed the advent of hordes of invading Arabs in A.D. 640, considering them as deliverers from the Roman oppressors.

43. *Ur of the Chaldees*

MY FIRST PERSONAL INTEREST in Sumerian civilization came from Reisner's having taught cuneiform at Harvard University long before he decided to become an Egyptologist. Therefore, he had a scholar's knowledge of the vast Sumerian literature. From time to time, authorities on the subject turned up at Harvard Camp. I heard about "literary" clay tablets dating from as early at 3000 B.C., containing Sumerian epics, myths, proverbs, and royal hymns composed for the kings of Dynasty III at Ur. I was told that a quarter of a million was a conservative estimate of the number of such tablets, covering many subjects other than purely literary ones, that were owned in America alone. By 2000 B.C., Sumerian cuneiform, which began as pictographic writing, was all over the Near East. The Hebrew contribution to the Western World came, in fact, from Sumeria through Babylon.

Reisner believed that, in Egypt, the art of writing was known even in the prehistoric period. Picture signs, he indicated, had developed rapidly during Dynasty I. He used to say that the primitive form of hieroglyphs, as they appeared on the stela at Abydos giving the name of Zer(Ity), the second king of Dynasty I, had traveled a long distance as a language before it reached the beautiful gold lettering on the furniture of Queen Hetepheres.

At times in Reisner's office, I sat in at heated discussions about whether the Sumerian was an older civilization than that of Egypt. The matter was still undetermined, as far as I could find out, when Corinna and I, early in December, 1930, were to leave Egypt for an extended trip that was to include a visit to Ur, the city of Abraham.

This is how it came about. C. Leonard Woolley, the English archaeologist, was, from 1923 on, in charge of a joint expedition of the British Museum and the University of Pennsylvania to excavate at Ur. In 1929, he came to America on a lecture tour, and during his stay in New York, he talked informally one evening about his excavations of the great flood pit at Ur (1927–29). Woolley described going down through nine strata of civilizations before reaching the original marsh, the "bottom" of Mesopotamia. Just above the marsh level, he came to an eight-foot bank of clay laid in clean water. He realized, he told us with unusual emphasis, that this amount of water was impossible to account for by an inundation. "Only the Flood of Sumerian legend could explain a clay bank that marked an abrupt break in the continuity of history and a complete change in the culture after it," he said.

That evening the Woolleys invited us to come to Ur. Corinna was all for it, and Reisner urged us to go. The flood pit fired my imagination, but, above all, I wanted to see in the Baghdad Museum the famous harp Woolley had discovered and judge for myself how much it resembled the harp I had painted from the walls of a Saqqarah tomb.

Our ultimate trip took us from Egypt to Damascus by train, and early the following morning we were off for Baghdad by the Nairn Transport Service. Because of nomad tribes, the desert trek of twenty-four hours by bus was made in a caravan with police escort. I was anxious to push on to Ur and I therefore allowed only a brief two days for Baghdad. At the moment, my mind was preoccupied with flood potentialities in Mesopotamia, and Paul Knabenshue, our American minister to Iraq, good naturedly drove us along the Tigris within a radius of several hundred miles to examine a number of places where recent inundations had been extensive before the flood water receded. The surface of the area looked to me like the stretches of desert in Egypt that I had been over after a heavy sand storm. A similar phenomenon occurs in Arizona and New Mexico, where the effect of whirling "sand devils" and cloudbursts were indistinguishable on desert land. Knabenshue, who also knew desert country, concurred in my opinion that traces left by flood water and sand were identical.

In the museum I paid homage to Woolley's great finds, which were well displayed, but I was disappointed that the harp was temporarily not on view. Some of the gold and silver vessels and bowls had the simplicity of line and perfection of workmanship so noticeable in the objects found in the tomb of Queen Hetepheres, and an interesting feature on the gold sheath of a magnificent dagger was an open-work pattern derived from plaited grass, suggestive of the reed mat design dating to the Archaic Period in Egypt. Amazing golden headdresses had tiny trees, flowers and petals inlaid with lapis lazuli, and shell with masses of intricate pendants. Other jewelry in the form of lunate earrings and bracelets was equally elaborate. There were engraved shell plaques, amulets in the form of fish, and on them gazelles and endless other delicate details.

That the civilization of Mesopotamia was older than that of Egypt, if calculated on the premise that it took a long time after a climax in traditional art had been reached before a decline set in, had confirmation in this sophisticated workmanship, on the verge of being a decadent art.

The low, flat country of Mesopotamia we passed through by train to reach Ur of the Chaldees was not inspiring, but seeing the Euphrates for the first time, muddy and unimpressive as it was, did stir my pulse. Soon after our arrival I made a sketch of Woolley's flood pit. The site fascinated me, as I sat on the edge and looked down into space, my thoughts on the history that had been revealed in a "cut" two hundred feet wide and going down to where all traces of human activity ceased.

Certain facts that Woolley mentioned as discoveries in different strata stood out, such as a single brick of burnt clay not far above sea

240

The Greek influence in Egypt. Ptolemaic Temple at Edfu. Photograph courtesy Ray Garner for the American Research Center in Egypt.

Persepolis, the Apadana Stairway from the northwest. Photograph courtesy the Oriental Institute, University of Chicago.

Detail from the Apadana Stairway: Scythian tribute bearers. Painting by Joseph Lindon Smith. Courtesy the Oriental Institute, University of Chicago.

level, which was evidence that Ur had been a center of civilization at a very early date. Later ruins indicated a high state of culture in an antediluvian age, and that probably the art of writing was known. What I liked best was Woolley's description of reaching a wide stratum where all signs of buildings had disappeared in a belt composed of ashes and broken pottery. In it he found fragments of potters' wheels, and inside one intact kiln were vessels neatly stacked, ready for final firing. This incident made me feel as though I were wandering about Pompeii.

I left the flood pit with reluctance to follow Woolley, who wanted to show me about his other excavations. Before going to the site of his sensational finds of the burial places of the three great kings of Dynasty III, he pointed out a place where four roads met. There, by pure chance, he had come upon a chapel dedicated to the little-known deity, Pa-Sag, "protector of the desert paths." The one room in this house far underground contained a tiny sanctuary with a statue of white limestone still in its niche. It was a squat little figure, broken in antiquity and mended for continued use in this wayside shrine. When I handled the odd little mended figure, it gave me the same thrill as seeing the chair that had been used in life and repaired for "grandma" by her granddaughter, in the Tomb of Ouiya and Touiyou.

In this same shrine, the door, made with a wooden frame and an inset panel of reeds, had been left half-open. Reeds and wood had vanished, but their impression was stamped on the hard soil, and Woolley got a photograph of it. This was the same kind of experience as the one I had had, when, in a side room of the unfinished Tomb of Tuthmosis IV, I saw in the sand the impression of a workman's shirt that had fallen from a wooden peg, which had been stuck in a crevice of the rock, and the peg was still there; or, again, the clearly defined footprints of the high priest and the chief mourner in a burial chamber with the seals on the outer door. These are incidents that made the past linger on as a reality, a past made vital by human beings like ourselves.

Woolley told me that Ur-Nammu, the founder of Dynasty III in 2079 B.C., built the Ziggurat. His son Dungi and his grandson Bur-Sin were the other two kings of this great Sumerian dynasty. The descent to

241

their buildings was through a labyrinth of stairways under corbelled vaults surrounded by massive walls and buttresses, into huge rooms, some of them fifty feet in length. Woolley seemed to find an added charm and mystery in having these temple tombs so deep down in the dark. I tried to keep pace with his imagination in visualizing the buildings in their former magnificence, ornamented with gold plaiting and mosaics in lapis lazuli and gold. He could reconstruct their appearance from scraps overlooked by the Elamites when they tore down the decorations on the doors and walls at the time they swept down in force from the Persian hills and put an end to Dynasty III (1960 B.C.).

The Sumerians during the period of Dynasty III had the peculiar conception that a king was to be worshiped as a god after his burial. But to them he remained alive, and his human past called for a house similar to houses in the residential quarters of the ancient city, with the usual courtyard and rooms, the only difference being that in these rooms were altars for offerings.

Like everything else at Ur, the *sati* royal burials with human sacrifices were on a gigantic scale. Woolley mentioned finding a queen with twenty-five people interred around her, and with them a wooden sledge chariot adorned with golden heads of lions and bulls. There were crushed skeletons of two asses with the bodies of grooms beside them. In another burial was a wagon drawn by three oxen with the skeleton of one of the animals so well preserved it could be removed. Drivers were inside the wagons and grooms lay near the heads of the oxen.

The Ziggurat, or temple of heaven, dedicated to the moon god of Ur, was a solid mass of brickwork. The walls, built with a pronounced inward slope, rose sheer on three sides to the level of the first stage, with three stairways converging at a great gateway; from there a single flight of steps led to the shrine on top, past terraces and towers. Long recesses in shallow buttresses were not paved but contained soil in which trees were planted. This was the plan used later for the "hanging gardens" of Babylon, and the towers above, for the "Tower of Babel." The construction of the Ziggurat was one of calculated curves, and by their use the architect had created an optical illusion copied by the Greeks in the Parthenon many centuries later.

We sat on the corner of the shrine looking over a vast distance of flat country. Woolley said we could understand how much excavating had been done at the Ziggurat, because, when he had first come to Ur, in 1923, it was possible to ride to the top on horseback. He pointed out stretches of the massive surrounding wall of the ancient city of Ur, still extant, and I was delighted to find out the kind of house which Abraham had lived in. When archaeologists had started excavating the residential district of the period of Abraham, they had expected very modest dwellings. Instead, digging revealed homes built on solid foundations, with a central court providing height and air, and thirteen or fourteen rooms on two stories, with plaster and whitewash hiding the brickwork. He also showed us the site of Jacob's house, quite close to the Ziggurat, and from the main court, evidence of a causeway which led from it directly up to the shrine. This causeway, we now know, was originally lined with gold. It was another touch with reality to be in the city where both Abraham and Jacob had lived, and to know that in this causeway was, perhaps, the source of the "ladders of gold" leading from Jacob's house to "heaven," as the shrine at the top of the Ziggurat was called.

Soon our conversation turned on other problematical details of Ur and the Sumerians. Ur had been one of the so-called "islands" in the original marsh, like the other ancient centers of the lower Euphrates Valley. The mounds of Ur had accumulated one above the other until the city was above the level destroyed by the ancient Flood. There remained no trace of the pottery that had been prevalent through the neighboring centers in the pre-Flood period. Therefore it was probable that none of the inhabitants of the places who made it had survived.

Ancient annals referred to kingship as having descended again after a gap. The Sumerians were thought to have come to Ur from a hilly country to the east and brought with them a highly organized civilization of the urban type. Scholars generally have accepted a later date than was at first calculated for the beginnings of the dynastic period in Egypt,

243

and the same is true for Ur. I understand that Woolley's great Dynasty III is now placed from 2079–1960 B.C.

Dates in ancient times have proved to be variable, but certainly the evidence of the great culture of Ur during the period of her magnificent buildings cannot be disputed. Her architects were familiar with the basic principles of construction, and her craftsmen in metal had a technical skill that was seldom reached by ancient peoples. To me, one of her most far-reaching contributions was the "Standard of Ur," a small mosaic with delicate figures silhouetted in shell, charming in detail and revealing a background of lapis lazuli.

On one side of the mosaic, the king and the royal family are seated at a feast, in costumes of sheepskin, seemingly kilts or petticoats. Servants are waiting on them, a musician is playing a harp, and a singer is performing vocally. In contrast with this peaceful scene, the reverse side shows the king in his war chariot, prisoners are being brought before him by soldiers, infantry forces are indicated wearing copper helmets and long cloaks of the type in use today by Anatolian shepherds. This mosaic is the earliest-known detailed picture of the organization of the Sumerian army, with the phalanx formation, the use of chariots, and the existence of infantry. It was a combination destined to bring victory to many countries at war down through the ages.

I realized that the relations between Egypt and the Sumerians at Ur were difficult to determine from the historical and artistic points of view, but I had been prepared to accept what I had heard from many intelligent sources and what I now saw for myself, and I thought I could reach some conclusions. For a final decision on one phase of the situation, I went again to the Baghdad Museum.

This time I examined the much-publicized harp. It was strikingly beautiful and a real musical instrument, as well. The sounding board was bordered with a broad edging of mosaics, the uprights separated by gold bands, and there were crossbars of plain wood, decorated with silver in front and surmounted by splendid heads of bearded, golden lions at each end.

The harp I had painted in Egypt was in the tomb of Mereruka on the wall of a small room. The scene was one of extreme domesticity, showing Mereruka and a young woman seated on the floor opposite each other, as she amused him by "playing the harp."

There was no question in my mind about the similarities in essentials in these two musical instruments, peculiarly intricate, each exhibiting the same features.

The fact that, in a royal burial in Ur, there were frequently three or four harps of this same general type, while in Egypt the harp in the tomb of Mereruka was unlike the ones known there, was direct evidence of a contact between the two countries during the lifetime of Mereruka, which was at the beginning of Dynasty VI, 2420 B.C.

That harp of Woolley's put me unequivocally in the list of archaeologists who believed in the continued connection between Egypt and the Valley of the Euphrates in ancient times—in spite of the silence of clay tablets on business transactions.

THE MAJESTY OF PERSIA

44. *Persepolis*

BREASTED HAD CABLED ME in Egypt in March, 1930, asking if I would be interested in going to Persepolis to paint the ruins for the Oriental Institute of the University of Chicago, after I had finished my season's work for Reisner. My answer was, "Thanks, yes." The cable was followed by a charming personal letter from Breasted imbued with his wonderful enthusiasm. He offered a bewildering list of suggestions as to subjects, but ended by saying, "Of course, no definite decision is possible until you have studied the ruins themselves from an artist's standpoint." I was delighted with the elasticity of this commission and with the opportunity afforded for me to visit a country that had remained an unfulfilled desire over a period of years, and all the more so because Corinna was invited to go with me.

A personal letter from Secretary of State Cordell Hull stated that Breasted had been in to see him personally, to secure the department's assistance in a permit for the entrance into Persia of my canvas and painting equipment in a tin cylinder. His friendly letter intimated that two months was none too much time to get permission for the entry. Even more important, the exit of my painted canvas, also contained in a tin cylinder which Breasted had vaguely described as "tall," would require negotiation. He requested me to cable the exact dimensions before the Persian minister in Washington was approached officially by the Department of State. I was greatly reassured when he said that Breasted's file on my Persian "project" would remain on his desk. I cabled the Secretary that the tin cylinder would be 7 feet 4 inches in height and 24 inches in circumference, and that it would contain 38 yards of canvas. This communication elicited a prompt reply, which said:

"State Department considers error made about height. Kindly confirm dimensions cylinder."

I did so, and in due course there came a formal letter signed by Cordell Hull, enclosing a copy of a letter from Riza Shah Pahlavi's representative in Washington, saying it was his "intention" to write to the Persian minister in Cairo. "The cylinder may yet become a *cause célèbre*. Regards," Hull had added in longhand.

We spent the night in Alexandria and then took an Imperial Airways plane, the *Hannibal,* to Baghdad, and left at once by a night train for Khanaqin, where early next morning a motor was waiting to take us over the road to Tehran. When we arrived at the Persian frontier, the much-dreaded Khosrovieh, I was met by a group of police in pale blue uniforms, who spoke to me in non-Parisian French. They escorted me as a guard of honor inside a building, where I was received with great ceremony by important officials in a fair-sized room. One of them introduced himself as the chief examiner of Customs, who said, "The banquet will be at noon." This formality finished, I produced our passports and police permit; both were waved aside graciously, as was the officially recommended tin cylinder. Fortunately, the banquet was served punctually at noon and the meal was short. We got into the car, the driver tooted his horn loudly, and the last barrier separating us from Persian soil was raised. We were on our way to the land of "poets and roses."

Soon the scenery became fine, and villages with simple, flat-roofed houses were in color like the desert and rocky ledges, of which they seemed to form a part. I rejoiced in their resistance to all visible signs of modern progress. And each time my weary old bones got a particularly fundamental jolt, I was consoled by the exhilaration of being in a country ahead of the railroad, with only one highway intersecting it from north to south. There were no bridges, and the many streams crossing the road were often increased to river proportions. Extreme skill was needed by the driver, who listened attentively as the springs of our car began to creak ominously and the engine spluttered in ridding itself of water. It was always doubtful whether the attempt to climb the abrupt opposite bank of a river bed would succeed, and each time it did, we breathed a sigh of relief, and the driver murmured, *"Hamdu lillah!"* ("God be praised"!)

Huge lorries, laboring noisily along, swaying perilously, in crossing difficult high passes with hairpin turns, steep grades, and incredibly rough surfaces, were a menace. One had also to reckon with lines of carts carrying slender poles made from peeled saplings extending far out behind. More than once we narrowly escaped being pushed over a cliff by a truck suddenly skidding backward or by a lurching cart. By the time we reached Kermanshah, a provincial seat of government. we were so tired that we roused ourselves with difficulty to be interested in the fact of the surrounding district "being rich in monuments of the Achaemenids and Sassanids." However, when our driver said, interrogatively, *"Taq-i-Bustan?,"* we dutifully opened Sir Denison Ross's book, *The Persians,* and with it as a guide, examined the famous sculptures mentioned in it. We felt repaid for our effort.

Strengthened by nibbling *petits beurres* and chocolate bars bought in Baghdad, we got a real thrill when the driver stopped the car by the roadside and pointed to a high, smooth cliff close by, on which was carved an inscription in three parallel lines. Suddenly I recalled Reisner's story about Sir Henry Rawlinson, who, in the late 1830's, at the risk of his neck, slid down the face of a steep rock to reach an inscription. Darius had used this smooth rock surface of vast extent, near the modern town of Hamadam (built on the site of the capital of the Medes). This trilingual inscription, in Babylonian, in the language of the Elamites, and in Persian, was deciphered by Sir Henry, whose feat made possible the reading of a great cuneiform literature which had baffled interpretation. Even though our climb was in the reverse direction, and an easier one than Rawlinson's, we reached the inscription with great difficulty, but again felt repaid for having done so.

Snow banks were now close, although not yet down to the roadside. After a descent, just as the twilight began to fade, we rose abruptly again to find ourselves on an ice-covered road, which indulged in rapid twists. Suddenly the cold became intense. We realized that we had reached Asadabad, the highest pass in Persia—ten thousand feet.

Within an hour, we had arrived at our stopping place for the night, the town of Hamadan. Next day, when we resumed travel, the passes were neither so high nor so sensational, but the scenery was again fine, with dolomite-shaped mountains on all sides, beautiful in color. Imagination offered full play in journeying along this route, which since time immemorial had been the only means of communication between the low plains of Mesopotamia and the high plateau of Iran. At first a simple mule trail, it had been gradually widened through the centuries by countless hordes of invaders and defenders sweeping over it. Crumbling walls of abandoned caravanseries and frequent gangs of road workers living in tents were constant reminders that the passenger motors and the lorries were forerunners of a complete change, and long caravans of animals soon would be relegated to the past, together with the unspoiled villages so satisfying to the eye.

Every few miles was a square fortress with a sentry in the doorway, or in a sentry box, and soldiers in pairs were met and passed patrolling the road. One sensed the military character of the government, as in the times of Cyrus and Darius.

The environs of Tehran broke the charm of suburb scenery. A tall factory chimney belched forth black smoke, and near by a modern, red-roofed monstrosity held my startled attention, to the exclusion of the first glimpse of the summit of Demavend, brought out sharply by the sunset glow, as it towered above the half-circle of mountains at the northern end of the town. What Fuji is to the Japanese, Demavend is to Persian imagination! We went to Hotel Naderi, and were shown by an Armenian clerk into a villa across a charming garden. Next morning, in a small droshky drawn by two horses, we headed towards the mountains directly above the residential district, where all the houses had some kind of garden.

The Antiquity Service in Persia, as in Egypt, functioned under the Department of Education, with Hekmet as minister. In the late afternoon, as we were about to go out to have tea, Hekmet called at our hotel to pay his respects. Corinna and I took to him at once. He had a fine face and alert manner, his English was excellent and spoken without an accent. Formal greetings took place. Then he asked for the famous tin cylinder. After a quick glance, he roared with laughter. "I defy anyone to call our frontier authorities difficult when they let *that* in," he said.

The home of the American minister was next to the Shah's palace on a broad avenue with fine trees. The minister was cordial and said he had communicated with Hekmet to get in touch with the frontier about letting my painting equipment in unopened, but when Hekmet reported that customs had planned a "banquet" in my honor, he believed everything was satisfactory.

We made an early morning start for Persepolis. The road was pretty bad, especially through a district where contorted mounds of mud had been homes before destructive floods broke loose more than a year before. But in many places the scenery compensated, for there were long stretches of fruit trees in full bloom, and tall poplars had fresh green leaves. The climbing over mountain passes gave variety, and when we reached the sacred city of Qum and the sunlight played over the golden dome above a shrine, that was something to remember!

As we approached the vicinity of Isfahan, the mountains were too far distant to compose themselves as part of the view, but I saw traces of a straight, broad highway under construction, leading to a bluish-green high dome so lovely as to raise excited anticipation of a nearer view. We took a circuitous route along the twisting banks of a river for some time before we passed through a tall entrance gate and were on a very wide main street, with a path for foot passengers shaded by a double line of superb trees down the center. We were in Isfahan, which Sir Denison Ross described as "the loveliest of all Persian cities." The light was perfect as we drove into the Royal Square, the Maidan-I-Shah. It was nobly conceived architecturally, with buildings of splendid proportions, combining graceful tiled arcades, magnificent domes, and minarets brilliantly ablaze at this sunset hour. I did not wonder at the Persian proverb, "Half the world is Isfahan." Through the eyes of that most insolent of adventurers, the fictitious Hajji Baba, I seemed to be seeing as a live entity Shah Abbas I on the balcony, surrounded by ambassadors and local grandees, wearing garments of gold and silver cloth, assembled for a polo match.

I did not need the tangible proofs of stone goal posts of the period still standing at either end of the Maidan actually to hear the click of mallets and the pounding hoofs of ponies with emeralds, diamonds, and pearls embroidered on the magnificent stuffs of their flapping saddle blankets, as they followed the ball back and forth, while the gorgeous spectators leaned far forward over the narrow balcony rail to acclaim the victors.

The contemporary of Shah Abbas I, Queen Elizabeth, could not herself have staged a greater pageant in England!

We stayed over in Isfahan in order to see Myron B. Smith, an authority on Islamic art. Among the splendid buildings he showed us was the famous Masjid-I-Shah, the oldest mosque in Isfahan, dated to A. D. 850, now unused. This mosque had a great square substructure and an ingenius octagonal dome rising from square towers that never failed to arouse the enthusiasm of modern architects, he told us. Both Myron and his wife were thoroughly familiar with all that was worth while in Isfahan, from living and working there.

The day following, at about noon, we saw a sign post marked "The Province of Fars," and there came to me in a flash a definition I had read: "Fars, the cradle of the Persian Nation." Cyrus, Cambyses, Darius, and Xerxes! All had lived and reigned here! At sunset, on emerging from a particularly rocky gorge, my eye rested on the finest collection of mountains we had yet seen, extending the length of a great plain, and on the latter were the far-famed columns of the buildings on the terrace of Persepolis. We stopped before a long portico facing a garden in embryo. An American stood in the doorway. "My name's Donald Mc-Cown," he said. Tea was served in the dining room, where McCown introduced two Germans, an archaeologist and the expedition photographer. Frederick Krefter, in charge, was temporarily away in Tehran.

Until dark I wandered about the ruins on the terrace. It was certainly an *embarras de richesse* from which to choose subjects to paint. Finally I gave it up, and seated at the edge of the terrace, facing the wide stairway rising from the plain below, my conscious self yielded to the magic of the changing color which, the sun near setting, suffused with an indescribable light over the mountains and columns alike, and I pinched myself to be sure I was awake. After ten hours' sleep in an American "Beauty Rest" bed, I was in a mood to overlook in the apartment allotted us such anachronisms as a comfortable sofa and an open fire in the sitting room of the restored harem quarters of the palace of Darius.

In the long, arch-roofed corridor off which rooms opened on both sides, the black tile pavement was on the original level, and here, as elsewhere in the building, the modern construction was an exact reproduction of the original, as to dimensions, details, and even the materials used, including a mixture of wood and mud brick. Krefter, who was the architect, had for his guidance half-standing walls with recesses and doorways. Several of the latter, with colossal reliefs of the "King of Kings" carved on their sides, were still in place and gave the illusion of his being our living host.

My painting program was an ambitious one to cover in six weeks. The three landscapes would comprise all the best that the great, artificially built-up terrace had to offer. One of my landscape subjects was of five columns and a generous supply of mountains and much blue sky; another took in the whole of the Apadana stairway, which Breasted's expedition had uncovered. In the immediate foreground was a long line of carved figures, and, to the left, four columns. The third was to be a panorama view, including the gate of Xerxes, utilizing its semi-ruined bulls sculptured on the sides as a foreground, also some of the remaining stately, slender columns, once a part of the great "Apadana" audience hall of Darius.

The carpenters began promptly to make boxes of very thick planks to hold the canvas in place while I worked. It was interesting to watch them handling a long saw. Without any indicating line on the peeled logs in the round, they cut the boards the desired length, and to an even thickness throughout, a feat that hardly any European carpenter could achieve.

Two significant events happened on the first day of our arrival. An amusing message came from Cordell Hull:

DELIGHTED TIN ROLL RECEIVED AS GOOD-WILL. PERSIAN AMBASSADOR WASHINGTON CONSIDERED SITUATION FAVORABLE OMEN FOR BETTER RELATIONS BETWEEN IRAN AND OUR OWN UNITED STATES OF AMERICA. CONGRATULATIONS.

The other was disconcerting. It seemed that official information had been given already to the expedition staff that the Shah had issued an edict forbidding his post-office authorities to deliver letters addressed to "Persia." Henceforth "Iran" was to be the name of the country. We Smiths had not been warned of what had happened, but this explained Reisner's cabled message to the effect: "My two letters returned country unknown mystified."

Donald McCown took us to prehistoric ruins of the Proto-Elamite period of about 5000 B.C. which had been excavated by the Breasted expedition. It was a pleasant walk of about a mile in the plains below the terrace of Persepolis. The site had yielded pottery and mud seals. Later I spent an interesting afternoon in the workshop looking over specimens of this pottery.

Many of the designs were reminiscent of the work of our Pueblo Indians. The craftsmen had developed a high perfection in simple design, their glazes very thin and smooth in texture. I also inspected innumerable seals, some in the form of buttons bearing the same kind of attachment as is used today on the reverse side to fasten them to garments. McCown told me that painted pottery had already become conventionalized before 4000 B.C. in Elam and Sumer, and that its origin must be much earlier.

He shared the hope of Frankfort (now in charge of Breasted's expedition in Mesopotamia) that a link between the Elamites and Sumerians in ancient times would be found. The French had been searching for it for some time before Breasted's expeditions had taken it up.

When I inquired about the use of cuneiform for expressing the Persian language on monuments, McCown informed me that the innumerable varieties employed by the Babylonians and Assyrians had been reduced to forty-three by the Persians. These, having fixed alphabetical values, probably dated to the time of Cyrus. No instance had been found of the use of Persian cuneiform later than the fall of the Achaemenid Empire.

I asked to see the dipping of cuneiform tablets into paraffin wax heated over spirit lamps, which was taking place in an agreeably warm room. Under supervision, six or eight small Persian boys were assisting their elders. After the immersion was completed, the youngest wrapped up the tablets in dark blue tissue paper before placing each one separately in pasteboard boxes containing cotton wool. The tablets were then ready for shipment in the boxes of wood prepared by the carpenters. The boys at work seemed to have deft fingers and to be enjoying what they were doing. Each boy, moreover, seemed to know the limit of his ability and did not have to be given orders. It was a delightful scene.

A supply of paraffin wax for dipping, sent by truck three weeks earlier by our American minister to the bank in Shiraz, where the expedition did its business, had not been heard from, and twice a car had gone the eighty miles there and back in the hope of getting a trace of it. McCown said they had melted all the candles to be found in the village near Persepolis or in Shiraz, and with today's dipping, the supply would be exhausted and the workers idle again. The way of the archaeologist in Persia was not easy!

I know that Ernst Herzfeld had inaugurated the Breasted expedition at Persepolis. At a dinner, I asked Krefter, who was present, about the well-known German scholar. He said that Herzfeld had first come to Persia in 1903 under the auspices of the Kaiser Wilhelm Institute. He lived in Tehran and was recognized as an authority on Persian art. His influence had been used in furthering German interests through his close connection with the German Legation in Tehran, and the concession to excavate Persepolis was given him personally by the Persian government. Later he had advocated turning over Persepolis to an American expedition. Negotiations resulted in our Secretary of State's approaching Breasted to find out whether the Oriental Institute would take over the concession, provided the American government got the Persian authorities to agree. This arrangement was made, and Herzfeld was put in charge. Much of the furniture and rugs in the expedition building belonged to Herzfeld, who left everything behind when he went to America. The library contained his comprehensive bibliography of ancient books on Persia and was considered the most complete collection in existence in many other scholarly fields, including comparative religion.

McCown announced that, for the first time, the expedition staff had been invited to join in the native celebration of Noruz (New Year) on the evening of March 19. The three of us walked to the edge of the terrace on the garden side close to our rooms. Down in the plain below, there were bonfires in a long line and men and some boys leaping high through the rising flames. We stood near the bonfires to watch this ceremonial done with perfect rhythm and timing. A small crowd of excited women and children and eager-eyed young girls were watching the scene from the top of the steep flight of steps leading into the valley.

We next saw what appeared to be a red star, which proved to be a fire balloon, then watched the preparations for the ascent of a second balloon. A wad of lighted cotton had been placed inside, and impelled by the resulting heat, the balloon slowly inflated, moved a little, then tentatively rose by its own momentum. The men, following the directions of our head boy, Hassan, let go. The large paper bubble slowly left the ground and, amid clapping of hands and breathless "ahs!" and "ohs!," soared upwards, seemingly to join the stars. Quite suddenly it wavered and fell to earth, and the village Persians vanished abruptly in absolute silence. The ceremony was over! The staff agreed that what we had just seen was a very old custom going back to Zoroaster's time of fire worship, or earlier.

Later on in the evening, with one accord the staff started for the terrace. The ruins of a fire altar stood out compellingly in the plain. The shadows on the stately columns of the Apadana were perfect. I looked up the fluted groove of one, holding my face close. In a straight line, the cutting went up fifty-five feet before it reached the damaged capital. The moon just overhead turned the stone reliefs on the great stairway into groups of real men of many conquered nations bringing the annual New Year tribute to the great King of Kings. Fire worshipers with their roots in the remote ages! Sculptors and artisans from Greece, Egypt, Babylon, and Assyria, assisted by the moonlight, had created a living pageant for our benefit.

The remains of a fire altar that I saw daily on the terrace and the one conspicuous in the valley below were both connected with the belief of the Zoroastrians in fire as a symbol of worship of the *one* great god Ahura-Mazda. They interested me in their connection with the Persian celebration of Noruz. When McCown told me that Herzfeld thought the square building at Naqsh-i-Rustam, near the tomb of Darius the Great, was the burial place of Zoroaster, I decided to knock off work and join a trip of inspection on horseback. We stopped at the rock-cut tomb of Darius, which was too high to reach, and then walked quite a distance to two impressive fire altars.

McCown said that Herzfeld placed Zoroaster in the reign of Darius, 522–485 B.C., who accepted his religious teaching, rather than at 1000 B.C., the date given by the *Cambridge Ancient History*. It was pleasant to find myself, at the same moment, near the tombs of two such outstanding personalities as Darius and Zoroaster. Only Darius the Great of the Achaemenians could have been great enough himself to follow the precepts of Zoroaster, who strove to free religion from superstition, magic, and evil spirits and taught immortality and the worship of one God.

Persepolis was a storehouse for treasures, and the Apadana, or great audience hall, was used mostly on ceremonial occasions, when the court assembled to receive tribute at Noruz from vassal nations or to entertain official emissaries—functions which became less frequent as the power of the empire waned.

On our way to study in detail the groups from vassal nations depicted on the Apadana stairway, McCown gave a dramatic account of the burning of the buildings on the terrace by Alexander the Great, to gratify his Greek mistress, Thais, in revenge for the Persians' destruction of the Acropolis in Athens. This, in turn, was in retaliation for the Greeks' destruction of Sardis, the capital of the Lydian allies of the Persians.

Even though Persepolis was set afire during a drunken orgy, the Macedonians involved removed the gold and other treasures before the flames swept over the terrace and column after column fell. I stooped and picked up a handful of ashes from a step, a small heap that had withstood the wind of centuries. The conflagration resulted in such a mass of ashes that this Apadana stairway was completely covered, and the reliefs, with the record of group after group of vassal nations, remained concealed until Breasted's expedition came to Persepolis five years before our trip.

I struggled hard to memorize the three-tiered frieze of the tribute bearers advancing in the following order:

Nubians	Caucasians	Parthians
Ethiopians	Sogdians	Gonds
Oasis of Merv	Hindus	Bactrians
Arabs of Oman		
Kermani		
Egyptians	Armenians	Heratis
Scythians (European)	Cilicians	Babylonians
Lydians	Cappadocians	Syrians
Susians	Arachosians	Medes

Each group was preceded by a Persian court official and divided from the next by a cypress tree. The attitude of the figures was not varied, the

257

faces were the same, except for the degrees of aquilinity of the noses, but there were minor differences in beards, headgear, garments, personal adornments, and equipment, which furnished the distinguishing data as to race, and the identification was further assisted by the kinds of tribute offered by the different groups. The animals shown among the gifts were horses, camels, bulls, a lioness with her cubs, antelopes, giraffes, and goats with long curved horns. There were many vessels and other specimens made of gold.

Conventionalized papyrus plants and the lotus blossom with an exaggerated number of petals became a rosette design above and below the carved reliefs of the groups. This design was used also in each triangle formed as a flight of stairs reached a landing, where the further decoration was always the lion, symbolizing the power of the empire triumphing over the bull, representing a conquered people. On the frieze along the tessellated wall at the top of the stairway, a human form had been roughly chiseled, and three other such forms next to it were in varying stages of completion. Obviously, unskilled artisans did the preliminary cutting on each figure, more expert ones carried the cutting a step further, and the final touches to the face and the important details of the figure were done by skilled sculptors. The Apadana of Darius depended on the genius of a single master mind. An open portico with thirty-six columns of fine proportions surrounded the hall proper, which had the same number of columns. This edifice extended over a vast area. It was indeed an architectural gem even in ruin! The thrilling discovery of the gold and silver foundation deposits bearing the name of Darius was made two years before our visit, at the four corners inside the portico.

At the far end of the Apadana was the "Tachara," the palace of Darius, which consisted of a large covered hall in the center, from which rooms opened out. On the doorways were a number of colossal-sized portraits of the King, holes on the chin showing where a lapis lazuli beard was attached. At one time gold bracelets adorned the arms. His private apartments could be identified by a servant carrying a towel over his arm. A great columned hall had belonged to the Queen. Behind the royal apartments were servants' quarters, and probably those of the

King's personal guards, since their figures were carved on the inside of the entrance doors of some of the chambers. On the outside wall of the Tachara facing the plain, a tall tablet gave the parentage of Darius and recorded the boundaries of his dominion.

Xerxes' palace, the "Hadish," was of poor workmanship throughout. It had a "tripylon" gate that gave quicker access to the harem than from his father's private apartments, and he had enlarged the harem building. The original plan of the hundred-column audience hall of Xerxes could still be determined. The stone used was poor in quality, and if an attempt were now made to set up the prostrate columns, they would disintegrate as an ugly mass of fallen stones, because Xerxes, in building, aimed at quantity rather than quality. But in his father's Apadana the tallest and slenderest columns extant in any ancient country still entranced the senses of the beholder.

Across the rocky hill, beneath the Artaxerxes tombs, in the remains of massive, thick mud brick, were a series of small rooms connected with one another by narrow alleys, with apertures hardly more than slits. From a few of these rooms, over thirty thousand cuneiform tablets were taken before the "dig" was discontinued to Chicago for the reading by the assyriological staff of the Oriental Institute. There could be no staff better qualified to undertake this momentous task.

I walked along the edge of the wide wall rising sheer from the valley, fifty feet or so below, the height making the terrace with its treasures impregnable to enemy attack before the days of gunpowder. Here one could feel an intimacy with the personalities that had trod these same steps long ago with different emotions, depending upon whether their stars were in the ascendant or declining. Here was the world as it was known to Cyrus and Darius through conquest: Susa, Ecbatana, Babylon, the Assyrian cities. Here swift horses in relays were sent out by the Achaemenid rulers over the same highway as today from the north to the Persian Gulf.

For years in the British Museum, I had hastily passed by huge Assyrian figures, clumsy and uninspiring, and again, years later, ignored them in Baghdad. But the familiarity of Darius the Great with the Assyrian motif in art was responsible for my having many hours of solid enjoyment as I wandered daily over the Persepolis terrace, thanks to the genius of Darius in skillful adaptation. I visited the King of Kings as he sat or stood, surrounded by his subjects representing many races, watched over by royal guards stiffly holding lances, bows, and buckles. The artificially built-up terrace, stone-faced, had its prototype in Assyria, where similar construction was bricked-faced instead. The god Ahura-Mazda, above the head of Darius in a winged disk, was the same as the Ninevite god Assur, guarding his sovereign. The colossal height of the king, his tall tiara, his curled hair and beard, the drapery of his royal robes, the high-backed throne supported by caryatid subjects, or soldiers, the winged bulls with human faces, were all inspired by Assyrian sculpture. But there the comparison ended. Refinement of treatment, perceptible even in the details of the groups of humans moving across the stone and the bull mauled so often by the lion, was a lasting tribute to the greatness of Darius, who knew what *not* to copy. However, the skilled artisans who chipped the stone at Persepolis slipped up dreadfully on legs and feet, which were, without exception, as clumsily executed as anything produced in Assyria.

In the unfinished tomb of Darius III, the crude representation, with a badly carved figure of Ahura-Mazda over the head, was evidence that the skilled craftsmen brought from Greece, Egypt, and Mesopotamia by Darius I had left no worthy descendants. With the last Darius, not only had the artistic genius of his predecessors vanished, but when he offered no military resistance to the invader, he deserved the fate he got at the hands of his disgusted generals. Long after their empire had fallen, the Persians continued to borrow the art of neighboring nations. The inspiration for ceramics, miniatures, textiles, carpets—all pre-eminent in medieval times—came from the outside world. Poetry alone was indigenous. I felt this fact might explain why, in our time, when the other so-called Persian arts are now lost traditions, insofar as real creativity is concerned, the poets, Sa'adi and Hafiz, who lived, respectively, at the end of the twelfth century A.D. and at the end of the thirteenth, continue to be living forces in Persia. Thus, good poetry is still being written. During the celebration of Noruz, villagers coming to pay respect to the Breasted staff all repeated lengthy verses that *sounded* like traditional poetry.

I took one more afternoon off to visit ruins that could only be reached by horseback. We went first to Naqsh-i-Rajem where there were two large Sassanian reliefs carved on the rock face showing Shapur receiving the crown from Ahura-Mazda. The type of sculpture was very unlike that of Persepolis, less refined but more realistic, and the modeling suggested an artist's painting rather than the restraint of a sculptor's work.

Sassanian reliefs during the period from A.D. 222 to 650 indicate a revival of Persian art, just as there was a revival in literature. But the sculpture at Naqsh-i-Rajem was not nearly as fine as that of Naqsh-i-Rustam, where there was a spirited relief of the Emperor Valerian kneeling before Shapur I, about A.D. 222. An even better piece of sculpture showed Shapur I receiving the crown from the Persian god. Both of them were on horseback with their heads touching. The devil was beneath the god's horse, and the conquered nations, symbolized as a man, beneath that of the King.

We also visited Istakhr, which was an inhabited city when Darius was building at Persepolis. The ruins, tremendous in area, were situated on a wide plain in view of a full quota of superb mountains. It was originally a walled town, and mounds surrounding it indicated its limits. Parthians, Sassanians, and possibly the Achaemenians built here.

The weeks passed all too quickly, and a second full moon had been enjoyed when the moment arrived for the tin cylinder to be of use again for the thirty-eight feet of canvas now covered with paint. I felt sad when the barred entrance to Darius's superb creation sprang open, then snapped back after our exit, probably, alas! never again to swing in to welcome the Joe Smiths. Before long the deeds of Elamites, Achaemenids, Sassanians, and others would fade from my memory like a broken dream, but Persepolis would remain before my mental vision. The great terrace, with its stately columns reaching into the deep blue sky, the stone stairway and carved doorways of the audience hall of Darius the

Great, I will never forget. Nor the King of Kings himself, as I had seen him day after day, with his tight curls, his attendants holding a canopy over him, and his personification of power. He stood also in mortal combat, conquering the forces of evil, symbolized sometimes as a bull, at others as a strange beast with a lion's head, a scorpion's tail, and a feathered breast and bird claws.

What an emotion was aroused in me by these hundreds of human figures of many vassal nations and captive animals moving in a dignified procession along the stone. Bulls torn by a lion's claws and monsters obligingly rearing to receive the royal dagger into their entrails were going through their ordeal in the same calm ceremonial tempo. The endless reduplication left me with no sense of monotony, no feeling of artistic weariness. Rather, it served to accentuate the awed mood in which I met them all, absorbing from the sculptured stone the symbolical purpose and reality of the power of Darius.

THE CLASSICAL WORLD

45. *Greece*

FAR MORE has been written on every phase of life in ancient Greece than on any other country. Therefore, I felt fortunate when I was given the opportunity to make a contribution on the subject of colored statuary in the classical period.

I knew Greece far earlier than I knew Egypt, having made my first trip in 1886 with Denman Ross. I continued to paint there with him for three consecutive years. Edward Robinson, curator of the Department of Classical Antiquities in the Boston Museum, was impressed by a preliminary research I had made on the coloring of Greek sculpture. Consequently, he invited me to go with him to a conference in Athens held in the spring of 1891, and urged me to continue to gather available evidence, and discuss the matter with classical scholars I would meet there through him.

In the Acropolis Museum, during my trips with Ross, I was instinctively drawn to figures of the Greek archaic period rather than to those of the later periods—possibly a forerunner of my subsequent interest running strongly to Egyptian stylized figures. Thanks to the traces of color in the early sculptures recently excavated on the Acropolis, there was a lifelike quality in the marble figures which made it easy for me to reproduce on canvas the spirit of the original master.

A European scholar who had made a study of the subject of color on statues, bought my picture, because he believed I had succeeded in per-petuating, through another medium, the work in marble where color had increased its beauty. He told me that he had made a careful examination of a relief on the Parthenon frieze in which plunging bulls were held by struggling men by an *imaginary* rope. The only plausible explana-tion could be that, originally, the rope had been indicated *in color*. He took me to see rare treasures of Tanagra figurines, exquisitely colored and in such a perfect state of preservation as to furnish invaluable evi-dence as to the methods used in applying body color in flat tones. Also with him I visited some collections of terra cotta with painted figures on them. He informed me that traces of color had been found on parts of statues protected by the earth in which they had been buried. He thought that color was used more delicately in Greece than was known to be the case in ancient Egypt, where the sculptured bodies of men were painted a bright red, and of women, a vivid yellow. Evidence which I examined made it seem probable that, originally, the statue of Athena Nike in her temple on the Acropolis was once gilded. I found many examples of bronze harness on horses, of gold ornaments on human figures, and of color on the hair, eyes, nostrils, and lips, as on Egyptian statues. I also found confirmation that body color in flat tones had been used on both draped and undraped figures. On the other hand, no absolute proof that a *majority* of statuary in the classical period had been tinted or the color applied at the time the sculptor executed his masterpieces. These were important factors still undetermined.

During this Athens conference, Robinson told me he had decided on a novel exhibition in a gallery of the Boston Museum which, he said, he had had in mind for some time. This was to put on public view two plaster casts of life-sized statues of the classical period in Greece, painted according to archaeological evidence, shown together with their dupli-cates in white. And he wanted me to do the coloring. I warned him that I already had felt the "pulse" of some of these Greek classical scholars, and that the proposed exhibition would be looked at by them, and many others, with traditional prejudice in the matter of classical purity, really a legacy from the Renaissance. These "interpreters" of pure form would insist (and violently) that the ancient Greek sculptor was inspired to show what he could do through the medium of *unstained marble*. I consented to go along with the experiment on one condition—that I be permitted to accept the challenge by "coloring" one of the best specimens of Greek sculpture known, the Hermes of Praxiteles. As a further condition, we agreed that we should go together to the museum at Olympia and apologize in advance to Hermes for what we were about to do to him. We went! Even the perfection of the muscular structure of a human body and the illusion of living tissues and flesh perpetuated in marble in the figure of Hermes, done by Praxiteles, did not shake Robinson from his purpose.

Casts of the Hermes of Praxiteles and of the Venus Genetrix in the Louvre arrived at the Boston Museum from Paris, and the preparations for the exhibition were concluded. Shall sculpture paint her face? This became a question of general discussion in cultural circles before the day of the preview, which was expected to arouse a furor among many art lovers from New York, Philadelphia, and other centers. It certainly did! Charles Eliot Norton gave one glance of agonized horror at the colored Hermes and, without a word, fled from the gallery. I followed him and said that both Robinson and I had personally apologized to Hermes at Olympia. Norton made no reply and left the museum.

An aggressive-looking group remarked that there was too much realism in having classics come down from their pedestals, so to speak, and change into wax figures such as might be seen in the dime museums of anatomy. Many elevated voices declared indignantly that the "experiment" conducted under the learned direction of the curator of the Classical Department did not exalt the good taste of ancient Greeks as artists, even if it afforded satisfaction to archaeologists who should leave art alone. But among the crowds that continued to come to the exhibition, I noticed a return of the same classical scholars and students, day after day, who usually asked Robinson and me intelligent questions. Gradually, objective and interesting criticism, based on thoughtful study, replaced the early, unreasoning opposition. This satisfactory change in attitude was reflected in editorial comments after Robinson, in a letter to *The New York Times,* calmly, but forcibly, analyzed the purpose of the experiment, which he considered had been lost sight of in a tendency towards noisy vituperation indulged in by critics.

Unexpected support came from a variety of sources and art critics. It was denied that Mr. Robinson and Mr. Smith had "yielded to a whim of modern minds" to startle the public. Their accurate research had relied in large part on the exquisitely colored Tanagra figures and those on terra cotta. This justified what would otherwise have been considered a bizarre contribution to the valuable discussion about how the Greeks treated their statuary. Whether critics and individuals happened to like, or dislike, painted statues was not germane. The demonstration was an approach to the question, carried out with an "unbiased judgment, combined with artistic knowledge," and the results were "highly educational."

46. *The Sarcophagus Found at Sidon*

ROBINSON never lost his interest in traces of color on Greek marble reliefs. In fact, he sent me on my first trip to Turkey in the spring of 1900 to paint for the Boston Museum life-sized copies of the colored sculptured reliefs on both sides of the so-called sarcophagus of Alexander the Great, found at Sidon in Asia Minor. Corinna and I arrived at Constantinople and established ourselves at a hotel in Pera, which was where diplomats and Europeans lived in the Turkish capital. The sarcophagus was in the government museum situated in the native quarter, accessible by the Galata Bridge.

I was informed that German museums had already sent artists to Turkey seeking permission to make studies of the sarcophagus, but that Sultan Abdul Hamid had refused. I was advised that this was a particularly inopportune moment to make a similar request on behalf of the Boston Museum, because of a recent incident between Americans and Turks.

Fortunately, I had brought a personal letter from the Reverend John P. Peters of New York, who some years before had been responsible for an archaeological expedition in Turkey, and I was told he was still *persona grata* to the authorities. My introduction was addressed to O. Hamdy Bey, director of the museum. I went there and refused to deliver the letter to anyone else. After a long delay, I was shown into Hamdy Bey's office, where that official gave me a cordial welcome. He said that we had been fellow students in Paris at the Académie Julien. He assured me he had remained interested in my career and was an amateur painter himself. He kept me for an informal luncheon, served in his office, and I departed with an impressive document stamped with a large seal, authorizing me to paint the sarcophagus and all other sculpture in Turkey.

From fear of the color fading on the sarcophagus reliefs, dark curtains were kept drawn across each side and removed only for a few moments at a time. Hamdy Bey was most co-operative in having the curtains opened during my painting hours. I started at once on a job which I expected would take at least two months.

At a brief noon luncheon with Hamdy Bey in his private museum quarters, the conversation would be on art and archaeology. Frequently the grand vizier, who was a patron of art, would drop in and stay on to watch me paint. The fellow guests were cultured Turks and an occasional European scholar. Usually we looked at a new museum acquisition, or a particularly fine piece of sculpture, before I took up my brush again.

In spite of constant political crises I managed to continue a quiet painting regime in the seclusion of the museum. Also, I interested myself in securing all available archaeological data about the sarcophagus, which Hamdy Bey had unearthed in the Necropolis of Sidon in 1887. Some of the European archaeologists, notably Theodore Reinbach, agreed with his (Hamdy Bey's) premise that the evidence warranted the assumption that Alexander actually had been entombed in the sarcophagus, or at least it had been made for that purpose. Hamdy Bey attributed great importance to its royal dimensions and the character of its workmanship, the lower part being of one block of Pentelicon marble weighing fifteen tons and the cover about half as much. The sculptured reliefs consisted of two panels about eight feet long and three feet wide, one side representing a spirited battle, the other, a hunt. There were no inscriptions, but Hamdy Bey based his identification mainly on the resemblance of the reliefs to coins of Alexander, which had a battle scene on one side and a hunt on the other, and to a head of Alexander. Even without further strong evidence, the historical details in the battle so closely resembled those of the period that quite a few archaeologists upheld Hamdy Bey and Reinbach as having a "tenable theory." Others declared that, even if Alexander was depicted on the bas reliefs, this was not evidence that the sarcophagus had been made for his body. The argument on this score could go back and forth interminably, I warned Hamdy Bey.

It seemed to me that much of the strenuous action of the warriors and hunters and their horses was clearly explained by the addition of the original coloring. Otherwise it would be somewhat obscure, as in the case of the metopes on the Parthenon. One day I made this statement to Hamdy Bey and the grand vizier, when the three of us were lunching alone. They whispered together for a few moments, then Hamdy Bey said that, for obvious reasons, I had been forced to work through the intercepting medium of glass. But they had decided to give me a privilege never before accorded to anyone; they would remove the glass for several hours. I felt complimented that the reasons given for this proposed action were my enthusiasm for the sarcophagus and an intelligent approach to the study of the use of color as an integral part of the design on the panels. Therefore, it was said, if I were permitted to examine minutely the method of treatment of color on the details, my trained eye as an artist would not fail to produce interesting results.

I wished that the archaeologist who happened to be in Sidon at the time of the discovery of the sarcophagus, and who was supposed to be the only foreigner to see the reliefs before they were protected by glass, could have been at my side. I would have liked to ask him whether he had made the same exciting discovery, that, in two cases, the weapons held by men began in high relief, subsided into lower relief, and ended in *pure color*. Hamdy Bey, as an artist, was as thrilled by what I pointed out to him and by its significance as I was.

268

It is known that Alexander died in Babylon in May, 323 B.C., and that his body had been kept there for at least a year and one-half. Connecting this sarcophagus with his body took surmise, and a lot of it, in my opinion. Art critics appeared to agree that the sarcophagus had been made between 330 and 320 B.C. If it had been ordered for the sepulchre of Alexander by either of the parties struggling for the succession, it would have taken a minimum of two years for even the skilled sculptors of the Peloponnesus to complete the elaborate bas-reliefs. All that was known with certainty was that the sarcophagus had reached Sidon, then the chief port of Asia Minor, since this was the "site" where it was excavated. But when Hamdy Bey found it, the necropolis had been plundered by natives, and the sarcophagus was empty—with no trace of a burial in it.

In the fall of 1930, I happened to be in Constantinople (by then known as Istanbul). I went at once to pay my respects to the sarcophagus of Alexander the Great. Once again, as so often thirty years before, the dark curtains were drawn aside for me. But I did not see the exact replicas of my paintings in the Boston Museum—on the original the color was gone!

47. Baalbek

BAALBEK WAS THE FIRST great caravan center in the same general area of the Roman Empire in the Orient as Petra and Palmyra, all three of which I visited. This was in the spring of 1900, and even after Damascus, which was called the "Emerald City" from the brilliance of its vegetation, my impression of the temple enclosure of Baalbek was of columns and other signs of ruins, set in the midst of one great garden. For sheer natural beauty of surroundings, including the distant, dramatic mountain ranges of Lebanon, I never saw an archaeological site to compare with it. Baalbek had a spring with a practically unlimited supply of water. As a consequence this oasis in a wide expanse of desert became a meeting place of roads, with such romantic sign posts as Tripoli, Sidon, and Tiberias, and rapidly developed into a great caravan center.

From the earliest times, Baalbek had been associated with the worship of Baal, and even after it became a Roman colony under Augustus (31 B.C.–A.D. 14), it continued to be famous for the number of its temples. People of all races were welcomed by a great variety of gods. Mighty Roman Jupiter supreme, Bacchus was there to compete with Bel at Palmyra, and also a number of Syrophoenician deities. Later, an oracle in Baalbek became popular, after Trajan was supposed to have consulted it with success.

Here in Baalbek was to be found by an interested spectator like myself visible evidence in stone of civilizations and ideas having jostled one another, as inevitably occurred when the original Roman buildings had superimposed on them structures of a later date.

Certain it was that Roman architects conceived stone monuments where a tremendous desert space was available, as here, in terms of size and elaborate decoration, rather than in terms of quality and fine detail. As an artist, I was rather pleased that Islam, in a negation of the human form in art, simplified the appearance of Roman temples in Baalbek by destroying endless rows of statues on high pedestals made at too late a date for good sculpture.

In a very sympathetic mood for what Baalbek offered in the way of ruins, I camped in the environs of the temple enclosure with painting equipment, and after rambling about the ruins speculatively for several hours, I placed my easel where there was a good view of the six remaining Corinthian columns of the Temple of Jupiter proper. Originally it had been surrounded by a peristyle of superb columns of vast size. They were unique in classical construction. Each column rested on a separate huge, square block, high in itself, and a great entablature crowning the columns added many more feet to the height.

Withal, the dimensions were in fine proportion, and a restraint and severity had been maintained in spite of rather elaborate details on the entablature. Therefore, there was a sense of rhythm and majesty about these columns, yellowish in color, that made them uncanny in beauty when the glow of the setting sun was on them. I never missed that breathtaking sight.

I felt a renewed thrill each time I passed by the wonders of Baalbek to and from work, which began the moment that I stepped onto the great artificial terrace, where the ruins of the temple stood on the Acropolis to the west of the present town. Many times, the thought struck me that probably in no other place had the various gods achieved temples of comparable magnificence or in more beautiful natural surroundings than here.

For instance, Bacchus had what was referred to as a "small" temple, but it covered more ground than the Parthenon. Venus had a charming little round temple which, incidentally, the Christians later took over.

Once I paused to go to the part of the enclosing wall where the three famous stones were discovered that gave Jupiter's temple the name of "Trilithon." It must have taken giants to raise them to twenty feet above the ground level where they were now. It has been said that these were probably the largest stones ever used by man in building.

I got sufficiently interested to make a special trip to the quarries from which they were brought. There, *in situ,* was an even bigger stone only partially disengaged from the bedrock.

Men in Egypt had also done a good deal in the quarries of Assuan and elsewhere in handling huge blocks. I personally believed a measuring tape would not have given all the odds to the feats of mass labor in handling enormous blocks of stone to workmen at Baalbek over those of Egypt. The Egyptians had disengaged tall obelisks in a single piece from the living rock and moved them long distances by raft on the Nile. And the colossal recumbent statue of Ramesses, also in a single piece near the Ramesseum, on the Theban Plain, had once stood erect. Its overthrow had inspired the poet Shelley to write: "My name is Ozymandias, king of kings! Look on my works, ye Mighty and despair!"

The stupendous scale of the Temple of Jupiter, and the immensity of each structural detail can be imagined from the dimensions of this terrace. In the Mameluke period the Arabs had done a thorough job in demolishing a stairway fifty feet wide that provided the approach to the temple area, since its position interfered with a moat needed for the protection of their fortress.

Nothing remained except a remnant of a tremendous portico which

271

formed the entrance into a great hall formerly having columns in front, the entire façade flanked by stone towers. But the width of the stairway gave an adequate clue to the dimensions of the rest of these architectural features.

Only the foundation stone and several niches of excellent workmanship remained of a great forecourt, entered from the portico by a triple gateway. The foundation, as I traced its length on foot over difficult ground, was incredibly extensive and revealed by its shape that the original had been hexagonal.

From this visual proof of the size of the outer court, I could accept the fact that the great altar court beyond was believed to have covered an area nearly five hundred feet in length, and, that it was surrounded on three sides by Corinthian columns and had an "undercut" entrance, used by chariots.

Originally, a series of steps led from the altar court into the Temple of Jupiter proper, where I had installed myself and my easel.

I was in daily proximity to the area of the court dedicated to this god, which Constantine (or one of his successors) had changed into a Christian church.

By the sixth century, the church had developed into an important basilica, erected on a scene where once chariots had brought Romans to worship their most important god. Christianity had replaced Roman paganism.

Soon after the Hegira (A.D. 622), the Moslems took possession of Baalbek. By another turn of the wheel in the Orient, the great gilded dome of the Christian basilica in Baalbek traveled to Jerusalem under Moslem custody to adorn the famous mosque known as the "Dome of the Rock."

48. *Palmyra*

THE CONCEPTION OF TRADE as the dominant occupation of men has been lost sight of all too often through the ages. Interpretative emphasis has been placed upon war instead of the peaceful pursuits that serve to bring peoples into contact with one another for their mutual advantage.

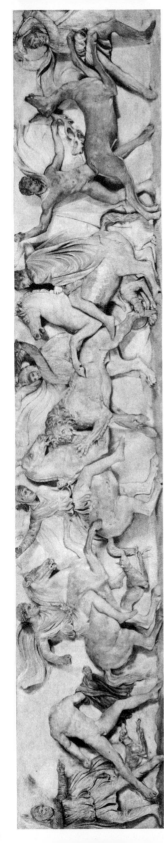

Details from the so-called Sarcophagus of Alexander the Great found at Sidon, now in the Museum, Istanbul. Paintings by Joseph Lindon Smith. Courtesy Museum of Fine Arts, Boston.

Façade of the Treasury at Petra. Painting by Joseph Lindon Smith.
Courtesy Robert P. Bass, Peterboro, N.H.

Desert caravan routes in ancient times and trade centers have long fascinated me for this reason. My active interest in them began in Egypt when my archaeological work gave me the opportunity to be in out-of-the-way districts seldom visited by foreigners. I began to think of rulers in terms of "business as usual" instead of in terms of war achievements.

For instance, an enterprising pharaoh easily became a great merchant prince, personally conducting expeditions to the regions of the Upper Nile, far beyond the outposts of civilization, pursuing trading occupations as only commercially aggressive people have done for millennia.

I have lived for weeks at a time in the same lonely regions these intrepid rulers visited, and from which they shipped their purchases back to Egypt. Fortunately, the record of them has remained. One can read today long lists of a variety of commodities, such as ostrich feathers, worn by gods and men as headdresses; porphyry, popular for special columns in temples and shrines; and slaves, always in demand for labor in Egypt's vast construction projects.

A few years back, I crossed from Luxor to the Red Sea over the same trackless desert used by caravans from prehistoric times on. Among the most energetic of early travelers was Queen Hatshepsut. She had recorded on the walls of her temple on the Theban Plain many details of her expeditions to the Land of Punt on the Red Sea. The stone record itemized metals and other materials not found in Egypt, needed in construction or for adornment.

On the much frequented routes across desert wastes to the Red Sea, most of the voyagers left behind something inscribed on a stone surface, which today has served to identify them and their enterprises. Scholars have studied a number of all but forgotten languages in which such inscriptions were written. The names of royal personages, appearing in their cartouches, drawings of unusual animals, and many other "feature stories," have been preserved from modern vandals. My own journeys over many such popular caravan routes of the past, and in many different countries, have warranted the assumption that an impulse to leave one's name on public monuments was no invention of the American tourist.

The distinction has been made, however, that, when a Greek soldier in the early days carved a long inscription on the leg of one of the colossal figures at Abu Simbel, he did it so long ago that, by now, it has become historical confirmation of his presence there rather than a considered desecration of a statue.

I remember that Reisner once said to me that he had been asked to write an article on the subject of the probability that a canal connected Luxor with trade centers of the Near East as early as the New Kingdom. This was offered as a rumor by Strabo and other Greeks. Reisner's answer was that, until the Greco-Roman period, the volume of trade in that area could easily have been handled by camel transport.

Trade conflicts between the countries of ancient times were not really acute, because life was less complicated then than now. But the principles governing the search for and seizure of raw materials, and the law of supply and demand, were the same then as now. Who owned them? Who wanted them? And who was in a strategic position to get them against a competitor?

Whenever I saw mummies in their tombs or in museums, I used to speculate about the markets that supplied the precious and semiprecious stones that they wore in necklaces and bracelets.

Darius the Great must have required a quantity of lapis lazuli to make the beards that were attached to the stone portraits of himself placed in his private apartments at Persepolis. Probably at all times the world supply of jewelry was reasonably adequate to meet the demands that were joined with the ability to pay.

Alexander's life ran too short a span to permit him to develop a world trade syndicate based upon the principle of partnership with his vassal states. This he might well have done in the development of trade as a part of his brilliant and original plan of conquest by mind and methods instead of military force.

His methods were entirely different in Egypt from those of the Persians, and they were effective! In a curious repetition of history, more than two thousand years later, Napoleon's adventures in Egypt were of a similar nature. Although he was kept there by the British fleet against his will, he was virtually the ruler of Egypt.

Under the Ptolemies, Egypt's trade connections with her Near East neighbors developed greatly. Later, when Egypt became an integrated part of the Roman Empire, this trade flourished. It was not until this latter era that Palmyra became a successful competitor of—indeed superseded—Petra as a trade center.

I believed that a visit would be stimulating intellectually, in addition to my enjoyment as an artist in seeing the monuments of Palmyra. It still was to be another five years before I was to go over the long road that from time immemorial has been the only communication between the lowlands of Mesopotamia and the high plateau of Persia. In the early spring of 1930, Corinna and I had the opportunity to visit Palmyra after a winter's work in Egypt. The final lap of the hundred-odd miles from Damascus was by horseback in company with a friend.

The modern town of Palmyra, with its humble Arab homes, was not much of a place to see. But the mountains in the vicinity were superb, and a vast number of colonnades in an imposing display of ruins were tangible evidence of Palmyra's former greatness among the cities of Asia Minor. Like Petra, it was mentioned in the Bible: "He [Solomon] built Tadmor in the wilderness . . . ." He had found it well supplied with water. It formed a link between East and West in a strategic situation between the Mediterranean and the Euphrates. Later this position was to be of primary advantage during the rise to power of Darius and Xerxes.

The continuity of Palmyra's history was in strong contrast to the historical vacuum that surrounded Petra. Even the date for the climax of the latter's decline, given as A.D. 105, was found in Palmyra's annals. Pliny referred to Palmyra as being in the midst of two "powerful and hostile kingdoms," i.e., Parthia and Persia, in an "almost impassable desert" (the Syro-Arabian). The earliest inscription in the annals of Palmyra mentioned the dedication of the Temple of Baal soon after the birth of Christ. Even in ruins, that temple was all-pervasive.

A panoramic view was my first introduction to the ancient city. It revealed columns on one level and in line, extending a distance of miles.

Here I was forcibly impressed with an agreeable feeling of the space between buildings. And for good reason: Palmyra's builders had the benefit of a vast stretch of desert to meet the requirements of town planning.

The Greek Pericles, on the other hand, had the disadvantage, in creating the same kind of monuments at a far greater period, artistically, of being compelled to crowd one building almost on top of another on the top of a rock called the Acropolis.

During long tramps through these enormous ruins at Palmyra, I noted differences as well as similarities in architecture, which was in large part Corinthian and restful to the eye. Fyfe called the Temple of Baal "the grandest classical monument in Syria." Granted, but I found particularly effective the Kufic inscriptions on the massive bastion entrance and the remains of a sacrificial altar in front of the temple proper.

One of the most amazing spectacles I have seen in my travels in any part of the ancient world was that of the long colonnade at Palmyra with the superb mountain range extending the length of my vision beyond it. A fitting climax to such an experience was reaching, on the east of it, the temple built to Baal, the sun god and principal deity of Palmyra. The simplicity of its construction was exhibited in vast walls with a fine group of columns at one end.

Equally amazing was a monumental triple arch, a very complex structure that stood on the threshold of the vast colonnade. It had been well restored and was as interesting to modern architects as the gigantic arch of Ctesiphon near Baghdad, built by the Parthians. Both were constructed without mortar and towered above the surrounding landscape, having defied earthquakes and the passing of the centuries.

The colonnade itself was a stupendous achievement of magnificence and dignity. It consisted of three hundred columns more than fifty feet tall. As the main street of a city, it was unique. But when commemorative statues were on pedestals part way up the columns, the effect must have been too ornate, especially if the sculptured figures in themselves had been unworthy of the architectural conception as a whole.

The other monuments included the important ones in existence in a

great city of the period, such as the agora, and an assembly place combined with a theater, similar in status to the theater of Dionysius in
Athens. Also a typical caravansery of the Orient, built on the general
lines of the Turkish khans in medieval times.

I visited some of the numerous temples and tomb towers, and found
charm and variety in the signs of Semitic and Arab influences, even in
the buildings predominantly Corinthian in feeling.

During our brief stay of a few days, I devoted many hours to sitting
quietly by myself at a point where I could absorb the panoramic view.
This was the city of Zenobia, a woman whom I consider to have been
the match in wits of Hetepheres II in Egypt. In statesmanship, however,
she would have had more in common with Queen Hatshepsut.

Among the city's greatest assets were her sulphur springs, which
attracted the wealthy from afar. The wealth they left behind added materially to Palmyra's great commercial prosperity. Her silks were the first
found in the Near East, received as imports from China, and her textiles
dated to the first and second centuries A.D. Even in the days of Solomon,
there was mention of his having fortified Palmyra so that wealth from
India could be brought into "his kingdom." Also, with the worship of
the sun and other deities, Palmyra became a religious center. Finally, as a
neutral between Rome and Parthia, Palmyra played one against the
other to her own financial and political advantage. When it became
necessary for her to decide between them, she chose Rome "because she
was the more distant."

Trajan, Hadrian, and other Romans drifted across the stage in
Palmyra. Contemporary records tell of a definite system of colonial gov-
ernment under Rome and mention taxation, revolts, and policies. In
Petra the same Romans drifted across the scene in absolute silence.

49. Petra, 1930

I ARRANGED ON IMPULSE to go to Petra, even though it was difficult to
reach from Palmyra. It meant a cross-country plane trip to Jerusalem,
and from there a day of motoring to Amman, Transjordania, head-

quarters of the Arab Legion. Permission for foreigners to camp in this out-of-the-way part of Transjordania, among rather lawless tribes, was a responsibility of the Legion to be granted only by Peake Pasha, the Englishman in charge.

Russell Pasha, commandant of the Cairo police, telegraphed Peake Pasha of our expected arrival, and Reisner arranged for a guide to meet us at Jerusalem. At sight, I felt complete confidence in the guide, a Sheikh Isa, and shortly we were on our way.

At the frontier between Palestine and Transjordania, we received the welcome news that Peake Pasha was expecting us to dine with him in Amman, the seat of Arab government in Transjordania, of which Abdullah was Emir under a British mandate and a high commissioner. On our arrival there, we left our luggage at the hotel and went directly into the amphitheatre built by the same Ptolemy known as Philadelphus (285–247 B.C.) who was responsible for the temples on the island of Philae. We were climbing among the steep tiers of stone seats in the well-preserved ruin when a commotion in a group of native police warned us of the approach of Peake Pasha. He said the necessary permits had been issued and orders given for police protection, and assured us that we would be safe in Sheikh Isa's hands, for the tribes "liked and feared" him. He emphasized the latter word and added, "A good thing that, in a region where there is always trouble and raids." Dinner was brief, but every second an event. The romance of the Arab Legion with its daring exploits sounded like a ballad of old-time chivalry, as told by our host. He said we were lucky that the weekly train from Amman left the following morning for Ma'an, our immediate destination, where we would be met by an English officer of the Legion.

It was an all-day journey on one of the casual railroads in the Near East and afforded me plenty of leisure to think about the secret that had remained concealed in the bright-colored rocks of Petra.

Both Peake Pasha, who had been there many times, and an English archaeologist, whom I ran across by chance and who had once excavated at Petra, had information to spare about the Nabateans, especially of the

278

early period, about 600 B.C., when Petra was their capital city and known by the Hebrew word *Sela* (rock). Then there was a gap, followed by their reappearance in 200 B.C. By this time the city was called *Petra,* the Greek word signifying rock. They had carried on a lively trade as the center of a caravan route, and had wrested from a weak ptolemy the control of the country as far north as Damascus and as far south as the Red Sea. After that came the Roman period, and by the time of the Emperor Severus (A.D. 222–235) Palmyra had become powerful and attracted the caravan trade, and Petra was "by-passed."

There had followed the usual sequence of Crusaders and Arabs in that part of the Near East. I was warned of the masses of ruins on every mountain peak of Petra—many hundreds in number, all Nabatean.

But both Peake Pasha and the archaeologist were discouragingly vague about the monument I was traveling so far to see, and left me to remove my own question marks concerning the identity of the people who had carved from a huge boulder a building reputed to be unique in many of its features, and who had vanished leaving no trace. And this in the reign of the Emperor Hadrian, when Roman records were fairly complete!

Where had they come from? What drove them away? Had enemy attacks cut off their water supply? What had happened? And when? I was still pondering the problem when, at the station of Ma'an, a British major, with a spectacular-looking escort of Arab Legionnaires, picked us up and deposited us at the hotel. We were off soon after sunrise by motor, hoping to sleep that night in Petra, *inshallah!* Our immediate road lay through two towns, Damascus Ma'an and Cairo Ma'an. "And much fighting goes on here," Sheikh Isa commented, after explaining that the office of the Arab Legion was situated between these two points. We passed rocky, monotonous desert, an occasional flock of black goats, a few cattle, and small patches of earth where Bedouins were plowing. I wondered what kept desert families from actual starvation.

It was about noon when we reached the village of Elji of the Wady Musa, where the motor part of our trip was to end. At one o'clock saddled horses with the single rein used by Arabs were waiting on the road above in a long cavalcade to take us and our simple camp outfit, including food supplies impossible to obtain in Petra.

Within a brief half-hour from Elji, we headed across the broad valley of the Wady Musa and struck a stream bed leading towards what appeared to be a cliff some hundreds of feet high without an opening. But a very narrow defile did give entrance to our horses, single file, through a *sik,* or gorge, with abrupt turns. Tall rock walls varied in height as we progressed. The width of the track under foot increased, but there was no change in the charm of the reds and purples on rocks of fantastic shapes. The first sight of the temple dedicated to Isis, as it emerged from a giant boulder, was so overwhelming in its unreality that my mind registered only the sensational brilliance of a flaming rose building with columns and alcoves, but otherwise absolutely unlike any Greco-Roman building I had ever seen. I stared at the perfection of this fabled el-Khuzneh (the Treasury), so called because the Bedouins believed a pharaoh's rich treasure was once in a huge urn that towered into the blue sky from the top of the building. I dismounted and, walking to the entrance, stood in silence taking in the details as well as the amazing color of a subject that was definitely worth the effort of getting to it.

When I saw Sheikh Isa was becoming restless, I reluctantly turned away and remounted my horse. A short distance beyond, I had an uncomfortable sensation of being completely hemmed in by ruins. They were here, there, and everywhere, situated on a wide plateau. It was almost a relief to pass on to what suggested a modern restricted residential district in the vicinity of the Petra Acropolis. Two tents were pitched close by, on a level plateau, and were equipped with the essentials for our comfort. Above us were sharp boulders, and behind, a long line of lower cliffs dotted with caves at an accessible level. Just before dark a "lady," as Sheikh Isa called female Bedouins, shouted down from the heights. Much talk ensued between them. He said she was telling him that an airplane with two men had "fallen too quick from the sky." When I inquired how far away this had happened, her answer was, "As far as a woman throws a stick." At dawn, what I termed a "shouting" acquaintance with Bedouins had recommenced with dim figures on the sky line, understudies, as it were, for the characters in Lady Gregory's Irish play, *Spreading the News*. I felt that the Bedouins would substitute for the morning radio broadcasts. And my prophecy was fulfilled! News was to fly fast and far from one crag to another during our stay!

While I was at breakfast, the early sun was accentuating the caves, from which a number of natives were emerging, their cheerful chatter permeating the silence. "Who are those men?" I asked Sheikh Isa, to learn they were all in my employ and glad for the warmth and protection afforded them in the caves of the Edomites. This was my introduction to the Edomites, the first known inhabitants of Petra, mentioned in the Old Testament by David, who exclaimed (*Psalm xl*), "Who will bring me into the strong city? Who will lead me into Edom?" Except for the caves, no trace remained of the culture of the Edomites. There were about twenty buildings extant of the classical type that would be easy to distinguish through my familiarity with Greek and Greco-Roman construction, dating from the same epoch as the Temple of Isis.

Among the most ancient of the monuments were strange, huge, four-sided block towers. We examined one that had been partially hollowed out to form an interior chamber. These towers were probably associated with Petra's principal god, Dhushara. His symbol was a black rectangular stone somewhat like the Ka'ba of Mecca. Also, in addition to these stones, scattered about in niches, were a number of signs of the Arabian female goddess Allat. But these ruins, connected with a primitive pagan religion, were relatively uninteresting.

Sheikh Isa told me that the majority of the available rock tops within view were used by the Nabateans when Petra was their ancient capital in 600 B.C. Some were designated merely as "tombs"; sacrificial arrangements in a few of them indicated they were holy places; others were temples.

On the first afternoon we were soon scrambling up the face of cliffs with the aid of spiked sticks that prevented slipping. It was an experience reminiscent of my youthful days in scaling the natural rocks of the

Acropolis of Athens. Equally impregnable was this former fortress, Acropolis of the Nabateans. I drew back hastily from a great black and yellow snake coiling so realistically about a boulder that I thought it alive. This was near a mass of rubble and loose stones that we had to cross to reach an imposing entrance to an unfinished cave. A carved doorway interested me from the fact that the carving was from the top downwards, a characteristic I had noticed in other decorated caves of the ancient Edomites. We crawled into another cave, which must have been very fine, judging by the remains of statues over the columned door. Inside, on the right, were rooms, and directly opposite, a door led into the harem quarters, where there was a very legible Nabatean inscription. Sheikh Isa remarked that Peake Pasha, on his visit to Petra, lived in an Edomite cave almost as elaborate. But the Smiths still preferred tents.

On a flat rock plateau above was a temple, or church, with fluted columns in a large circular interior. These columns, of a delicate rose color, were the only fluted ones we saw in Petra, and on one of them was a long Nabatean inscription. Another afternoon trip gave us the opportunity to see one of the monuments of the classical type, which Sheikh Isa called *el-Deir* (convent), and which he had strongly recommended. We arrived rather out of breath from crawling along a trail that meandered over rocky ledges and up steps in no better condition. In spite of the name, this building could only have been a temple. As one approached, the first impression was one of great majesty, for the monument possessed an enormous façade, wider than that of Westminster Abbey, a central section with three engaged columns on each side of a doorway of great height, and a massive tower surmounted by a gigantic urn. A niche, originally intended for an idol, had in it a few small crosses carved on its walls, doubtless made by Crusaders. Sensational as this building was because of its size and dramatic situation, it seemed to me rather a poor imitation of the Treasury, and its color (surprisingly for Petra) was a monotonous khaki. I considered *el-Deir* among the less successful monuments of a classical trend.

I had to take a day off for the *Zibb Atafar,* or Mount of Obelisks, and the great High Place. Abdullah, our favorite native guide, led the procession, carrying a large, round basket containing lunch and heavy coats Sheikh Isa insisted we would need. The Arab guard was among several additional ones who had recently arrived, and was a fierce-looking man with a heavy-bearded face. We had reached quite a height, after a stiff climb of several hours, before we came to an original flight of wide steps with an unusual quality about them. They were curiously similar in construction to the ones by which we had descended into the Dieng Plateau in Java during a Far-Eastern expedition. We left the staircase at a point where a massive construction of masonry formed one end of a tank above a charming little temple with fine columns and good details, cut out of a boulder beautiful in form and color. A splendid, jagged sky line and a view of superb rocks across a valley made it a subject to tempt an artist's brush. Frequently, as we continued to mount higher, Sheikh Isa pointed out trenches in the face of the rock for taking rain water into storage tanks. Certainly the people who lived here, who-ever they turned out to be, preserved every drop of precious water.

We all began to get out of breath, and I asked Isa the height of the Mount of the Obelisk we were approaching. When he told me six thousand feet, I understood both our puffing and the reason for our over-coats. We did not linger at the gigantic ruins of a Crusader's castle which had not been destroyed when Saladin drove the Crusaders from their strongholds, even in this isolated district. We pushed on, turning towards the *sik* at a slightly lower level. Near us were two tall obelisks, as stone sentinels, with their tips marking the original height of the rock (now a plateau) from which had come the huge blocks for building the castle. We sat overlooking the great boulder that contained the cameo-like gem of the Temple of Isis. The cloud effects were perfect. Beyond the green village of Elji was the winding road that had brought us from Amman to the enchantment of Petra and the artistic triumph of this classical monument, where builders with true creative genius, instead of marring the natural beauty of the site, had added to its perfection.

Immediately above the Mount of Obelisks, we were on the great High

Place, amidst mountain tops, but all else was lost in a vast expanse of level rock that stretched on and on as though into eternity. If this was not the spot where Abraham offered up his sacrifice, surely it was exactly like that biblical place. The altar facing the rising sun, with the significant cuttings upon the altar block! The place where the priest stood, with the basin for his ablutions! The drain where the water trickled away! The great slab whereon the sacrifice was slain! The trench that carried the blood away! And the carved bench for the beholders! Nothing was missing, and at last I knew exactly how a holy place of sacrifice of a primitive semitic people looked.

There were several ruins of the "classical" type worth seeing at Petra. They usually had façades carved in a single piece from the face of the living rock. The façade had four doorways, each enclosed by a pair of pilasters and a cornice. The "Palace Tomb" varied from the pattern by having the upper story constructed of masonry. The "Daughter's House," situated near our camp, was fairly late Roman, and had been built, not cut from the rock. More of it remained than was the case with any other building of this kind in the area, and it had a quite impressive colonnade. On both sides of the rocky stream bed which ran through the *sik* were ruins huddled close together. From the original construction and the amount of ground covered, I judged the buildings must have been used as trading centers or were imposing private buildings.

We had interesting guests from among our Bedouin neighbors. They would come near our tent, stand silently staring for a while, and then disappear. One day, the lady Bedouin of shouting acquaintance came unannounced to the tent and handed me a beautiful, small Phoenician glass vase in perfect condition. I told Sheikh Isa to ask how much she wanted for it. Her answer was, "It is a present."

All the guards and native guides accompanied us on a final walk up to a superb plateau of some extent, where the cliffs were dotted with cave homes formerly occupied by Edomites. Bedouin families now occupied the latter. We accepted an invitation to have coffee in one of them. The experience was similar to those we had had in the Nile villages, where we received the hospitality of people in mud brick homes. Such a cackle of voices and rushing about, as the people crowded on to that plateau from every direction to welcome the strangers!

Next morning we mounted and rode away from a camp to a mournful wailing of Bedouins. The rosy glow of the rising sun brought out the consummate skill of the original workmanship of Pharaoh's Treasury.

Just before the exit to the *sik*, we paused, got off our horses, and followed Sheikh Isa to a long line of ruined masonry, obviously once an aqueduct, and also obviously one that *deflected* the water supply from Petra.

"They couldn't capture the city," he said, "so they cut off the water and then Petra was finished."

"Who did this?" I asked.

"The peoples who wanted the city, when they came to get it," he replied, with a vagueness shared by archaeologists still awaiting "scientific explorations of Petra's secrets, concealed in her bright-colored rocks."

QUEST IN THE FAR EAST

50. *Japanese and Chinese Monuments*

THROUGHOUT MY PAINTING CAREER I have been called, often with little notice, to many parts of the world where traditional arts existed. For this reason, my chronology frequently doubles back on itself. The Far East is, like Greece and Imperial Rome, another case in point, since I was there much earlier than the period covered in the chapters on Baalbek, Palmyra, and Petra.

The great single fact of art in its historical perspective is the steady continuity, age in and age out, of man's drive towards durable and striking artistic expression. In the countries of the Far East, religion, in every development of civilization, has been a reflection of that civilization and expresses the energy which imbued it. What we see in Japan, Korea, China, Indo-China, India, and Java in the form of temples and royal state apartments adorned with superb sculpture, whether inspired by one or the other of several ancient religions, are joined together by a bond of unity in some inexplicable process. The same is true of ceramics and paintings, in black and white or in color, on silk, cloth, or wood panels.

I intend to comment briefly on an interdependence in art expression during a period extending from the early part of the Christian Era and lasting into the fourteenth century in these Far Eastern countries with which I am familiar. For my purposes, I will consider them in two

286

groups, one comprising China, Korea, and Japan, the other, Indo-China, Siam, India, and Java.

My first direct contact with an Asiatic country occurred when Corinna and I spent the better part of the year 1901 in Japan. Later, Denman Ross and I were in Korea and China. On this and subsequent trips, I came to know the monuments of Peking and other centers of China, temples with flaming red and gold ornamentation, monasteries, pagodas, arches, gateways, all with the characteristic architectural features of the period to which they belonged. I studied the enormous figures of Buddha, monuments to Confucius and Taoism, and the striking tombs of the Ming emperors, with their huge tablets inscribed with poems, supported by tremendous turtles and processions of fabulous animals in stone.

I considered some of the most productive hours were those spent in the native quarters of Hanchow, Suchow, and Canton in search of antiquities. I would edge my way on foot through narrow, dark alleys, jostled by dense crowds, but often to be rewarded by a find. Once it was a splendid specimen of Sung pottery, discovered in a small shop selling dried rats, frogs, snakes, and bears' claws. An equally unlikely spot yielded a Han piece, made at a date when the quality of the glass and beauty of color were valued above shape. At a particularly congested corner in Canton, I caused a traffic jam during the process of buying my most important acquisitions, a superb Sung painting and two of the Ming School, curious rather than attractive, landscapes of sponge-shaped rocks combined with bamboo, willow, and temple and villa architecture, with mountains beyond.

In China, I always traveled too rapidly to paint, but in Japan quite frequently I settled down for weeks at a time to a painting regime at Nara, where superb wooden statues tempted my brush, or at Kyoto, where the beautiful interiors of temples suggested fine possibilities. Nara was the ancient capital of Japan, and the countryside had remained largely unchanged since the middle of the sixth century of the Christian Era. Indian gods of Buddhism had come by way of China and Korea and reached Japan. During the eighth century, foreign craftsmen erected magnificent buildings in great parts at Nara and its vicinity, in honor of these imported gods. The finest was the Monastery of Horyuji. The superb Ni-o-non Gateway to the group of sacred buildings showed the genius of Korean architects in this and earlier periods. Moreover, "classical" form in architecture was maintained by the Koreans in their construction of the "Hall of Dreams" at an even later date.

When I painted in an Egyptian tomb, I was pleasantly conscious of its owner's possessions, but in the Monastery of Horyuji, the absence of material things created an atmosphere of peace and contemplation suggestive of Buddha himself, an atmosphere that was enhanced by a spiritual quality in the expression of the faces of the statues. I worked in many different apartments of the monastery. One of the subjects I enjoyed particularly was a standing Kwannon in the huge Kondo Hall. There was a dignity and reverence about the figure, and also in a dark idol I painted in the neighboring Nunnery of Chuguji. It was seated in a deep gold shrine, with one leg crossed over the lap, conveying a sense of rhythm.

But supreme among Nara's many treasures was the Kwannon of Yumedono in the Nara Horyuji Temple, dating to the Suiko period. When the doors of the shrine containing it were opened for me, before I was to begin to paint, I stood for some time gazing into that extraordinary, mysterious face. I still believe that this Kwannon is the last word in the conception and execution of the great religious sculptures of the Far East.

The Korean statues at Horyuji and in the museums of Nara and Kyoto were really splendid, with their closed, mongoloid eyes, raised eyebrows, and elongated ears. The drapery, strictly traditional in form, made me appreciate Korean sculptors as apt pupils of the Chinese. Also, among many wonderful embroideries I saw in Japan, some of the best were Korean, and the Korean contribution to ceramics was equally persuasive. A number of ornamented pieces of ceramics, made by Korean potters and suggestive of Sung influence, were found in Japan, and a green and blue glass bowl, a familiar type in Japan, was Korean in origin. All in all, I found many examples of the centuries during which

Painting of the Daibutsu Buddha at Kamakura, Japan, by Joseph Lindon Smith. Courtesy Mrs. Joseph Lindon Smith, Dublin, N.H.

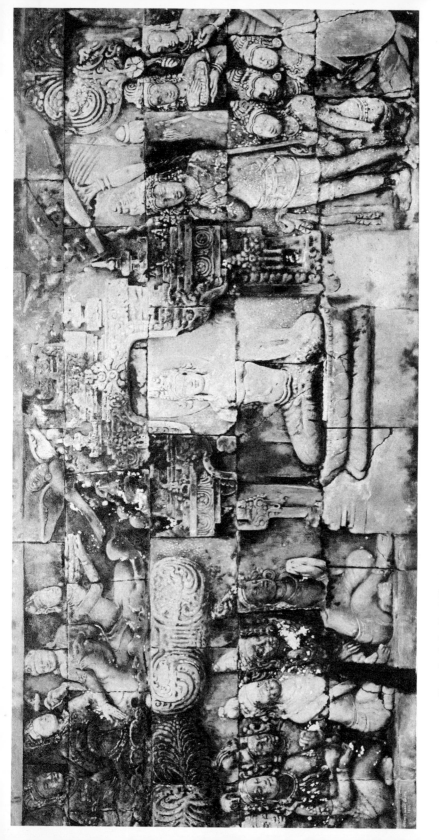

Detail of the Buddha Monument at Borobudur, Java. Painting by Joseph Lindon Smith. Courtesy Museum of Fine Arts, Boston.

the Koreans had assimilated the traditional art expressions of China to the advantage of other countries.

In the Nara Museum there was an entirely different, but very remarkable, aspect of Japanese wooden sculpture represented by Unkei in the Kamakura period (A.D. 1185–1392). He was not only an "innovator" in technique but a master craftsman. The fierce energy displayed in his carved wooden faces and tremendous muscular development of limbs and body occasionally reached the mighty conceptions of Michelangelo, I painted an expressive statue by Unkei of a deva king guardian outside the temple of Todaiji, Nara, whose duty it was to drive away evil spirits.

Kyoto superseded Nara as the capital of Japan from the year A.D. 745 until the Kamakura period beginning A.D. 1185. The Fujiwara family was the important factor in the creation of an art entirely freed from the Chinese influence that had dominated ancient Nara, and in the development in Kyoto of a medieval culture purely Japanese. It was to me interesting to witness a metamorphosis as definite as the break from the old order which had occurred in Akhenaten's period in Egypt.

Occasionally Chinese influence lingered on, as in the Ho-o-do, or Phoenix Hall, an architectural monument that depicted court life of long ago, now in a sad state of decay. The wall paintings were about gone, the garden no more, but as I sat on the edge of what had been a lotus pond of great beauty, the building with slender, spreading wings ending in charming belvederes and other lovely details, came back to me, as depicted in Buddhist wall paintings in China of the T'ang Dynasty (A.D. 618–907).

Never in China or any other Eastern country could there be such an all-satisfying temple dedicated to religion as Chion-in, the chief monastery belonging to the Jodo sect of Buddhism. I was completely overcome by the beauty of the Kondo (hall) of vast extent, flooded by sunlight in unexpected places, and very lovely throughout with deep velvety blacks and browns contrasting with wonderful scintillations of gold and lacquer. For form, color, varying lights, superbly sculptured and gilded shrines, tall pillars, and huge, gold lotus in old Chinese vases, no interior can be comparable.

In Kyoto, I became daily more thoroughly impressed with the inspired work of Japanese artists. I examined with interest an outstanding example, in an ink study on paper, of deer that maintained the individuality of each deer, never losing the detail to the mass, and with no confusion. And how I admired the artists who, with a few bold strokes, produced a rugged rock, an outline of a mountain, a river scene gay with boats, or one with a single fisherman, birds, a superb tree, or a portrait of a peasant, priest, or samurai with distinctive personality.

In Kyoto, too, the past lived on, as in Egypt: for instance, in a religious procession held in the summer and therefore rarely seen by foreigners. This was the procession of the Gion, when four huge metal shrines, heavily gilded, were carried on men's shoulders from one temple to another. They were preceded by priests, gentlemen, and warriors, who looked as though they had stepped out of screens or other Japanese paintings, dressed, as they were, in rich robes and armor borrowed from museum collections. I found similarities between this observance and those of Egypt.

The third capital of ancient Japan was Kamakura (A.D. 1185–1392). I went there to paint the Daibutsu Buddha, modeled and cast in bronze by the Japanese sculptor Goroyemon, who lived in the early part of the Kamakura period. The great seated figure, almost sixty feet in height, was in the open, surrounded by a sacred enclosure of low trees. When I first saw the Daibutsu, after a light shower, the bronze patina of six centuries was shiny and richer in color from the rain, which brought out delightful harmonies of greens in light and shadow.

I began to paint at once, and fortunately, the rain obligingly continued until I had finished my picture. I always found fishermen abroad early as I passed along the shore of the sea to reach the Buddha, and the scenes were a reminder of the armed camp on the coast, in a small fishing village which became the Kamakura Shogunate. Both warriors and fishermen were characteristic of the paintings of the Kamakura era. The Daibutsu was like the great seated Colossi of Abu Simbel in symbolizing the calm serenity of eternal life, but the draperies were archaic Greek—an effective combination. Yet I found in Japan, as I had found elsewhere, that the great shrines did not attract little people, whose devotions seemed more natural, and perhaps more effective, at the little shrines in paddy fields and along the roads of their country.

51. *Angkor Wat, Angkor Thom*

To REACH ANGKOR WAT from Hongkong, as I did on my first trip with Ross in 1910, required two days at sea to Saigon, the port of Indo-China. There we changed steamers and headed north on the Mekong, one of the great rivers of the world, which penetrated far into China. Our destination was Cambodia. The second morning, I awakened at dawn to find that we were in the midst of enormous submerged trees, in a part of the country flooded by the Mekong during certain months of the year. Marabou storks and pelicans were flying overhead or fishing along the shores, as were herons, loons, and bright blue and green birds of a species I did not recognize.

On leaving the coast, if the area of treetops can thus be termed, we entered again a vast stretch of open water such as we had been on for most of the river trip. After quite a distance, we approached evidence of man in the vast solitude. There was only a light perched high on a pole. The captain informed us that we had arrived at our getting-off point for Angkor Wat. The nose of a long narrow boat pushed out from the direction of the light and headed towards our steamer. Soon we and our luggage were installed in it: A skillful Indian guide poled the boat through submerged woods, and then of a sudden we plunged into tropical vegetation of bamboo and mango and thick vines. The scenes on either bank were like those of the Congo, with natives peering at us from dark huts. The women wore skirts but were bare above the waist, and the children were clothed in anklets and earrings.

After quite a struggle with the swiftly rushing stream, here only thirty feet wide, we went ashore and mounted elephants. Almost at once we turned into a deep forest. The long ride had been devastating to the anatomy and we were glad to dismount at an unpretentious bungalow built by the French government, where visitors to the temple of Angkor

Wat were lodged. A French official, M. Comyus, who was in charge of the Cambodian monuments, looked us up that evening soon after our arrival. He told us he had finished excavations and repairs at Angkor Wat and was about to do similar restoration at Angkor Thom.

By 5:30 the next morning, I was looking into the eastern sky, where the wonderful towers of the temple of Angkor Wat stood out dark blue against the sunrise. Columns of pale smoke rose slowly from brush fires, where workmen were clearing the ever-encroaching, tangled jungle and the rapidly growing trees from walls of the temple. Comyus joined us on the huge stone causeway that took us across a broad moat surrounding the enormous temple enclosure. Buffaloes were enjoying themselves in the water of the moat, and lovely white egrets were riding on their backs. As we approached the temple, we saw five massive towers, the central one soaring far above the others, which dominated the view.

The construction was on such a gigantic scale that I felt my imagination must have deceived my eyes. It seemed almost impossible that mere men could have handled this great mass of grayish-colored stone, which must have amounted to thousands of tons.

"Where did all that stone come from?" I asked. Comyus said that it had been brought from quarries about twenty miles away, and added, "But we don't know by whom or how."

In the way of history, he mentioned that Angkor Wat dated to the end of the thirteenth century, built by the Khmers, who were obviously a powerful people, supposedly from India. How they had got there and why they left, he dismissed as another secret concealed in the Cambodian jungles. It was a French naturalist, while searching for specimens, who had accidentally discovered these massive ruins, which had been engulfed by nature and all trace of their existence lost. The discovery had occurred in 1860, and the French government had assumed archaeological responsibility for the preservation of the monuments.

We entered through the first portal and then walked along a wide, stone-paved avenue which ended in steps ascending to the entrance to the temple proper, which was built in cruciform shape. Inside, a flight of high steps mounted to a shrine dedicated to Vishnu. Endless corridors and a veritable labyrinth of long galleries showed signs of the ceaseless activity of many sculptors on the stone surface inside and out, including the ceilings. It was as though Vishnu, Siva, and Buddha had vied with one another to determine which of them could have the greatest number of intricate designs and figures carved in their honor.

I examined walls high and low. On them all were bas-reliefs and ornaments, seen and partly seen. In the four great halls, was a series of reliefs, historical and religious, with hundreds upon hundreds of figures, men, animals, reptiles, birds, battle triumphs, court scenes, hunts, games —the history of Cambodia written in stone and the color, a beautiful moss-green where water had trickled down over the surface, lavenders, blues, browns, and purples.

Even on that first day I quickly placed my easel before a dancing girl or priestess, life size, with elaborate foliate ornament above her head, and for a second subject, I decided on a detail of a seated Siva from a wonderful frieze from the south gallery of the temple.

During the length of our stay, I never lost entirely a feeling of bewilderment, even artistic weariness, from the lack of a central idea in all the splendor. But, finally, I succumbed to the majesty of this unique temple, with its tremendous towers above the tallest of the near-by forest's tall trees. I remained in a state of awed wonder at the rendering of a battle scene between Hindus and unknown enemies, and one of a struggle between men and monkeys; stories told in terms of a pageant master in great processional epics that would have taken hours merely to cross a hippodrome stage.

Gradually, I got accustomed to the superabundance of decoration and yielded to the rare beauty of detail and delicate grace of the reliefs, particularly in feminine figures, which had a charm and vitality amazingly captured in stone. Many of the motifs showed the influence of India. Even so, Angkor Wat's sculptures were less exotic and sensual, and avoided a tendency to coarseness noticeable in Indian art.

As I painted a warrior in his chariot on the terrace of a turret, I could hear the priests chanting in a little scattered settlement, under the trees below, just inside the temple enclosure. They presented a gay note in their robes of saffron, orange, and deep yellow. Often, while I worked, groups of them sat around me and talked incessantly a language that sounded like the buzz of a stringed instrument. The bats squeaked angrily overhead, and every now and again the raucous croaking of a large lizard reverberated through the halls and courts, causing an amusing diversion.

Angkor Thom was twelve miles away, which meant a day off and an elephant ride. It was fortunate for Ross and me that Comyus arranged to accompany us, otherwise we would have been completely lost in an area of jungle monuments so vast that it made those of Angkor Wat a mere pocket handkerchief in comparison. Angkor Thom had been the great capital city of Cambodia, its king and court living inside its massive walls. It was built during the ninth century after Christ, and its earlier origins were reflected in an art that was of a far higher quality than that of Angkor Wat.

Comyus told us of two known references to Angkor Thom in early times, both Chinese in source. One record mentioned a kingdom of the Hindus in that area, at the beginning of the fourth century. Again in the thirteenth century, a Chinese traveler visited Angkor Thom and wrote of its marvels. His account was confirmed by subsequent scholars, who were able to date some of the stone reliefs and inscriptions to the latter part of the thirteenth century, the period during which Angkor Wat was built for the people of Angkor Thom. After this, and apparently with finality, the Khmers disappeared into the Cambodian jungle.

Everywhere throughout the ruins of Angkor Thom, masses of amazing, very spirited bas-reliefs were partially covered with vines and plants, and great trees were pushing and pulling the masonry to pieces. But even nature was powerless in preventing the overwhelming emphasis of Buddha in Bayon, the most stupendous and artistic monument of them all. Here, in row after row of mighty towers, Buddha's face was carved so that it might look toward the four cardinal points of the compass, on each and every tower. And this in a city where Siva, the destroyer was the patron saint!

Angkor Thom was the most perfect tangle of nature and art of a great early Asiatic period I ever hope to see. Monkeys followed us about, and when we ignored their presence, chattered shrilly in frustration. They, and snakes to avoid underfoot, gave just the right note, somehow. On the return ride to Angkor Wat, we stopped to climb a solitary tall monument, where, from the summit, we saw miles and miles of enormous trees, doubtless covering numberless more ruins of the Khmers. A beautiful lake was encircled by a broken line of charming mountains and the towers of Angkor Wat were prominent even at a distance.

An unforgettable experience occurred on the last evening of that first visit, when, by the light of a full moon, Cambodian girls of today performed inside the temple the traditional dances of long ago. Every detail of their headdresses and costumes, each posture, the use of the hands, and facial expressions were so like those of the dancers carved in stone on the wall above them that it seemed as though the latter had come to life.

Corinna and I spent a couple of weeks in Bangkok in 1921. I particularly wished to see Ayutthaya, where some of the remains of early Thai civilization, dating from the fourteenth century, might still be seen. I wished particularly to find out whether there were similarities between the ruins of Ayutthaya and Angkor Wat. A Siamese (or Thai) historian took us by river to Ayutthaya, situated on an island about fifty miles from Bangkok. A modern town had grown up near the ancient site and a railroad station was in process of construction. No Siamese seemed willing to lend us a cart, and I did not blame them when we found what we had to get through in the way of old bricks and an almost impenetrable tangle of bamboo and vines of the clinging variety.

It was a rough tramp of several miles and there was not much to reward us in the way of ruins. There had been two principal temples, or *wats*. One had several spires in a dilapidated state, towards which we clambered over a brick wall that once had surrounded the ancient city. The brick spires were neither reminiscent of Angkor Wat's towers nor distinctive in themselves.

The other *wat,* Mongkol Bopitr, had once been one of the famous

295

temples of medieval times. But it, too, was disappointing as a roofless ruin, with walls fallen into mere heaps of formless bricks. There was, however, a single, rather large figure of a Buddha, not good in workmanship but impressive from the fact that it *was* there.

We also made a visit to Lopburi, which had been the capital of Siam after Ayutthaya was sacked by the Burmese in 1767. As guests of the governor of the province, we were to be lodged in a floating bungalow moored to the river bank. A delightful old Frenchman named Montocchio, who had a Siamese wife, was delegated to look after us. We left Bangkok before daylight on a five-hour railroad journey, passing vast rice fields on both sides of the track. At the station for Lopburi, we were welcomed by a pleasant-faced Cambodian, accompanied by several aides, who introduced himself as secretary to His Excellency Phra Titsamulake. He later saw us to the ancient ruins.

Lopburi had been on a main route of travel that connected with Angkor in ancient times and, as in Ayutthaya, I wished to examine for any trace of temples dating to the eleventh century, when Siam was under Cambodian rule. The secretary led us through a primitive village of today, and some distance beyond it, we reached a site where several towers were reminiscent of Cambodian towers. There were other ruins of this early period in the midst of cactus bushes and roses in bloom. The best were in the vicinity of a banyan tree, hundreds of years old, with the branches growing down into new roots and coming up again to repeat the process, thus forming an intermingling of roots and branches that was an extraordinary freak of nature.

The decay of temples, built of brick and faced with mortar, was nearly complete, but I saw a number of fragments of carved stone that were excellent artistically, and among them, a few small heads in the round that had features in common with the Khmer reliefs of Angkor Wat. I found far less interesting the ruins generally visited, which were those of a palace belonging to the Siamese King Narai, who lived in the days of Louis XIV of France. There was not much left of either the palace or an adjacent temple. What was really worth seeing were doorways of sandstone at the entrance to a shrine that showed a strong Chinese influence, and although blackened by fire, they were still magnificent. My thoughts were too much occupied with trying to evolve some plan for the protection of these doors and of the lovely Khmer heads to listen to anecdotes and legends of the secretary connected with King Narai.

The Governor, Phra Titsamulake, entertained us at an elaborate dinner in his palace of many large rooms. During it, a group of Siamese girls gave a series of traditional dances. Every detail of their costumes and movements, as in the case of the Cambodian girls I had seen performing at Angkor Wat, was reflected in the ancient depictions of dancers carved on the temple walls of Cambodia.

At Pnomb Pneng on the Mekong River, among a conglomerate architecture, there was a group of pure white buildings that were very beautiful, and everything about them in construction, decoration, and detail was Indian.

In the temples of central Java, on the other hand, Siva was often in evidence, but at Borobudur one felt the power of Buddha consecrated in stone. I had been there for a brief stay with Ross after Angkor Wat. Both monuments have the artistic expression and the qualities essential to the finest sculptured reliefs. For architecture and dignified magnificence, Angkor Wat was far superior, but in addition to fidelity of the human form, the reliefs of Borobudur expressed *ideas* to a far greater degree. It was to Borobudur that I wanted to return, and I was glad of the opportunity to be there for a month with Corinna after our trip together to Siam. We had driven for several hours in a carriage drawn by four horses through the morning drizzle of the rainy season, over narrow roads between tall trees. Suddenly, our driver pointed to a hill ahead of us and said one word, "Borobudur."

In a setting of vivid green, great cupolas rose above a vast superstructure and its forest of pinnacles. At the top was a tremendous dome dwarfing everything in its vicinity. A sharp turn to the left brought us abruptly to the government "rest house," close to the monument. We were shown into a large, airy room, from the doorway of which we looked directly into the center of Borobudur. After persistent showers at intervals, the clouds rolled away and we started to go up the steep stairway, past the long terraces where, in a splendid series of reliefs, men and animals were rendering homage to the Buddha, who sat calmly in contemplation. We walked past circular galleries with myriads of pinnacles and projecting cornices, up to the great round *dagoba,* the place of mystery, and sat on the ledge. It was a peaceful scene of flooded rice fields with reflections of green hillsides in their still surfaces. Dark figures of men were emerging from the fields to disappear with creaking bullock carts toward little villages. We were facing the three active volcanoes, Merapi, Soombing, and Meraboe, from the ancient molten stone of which grew this and other art treasures in Java. There was a solemnity and spirituality in the surroundings that made me understand why men of genius in every country have always looked beyond material things for guidance.

During the succeeding weeks, as I painted hour after hour, I gradually absorbed the fundamental attributes of the bas-reliefs. The ornament, although elaborate, never became meaningless, because both builder and sculptor kept to straight lines and empty spaces. The carvings on the inner walls of the first gallery represented the life of Buddha from birth to death, showing gatherings under the bo tree, pilgrimages to sacred spots, Buddha's admonitions to virtue, tolerance, and abstinence, and his own emphasis upon the desire to sacrifice himself for his fellow creatures. In the late afternoon of our last day at Borobudur, I mounted at random, pausing to notice in passing with what an admirable sense of proportion the gateway and stairways were constructed with moldings of classic simplicity. I continued up through the three circular galleries, which were open on all sides and without ornament or sculpture, since, according to the belief of the "initiated," the higher they rose toward an understanding of Buddha's teaching, the less the outward symbol of it was needed. I saw nothing except dimly visible Buddhas behind latticed stonework. The last flight of steps took me to the unfinished, unseen, but all-pervading Buddha within the *dagoba*. To me this monument was as religious in feeling as mortal hands could create, but as I looked from the radiant sky down to the rich soil I could not accept Buddha's concept of a principle that was intent upon the extinction of self, the losing of the individual in the eternal void.

The unsolved mysteries contained in stone amidst the jungles continued to fascinate me during my travels, therefore, after I had finished painting at Borobudur, I decided to add the Dieng Plateau to Petra in Transjordania and the Khmers of Cambodia. Dieng Plateau of central Java had several hundreds of temples, most of them dedicated to Buddhism, but many Hindus of Java were supposed to have been buried there. The monuments were last heard of in the early part of the fifteenth century, and the mystery connected with them has remained unsolved.

The starting point to Dieng was the town of Wonosobo, situated at the base of Soombing and its twin but quiescent volcano, Sindoro. It was an ascent of three thousand feet on horseback from a small place called Garoeng, over a steep, stony path on the knife-like edge of the ridge of a mountain. We rode along this ridge for several hours, but seemingly far above us always was the top of the path. Swift brooks made a delightful sound over the stones, and we crossed waterfalls frequently by quaint bridges. The trail soon became really steep, ferns and moss clung to the banks with the paler camellias blending with the cerise of fuschia hedges. Fantastic shapes of green-covered cones surrounded us, and the volcano Soombing looked threatening with black smoke issuing from its summit. We dismounted at a small village marked "Half-way," took twenty minutes for breakfast, and started off again. Rain fell and the path was very muddy. Our ponies stumbled as the trail became almost vertical over wet rocks. I had the sensation of being lifted into the clouds. There was no sound but the quickened breathing of our guides on foot and of the ponies from the struggle to reach the top of a pass that was no longer visible. Suddenly, as though by magic, the sun was shining brightly on high cones, and the guides were explaining by pantomime how fortunate we were to have it clear on the Dieng Plateau during the rainy season. Soon we began a rapid descent by a long flight of steps, over which master builders had traveled centuries ago, to reach at its foot an easily defended, narrow entrance to the holy city.

It was an extraordinary sensation, on reaching the plateau, to find ourselves in the midst of steam rising gently from rocks, and with sulphur bubbling up from a deadly green morass. Dark gray ruins seemed to reach almost to the top of extinct volcanoes all around us. I wondered, as had many others before me, how this ancient sacred city came to be built up in the clouds, far from the haunts of men—and when did it perish? We dismounted to walk over some of the roads. After a short distance, our feet began to sink deep into the morass. It was quite a struggle to extricate ourselves and reach a ruin in which the larger niches had been despoiled and the decoration had not been completed, but the heads on reliefs that had survived were magnificent, the double lotus of the cornice was exquisite, and the bo trees were of unusual shape. Broad stretches of morass surrounded remnants of temples little more than heaps of stone, but a few remaining fragments were so beautifully carved as to arouse my admiration for the genius that had created this city. At one point we saw in the distance lakes yellow in color from the fumes along their shores. Others were of changing blues and greens, and tall grasses swayed from the bubbling sulphur beneath them.

We took a high trail and crept over slippery stone that gave beneath our tread, but it was worth the effort, since we had reached temples that were definite now in form. They had the appearance of having once been pyramids. Many of the structures had a strange, unaccountable resemblance to the buildings of the Maya in Yucatán.

In Japan, China, and other Asiatic countries, there was nothing I saw that reminded me of the great Maya achievement in building in Yucatán, Honduras, and Guatemala, about which I shall have more to say later. Even in the temples of Angkor Wat and Angkor Thom, situated in the same kind of jungle surroundings, there were no similarities. It was in Egypt, of all countries, that I found striking features in common between the material cultures of the Maya and the Egyptians. It had nothing to do with pyramid construction suggested by the Dieng Plateau. In Egypt, the approach to a temple was through a series of great courts leading to enormous pylon gates. The idea of space in an approach to temples was carried out by the Maya with the same sense of majesty and space, and through similar great courts, but they used, instead of pylons, carved monoliths of incredible size.

ANCIENT MONUMENTS OF THE AMERICAS

52. *The Maya: Quiriguá and Copán*

T HE LATE SYLVANUS GRISWOLD MORLEY wrote an appreciation of
Maya architecture and sculpture for distribution at an exhibition held at the Carnegie Institution of Washington in December, 1941. The exhibition was a collection of my Maya paintings lent by
the various museums which owned them.

Maya civilization in Guatemala and Honduras dates from the beginnings of the Christian Era. Its great period was from A.D. 564–663,
span of the so-called Old Empire. In northern Yucatán, Maya civilization
also had its beginnings as the Christian Era dawned. The Itzá period,
characterized by the Toltec-Maya fusion as a result of Mexican conquest, started about A.D. 900 and had its classic florescence, lasting until
about A.D. 1400 or 1450. It had declined, therefore, prior to the arrival
of the Spaniards.

Morley mentioned great civic and religious centers of cut masonry
built around spacious paved plazas, scattered through the forests of Guatemala and Yucatán. There were lofty pyramids crowned by glistening
white temples, colonnades with impressive courts, causeways, astronomical observatories, ball courts, platforms, and hundreds of other structures.

Door lintels, wall panels, balustrades to stairways, and cornices,
elaborately sculptured, gave these buildings an effect of barbaric splendor unique in ancient America. Today they bear eloquent testimony to

the extent and former magnificence of these Maya cities. As with all other material cultures, the presence of satisfactory materials was of the essence to these developments. Native limestone furnished an easily worked building stone for a people who were without metal tools. Their inventiveness moved them to use lime and a coarse gravel for making mortar.

In sculpture the Maya were equally gifted. Working with chisels of a hard stone such as diorite, they carved great statues or stelae from single slabs ten to twenty-five feet in height and standing free and erect on platforms. Particularly in Quiriguá, Guatemala, and Copán, Honduras, these statues were striking examples of portraiture, revealing distinctive personalities. The figures were elaborately garbed, and tall headdresses with tremendous plumes towered above them. The sides and backs of these stelae were usually covered with hieroglyphic writing, superbly executed, and the entire surface of the stone was rich in color.

To sum up, Morley said, "Their architecture clearly demonstrated a fundamental feeling for the principles of harmony, balance, mass, and design, while a complete mastery of the technique of stone and wood sculpture amply justifies our calling the Maya the Greeks of the new world."

I had made three trips to Greece, had had two working seasons in Egypt, and was recently back from a trip to Turkey. It was the early fall of 1900, and I had planned to remain in Boston until leaving for Japan soon after the first of the year.

I chanced to see in the Fogg Museum of Harvard University, on loan from the Peabody Museum of Boston, a sculptured head in the round of the corn goddess of the Maya. I was greatly excited by its beauty and felt it was unquestionably a portrait and one of the world's great ones. In ancient times, there was no such specialization in artistic creations as exists today, and where a pre-eminently fine piece of sculpture was found, there were certain to be other works of the same period which would be of interest to a young artist like myself, reasonably catholic in his tastes.

I yielded to a sudden impulse and at once looked up a friend of mine

in the United Fruit Company. It was an expedition sent by F. W. Putnam, the head of the Peabody Museum, that had discovered the corn
goddess in Copán about 1890. When I went to see Putnam, he expressed
himself as being delighted with my desire to see an ancient American
civilization that meant so much to him, and he accordingly gave me
many introductions to authorities at the various sites I planned to visit.

Inside of two weeks, one of the company's steamers had landed me
on the coast of Central America, and I was staying in a hacienda in
Antigua available for its guests. Antigua was a delightful city, situated
in a valley of Guatemala, with rivers furnishing water for cultivation
and enough to spare for fountains that were a pleasant feature of the
squares. The mountains near by were superb.

Three volcanoes, Agua, Acatenango, and Fuego, were well behaved
at the time of my visit, but many times through the centuries erup-
tions had wrecked this peaceful, smiling countryside and destroyed the
crops of corn on which its civilization was based.

My immediate objective was Quiriguá, lying between Puerto Barrios
and Guatemala City and dating from the early classical times of Maya
civilization. I refer, of course, to the ancient city, not the modern village.
Having arrived, I was at once introduced to the jungle growth, consisting of imposing cedar and mahogany trees of vast proportions, in which
were to be found the famous stelae of sandstone and the stupendous
altars of the same material. Needless to say, I was impressed—all the
more so because I knew already a good deal about the great monuments
of early man's creation in other parts of the world.

It may be important to point out here a few facts about the development of this material and artistic culture. Vast oceans, as well as great
land distances, separated this and other centers of Maya civilization from
any probable cultural contacts with Asia and Europe. Here, civilization
had reached a climax before the Spaniards arrived. The conquest was
not responsible for the wonders still to be seen in our time.

In Honduras and Guatemala, the art life of early civilizations had
been brief, compared with that of Egypt and China. It flowered from
approximately the second century after Christ to the seventh. Neverthe-

Maya Corn Goddess. Painting by Joseph Lindon Smith. Courtesy Peabody Museum, Harvard University.

Head from a stela sculptured by the Maya at Copán, Honduras. Painting by Joseph Lindon Smith. Courtesy Peabody Museum, Harvard University.

less, this splendid, vigorous Maya art sprang from the same basic roots as those of all the great arts of the known world. It had the same human figures, animals, birds, reptile forms, and geometric shapes. But the "animal-formed" altars of Quiriguá were unique. The stelae were hardly less remarkable.

I stood in front of the largest stela known to Maya civilization, which was reminiscent of the monoliths of Stonehenge in England. But here was to be seen a barbaric splendor in an assertive mass of stone, richly carved, standing defiant in the desolation and companionship of trees and vines on the same spot where once it had formed an integral part of an important ancient city.

The subject matter covered in the carvings on the surface of the stela appeared in bas-relief and evidenced remarkably few changes from the assaults of time. The principal composition, dominated by a single male figure, elaborately costumed and with a tremendous plume-bedecked headdress, remained sharp and impressive after the centuries.

Even in a complicated style of stone carving, where the incised details on the raised surfaces ranged back and forth between high and low relief, there was an extraordinary restraint maintained by the sculptor, who produced a sense of harmony in an achievement of outstanding artistic merit. I welcomed with enthusiasm this opportunity to reproduce on canvas a type of art that, at the time, was the most challenging I had encountered in the reproduction of stone-sculptured surfaces.

I finished painting two of Quiriguá's marvelous stelae, and during the process had learned much about "pure design" and the handling of lights and shadows on canvas, to accentuate artistic values as the Maya saw them.

I made a brief stop in Guatemala City, noted for the natural beauty of its mountain scenery. But my primary reason for going there was to inspect the pyramid at Kaminaljuyú, on the outskirts of the city, to see whether it had features in common with the pyramids of Egypt made by Cheops and his family. I found there was not even a remote similarity between them. The Maya one was flat-topped and rectangular, only about sixty feet in height, and made chiefly of adobe without a facing of stone.

It did suggest, however, the Ziggurat of the Sumerians. I felt repaid for a visit that had at least served to satisfy my curiosity about this form of construction by the Maya.

Putnam's introductions resulted in my having courtesies extended to me in many ways. I particularly appreciated being shown specimens of mosaic work in shell and feathers and ceramics in which the Maya excelled. Weaving and embroidery designs in cloth deserved special study. They were the same as the costumes worn by Mayan religious and civic dignitaries portrayed on ancient bas-reliefs on the temple walls. Some of these same designs might be found in villages of Central America today.

The genius of the Maya as lapidaries of jade has been recognized in collections of many of the world's great museums. I saw much of this remarkable work during my visit.

It was not until 1926 that I had a chance to visit another Maya center of classical times. The invitation came in a telegram signed "Sylvanus," requesting me to join him in Mexico City the week following for a trip to Copán to last about a month and returning with him to Chichén Itzá. The Carnegie Institution of Washington had established headquarters at Chichén Itzá, Yucatán, in 1923, having rented the hacienda owned and previously occupied by E. H. Thompson, the American consul, who had an able amateur's interest in archaeology. Thompson had managed to purchase and get out of the country an important collection of jewelry worn by victims sacrificed in the near-by *cenote,* or well. The Carnegie Institution had put Sylvanus Morley in charge, and from Chichén as a center, archaeological expeditions were to function in Yucatán and Guatemala.

My good friend, Alfred M. Tozzer, had become a significant figure at the Peabody Museum and at Harvard through his famous Maya seminars. In addition to a heavy teaching schedule for an ever increasing number of enthusiastic students, he devoted himself to extensive travel through Maya ruins and to work on important research publications. He persuaded me not to miss this opportunity to be with Morley. At the time, I knew Morley only slightly, but, like everyone else, had instantly succumbed to the charm of a personality that was unique. I sent word at once that the answer was "Yes." To this he replied: "Bring all the insecticide powder Massachusetts will spare!"

I was as eager as Morley to lose no time in being on the way to Copán. Customs was on the Mexican side on entering Guatemala en route for Honduras. I presented my passport to a Mexican, who made no attempt to take it but, staring at me, said, "Who are you?" I told him I was Joseph Lindon Smith, as described in the little green book which I now shoved into his reluctant hand. Then, abruptly, he said, "Have you a mother?" I answered, "Yes, but she is dead." Whereupon he offered his condolences at great length. Meanwhile, he kept dipping a pen into ink and poising it over my papers. "Was your mother black?" he asked.

Morley, sticking his head in at the door, came to my rescue. "What's the trouble?" he inquired. In voluble non-Castilian Spanish, he straightened out the difficulty in no time. When I wanted to know whether his passport had been attended to, he said that he had "left it behind by mistake," but that customs authorities at frontiers in that part of the country never bothered to check his credentials.

Morley enjoyed seeing the country from the back of a mule, which was the method of our final lap to Copán. Everywhere we stopped, crowds gathered around him. From his response to their attention, each one seemed a very special friend.

I took a dim view of the situation when he accepted an invitation for us to spend the night in the home of an *alcalde* who was of mixed blood. There was too much thatched roof and too many other possible lurking places for vermin, and too little floor space for the *alcalde's* large family and livestock, to make our presence seem advisable to me. But Morley was adamant.

The wife made very superior *tortillas*. Morley was in grand form and chatted gaily in a strange jargon that apparently was understood by everyone except me. He consumed a vast number of *tortillas* before we settled ourselves to sleep on mattresses that obviously had been slept on by many others before us. I kept up a steady scratching of my legs and arms, but the torture only increased as new species of vermin joined the onslaught upon me.

When scorpions began to drop from above, just missing us, even Morley felt that the limits of courtesy had been passed. We crawled outside into the open, where the path to a stream was outlined in the moonlight. At the water's edge we shed our inhabited pajamas and jumped in. When we had given the insects on our bodies time to sink or swim away from us, we climbed out on to the bank and enveloped ourselves from head to foot in clouds of yellow powder.

We put on clean garments from our travel kits and, abandoning the pajamas and finding a spot at a satisfactory distance from thatched homes, we slept soundly until awakened by the morning sun shining in our faces.

Morley was a stimulating companion. I admired him for his vast fund of scholarly knowledge about everything concerned with the Maya and their ways. Even more for his method of imparting it casually and without apparent continuity until, unexpectedly, I found that every word he uttered fitted into a whole, forming a pattern as clear-cut as a cameo and told with an inimitable humor and vividness that made valuable information "stick."

Each day was much the same, yet different, before the climax of Copán was reached. In the heat of midday, our muleteers rolled their trousers far above their knees, and their shirts came off. We paused at moments to cool off under the shade of a spacious tree, frequently a mahogany with roots sprawling as though alive over an adjacent rock. Broad-brimmed straw hats protected our heads from the direct rays of the sun. A splash of color was quickly identified as a parrot, a white egret, or the exotic bloom of some jungle plant.

Occasionally our trail led past open spaces, planted with Indian corn, still today, as in ancient times, the mainstay of the people. In several places we came upon the ruins of a church, or a church starting to fall.

In a mood of eager anticipation of what lay ahead, we rode over the boundary line between Guatemala and Honduras. The village of Copán was not impressive. To reach it, we crossed a river and faced, in our immediate foreground, quite a bit of an ancient wall, where supposedly the cacique of Copán had put up a stiff fight before being overwhelmed by the Spaniards.

Morley devoted the better part of a day to giving me a general idea of the extent of the ruins and an explanation of them. Then we were to settle down to the purposes that had brought us to Copán—his, an examination of some of the ruins, and mine, to paint stelae that I expected to find (and did) even better subjects, artistically, than those in Quiriguá.

At one charming spot, the plaza overlooked the river; at another, a gigantic wild cotton tree, known generally as the Ceiba, was growing with its wide branches stretching dramatically over the ruins of a temple and an adjacent altar. We stumbled over enveloping roots and came upon columns with complicated sculptured designs, and a colossal head, which obviously could only have been a portrait, judging from the individual characteristics of the face.

For portraiture Copán was remarkable. Personalities emerged from the stone surfaces of the great stelae and from among the seated figures on friezes. As for architectural achievement, I would match the enormously high flight of stone steps known as the "hieroglyphic stairway," from being covered with beautifully carved inscriptions, against any stone stairway I have ever seen.

To me, Morley's interpretations, like a verbal Rosetta stone, made this city of Copán live again in its original grandeur. He summarized what it must have looked like as a flourishing cultural center, where splendid architecture and sculpture rejoiced the eye of the beholder, and ambition and glory had their moment in space.

Later my few leisure hours from painting, were devoted to a careful scrutiny of door lintels, wall panels, and other structural details. I found it hard to believe that stone chisels had accomplished such a complete mastery of the technique of stone sculpture.

And Maya architecture included religious "complexes" (as Reisner used to term their counterparts in ancient Egypt), comprising, as a unit, a pyramid, a plaza with stelae, and temples and altars carved ornately.

The designs represented symbolism used in the ceremonials of a highly organized religion of many gods with specialized attributes, around which developed an elaborate mythology, all in the hands of the priesthood.

I heartily concurred in Morley's conclusion that the Maya were the "Greeks of the New World."

Our ultimate departure from Copán was a harrowing experience, because Morley had been stricken with one of the periodic attacks of fever which knocked him completely out. He refused to have natives carry him on a stretcher, so his limp body was swung under the belly of the gentlest non-kicking mule that the village could provide.

I rode behind, rather than in front, to do something (I never knew quite what) if catastrophe threatened; and a muleteer with a watchful eye tramped along on either side of Morley's mule. Morley never lost his courage and joked incessantly as the strange-looking procession moved along at a snail's pace.

After many adventures on the trail phase of the trip, the remainder of the return to Chichén was easily accomplished.

53. *With the Carnegie Staff at Chichén Itzá*

To COME to Chichén Itzá after Quiriguá and Copán was not the anticlimax I had feared. In my several journeys through Mexico, I had known the jaguar, the eagle, and the vulture as decorative motifs, but they seemed to have acquired an added charm in Yucatán. As for the feathered serpent god, proud Quetzalcoatl, he looked magnificent as an adornment to balustrades and cornices.

The monuments in Chichén, such as the Temple of the Jaguars, the Temple of the Warriors, the Jaguar and Eagle Mausoleum, and the Great Ball Court, were effective architecturally. The buildings in old Chichén were most attractive in themselves and instructive in giving a realistic conception of the outward appearance of palaces and civic centers.

But my trip to Chichén in 1926 was only the first of many. I made a number of short visits there as a guest of the Carnegie staff in subsequent years, and painted innumerable and varied details on the monuments. The more familiar I became with Maya sculptured reliefs, the more I appreciated them artistically. But just as in Egypt no later sculpture ever equaled the great portraits and other masterpieces of the Old Kingdom, the Maya stone sculpture of this great classical area had remained without a rival on our American continent.

These ruins at Chichén compared very favorably with those in the part of the Valley of Mexico where I had once stayed with George Vaillant after he had joined the staff of the American Museum of Natural History (1928). I first knew him when he was with Reisner's expedition in the Sudan in 1924, and we were all sorry to have him desert Egypt for the American field. Vaillant used to say that it was being with Reisner and having the opportunity to come in contact with Petrie's brilliant work on classifying pottery that developed his first interest in the chronological significance of Maya ceramics, in which Vaillant was to become an authority.

I also was familiar with the results of Herbert J. Spinden's extensive wanderings in search of ruined cities in Central America, and had seen his exhibits on the Aztecs as well as on the Maya.

During the 1940 working season, Corinna and I occupied one of the houses that the Carnegie provided within its concession at Chichén for married couples on its large staff. At the Boston Museum expedition in Egypt, I had lived for many years with Cheops' great pyramid in the "front yard," figuratively speaking. El Castillo, the important pyramid dominating the ruins at Chichén, was even closer.

A climb to the summit of Cheops' pyramid was a major operation. One had to be hauled upwards over huge blocks of a great width, uncertain of one's footing, a native on either side and a third pushing from behind. The descent was even more difficult, requiring the same natives to keep one from plunging forward to land face downward on a rock.

This situation I contrasted with what the pyramid at Chichén offered me. Its "step-sided" construction gave easy access to the square temple on its top, by a gradual rise up a long flight of steps that I could take at a run for daily exercise.

311

Mexican archaeologists had been making some repairs to El Castillo pyramid when, unexpectedly, they came upon a sealed-up, narrow inner flight of stairs leading from the ground level to a small chamber about four feet square near the top of the pyramid. There, in the darkness, stood a bright red jaguar entirely alone on a pedestal, his body and legs dotted by bits of jade to represent the animal's spots.

Morley got permission from the Mexican authorities for me to paint an oil study of the jaguar. This was given on condition that an inspector was inside the chamber with me while I painted, and that both of us were locked in. Artificial light was necessary and the ventilation very bad. The inspector and I mounted the steps together, accompanied by a higher official. Before leaving us, he solemnly counted the jade pieces. There were seventy-two in all, of an apple-green color. After this ritual, he left the inspector and me, and I heard the heavy metal key making quite a noise as he turned it in the lock.

The official's returning footsteps at noon made a pleasant sound. Immediately on re-entering the chamber, he counted the jade, making quite a ceremony out of the performance. This occurred three mornings in succession. Fortunately, at the third and final counting, when my picture was finished, the jade tally was still seventy-two.

The Temple of the Warriors was a wonderful studio, and on its long walls and doorways I was surrounded by splendid details to paint, of easy access, thanks to the excavations and restorations done by Earl and Ann Morris for the Carnegie Institution.

Fred Walcott, the chairman of the Finance Committee, spent a number of weeks with us. His companionship was stimulating and he had an amazing knowledge of the Maya. He was an enthusiastic amateur painter, with a good color sense for landscape and a feeling for form excellent for architectural details. I felt flattered when he became my pupil. We were an odd contrast as we sat together hour after hour, I engaged in covering the enormous expanse of canvas it took to render the stupendous subjects of my choice, and he doing rather small pictures.

His painting equipment was the result of high-powered salesmanship in New York. It consisted of an armchair, which occupied a good deal of space when opened out, and an easel, which was heavy to move because of the number of gadgets required for opening drawers containing an assortment of paints and brushes. The uncertainties of a tropical climate made it necessary to summon the expedition carpenter frequently when the machinery refused to function. After a few days, Fred adjusted himself to my simple methods, sat on a jagged rock and produced the desired paints and brushes from his pockets.

A member of the staff whom Corinna and I particularly appreciated was George W. Brainerd. His specialty was Maya pottery; he was young and had come from Colorado at Kidder's suggestion. Brainerd installed himself in a rambling, disused old chapel on the grounds, in bad repair and with very little light, and went to work to restore order out of chaos, in classifying literally some hundreds of boxes containing dust-covered shards from everybody's expeditions over the years, the labels for which were often misplaced or lacking.

We usually dropped in to spend half an hour with him at the end of my painting day. He always had something of value to explain in the way of a progress report, and I early formed a conviction that his systematic work would eventually prove of great scholarly importance in determining Maya dates. Therefore, I was delighted at the decision of the Carnegie at the instigation of Kidder to have Brainerd continue his research the following season. The Chichén expedition was to be closed, but we Smiths were to be with the Morleys in a hacienda in the vicinity of Mérida. Brainerd, living near by, was to use a part of Morley's workshop and possibly have a small dig. Meantime, he was to marry Katharine Babcock.

Ted and Madeleine Kidder turned up from one of their jaunts to Guatemala, and Kidder's presence, even for a short time, meant much to Morley, who was facing the end of a working era in surroundings that, under his leadership, had added greatly to the prestige of the Carnegie Institution as a great archaeological center. An early friendship between Kidder and Morley had been strengthened by a closer contact when, in 1929, the Division on Historical Research of the Carnegie Institution was reorganized by Kidder to include other angles of approach to the problems of Maya research than those for which Morley's genius had been responsible.

All of us who were there that winter admired Morley's wife, Frances, who not only safeguarded his precarious health, which he himself ignored, but kept him in good spirits and shared in his work. She was a real helpmate.

The cottage given us originally was on the edge of old Chichén. From it by a short stroll at sunset, past an elaborate ancient doorway, we could reach the broad terrace on which was built the Caracol, visible from our stone veranda. This circular observatory of the Maya was a dramatic landmark. Several times at full moon, we scrambled to the top for a picnic. The surrounding bush had special features, and as I watched nature's display, I paid tribute to Karl Ruppert and Harry E. D. Pollack for their construction job in repairing the Caracol and the wide terrace below. On several trips with Morley in Yucatán, I had seen some of Harry's other work as an architect, and I liked his restraint in what he left untouched in a ruin, a characteristic I have too often found lacking in those entrusted with the preservation and restoration of ancient buildings.

The Italian Giacomo Boni (later in charge of the Roman Forum) was a rare exception. I used to be with him for weeks at a time in Italy, during the early period when, as the favorite pupil of Ruskin, he was in charge of Italian monuments. His reverence for age-worn surfaces of stone or wood was only equaled by his ingenuity in strengthening or rebuilding surroundings of which they were a part, with no visible sign of modern workmanship.

Although tropical medicine was entirely out of my line, Dr. George C. Shattuck could make the habits and habitat of the malarial mosquitoes he had known personally so exciting as to distract my attention from archaeology and art. His adventures were shared by his brilliant wife, Virginia, on trips in small boats up remote rivers or along coasts seldom visited, and into the bush in search of scientific information, which, incidentally, they always secured! The matter-of-fact way in which both described (on request) hair-raising episodes enlivened the leisure hours of the staff. And how they were missed on their departure for Boston!

It was during this stay at Chichén that I became intensely interested in certain details of Maya art. In murals and on sculptured walls of the monuments the clothing worn by Maya dignitaries was very spectacular and used by the craftsmen as a part of the decorative design. Never in any other part of the world have such magnificent garments been reproduced in stone, and originally they were painted. Tremendous headdresses with sweeping curves represented brilliant feathers of tropical birds. Great earplugs, breastplates, and necklaces were effectively suggested, and ornaments were attached to legs and arms and around the waist.

The priests were the most magnificently garbed of them all in costumes of intricate embroideries and weaving. Dressed as they were, to represent gods, they must have evoked awe among the people.

Large parasols and litters were in evidence in a general design where rulers were seated cross-legged on thrones covered with jaguar skins. Monuments at Chichén Itzá, for the most part, commemorated calendar events rather than political ones. But there was a battle scene in an inner chamber of the Temple of the Jaguar in Chichén Itzá.

Victims in sacrifice scenes could be identified by the absence of headgear, the simplicity of the loin cloth, and their braided hair. Certain bas-reliefs, murals, and also the designs on gold disks from the Sacred Cenote at Chichén Itzá showed warfare in which the Maya were losing out.

One mural dealt with human sacrifices, showing the heart being removed through the abdomen in a manner characteristic of the Aztecs.

Jaguars and vultures were very similar in the bas-reliefs at Tula and at Chichén Itzá, as were very stylized figures at the two sites which seemed to represent the Mexican rain god.

Morley emphasized the intellectual attainments of the Maya as being of a high order. He claimed that in astronomy their knowledge surpassed that of the ancient Egyptians prior to the Ptolemaic period. He felt that they had produced the only graphic system of hieroglyphic writing known in the Americas and that their chronology was as accurate as that made possible by our own Gregorian calendar.

The Egyptians had irrigation systems in the Nile Delta as early as the Middle Kingdom. I was surprised that the Maya had developed no proficiency in irrigation or fertilization in the areas where both must have been needed. Thus the many *cenotes* in Yucatán had doubtless attracted people to settle there, abandoning their own "thirsty lands" elsewhere.

The Maya gods had attributes based upon a simple agricultural pantheon of earth, rain, and sky, a good deal the same as in the early religion of Mesopotamia and Egypt. The Maya religion, however, contained the element of human sacrifice to propitiate the gods, so that they would provide the yield of corn on which the Mayas' very existence depended.

I found it interesting to study the changes in architecture that were introduced into Yucatán during the Mexican period. The walls of temples, palaces, and other buildings sloped to the ground at an angle, whereas the Maya built them in a straight line to the ground. Another difference was that columns were round instead of square, as in Maya construction, and designs in general were more elaborate and ornate, and rosettes were introduced.

I enjoyed greatly a brief trip to Tulum, on the east coast of Yucatán. Here I saw the best-preserved monument of the late post-classical Maya ruins. Tulum was a walled Maya site and had a splendid *castillo,* with two temples exactly alike separated by a broad flight of steps.

54. *The Persistent Past in Yucatán*

IN QUINTANA ROO, far to the south in a region of trackless "bush," there live today a group of seven hundred primitive Indians in a series of nine villages of a settlement known as Tixcacal. Although no priest had ever been among them, they worshiped *"Cristo"* and *"La Madre Sancta"* in a church they had built by themselves without outside advice. In it they celebrated Mass on the Catholic Saint days.

Morley told me that these were among the last Indians he knew of living as an isolated ethnological group scarcely advanced socially since the Spanish Conquest in 1540. Their government consisted of a cacique, "head man," whose authority was absolute except over the Indian chosen as "priest." This office of priest was held for a period of six weeks by each male in turn. These Indians continued to refuse to learn Spanish or to permit the hated Mexicans to teach their children in school. Their language remained Maya.

A delegation of them had turned up some years back at Chichén to ask Morley's intercession with the Mexican authorities in their behalf.

We were all seated at tea one afternoon in late January in the corridor of the hacienda when a large group of these primitive Indians appeared, looking like a flock of tropical birds as they approached from the entrance gate. They mounted the steps to the corridor and with old-time courtesy took off their hats and made low bows as they shook hands first with Morley and with each one of us in turn, and then perched immobile and silent on top of the stone railing facing us. They might have stepped from a Spanish engraving of the sixteenth century, with extremely tall straw hats perched on top of coarse black hair; all had distinctive features, some with Oriental cast.

They wore cotton drawers cut according to a style at the time of the Conquest: short, reaching only half down the leg, at both sides triangular openings disclosing dark skin, and fastened at the back with gathered frills. High-waisted blouses were also frilled across the front and back. Two blouses were a brilliant pink, others orange, and several were vivid blue. Each Indian had slung across his shoulders a small knapsack made of cotton embroidered in bright-colored flower designs, with roses predominating.

The head cacique, Concepción Cituk, was an amazing personality with ageless wisdom in his slant eyes that never left Morley's face. In a quiet, yet ringing voice he engaged in a long, earnest conversation with Morley through Exedra, one of the expedition's houseboys, who served

317

as interpreter. The rest of the group kept their eyes also on Morley with a pathetic expression of confidence in his power to right their wrongs. It was a solemn occasion as Concepción related abuses in their dealings with Mexican *politicos* and contractors who cheated them in the trading of their chicle and in the collection of taxes—both abuses, which they were helpless to combat, steadily on the increase.

Morley offered to assist in drafting a letter to be sent directly to the President of the Republic of Mexico, and assured Concepción that he could arrange to have the letter reach the President himself through friends in Mexico City. A slow smile spread over the impassive features of the old cacique, tension relaxed, and Juan Bautista, the young cacique, played a melancholy but stirring refrain on an Indian drum that he found in the dining room.

Morley, practical and efficient as ever, had disappeared to make arrangements for the feeding of these guests, which took some doing since after counting them and making a rapid calculation on his fingers, he declared, "They will eat 1,400 *tortillas* a day." He dispatched a truck to Pisté for sacks of corn, already ground, and also arranged for sleeping quarters in the loft above the garage. Later, I went to visit the homes of our Maya servants and found all the women busily engaged in making *tortillas*. Their agile fingers flew back and forth in this complicated art of preparing and baking *tortillas,* each hand occupied with a different process at the same time. We Smiths, as guests, were offered some of these small cakes as they came hot from the coals.

I had an amusing experience when, accompanied by Exedra and me, the entire group entered the great Ball Court to listen to the echo. Exedra explained what an echo was, and how to get the response from the distant end wall. One of the Indians, timid in the presence of his cacique, spoke in a low voice and a small echo responded. A lesser cacique tried in a somewhat louder voice and a louder echo came back. Then Concepción Cituk roared a few words and a tremendous volume of sound thundered back. He was delighted. "Even our ancestors know who is chief today in Tixcacal," he remarked chuckling.

The next day these Indian visitors spent much time scrambling over the many ruins of Chichén and later I showed them my paintings. They stood over them as they lay spread out on the floor of the long porch of our house, gazed intently but in silence, and suddenly vanished. I asked Exedra why they had gone. "They will be back," he said. In about ten minutes they reappeared, out of breath as though from running. Again they gazed intently, then began to pat me approvingly, with wide grins and admiring glances, talking rapidly.

"What do they say?" I said, appealing to Exedra. "They are much pleased; they have repeated many times, 'He worker in magic—he went to ruins and brought eagles, serpents, jaguars and placed them on this floor. So we ran fast back to ruins, but his magic very big, he'd put every animal where we saw them before, and now we come back, and again his magic faster than our feet.' "

After this, they stared for some time with puckered brows at a part of a canvas where the yellow underpainting covered what should be sky. "What are they thinking now?" I asked. "What they say," Exedra explained, "is that yellow is evil and better put blue for sky." When Exedra interpreted for me that the blue would come later, they grunted their satisfaction.

During their visit I painted a portrait of Juan Bautista, who sat immovable for it, and at the end all looked at the picture, laughing loudly. "That means they think paper look just like Juan Bautista," Exedra stated.

A week later we watched these Indians trudge away again to a future that must inevitably be more and more difficult, but for the moment they looked absolutely contented, and why not? Provisions in quantity were loaded on the back of a horse, and the last I saw of Concepción Cituk he was swinging the long end of a belt of finger-weave done in various shades of bright red, the work of an Oklahoma Indian, and with which Morley had many times declared he would never part.

The story of the Xiu dynasty of Uxmal that started in A.D. 960 and had an "heir apparent" in the year of grace 1940 (whom incidentally I came to know) was another striking example of the persistency of the past in Yucatán.

Morley, in searching for facts concerning the dynasty that had founded one of the greatest Maya centers of the New Empire, had been impressed by the continuity of the family through direct male descendants. For instance, in Spanish chronicles he found the following statement: "Seventeen days after the city of Mérida had been founded [January, 1542] the Xiu, 'King of all Yucatán,' appeared in the capital bearing gifts of corn, fruits, chicken, and woven cloth. He was baptized into the Catholic church under the name of Melchior and was appointed a *hidalgo.*"

After a comprehensive examination of genealogical records since Spanish colonial days, a male descendant of this Melchior, and therefore the present heir of the Tutul Xiu of Uxmal, was discovered. He was a Maya peasant, Nemesio, who lived in Tulum, Yucatán, and he had a son named Dionisio.

Morley sent for them, and after the first meeting his interest in Nemesio, but more particularly in the son, Dionisio, had continued. When he and I decided to go to Uxmal for a week's camping trip, I suggested that the "heir" and "heir apparent" to a kingdom no longer theirs should be invited to join us.

They were a delightful addition. Both of them could have posed for their counterparts in stone all over the place. It was an amusing experience to stand with Nemesio and Dionisio within the ruins of the Governor's Palace at Uxmal, considered by modern architects one of the most splendid buildings ever erected by the Maya or anyone else.

No palace for these representatives of the former great Xiu dynasty—only a palm-thatched home in an isolated village. Instead of the stiff-bosom front of a ceremonial garb, the rolled-up short sleeves worn by their peasant neighbors, with whom they cleared, planted, and reaped their *milpas* (cornfields).

We sat among the ruins of the glory of their ancestors, and Dionisio told Morley his troubles and sought his advice. He was in love with a girl of fourteen, but her grandmother, as head of the family, refused to consent to their marriage. She had referred to Dionisio and his suit with insulting epithets and had beaten the girl. Morley found it difficult

Passage between the Nunnery Annex, left, and the Iglesia, right, Chichén Itzá.
Painting by Joseph Lindon Smith. Courtesy Carnegie Institution of Washington.

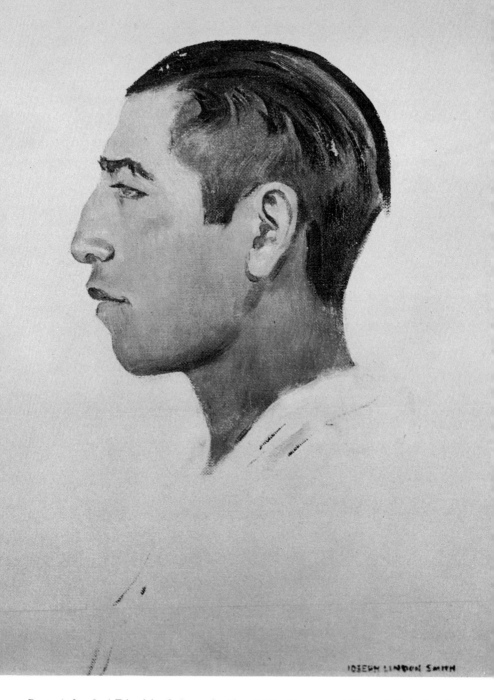

Portrait head of Dionisio, heir to the Tutul Xiu Dynasty of Uxmal. Painting by Joseph Lindon Smith. Courtesy of the Carnegie Institution of Washington.

to restrain his indignation at an old peasant woman's considering the heir apparent to the Xiu of Uxmal dynastic fame not good enough for a girl whose family name was "Pech," Maya for *garrapata,* the most common insect pest in Central America.

He wrote a suave, tactful letter to the old lady, stating that he had personally known Nemesio and Dionisio Xiu for many years and greatly esteemed them; he reviewed their distinguished ancestry and added that he and his wife intended to stand as godparents for Dionisio at his wedding, and be begged to remain "your obedient and attentive servant."

Dionisio came to Chichén to await the reply to this letter. He became devoted to me, and I made an oil sketch of him which might have been a portrait of the original Tutul Xiu of Uxmal. Nemesio, the father, turned up. There was strong character in his deeply lined face and he was even more Maya in type than his son. I sketched him also, which made me painter-in-chief to the Maya royal family, without a kingdom at the moment.

The answer to the letter came. The Pech grandmother was equally suave and polite. She withdrew her opposition to the marriage at Dr. Morley's request and would accept Dionisio as the official fiancé of her granddaughter, but declared that the marriage could not take place for another ten years. This was stalemate! Fred Walcott offered to delay his departure to make a personal appeal to the obdurate old lady. Morley dissuaded him. Dionisio said the girl was willing to run away with him, but that a Xiu must marry with the formal consent of all contracting parties.

A month passed. Then Don Pedro arrived one day as an emissary from Nemesio with a formal request for Morley's consent to Dionisio's marriage to a different girl, from Tulum, from which place, incidentally, brides of the Tutul Xiu came during the great dynastic days. Don Pedro produced a photograph. The girl was very pretty. He pled the cause well, stating that she was serious minded and an excellent *tortilla* maker—the latter a necessary qualification in a country where the woman's lot is to bake *tortillas* twice daily and nurse her babies.

Morley gave his consent. Later Dionisio came to Chichén, bringing a letter from his father requesting that the contemplated marriage be performed in the church of Tulum, with the bans published April 3 and the ceremony April 22. The girl insisted on a modest wedding reception, "since we will be poor."

Corinna and I felt honored at being allowed to give the gilded silver chain, worn by a bride on her wedding day for the first time and then during the remainder of her life. Thus, the ancient Maya lived still in the young people of Maya descent, carrying forward quietly the customs of other times, the slow but persistent stream of human destiny.

BIBLIOGRAPHY

I. EGYPT

Baedeker. *Egypt and the Sudan.* Ed. by Georg Steindorff. 8th Edition. Leipzig, 1929.

Bevan, Edwin. *A History of Egypt: The Ptolemaic Dynasty.* London, Methuen & Co., Ltd., 1914.

Breasted, James H. *A History of Egypt.* New York, C. Scribner's Sons, 1905.

—— (ed. and trans.). *Ancient Records of Egypt.* 5 vols. Chicago, University of Chicago Press, 1906–1907.

——. *Development of Religion and Thought in Ancient Egypt.* New York, C. Scribner's Sons, 1912.

——. *Ancient Times.* New York, Ginn & Co., 1916.

——. *The Edwin Smith Surgical Papyrus.* Chicago, University of Chicago Press, 1930.

——. *The Dawn of Conscience.* New York, C. Scribner's Sons, 1933.

Brunton, W. M. *Kings and Queens of Ancient Egypt.* London, Hodder & Son, 1925.

——, and others. *Great Ones of Ancient Egypt.* London, Hodder & Son, 1929.

Budge, E. A. W. *The Book of the Dead: The Chapters of Coming Forth by Day.* 3 vols. London, 1898.

——. *The Mummy: A Handbook of Funerary Archaeology.* 2nd Edition. Cambridge, Eng., The University Press, 1925.

Carnarvon, The Earl of, and Carter, Howard. *Five Years Exploration at Thebes, 1907–1911.* London and New York, H. Frowde, 1912.

Carter, Howard. *Tomb of Tut-ankh-Amen.* 3 vols. London, Cassell, 1930.

——, and Mace, A. C. *The Tomb of Tut-ankh-Amen.* Vols. II and III. London, Cassell, 1930.

323

Černey, J. *Ancient Egyptian Religion*. London, Hutchinson, 1952.

Chapman, Suzanne E. *Early American Design Motifs*. New York, Dover Publications, 1952.

——, and Dunham, Dows. *The Royal Cemeteries of Kush, III, Decorated Chapels of The Meroitic Pyramids at Meroe and Barkal*. Boston, 1952.

Davies, Nina M., and Gardiner, A. H. *Ancient Egyptian Paintings*. 3 vols. Chicago, University of Chicago Press, 1936.

Davies, Norman de Garis. *Five Theban Tombs*. London, Egypt Exploration Fund, 1915.

Davis, Theodore M. *Tomb of Iouiya and Touiyou*. London, A. Constable & Co., Ltd., 1907.

——. *Tomb of Siphtah*. London, A. Constable & Co., Ltd., 1908.

——. *Tomb of Queen Tiyi*. London, A. Constable & Co., Ltd., 1910.

Dawson, Warren R. *Who Was Who in Egyptology*. London, Egypt Exploration Society, 1951.

Drioton, E. *La Religion des Egyptiens*. Paris, Service des antiquités, 1937.

——, and Vandier, J. *Les Peuples de'l'orient Mediterranéan: l'Égypte*. 3rd Edition. Paris, 1952.

Duell, Prentice. *The Mastaba of Mereruka*. 2 vols. Chicago, University of Chicago Press, 1938. Oriental Institute Publications XXXI, XXXIX.

Dunham, Dows. *Naga-ed-Dêr Stelae of the First Intermediate Period*. London, Published for the Museum of Fine Arts, Boston, by the Oxford University Press, H. Milford, 1937.

——. *The Royal Cemeteries of Kush, I, El Kurru*. Cambridge, Published for the Museum of Fine Arts by Harvard University Press, 1950.

——. *The Royal Cemeteries of Kush, II, Nuri*. Boston, 1955.

Edwards, I. E. S. *The Pyramids of Egypt*. New York, Penguin Books, 1947.

Emery, Walter B. *Excavations at Saqqara: The Tomb of Hemaka*. Cairo, Government Press, 1938.

——. *The Royal Tombs of Ballana and Qustul*. Cairo, Government Press, 1938.

——. *Excavations at Saqqara: 1937-1938, Hor Aha*. Cairo, Government Press, 1939.

——. *Nubian Treasure: An Account of the Discoveries at Ballana and Qustul*. London, Methuen, 1948.

——. *Excavations at Saqqara: Great Tombs of the First Dynasty*. I. Cairo, 1949.

——. *Excavations at Saqqara: Great Tombs of the First Dynasty*. II. Oxford, Egypt Exploration Society, 1954.

————, and Kirwan, L. P. *The Excavations and Survey Between Wadi es-Sebua and Adindan, 1929–1931.* Cairo, Government Press, 1935.

Engelbach, Reginald. *Introduction to Egyptian Archaeology.* Cairo, Service des antiquités, 1946.

Erman, Adolf. *The Literature of the Ancient Egyptians . . . from the Third and Second Millennia,* B.C. Trans. by Aylward M. Blackman. London, Methuen & Co., Ltd., 1927.

Firth, Cecil M. *The Nubian Archaeological Survey.* Service des antiquités Publication, *Reports, 1909–10 and 1910–11.* Cairo, 1910–11.

Firth, Cecil M., and Quibell, J. E. *The Step-Pyramid: Excavations at Saqqara.* 2 vols. Cairo, Service des antiquités, 1935.

———— and Gunn, B. *Teti Pyramid Cemeteries.* 2 vols. Cairo, Service des antiquités, 1926.

Frankfort, Henri. *Cenotaph of Seti I at Abydos.* 2 vols. London, The Egypt Exploration Fund, 1933. 39th Memoir of the Egypt Exploration Society.

————. *Ancient Egyptian Religion.* New York, Columbia University Press, 1948.

————; Frankfort, H. A.; Wilson, John A.; Jacobsen, T; and Irwin, W. A. *The Intellectual Adventure of Ancient Man.* Chicago, University of Chicago Press, 1946. Republished (without chapters by Irwin) as *Before Philosophy* (New York, Penguin Books, 1949).

Gardiner, A. H. *The Attitude of the Ancient Egyptians to Death and the Dead.* Cambridge, Eng., The University Press, 1935.

———— (ed.). *The Temple of King Sethos I at Abydos.* Vols. I–III. Copied by Amice M. Calverley and Myrtle M. Broome. Chicago, University of Chicago Press, 1933–35.

Garstang, John. *The Burial Customs of Ancient Egypt.* London, A. Constable & Co., Ltd., 1907.

Glanville, S. R. K. *Daily Life in Ancient Egypt.* Routledge Introduction to Modern Knowledge, No. 16. London, G. Routledge & Sons, 1930.

Griffith, F. L. *A Collection of Hieroglyphs.* London, Egypt Exploration Fund, 1896. 5th Memoir (Part III) of Archaeological Survey of Egypt, ed. by F. L. Griffith.

Hayes, William C. *The Scepter of Egypt, Part I: From the Earliest Times to the End of the Middle Kingdom.* New York, Metropolitan Museum of Art, 1953.

Hölscher, Uvo. *The Excavations of Medinet Habu.* 5 vols. Chicago, University of Chicago Press, 1934–54. Oriental Institute Publications.

Lacau, Pierre. *Sarcophages anteriéurs au nouvel empire. Catalogue général des antiquités Égyptiennes du Musée du Cairo,* Nos. 28001–28126. 2 vols. Cairo, 1904–06.

———. *Stèles du nouvel Empire. Catalogue général des antiquités Égyptiennes du Musée du Cairo,* Nos. 34001–34186. Cairo, 1909.

Lauer, J. P. *La pyramide à degrés: l'Architecture. Fouilles à Saqqarah.* 3 vols. Cairo, Service des antiquités d' Égypte, 1936–39.

Legrain, Georges. *Statues et Statuettes de Rois et de particuliers.* 3 vols. Cairo, Service des antiquités, 1906–14.

Lucas, A. *Ancient Egyptian Materials and Industries.* 3rd Edition, Revised. London, E. Arnold & Co., 1948.

Mace, A. C., and Winlock, Herbert E. *The Tomb of Senebtisi at Lisht. Publications* of the Metropolitan Museum of Art, Egyptian Expedition. Vol. I. New York, 1916.

Mariette, A. *Catalogue général des monuments d'Abydos découverts pendant les fouilles de cette ville.* Paris, L'imprimerie nationale, 1880.

———. *Les Mastabas de l'ancien empire.* Paris, F. Vieweg, 1889.

Maspero, G. *Études de mythologie et d'archéologie Égyptienne.* 7 vols. Paris, Bibliothèque égyptologique d'études, 1893–1913.

Naville, Édouard. *Das aegyptische Todtendenbuch der XVIII. bis XX. Dynastie.* 3 vols. Berlin, Asher & Co., 1886.

Nelson, Harold H. *Medinet Habu.* Vols. I–V. Chicago, University of Chicago Press, 1930–56. Oriental Institute Publications.

———, and Hölscher, Uvo. *Work in Western Thebes, 1931–33.* Chicago, University of Chicago Press, 1934. Oriental Institute Publications.

Newberry, P. E. *Egyptian Antiquities, Scarabs: An Introduction to the Study of Egyptian Seals and Signet Rings.* London, Institute of Archaeology of the University of Liverpool, 1889.

Parker, Richard A. *The Calendars of Ancient Egypt.* Chicago, The University of Chicago Press, 1950. Oriental Institute Studies in Ancient Oriental Civilization, No. 26.

Petrie, W. M. F. *Historical Scarabs: A Series of Drawings from the Principal Collections Arranged Chronologically.* London, D. Nutt, 1889.

———. *The Royal Tombs of the First Dynasty.* Part 2. London, 1901. 21st Memoir of Egypt Exploration Fund.

———. *The Arts and Crafts of Ancient Egypt.* 2nd Edition. London and Edinburgh, T. N. Foulis, 1910.

———. *A History of Egypt from the Earliest Kings to the XVIth Dynasty.* 11th Edition. London, Methuen & Co., Ltd., 1924.

————. *Objects of Daily Use*. London, British School of Archaeology in Egypt, 1927.

————. *Egyptian Architecture*. London, British School of Archaeology in Egypt, 1938.

————. *Seventy Years in Archaeology*. London, S. Low, Marston & Co., Ltd., 1931.

Pratt, I. A. *Ancient Egypt: Sources of Information in the New York Public Library*. New York, The Library, 1925.

————. *Supplement: Ancient Egypt, 1925–1941*. New York, The Library, 1942.

Pritchard, J. B. (ed.). *Ancient Near Eastern Texts Relating to the New Testament*. Princeton, Princeton University Press, 1950.

Quibell, J. E. *Excavations at Saqqara, 1906–1907*. Cairo, Service des antiquités, 1907–1908.

————. *Archaic Mastabas: Excavations at Saqqara, 1912–1914*. Cairo, Service des antiquités, 1923.

————, and others. *Excavations at Saqqara, 1907–1938*. Cairo, Service des antiquités, 1927– .

Randall-MacIver, D., and Woolley, C. L. *Eckley B. Coxe, Jr., Expedition to Nubia*. Vols. VII, VIII. 2 vols. Philadelphia, University of Pennsylvania, Egyptian Department of the University Museum, 1911.

Reisner, G. A. *The Hearst Medical Payprus*. Leipzig, University of California: Egyptian Archaeology, 1905.

————. *The Archaeological Survey of Nubia: Report for 1907–1908* (2 vols.), *Report for 1908–1909* (1 vol.). Cairo, National Printing Dept.

————. *Excavations at Kerma*. Cambridge, Mass., Peabody Museum of Harvard University, 1923. Harvard African Studies, Vols. V, VI.

————. *Mycerinus: The Temples of the Third Pyramid at Giza*. Cambridge, Mass., Harvard University Press, 1931.

————. *The Development of the Egyptian Tomb down to the Accession of Cheops*. Cambridge, Harvard University Press; London, Oxford University Press, H. Milford, 1936.

————. *A History of the Giza Necropolis, I*. Cambridge, Harvard University Press; London, Oxford University Press, H. Milford, 1942.

————, and Smith, William Stevenson. *A History of the Giza Necropolis: II, The Tomb of Hetep-heres, the Mother of Cheops*. Cambridge, Harvard University Press, 1955.

————, and Mace, A. C. *The Early Dynastic Cemeteries at Naga-el-Dêr*. 2 vols. Leipzig, J. C. Hinrichs, 1908–1909.

Riefstahl, Elizabeth. *Toilet Articles from Ancient Egypt*. Brooklyn, The Brooklyn Museum, 1943.

——. *Glass and Glazes from Ancient Egypt*. Brooklyn, The Brooklyn Museum, 1948.

——. *People of the Black Land*. Series I. Brooklyn, The Brooklyn Museum, n. d. (Six illus. pamphlets for children.)

——. *Egyptian Writing*. Series II. Brooklyn, The Brooklyn Museum, n. d. (Four illus. pamphlets for children.)

Ross, E. D. *The Art of Egypt Through the Ages*. New York and London, Studio, 1931.

Sayce, A. H. *Reminiscences*. London, Macmillan Co., Ltd., 1923.

Sethe, Kurt. *Die altaegyptischen Pyramidentexte*. 3 vols. Leipzig, 1908–22.

Smith, William Stevenson. *A History of Egyptian Sculpture and Painting in the Old Kingdom*. London, Published on behalf of the Museum of Fine Arts, Boston, U. S. A., by the Oxford University Press, 1946; 2nd Edition, 1949.

——. *Ancient Egypt as Represented in the Museum of Fine Arts*. Boston, 1942; 2nd Edition, 1946; 3rd Edition, Revised, 1952.

Weigall, Arthur E. P. *A Report on the Antiquities of Lower Nubia: The First Cataract to the Sudan Frontier*. Oxford, Service des antiquités d'Égypte, 1907.

——. *Guide to the Antiquities of Upper Egypt from Abydos to the Sudan Frontier*. London, Methuen & Co., Ltd., 1910.

Wilbour, Charles Edwin. *Travels in Egypt . . . Letters of . . .* Jean Capart, ed. Brooklyn, The Brooklyn Museum, 1936.

Williams, Caroline Ransom. *The Decoration of the Tomb of Perneb: The Technique and the Color Conventions*. New York, The Metropolitan Museum of Art, 1933. Department of Egyptian Art Publications, Vol. III.

Wilson, John A. *The Burden of Egypt*. Chicago, University of Chicago Press, 1951.

Winlock, H. E. *Excavations at Deir el-Bahri, 1911–1931*. New York, The Macmillan Co., 1942.

——. *The Rise and Fall of the Middle Kingdom in Thebes*. New York, The Macmillan Co., 1947.

II. MESOPOTAMIA

Frankfort, Henri. *The Birth of Civilization in the Near East*. Bloomington, Indiana University Press, 1951.

———. *Cylinder Seals: A Documentary Essay on the Art and Religion of the Ancient Near East.* London, Macmillan & Co., 1939.

———. *Kingship and the Gods: A Study of Ancient Near Eastern Religion as the Integration of Society and Nature.* Chicago, University of Chicago Press, 1948.

Heidel, Alexander. *The Gilgamesh Epic and Old Testament Parallels.* Chicago, University of Chicago Press, 1945.

Kramer, Samuel M. *Sumerian Mythology. Memoirs* of the American Philosophical Society, XXI. Philadelphia, 1944.

Reisner, G. A. and others. *Harvard Excavations at Samaria.* 2 vols. Cambridge, Mass., Harvard University Press, 1924. (Palestine.)

Woolley, C. Leonard. *Ur of the Chaldees: A Record of Seven Years of Excavation.* New York, C. Scribner's Sons, 1930.

———. *Ur Excavations: The Royal Cemetery Text,* Vol. II. Oxford, Oxford University Press, 1934.

III. PERSEPOLIS

Breasted, James H. *Oriental Forerunners of Byzantine Painting.* Chicago, University of Chicago Press, 1924. Oriental Institute Publications, Vol. I.

Browne, Edward G. *A Year Among the Persians.* London, A. & C. Black, 1893. Reprinted Cambridge, Eng., The University Press, 1924.

———. *Persian Historical Texts.* London, Luzac & Co., 1901–1907.

———. *A Literary History of Persia.* London, T. F. Unwin, 1902–1906.

———. *A Literary History of Persia.* Cambridge, Eng., The University Press, 1929.

———. Memorial Fund Series. *The Reigns of Ardashuri and Shapur I.* Extracted from the *Shah-nama of Ferdawsi,* Vol. II.

Cameron, George G. *History of Early Iran.* Chicago, University of Chicago Press, 1936.

Curzon, George N. *Persia and the Persian Question.* 2 vols. London and New York, Longmans, Green & Co., 1892.

Dalton, O. M. *The Treasure of the Oxus.* 2nd Edition. London, British Museum, 1926.

Frankfort, Henri. *The Art and Architecture of the Ancient Orient.* Great Britain, Penguin Books, Ltd., 1954. (See also Egypt and Mesopotamia.)

Herzfeld, Ernest E. *Iran in the Ancient East.* Studies presented in the Lowell Lectures at Boston. London and New York, Oxford University Press, 1941.

Olmstead, A. T. *The History of the Persian Empire: Achaemenid Period.* Chicago, University of Chicago Press, 1948.

Pope, Arthur Upham. *A Survey of Persian Art from Prehistoric Times to the Present.* 6 vols. London and New York, Oxford University Press, 1938–39.

Ross, E. Denison. *The Persians.* Oxford, The Clarendon Press, 1931. (A small handbook. There is no guidebook for Persia.)

Schmidt, Erich F. *Persepolis I: Structures, Reliefs, Inscriptions.* Chicago, University of Chicago Press, 1953. Oriental Institute Publications, Vol. LXVIII.

Smith, Myron Bement. *Material for a Corpus of Early Iranian Islamic Architecture.* Ann Arbor, Ann Arbor Press (Series), 1935– .

———. "The Manars of Isfahan," in *Athar-E-Iran,* pp. 313–15. Haarlem, Holland, 1936.

Sykes, Percival. *Life of Zoroaster.* London, n. d.

IV. GREECE

Bieber, Margarete. *The Sculpture of the Hellenistic Age.* New York, Columbia University Press, 1955.

Burn, A. R. *Alexander the Great and the Hellenistic Empire.* London, Hodder & Stoughton, 1947.

Collignon, M. *Histoire de la sculpture grecque.* 2 vols. Paris, Firmin, 1897.

Ducati, Pericle. *L'arte classica.* Turin, Unione Tipografico, 1952.

Gardner, Percy. *The Principles of Greek Art.* New York, The Macmillan Co., 1914.

Reinach, T. *"Les sarcophages de Sidon,"* Vols. VII and VIII (1892), *Gazette des Beaux Arts.*

Richter, Gisela M. A. *The Sculpture and Sculptors of the Greeks.* New Haven, Yale University Press, 1950.

Robinson, C. A., Jr., *Alexander the Great: The Meeting of East and West in World Government and Brotherhood.* New York, Dutton, 1947.

Rostovtzev, M. I. *The Social and Economic History of the Hellenistic World.* 3 vols. Oxford, Clarendon Press, 1941.

Seltman, Charles. *Approach to Greek Art.* London, Studio, 1948.

Tarn, W. W. *Alexander the Great.* 2 vols. Cambridge, Eng., University Press, 1951.

Winter, Franz. *Der Alexandersarkophag aus Sidon.* Strassburg, Truebner, 1912.

V. IMPERIAL ROME (BAALBEK)

Baedeker. *Palestine and Syria.* Leipzig, 1894.

Frauberger, Heinrich. *Die Acropolis von Baalbek.* Frankfurt, Heinrich Keller, 1892.

Robinson, David M. *Baalbek, Palmyra.* New York, J. J. Augustin, 1946.

UNESCO. *Lebanon.* Museums and Monuments, VI, 1953.

Weigand, Theodore. *Baalbek.* Berlin and Leipzig, Walter de Gruyter & Co., 1923.

Wood, Robert. "An Account of the Ruins of Balbec, The Ancient Heliopolis in Coelosyria," in *The World Displayed,* XI, (1774), 120–28.

———. *The World Displayed.* 15 vols. 1762–90.

VI. IMPERIAL ROME (PALMYRA)

Baedeker. *Palestine and Syria.* Leipzig, 1894.

Champdor, Albert. *Les ruines de Palmyre.* Paris, Albert Guillot, 1953.

Seller, Abednego. *The Antiquities of Palmyra.* London, 1696.

Starcky, Jean. *Palmyra.* Damascus, Directorate General of Antiquities, 1948.

———. *Palmyre.* Paris, Maisonneuve, 1952.

Ware, William. *Zenobia, or the Fall of Palmyra.* New York, Thos. R. Knox & Co., 1840.

Weygand, Theodore. *Palmyra.* Berlin, Heinrich Keller, 1932.

Wood, Robert. *The Ruins of Palmyra, Otherwise Tedmor, in the Desert.* London, 1753.

VII. IMPERIAL ROME (PETRA)

Erskine, Beatrice. *The Vanished Cities of Arabia.* New York, E. P. Dutton & Co., 1925.

Forder, A. *Petra, Perea and Phoenicia.* London and Edinburgh, Marshall Bros., Ltd., 1923.

Hamilton, Norah Rowan. *Both Sides of the Jordan: A Woman's Adventures in the Near East.* London, Herbert Jenkins, Ltd., 1925.

Harding, Lankester. *Petra.* Amman, Department of Antiquities, n. d.

Kennedy, Sir Alexander B. W. *Petra: Its History and Monuments.* London, Country Life, 1925.

Laborde, Leon de. *Arabia Petraea.* London, John Murray, 1836.

Martineau, Harriet. *Eastern Life Present and Past.* Philadelphia, Lea & Blanchard, 1848.

Murray, Margaret Alice. *Petra, the Rock City of Edom.* London and Glasgow, Blackie & Son, Ltd., 1939.

Robinson, George Livingston. *Sarcophagus of an Ancient Civilization.* New York, The Macmillan Co., 1930.

VIII. THE FAR EAST—ANGKOR WAT, SIAM, AND JAVA

Banner, Hubert S. *Romantic Java, including Dieng Plateau.* London, Seeley, Service & Co., 1927.

Coedés, Georges. *Pour Mieux Comprendre Angkor.* Paris, Maisonneuve, 1947.

Coomaraswamy, Amanda K. *History of Indian and Indonesian Art.* New York, E. Weyhe, 1927.

L'École française d'Extrême Orient. Le temple d'Angkor Vat. Memoires archéologiques, Tome II, La galerie des bas-reliefs, Vols. I, II, III, Introduction Plaches 287 à 350 Pavilions D'Angle. 3 vols in 7. Paris, G. Van Oest, 1929–32.

Foucher, André. *The Beginnings of Buddhist Art and Other Essays in Indian and Central-Asian Archaeology.* Paris, Paul Geuthner, 1917.

Garrat, G. T. (ed.). *Legacy of India.* Oxford, Oxford University Press, 1937. Especially Poussin de la Vallee, essays on "Buddhism"; K. de B. Codrington, "Indian Art and Archaeology."

McMillan, Michael. *A Journey to Java.* London, Holden & Hardingham, 1914.

Marchal, Henri. *Guide archéologique aux temples d'Angkor.* Paris and Bruxelles, G. Van Oest, 1928.

Le May, Reginald. *The Culture of South-East Asia.* London, George Allen & Unwin, Ltd., 1954.

Raffles, Sir Thomas Stanford. *Antiquarian, Architectural and Landscape Illustrations of the History of Java.* London, 1844.

Scidmore, Eliza R. *Java.* New York, Century Co., 1897.

IX. THE FAR EAST—CHINA, KOREA, AND JAPAN

Binyon, Lawrence. *Painting in the Far East.* London, Edward Arnold, 1913.

Cohn, William. *Chinese Art.* London, The Studio, Ltd., 1930.

Eckardt, P. A. *History of Korean Art.* England, E. Goldston, 1929.

Fenollosa, Ernest F. *Epochs of Chinese and Japanese Art.* London, William Heineman, 1913.

Griffis, William Elliot. *Corea, the Hermit Nation.* New York, Charles Scribner's Sons, 1888.

Hamilton, Angus. *Korea.* New York, Charles Scribner's Sons, 1888.

Minamoto, H. Trans. by Harold G. Henderson. *An Illustrated History of Japanese Art.* Kyoto, K. Hoshina, 1935.

Paine, Robert Treat, and Soper, Alexander. *The Art and Architecture of Japan*. Harmondsworth, England, Penguin Books, Ltd., 1955.

Sanson, George B. *Japan: A Short Cultural History*. New York, Appleton, 1936.

Sickman, Laurence, and Soper, Alexander. *The Art and Architecture of China*. Harmondsworth, England, Penguin Books, Ltd., 1956.

Warner, Langdon. *Japanese Sculpture of the Suiko Period*. New Haven, Yale University Press for Cleveland Museum of Art, 1923.

———. *The Craft of the Japanese Sculptor*. New York, McFarlane, Warde, McFarlane and Japan Society of New York, 1936.

———. *The Enduring Art of Japan*. Cambridge, Mass., Harvard University Press, 1952.

X. THE MAYA REGION

Brainerd, George Walton. "Fine Orange Pottery in Yucatán," *Revista Mexicana de Estudios Antropologicos*, Vol. V (1941), 163–83.

———. *The Maya Civilization*. Los Angeles, Southwest Museum, 1954.

Catherwood, Frederick. *Views of Ancient Monuments in Central America, Chiapas, and Yucatán*. New York, Barlett and Welford, 1844.

Gates, William. *Codices. Dresden Codex*. Baltimore, The Maya Society, 1880. *Madrid Codex*. 1911. *Peresianus Codex*, 1910.

Gordon, George Byron, and Mason, John Alden (eds.). *Examples of Maya Pottery in the Museum and Other Collections*. Parts 1, 2, and 3. Philadelphia, Museum of the University of Pennsylvania, 1925–43.

Hagen, Victor Wolfgang von. *Maya Explorer: John Lloyd Stephens and the Lost Cities of Central America and Yucatán*. Norman, University of Oklahoma Press, 1947.

Kidder, Alfred V. *The Artifacts of Uaxactún, Guatemala*. Carnegie Institution of Washington *Pub. 576*. Washington, D. C., 1947.

———; Jennings, Jesse David; and Shook, Edwin M. *Excavations at Kaminaljuyú, Guatemala*. Carnegie Institution of Washington *Pub. 561*. Washington, D. C., 1946.

Maudslay, Alfred Percival and Anne Cary. *A Glimpse at Guatemala and Some Notes on the Ancient Monuments of Central America*. London, J. Murray, 1899.

Morley, Sylvanus Griswold. *The Ancient Maya*. Stanford, Stanford University Press, 1946.

———. *The Inscriptions at Copán*. Carnegie Institution of Washington *Pub. 219*. Washington, D. C., 1920.

———. *The Inscriptions of Petén.* 5 vols. Carnegie Institution of Washington *Pub. 437.* Washington, D. C., 1937–38.

———. *An Introduction to the Study of the Maya Hieroglyphs.* Bureau of American Ethnology, Smithsonian Institution *Bulletin 57.* Washington, D. C., 1915.

Morris, Ann Axtell. *Digging in Yucatán.* New York, Junior Literary Guild, 1931. (Popular book of exploration.)

Morris, Earl Halstead. *Temple of the Warriors.* New York, C. Scribner's Sons, 1931. (Popular book of exploration.)

———; Charlot, Jean; and Morris, Ann Axtell. *The Temple of the Warriors at Chichen Itzá, Yucatán.* 2 vols. Carnegie Institution of Washington *Pub. 406.* Washington, D. C., 1931.

Pollock, Harry Evelyn Dorr. "The Casa Redonda at Chichén Itzá Yucatán," Carnegie Institution of Washington, *Contributions to American Anthropology and History,* Vol. III, No. 17. (1937).

Recinos, Adrian (trans. and ed.). *Popol Vuh: The Sacred Book of the Ancient Quiché Maya.* English version by Delia Goetz and Sylvanus G. Morley. Norman, University of Oklahoma Press, 1950.

———, and Goetz, Delia (trans. and eds.). *The Annals of the Cakchiquels,* with *Title of the Lords of Totonicapán.* Norman, University of Oklahoma Press, 1953.

Ruppert, Karl. *The Caracol at Chichén Itzá, Yucatán, Mexico.* Carnegie Institution of Washington *Pub. 454.* Washington, D. C., 1935.

———. *A Medical Survey of the Republic of Guatemala.* Carnegie Institution of Washington *Pub. 499.* Washington, D. C., 1938.

———. *Chichén Itzá: Architectural Notes and Plans.* Carnegie Institution of Washington *Pub. 595.* Washington D. C., 1952.

———. "Temple of the Wall Panels, Chichén Itzá," Carnegie Institution of Washington, *Contributions to American Anthropology and History,* Vol. I, No. 3 (1931).

Shattuck, George Cheever, M.D. *Diseases of the Tropics.* New York, Appleton-Century-Crofts, 1951.

———. *The Peninsula of Yucatán: Medical, Biological, Meteorological and Sociological Studies.* Carnegie Institution of Washington *Pub. 431.* Washington, D. C., 1933.

———. *A Medical Survey of the Republic of Guatemala.* Carnegie Institution of Washington *Pub. 499.* Washington, D. C., 1938.

Spinden, Herbert J. *Ancient Civilizations of Mexico and Central America.*

American Museum of Natural History Handbooks, Series No. 3. New York, 1917.

——. *A Study of Maya Art*. Peabody Museum *Publications*, Vol. VI. Cambridge, Mass., 1913.

Stephens, John Lloyd. *Incidents of Travel in Central America, Chiapas, and Yucatán*. 2 vols. New York, Harper & Bros., 1841.

——. *Incidents of Travel in Yucatán*. 2 vols. New York, Harper & Bros., 1843.

Thompson, Edward Herbert. *People of the Serpent*. Boston and New York, Houghton Mifflin Co., 1932. (Popular book of exploration.)

Thompson, J. Eric S. *Maya Hieroglyphic Writing: Introduction*. Carnegie Institution of Washington *Pub. 589*. Washington, D. C., 1950.

——. *Ethnology of the Mayas of Southern and Central British Honduras*. Chicago, Field Museum of Natural History, 1930.

——; Pollock, Harry Evelyn Dorr; and Charlot, Jean. *A Preliminary Study of the Ruins of Cobá, Quintana Roo, Mexico*. Carnegie Institution of Washington *Pub. 424*. Washington, D. C., 1932.

——. *The Rise and Fall of Maya Civilization*. Norman, University of Oklahoma Press, 1954.

——. *Excavations of San José, British Honduras*. Carnegie Institution of Washington *Pub. 506*. Washington, D. C., 1939.

Tozzer, Alfred M. *A Comparative Study of the Maya and the Lacandones*. New York and London, Published for the Archaeological Institute of America by the Macmillan Co., 1907.

——. *A Preliminary Study of the Prehistoric Ruins of Tikal, Guatemala*. *Memoirs* of the Peabody Museum, Harvard University, Vol. V, No. 2. Report of the Peabody Museum Expedition (1909–10). Cambridge, Mass., 1911.

Vaillant, George Clapp. *Aztecs of Mexico*. Garden City, Doubleday Doran & Co., Inc., 1941.

——. *The Maya and their Neighbors*. New York and London, D. Appleton-Century Co., Inc., 1940.

Willard, Theodore Arthur. *The City of the Sacred Well*. New York, Grosset & Dunlap, 1926. (Popular book of exploration.)

INDEX

INDEX

TOMBS, TEMPLES, & ANCIENT ART

has been composed on the Linotype machine in eleven-point Granjon, with three points of space between the lines. The title page is hand-set in Michelangelo from Stempel Type Foundry, Frankfurt, Germany, and Arrighi from the English Monotype Corporation, Ltd., London. The illustrations have been printed separately by offset, wrapped around the text signatures, and sewn together in the binding of this book.